NEITHER BLACK NOR WHITE

by *Wilma Dykeman and James Stokely*

BELIEVING that the greatest service to the South and the nation currently lies in honest praise and constructive criticism, springing from affectionate concern for the region, the authors have produced this illuminating personal narrative of the contemporary South.

Southerners themselves, Wilma Dykeman and James Stokely have traveled through thirteen states since the 1954 Supreme Court decision ruling against separate, but equal, schools to collect this kaleidoscopic report on Southern views. Myriad interviews and conversations, here recorded, allow Southerners of all shades of opinion and background to express their individual approaches to the problems besetting them.

Touched off by the school-integration issue, the dilemma of the South—neither all black nor all white—is explained. Here is the dilemma of a traditionally individualistic region now demanding from all Southerners conformity on integration and all concomitant problems.

The positions taken by the press, clergy, universities, public school officials, politicians and citizenry are de-

(continued on back flap)

(continued from front flap)

scribed with understanding and respect in terms of both current events and historical forces.

In this book as nowhere else the myth of the "solid South" is exploded. The many Souths—agricultural or industrial, liberal or conservative, integrated or segregated, rich or poverty-stricken—are revealed in all their disparity. And Southerners caught in the drama of transition now taking place are shown in their attempts to cope with change and equality, to overcome fears and tensions, to maintain themselves and their institutions.

With intelligence and insight, this book measures the pulse of the South in this period of transition.

WILMA DYKEMAN and JAMES STOKELY have been married for more than fifteen years and this is their first book written together. Mr. Stokely is a poet, and his wife, Wilma Dykeman, is the author of numerous articles and short stories, and of *The French Broad,* a volume in the Rivers of America Series. Miss Dykeman is a native of North Carolina, while her husband comes from Tennessee. They and their children live in the South.

By Wilma Dykeman

THE FRENCH BROAD

By Wilma Dykeman and James Stokely

NEITHER BLACK NOR WHITE

By Wilma Dykeman and James Stokely

Neither **BLACK**
Nor WHITE

Rinehart & Company, Inc.   *New York   Toronto*

First Printing, October 1957
Second Printing, April 1958

Published simultaneously in Canada by

Clarke, Irwin & Company, Ltd., Toronto

This book is for

our parents

in remembrance of the best that is in our past

and for

our children

in anticipation of the best that can be in their future

Contents

Contents

Neither BLACK
Nor WHITE

"Each of us inevitable,
   Each of us limitless—each of us with his or her right upon the
      earth,
   Each of us allow'd the eternal purports of the earth,
   Each of us here as divinely as any is here."

Walt Whitman, New Yorker

"And everywhere, through the immortal dark, something moving in the night, and something stirring in the hearts of men,
and something crying in their wild, unuttered blood, the wild,
unuttered tongues of its huge prophecies—so soon the morning,
soon the morning: O America."

Thomas Wolfe, North Carolinian

1 ▓ The Reason

How shall we say when we began this journey? Was it when some distant ancestor shouldered his long rifle and made a dusty march to defeat the British redcoats somewhere in the Carolinas? Was it when our fathers came here, or remained here, despite the lure of other regions, because there was something in the South which held their attention and allegiance? Was it years ago, when we made our own first journey from the high pungent balsams of the Great Smokies down through the wide lonely country of the longleaf pine to the ancient stillness of the live oaks with their grey burdens of Spanish moss?

Or was it yesterday, when we rode in an airplane and looked at the tidy patterns of green field and forest and blue water and grey town, hills subsiding into flatlands, streams growing into rivers, and rivers spilling into ocean and gulf, the honeycomb and swarm of the city suddenly giving way to the solitary little farmhouse far down an unpaved road? Was it when we rolled along the roads, in bus and train and car, seeing the lighted windows at night and a sickle of moon above quiet pastures and deserted streets, waves of heat which shimmered up from a glazed pavement on August afternoons, and the miles marked by signs of the United States Government and the military installations? Was it when we walked on the red clay or black muck or white sand, among the dark shanties of "Jimtown" or "Jaybird" on a rainy afternoon, or along paths which may lead anywhere: to a weather-beaten country church, a state-park waterfall, a moonshiner's still. It's a journey begun a long time ago—continuing long after these words. And this is the journal, not so much of finalities discovered as of possibilities confronted.

Why the journey? Many reasons, some simple to explain and understand, others complex and possibly incommunicable—but two reasons above all others from the beginning. First, we had spent most of our lives (and more important to some people, our taxes) in the South. We knew that the South is not a place, it is many places; it is not a people, it is many people; it is not even a way of life, but many ways in many lives.

3

A man from another region of the United States meets a Southerner and says, "Oh, you're from down there!" The pigeonholes fall into place as to Southern intellectual, economic, phonetic, social and racial habits. The result, as far as friendship and understanding are concerned, is as disastrous as when a Southerner looks at a Negro he has been acquainted with for many years and says, "They're all like that." Each year of our life we had seen the South growing less and less homogeneous and we believed that in this time of transition, when the biggest, oldest, deepest tie of Southern homogeneity is being loosened, we should like to know firsthand, feel and hear and see, not only the loud public character, but these many Souths.

Second, we remembered something Robert Frost once said: "I am not a regionalist. I am a realmist." As much as, perhaps more than, a region, we undertook to discover, record and interpret a realm of experience, a republic of the human mind.

We searched out facts, but remembered that Mark Twain said there are three kinds of lies: plain lies, damned lies and statistics. We asked for the courage of judgment and clarity, recalling what one South Carolina woman told us: "If we're not frank when we speak about our faults, we won't be believed when we talk about our virtues." But even more frequently we remembered the mountain man on the witness stand in Tennessee, pressed to state whether the defendant, who was his neighbor, had a good or bad character. "Well now," he said, "I reckon a little of both."

Neither black nor white: the dilemma of the South, the wisdom we shall all need, the solution which will triumph.

This was not only a journey in space but in time. Great-grandfather's allegiance to Calhoun is no less real a bequest than great-grandmother's Sheffield on the sideboard, although each may be slightly tarnished at the moment. Grandfather's enthusiasm for Henry Grady is no less real a bequest than the brick mills dotting the countryside, although Utopia may not have quite arrived. The point of departure for our journey was respect for the past, knowing we cannot go back to yesterday; anticipation of the future, knowing it will not come until tomorrow; admitting that today is more than we will fill, and if we waste it, we have discarded the past and future as well.

"Down here we wear our heart on our sleeve and a chip on our shoulder," a woman in Georgia told us. We collected both hearts and chips on our journey.

"I treasure the South's innocence but I despise its ignorance," a man in Louisiana said. We encountered both the innocence and the ignorance.

Most of the talk about the South today seems to deal only with man to man, yet so much of the Southern experience has been between man and the earth. Perhaps the relationship among all living things has seldom been more beautifully balanced, more tragically unrealized, than in our region. Albert Schweitzer, seeking a phrase which would sum up his philosophy, tells of finding it one day as he sat in a boat in Africa: "Reverence for life."

How desperately we have need of this reverence which reaches out and embraces God and grass, man and mole, water and crag, fern and forest, in one total realization of the interdependence of all life. As we have misused our richest land, we have misused ourselves; as we have wasted our bountiful water, we have wasted ourselves; as we have diminished the lives of one whole segment of our people, we have diminished ourselves. Irreverence for one life blasphemes against all life—and perhaps only a man like Schweitzer, of profound culture, who has returned to the primitive at the edge of the jungle, can realize the refined irreverences civilization may indulge.

It is on these old debts of blasphemy that we are still paying interest today—not only in the South, of course—in all parts of our nation. But we talk of the debt and lament the cost in the South because that is the region we know and cherish most intimately.

The South is, above all, a region of living things. Late mechanizing, we have also been late to give up a close relationship with the earth, with the elements which rule rural life, and above all, with each other. But those relationships have not always been wise or just. In 1955, almost seven million acres of forest land were burned over in the South. North Carolina's State Forester estimates that North Carolina alone loses thirty-five million dollars a year in forest fires. And as anyone who has lived in the South knows, many of these fires are deliberately set. They flare from the dissatisfactions of Saturday nights and the lethargy of long Sunday afternoons in small towns where the movie palace and the dingy café and half a dozen filling stations are the social centers for bored boys and girls who seek something they cannot name and wait for a glory they will not confess—and a struck match, a blazing pine, provides one momentary diversion and excitement. They flame from the habits and repressions of country men who feel the vise of want and time holding them fast, and a tossed faggot, a burning forest, provides momentary release and action, and sometimes a job fighting the fire—or any easy way of clearing land, or "killing off the snakes" as lumbermen say. They are in the tradition of their ancestors, but while the earlier waste by fire was incalculable, the present waste is unforgivable.

Irreverence for life spreads out from one center to devitalize other areas, too. The central irreverence of the Old South was surely its acceptance, its use, its defense of slave labor. Historians are still debating the question of whether or not slavery as an economic system was profitable. But few will dispute the fact that it was wasteful. Enforced labor from the muscles of enslaved men was, of course, exactly contrary to the whole economic ideology upon which American "free enterprise" was based. Yet those who proclaimed most loudly against the motes which sometimes impeded the "American way" often failed utterly to behold the beam in their own vision, which denied "incentive" and "profit" and the "right to competition" to one large group of laboring Americans. Slave labor was considered in terms of overhead and underfoot—and because it was often a struggle of wills, uninspired by any large hope for the future, it was frequently work done as slowly and poorly as possible.

William Faulkner recently pointed out that work is the only activity man can engage in day in and day out all day long. If work is more than a man's livelihood and panacea, if it is also his challenge and response, then slavery (and some of the economic servitude which followed when formal bondage was abolished) robbed it of all dignity, perverted its deepest purposes and destroyed its meaning for both the individual and society.

It might well be claimed that one of slavery's worst legacies was an attitude toward work which it had fostered in some Southern areas among certain people. It is a cliché, as inaccurate as most generalizations, to describe the Southern man as a shiftless charmer, either in broadcloth or blue jeans, who would rather starve on mint juleps or turnips than eat by the sweat of his brow; and cliché to picture his wife as a debilitated belle who would rather live on large doses of patent medicine or smuggled cognac than cook her own dinner. The South has had hard work to do for a long time now—and has done it. And yet—perhaps it was, too often, the joy in work itself which was missing. As in many aristocracies the world over, in some parts of the South physical work, mental labor, the necessity to earn money, was too often considered slightly degrading, something to have over and done with at the earliest moment possible.

There is a story now making the rounds in the South about the part-time maid who came to her old Southern employer one morning and informed her that she was not happy in her work for a new housewife from the North, who had just moved into the town with one of the new industries.

"But, Belle, what's wrong?" the Southern mistress asked.

"Nothing, except that new woman's just not any lady."

"Oh, Belle, I'm sure you're mistaken. How do you know she's not a lady?"

"Well, for one thing, she washes her own windows."

"Now that's silly. Why, I wash my own windows."

"Yes, ma'am. But she knows how."

There are many here, of course, who "know how," who have put the strength of their arms and the power of their minds and the dedication of their hearts into fulfilling the best of the region. To them we owe a debt which can be repaid only by the same labor and love.

But it is in some of these large and obvious, small but important reverencies and irreverencies for life and its creatures, that the story of the South, and this account of a journey through it, has meaning beyond the South.

The meaning accumulates through remembered faces and the way a road turned through a flat piney woods in the Piedmont; a collection of sights and sounds and smells that remain as sharply defined in memory as the many Souths which produced them, yet also blend into one big portrait of land and people.

The memories are of:

—the greenness of Kentucky after spring rains, and the lush plenty of cattle lying in a hillside pasture at nine o'clock in the morning. ("You don't see cattle lying down early in the day like that unless they're mighty well fed. Folks around here put their land to work.") The marvelous green farms where the racing thoroughbreds are raised and miles of white walls lace the countryside; the roads northeast of Lexington where stone fences edge the smaller rolling farms and trees spread leafy shade over the pavement or gravel, and for a moment you feel as if you might be in Connecticut or Vermont or upstate New York. And not so many miles away, the steep hills and black slag and the mineholes that gape in the mountainsides above rows of sooty, grimy houses where children play with bits of coal and the sudden flowering of a japonica seems incongruous and sad.

—the lonesome look of a Negro man in "the falling part of the evening," or late afternoon, going down a long country road toward the little crossroads store in the distance, carrying a half-gallon jug for "lamp oil" to kindle the morning fires in the woodstove and fill the lamps for nightfall.

—the small, constant column of smoke from a pile of burning sawdust at a lumberyard deep in a deserted countryside, and the truck with bent fenders and smooth tires, from which three wild-eyed, blue-eyed boys unload pine logs.

—the smooth Caribbean music of the orchestra and the limp lovely girls dancing with their boys on the terrace of the country club. The relaxed laughter and the sweetness of wilting corsages, and down below the terrace the summer fragrance of new-clipped grass on the lawn leading down to the fairway of the golf links. There is the easy friendliness of people who belong and have always belonged here, and yet there is an unease, a trace of boredom, too. But the drinks are very cool and heady, and the music is like syrup pouring over the tables and the terrace and the people, and the night is warm and intimate as a cocoon.

—in the middle of a school morning in a little town in Alabama, the Negro boy about twelve years old, leaning against a penny weight machine, hands shoved in his torn overalls' pockets, gazing at the world from brown fathomless eyes, waiting, watching, silently, under the sign on the weight machine just above his head, which says: "Character Readings: What Is Your Future?"

—the Saturday washing at a Negro shack on a little red clay road: incredibly faded and tattered overalls of a half-dozen sizes, bedsheets made out of the bleached sacks that cow feed is sold in, shirts and a dress of indistinct color, two towels of the same feed sacking, and a single pair of socks—all hung on a sagging barbed wire fence, blowing dry and even more ragged. And the weary woman sitting on her littered porch on the shattered old sofa which has lost most of its upholstering, sitting and staring into the collard patch beyond the barbed-wire clothesline.

—the autumn afternoon in Georgia when a casually opened door becomes an entrance into another world: ladies in the latest cashmere coats and gentlemen in dacron-and-cotton shirts, living again the battle of the blue and grey. At Kennesaw Mountain National Battlefield, where Joseph Johnston and Tecumseh Sherman faced each other during the Atlanta Campaign of '64, local citizens and historians gather at the National Park headquarters to commemorate the event. In the season of nostalgia, with October sun and shadows bright on the grass and along the towering mountain, they sit sedately in the little room and speak of the dead—and in an exhibition case in the next room are newspapers of the years just after the Civil War: Nathan Bedford Forrest tells about the beginning of the Ku Klux Klan, and a correspondent explains the terrible consequences of amalgamation, and suddenly the dead do not seem altogether dead, and the past seems very present. The ladies fold a regimental flag lovingly, and the late sunlight slants through the western windows and across the slopes of the mountain where weary men once met and fought each other to the death.

—and in Virginia in the spring, the dogwood glistening pure and white among the second-growth of pine and oak growing in The Wilderness. Between Fredericksburg and Chancellorsville and Spotsylvania the road runs, a smooth road, and on either side are the gentle woods covering the once-torn earth. Deep in the shadows, the humps of old trenches, dug in the heat and hurry and frustration of war, are visible—but even they, too, are smooth with time. Wide-leafed lady's-slippers flower in the rich mulch, and the old raw wounds are healed to a lump of scar tissue now.

—the steep hill leading from the administration and classroom and dormitory buildings of the Piney Woods Country Life School down to the weather-beaten cabin where Laurence Jones taught his first class of boys and girls in the heart of Mississippi, almost half a century ago. When the "Little Professor" from Iowa first came to this county in 1909, it was estimated that eighty per cent of the Negroes were illiterate. They signed their grocery bills and yearly farm settlements with an "X" and lived bleak, hard lives. But the classes that began on a log under a cedar tree, and then in a sheep shelter, changed the lives of many a Negro—and, unconsciously, many a white person, too.

This three-room cabin is a link from the slave days, when it was built, to the real emancipation, through learning, in the large buildings atop the hill. The two chinked fireplaces at each end of the narrow building still hold the old iron pots and spider in which Dr. Jones and his pupils cooked their meals. (Jones so poor that some of the white folks in the community said he had only corn bread and black-eyed peas for breakfast, dinner and supper, and there was a community joke about "the man who ate peas for breakfast, drank water for dinner and swelled up for supper.") In the "classroom" one window: a square opening cut in the logs, no glass, only a wooden cover to slip through a slot and shut out rain or wind. One little bookshelf, of rough lumber, and the handmade shingles on the rafter poles all bear the old-silver color of age and weather. From this cabin under tall pines, used as a stock shelter until the young Negro teacher proved to the white owner that he could use it to better

advantage than the sheep, it is a few steps up the hill to the little frame
Rosenwald Building, the school's first expansion. From here the path
climbs sharply and at the top is the present school, where Negro boys
and girls find encouragement and training for their abilities, and become
capable citizens. There is the memory of the students who walked with us
around Piney Woods—their grave old courtesy; their brave, new self-confidence. And the memory of the words of the white man who told about
Jones's appeal for help in the beginning. "Jones came in the office one
morning looking down-spirited. My typist said he bowed plenty polite but
that he had lost some of his scrape. He came right to the subject at once. He
said, 'I am in trouble. I have gone about as far as I can go by myself.' 'Well,
what is it?' I asked. He says, 'Well, I have just got to have some kind of a
schoolhouse. I have got forty-odd pupils and no schoolhouse. We haven't
got anywhere to go except the little old log cabin we took from the sheep,
and it's getting cold from the fall rains and you know these little black
boys and girls haven't any very good clothes.'

"I interrupted him. 'Yes, Jones, it's pitiful. I know you need a building. Now, what is the least you can get on with?' He said, 'Beggars
mustn't be choosers.' 'Well, now, let me speak plain to you, Jones. I have
never believed that it was worth while to educate the Negro in the South
under the present environmental conditions. You know we regard the
Negro as a servant to the white man, but I must say that you have an
unusual proposition, through a new approach, and I will say that you
have more guts and determination than any man I ever saw. So I am
going to trust to your perseverance and integrity to the end, and I am
going to give you ten thousand feet of lumber for that school building,
and I will grant you credit as you need it from time to time.' "

Up the hill the buildings climbed, for that was the direction their
builder followed and led. And there are many such spots scattered through
the South today, all possible because someone made practical his reverence for life.

This was the area we considered the South: the eleven states which
belonged to the Confederacy—Virginia, North and South Carolina,
Georgia, Florida, Alabama, Louisiana, Mississippi, Texas, Arkansas and
Tennessee—with Kentucky and Oklahoma added. Twenty-nine per cent
of the continental United States, a little over twenty-seven per cent of
the nation's population, a little less than forty-two million people in
1950. The range is wide:

From Monticello on its tree-covered heights, where the innovations
of Thomas Jefferson's active mind and sense of proportion and dedication

to freedom, and the self-sufficiency of another age, all find concrete expression in house and gardens, with the smell of box hedge and growing herbs and damp old bricks in cellar passages—from this to the Alamo, silent in the moonlight, surrounded by its wall and gardens like an oasis of the past in the burgeoning city, ghostlike with the smell of mesquite and adobe and the stillness of night around it. From the wild breaking of the waves on the jagged Atlantic coast at Hatteras, to the rhythmic pumping of the oil wells on the very grounds of the capitol in Oklahoma.

From the golden strip of Miami Beach with its massed luxury as thick and fat as cream, to the spread-eagled plants belting out paper and aluminum and textiles and chemicals and lengthening lists of other products with massed precision. From cabins in laurel and rhododendron thickets to mansions in azalea and magnolia gardens. From the comfortable old frame house and the little laboratory in Fort Myers, Florida, where Thomas Edison experimented and gave the twentieth century much of its form, to the pleasant cottage at Warm Springs, Georgia, where Franklin Roosevelt came as a crippled man and a powerful President; to the Biltmore Estate of one of the Vanderbilts, in Asheville, North Carolina, where the first school of forestry in America was begun; to the simple dignity of Andrew Jackson's Hermitage in the rolling grasslands of middle Tennessee, where much of the commonness and uncommonness of America met in the character and life of one very human man.

And everywhere we realized our need and desire to listen to anyone who would talk—to hear the voices, learned and unlearned, bitter and kind, raw with hate, passionate with hope. We became increasingly aware of the graduated scorns which can find a whole range in white voices from "nigger" to "nigra," and in Negro voices from "white trash" to "White Folks." There were the conscious and unconscious deprecations of the constant inversions in white references to that most discussed of all organizations, the NAACP, which becomes the "NAPC," "NCAP," or "whatever it is that thing's called."

And there was growing awareness, too, of the subtleties and varieties of thought and feeling among all the people of the South, who must not be degraded by easy stereotype. Every statement we had made to us, every conversation—with white or Negro, bigot or brother or would-be onlooker; those frozen in certainty or trembling in uncertainty—each one was like glimpsing the tip of an iceberg. Underneath the visible evidence lay the great undetermined bulk of reality. There were the fears and beliefs, facts and myths, of which we only caught the briefest glance and which most of the people themselves could never have articulated beneath the bits of conversation, the revealing shafts of conviction; beneath the edge of the iceberg moved the powerful mass that will shape or wreck the ship to which all of us are committed.

Stephen Vincent Benét, years ago, gave the theme which binds together the voices we heard, the voices you hear, through the South today:

> And these you are, and each is partly you,
> And none is false, and none is wholly true.

"We talk to each other," Dr. Charles Johnson, mild-mannered, scholarly, wisely humorous President of Fisk University in Nashville, told us shortly before his sudden death in October, 1956: "The next step is talking with each other. How little we know other people! There was the elderly lady who visited the Indian Village at the World's Fair in Chicago several years ago. As she watched the exhibit there she was moved to speak a friendly word to one of these aborigines, and she asked him, 'How do you like our country?'

"Or there was the man who went to France and on a street corner in Paris he saw a black man, a fine-looking Senegalese. Being from the South, the white man went up to him and said, 'How you like it here, boy?' The African just looked at him. He asked again, 'Boy, you like it here pretty well?' This time the man just let out a great stream of Senegalese, and the American said to him, 'Look here, you've not been over here so long you've forgotten your own language, have you?' "

In a small town in middle Mississippi a stranger informed us: "We got one of the highest gasoline taxes of any state in the country, and most of it's being used by the Governor to equalize the nigger's schools. And you know niggers don't pay no tax much. They come in here, buy a little gas once in a while, but it's really us paying for all their schools. I hope we're not going to have any trouble here, afraid we will. It's something the government can't force on the people. Oughtn't to do it, can't do it."

"The chip on the shoulder is truly a burden," the Negro urban leader said. "I meet people who think that everything that happens to them happens because they're colored. Then they begin to hate themselves because they're colored. We must be emancipated from this, too."

The radio preacher we heard one hot Sunday afternoon as we drove through the upland South: "Now it may seem to some of you out there that you don't have much of this world's goods, that you're outcastes but

I'm here to tell you-ah, that you're a king's son. Oh, you may say, If I was a king's son, I'd be a-living in a fine palace and have the latest fixtures around my yard. I'd not be a-digging ditches, I'd be attending the big balls and wine parties. Well, you may not have the great lot of wealth down here, much property and such as that, but when you move across the river, you'll have it all. That's why this-here program is dedicated to them that are lost and undone.

"The harder the cross, the brighter the crown. Bread and all such as that will be taken care of when we get Home. When we reach that mansion over there, we won't never have to move on no more. They'll spread the welcome table for us. We'll all eat together up there."

"This whole question of segregation and integration, of Negro and white, has got to be seen as a community dialogue," an astute newspaperman told us one spring evening. "We've betrayed our best dream—not only in the South, throughout the nation. But now school integration is the least part of the issue—it's as citizens of a community that we must find our way back to the dream.

"Let me tell you about two Southerners, both born in Kentucky not a hundred miles and only a few hours apart. One moved as a child to Mississippi, went on to West Point, made a fine record there, returned home to Mississippi and identified with the power structure. The other moved to Illinois, became part of the frontier, moving, changing, growing, and he identified with humanity. Then these two men, born so close together in time and space, became presidents of two opposing governments in the bloodiest war America has ever known.

"I have never thought that complying with the Court decision on schools would mean a lot of integration. There are too many factors against it—but the big issue is permissiveness. The Negroes want to know they're decent, can live like civilized, self-respecting citizens."

A Southern university professor described an encounter he had had: "A colleague and I were eating lunch the other day and this boy came up to our table. He was in the Law School and he was very upset over two Negro students who had been admitted to the School, said he and some other fellows were going to organize a protest against it, going to write to other Southern universities—oh, he was very excited about it.

"Finally I asked him if he thought these students were really going to bother him in any way. And he said, 'I'm from Columbia, South Carolina.' I said, 'All right. Now, how are these Negroes going to hurt you?'

" 'But you don't understand!' he said. 'I'm from South Carolina. I can't let South Carolina down. My grandfathers were in the War Against the South and the Negroes caused the War, and I don't propose to forget that.' I pressed him a bit further on this point and he said the Negroes caused the War by stirring up the Abolitionists. It seemed to me this might be the way a fox caused a fox hunt, but I didn't tell him so.

"Then he went on, said something about going to Yale. I told him that I felt reasonably sure they had some Negroes in the Law School at Yale. 'Well,' he said, 'they don't like them up there as well as we do down here.' Finally my colleague told the boy he wasn't logical, just emotional. All right, the boy agreed, so he was emotional about it. That was that. It was one of the most frustrating attempts at communication I have ever engaged in."

There was the dinner conversation at which a handsome Japanese girl, who had married a Southerner of long lineage, asked, "Why do people here always point out with such pride, 'This was built by slave labor'?"

And the answers revealed each speaker's character, as well as a facet of the solution to the stranger's inquiry.

An elderly lady of kind countenance, who had lived most of her life in the United States and foreign countries doing religious mission work, replied, "Because they are proud of the fine craftsmanship of the Negroes in the early days. They are eager to show off the slave's accomplishments."

The Japanese girl's husband thought differently. "I think they say 'slave labor' because that dates the house, makes its history and antiquity authentic."

It was a young housewife who gave the sternest reason. "I believe Southerners point out the old smokehouse, the Big House itself, as having been built by slave labor because they know visitors from outside like to hear about it. And I think they like to say it and strangers like to hear it because of man's preoccupation with brutality and lordship. There's a vicarious fascination and self-projection into those older days. We'd all like to be superior, chosen people—but it's so hard if you have to earn your superiority!"

And a young Southern minister, living in one of Tennessee's most rural counties: "All life is one, and cannot be separated into sacred and secular, material and spiritual. One of the greatest opportunities of the church is to hold up this unity and wholeness of life under God. Souls cannot be saved apart from the rest of life—soil, society and souls belong together."

2 The Dawn Comes up Like Thunder

On May 17, 1954, in the hushed dignity of the chambers of the Supreme Court of the United States, Mr. Chief Justice Warren delivered the unanimous opinion of that court on the subject of school segregation. The voice and words were calm and deliberate. "We conclude that in the field of public education the doctrine of 'separate but equal' has no place. Separate educational facilities are inherently unequal." How distant and cool the words were compared to the dust and heat they would stir at a hundred little crossroads, in dozens of cities, across a whole countryside quick to anger and stubborn in pride. In the century of the atom bomb, these words set off a chain reaction which has resulted in a social fission of startling proportions.

Immediately after announcement of the decision, there was a brief interlude of stunned silence and occasional halfhearted acquiescence in the South—and then the explosion erupted. Through smoke-stained county courtrooms and lawyers' offices, through dimly lit clubs and brightly lit public auditoriums, up from offices of editors and down from boards of directors, the reaction boiled and increased. Its counterpart could only be found in the angry editorials of the Northern newspapers following the Dred Scott decision in 1857. Denunciations varied from former Justice of the Supreme Court James Byrnes's black-tie and dinner-jacket attacks to the overall-and-blue-jean shouts of "traitors, Communist sympathizers, carpetbaggers."

"At least we've demonstrated to the world that we have free speech here in the United States," a Tennessean remarks wryly.

Many Southerners and most Northerners were astonished at the bitterness, the wildness—indeed, frequently the fury—of the region's reaction. Suddenly we discovered that we did not even know ourselves as well as we had thought. Over the legend of the Old South we had spread the fiction of the New South. Both were deceptive, and we had deceived not only our visitors but also ourselves.

15

After all, the South learned long since that the truth about itself was complex and wearisome for strangers to try to comprehend, and so it obligingly accommodated to some of the folklore most readily consumed by outsiders. The legend was, in part, like cotton and pralines, for the export trade. Other regions of the country bought the mammies and magnolias and you-alls, and Southerners learned to whip them up with ease. "Scarlett" Leigh and "Rhett" Gable became the most vivid embodiments of Southern history; what chance, in the popular imagination, did the hosts of plodding reality have beside such exciting creations? Underneath the pretty legend, the self-deception fostered by segregation became more firmly impacted, however. It not only restricted knowledge, it did something worse—tortured specific areas of the knowledge that was common currency throughout the rest of the civilized world into false patterns and conclusions. Nameless fears became fortified behind barriers no facts could penetrate. The noble meaning of "tradition" was bastardized to include anything anyone remembered being done for as long as a generation. As Vann Woodward has pointed out to us, even *The Strange Career of Jim Crow* himself has been brief—actually our legal segregation is a habit learned in the twentieth century, and it is neither an inborn creed nor an antebellum necessity inherited by virtue of its vitality. Neo-Grecian architecture flourished with Neo-Gothic literature, and both were accepted as the Old South.

Then, with the coming of industries to the vacant lots outside town, and the arrival of grass on the gullied hills and leached-out fields, the New South and a new legend were born. Change was the watchword and the outward changes were many and varied. Mint juleps were replaced by Coca-Cola as the symbol of homebred hospitality. The smokehouses were torn down and food freezers installed on the back porch. Driving along the side roads you see petunias planted in the black iron washpots, and the army recently abandoned that old standby, the stubborn mule.

As an old mountain woman tells you, "Ever'thing's changing seems like. You take even the little ole flowers I try to raise here in my yard-patch; nowadays folks plant them gladiolas and tulips and such. But I can't break away from the old favorites, my prince's feather and golden glows and dahlias, and in the spring my peonies—oh, I do just cling to my peonies. That's the way it is with some of us, I reckon: hard to let go of the old things, the old ways."

But the mountain girls jolt down from the coves and hills on Saturdays, buy ballerina-style shoes and dirndl skirts and scarlet fingernail polish, and feel that they belong to the American dream of a permanent wave and true romance guaranteed for every girl. In the lowlands, the Negro women and the country housewives from the flat, burning farms swarm into town on Saturdays, buy plastic window curtains and hot dogs and shiny, skimpy rayon dresses—and at least momentarily they "belong."

In the towns and suburbs we build our ranch-style and our split-level houses handy to Woolworth's and the supermarkets, we subscribe to *House Beautiful*, switch to chlorophyll toothpaste, and set a picture window in our living room. We had begun to think that because we looked alike we were all thinking alike. We built picture windows and forgot that we look out of those windows with different eyes through different experiences and memories. We built bigger brick churches and thought that by some alchemy just the process of building would make us bigger persons. Examining polls and surveys, we trusted more complete statistics to make us more complete persons, and counted on an extra vitamin pill a day to ward off all troubles. The veneer is thin and the Supreme Court decision cracked it right down the middle and exposed the old rosewood underneath the "blonde moderne."

A Southerner, who has traveled the region and seen it more clearly at closer range than possibly any other man in the area, tells you, "You know what the big impediment is now to any outside understanding of the South? It's the visitor who drives though, stops at Howard Johnson's where they have the same twenty-eight flavors they have in Pennsylvania and Ohio, and calls up Joe who's the friend of an old roommate at Harvard. Joe asks him out to the house for a drink, and he goes to Joe's and has a gin and tonic and a steak Joe makes a big ritual of broiling on the portable charcoal burner out on the terrace, and they talk about income taxes or the new quiz program on TV or the way the baseball season's shaping up. Everything's fine. If the race situation is mentioned, Joe shakes his head and says sagely, 'It's a big problem.' And his visitor agrees, 'Yeah, we know. We got our problems too—the kikes, the wops, the Puerto Ricans, et cetera, et cetera.' And then our new authority on the South goes home and gives everyone the inside dope on all this violence and tension being just so much eyewash. 'Why there was this guy I met . . .'

"We—and I mean the North, South, all of us—deal in stereotypes and that's fatal, in literature or life."

The stereotypes of the New South are perhaps hindering us as much in this time of transition and adjustment as their more familiar counterparts from the Old South. Part of the problem of the South may be summed up in the realization that for generations we were a land committed to two races, one crop and no change. This led us into the deep dilemma which has been stated before but must surely be restated in any book dealing with the South today: pledged by our American citizenship to a national philosophy of human equality, we have clung to a regional myth of racial superiority; involved in a world which has as its fundamental requirement the constant process of change, we have tried, too often, to escape rather than to shape that change. Little wonder that we are sometimes confused and frequently on the defensive.

Reduced to a smaller personal level, the dread of both equality and change is echoed in the sigh of an elegant young professor in North Carolina who told a friend recently how good it was to visit in South Carolina. "In South Carolina you know right where you are. Everyone has his place and keeps it. But in North Carolina everybody's all mixed up, things are wishy-washy. Nobody knows precisely who he is, or where he is. It's uncomfortable and untidy."

Of course the South's conscious resistance to change in the past is made ironical by the fact that it has experienced more violent change than any other part of our country. Its memory includes not only war but the aftermath of war, not only defeat but the adjustments to defeat. After the Civil War, when the South saw almost everything it had built and collected and cherished crumbling to dust and ashes, as homes disappeared in smoke and the silver and hams were looted and the earth itself was stripped by hungry enemy and friend alike—then the Southerners clutched the only things that were left: their memory, their pride, their ideas. The physical ramparts of their world tumbled, and they cemented all their crumbs of glory and despair into a mental image. They welded their anguish and bitterness into an iron reality. Ideas became images cast in bronze. Their broken swords were beaten into plowshares, but they had forged new weapons in the fortress of their minds. Thus the defeated found victory, and the victor went too long unaware of his defeat.

A doctor in the capital city of one Southern state tells you, during an evening in his pleasant paneled library: "The South has a way of life the North has always envied. Conditions have made it impossible for them to copy us—and so they want to tear down what we have. They tried once, and almost succeeded, but we came back—without any Marshall Plan, either—and even though they'd won the war, we won the peace. Now, again, they want to destroy our way of life.

"What do they care about the Negro? They have plenty up there to look after, if they're so worried about them. We have real affection for the Negro here. We had a yard boy, Luke, who got hell-bent on going up

North about a year ago. One day I said, 'Luke, dammit, why don't you go on? You'll never be any good to us till you get it out of your system.' And he went. It wasn't three weeks till Martha got a letter: 'Dear Miss Martha, Can I have my job back? These folks up here wouldn't pick you up if you were lying in the gutter.' And Luke came back—in the back door, mind you, and not in school with our children either, but with somebody who wouldn't let him starve to death. Northerners can't understand why the Negroes like Luke come back. They're part of our way of life—that's why. And it's something we'll have when the Supreme Court is just a memory."

This resistance to change in the midst of a rapidly changing scene, this stubborn monolithic resentment of the Supreme Court at a time when the South is trying to offer its most fluid and amenable self to public view: these are two of the bewildering contradictions which recur throughout the South—and this book.

The recalcitrance seems to have grown by feeding on itself. A careful observer of the Southern scene tells you: "Actually things have developed much as I expected—not as I hoped; I had hoped for something much better. I hoped we were ready to join the twentieth century—but I guess this is about what I'd expected. I think there was a point, right after the decision, when the liberal South, the modern South—call it what you want to—fumbled the ball. Our political leadership might have come forward and led us, our newspapers could have been more constructive, our churches might have proclaimed the light with a little more heat—but nobody filled the vacuum until the White Citizens' Councils got under way and the politicians saw they could make hay on the issue, and then the main chance was gone."

"You can't imagine how deep the feeling runs here concerning the Court's decision," says a Deep South lady whose maiden and married names combined read like a page from the local history. "Recently I asked a very close friend of mine about some project an organization we belong to was planning for the Negroes. She said that was all impossible now, since the Supreme Court decision." The rest of the world may consider the atom bomb dropped on Hiroshima as a certain dividing point in international affairs and national outlook, but the South uses the 1954 Supreme Court decision on school segregation as its Before and After point of no return.

The attitude of defiance is not new in the region. Andrew Jackson said, over one hundred years ago, when the United States Supreme Court handed down an opinion with which he did not agree, that John Marshall had made his decision, now let him enforce it. It was this same Chief

Justice Marshall who pointed out something many present leaders in the
South prefer to overlook: "We must never forget that it is a constitution
we are expounding, a constitution intended to endure for ages to come,
and, consequently to be adapted to the various crises of human affairs."

Cecil Sims, a lawyer in Nashville, Tennessee, defined the fundamental thing that is going to have to take place before we can have a real¹
ground swell of constructive thinking on the decision or its implementation, and his point is, unfortunately, as necessary today as it was when he
made it in November, 1955, to a group of fellow Southerners:

"What is needed in the South now is a recognition of the fact
that the agency set up by ourselves in our democracy to determine questions of this nature has unanimously rendered a decision which establishes
with finality the illegality of compulsory segregation of the Negro in the
public schools. Our problem now is to examine the scope of the decision,
to accept it, and to provide a rational plan that will come within the man-
date of the Court and, if possible, one that will not destroy the public
school systems."

It is distressing to realize that only the most meager effort has been
made, so far, to carry out any one of lawyer Sims's three very reasonable
first steps: examine, accept, provide a rational plan. So irrational has the
reaction been in some areas that even deliberate examination of the decision or careful discussion of its implications is branded as heresy.

"I was born in Mississippi," a young newspaperman tells you. "I
lived there all my life till I started to work on other Southern papers. God
knows I thought I knew my state and folks as well as anybody. After all
this race situation started to build up, I thought I'd like to go back to
Mississippi. We'd been away eight or ten years. My wife and I went to
Jackson. We stuck it out a little over a year and then we had to leave—had
to come to a 'border state.' You can't imagine the bitterness of the people
there until you've brought up the subject and seen their faces grow red
and their necks bulge and heard them talk. There's no discussing—only
cussing. If you discuss integration, you admit its existence; and if you
even admit its possibility, you're for it; and if you're for it, then you're the
Enemy."

Because of this denial of fundamental discussion of even the decision, much less its issues, a murky haze of half-truths and half-measures
has descended over a large portion of the South while it endeavors, as
someone has said, to compound old errors under new labels. Just as segregated schools were scrupulously separate, but unscrupulously unequal,
so the movement toward desegregation has been marked by a deliberate-

ness which often precludes mobility of any sort. The value or harm of outside influences is difficult to assess. Cool winds are blowing down from the North, fresh breezes are blowing in from the West—but it is a matter for debate whether they are cooling the South's hot tempers or merely fanning the flames to warmer heights.

In this murky half-light, misconceptions flourish. There is a prevalent attitude among large groups of white people that, if they ignore the Supreme Court decision, it will go away. On the other hand, a majority of Southerners you talk with believe that the Supreme Court ordered integration. They are not aware that the 1954 decision did not even mention the word "integration" except in one direct quote from a previous case. What it outlawed was compulsory segregation because of race, and the first process which must be undertaken is desegregation—a far simpler business than integration.

Another basic misconception, which seems to have been accepted in some areas and fostered by certain leaders, is that equality of educational opportunity and limited desegregation of the schools would have taken place eventually in the South without pressure from outside forces, and would have proceeded much more smoothly without the Supreme Court decision. A sociologist in Florida sums up the realities of this opinion when he candidly tells you: "Let's face it! The Negroes have never won one single important contest for their rights, political or educational, without 'interference' by the Federal government. The real pressure for the steps forward has always come from outside, although, of course, there were always those in the South who stood ready to make their contribution when they could. No doubt about it, much was being done for improvement under the separate but equal formula, and some of that has been set back. In the field of recreation—beaches, for example—there has been retrogression, in that the Negroes have lost some facilities they had. But all this is simply the backward pull before the surge forward. And that surge will carry the Negroes, and ourselves, a lot farther ahead than we think."

Closely allied to this resentment of "outsiders" is the most firmly entrenched of all Southern misconceptions, which will recur like a thematic cry throughout this book, for that is the way it rises throughout the South today: "There is no Negro-white problem down here. We've gotten along fine until now; all our good relations of the past are breaking down now because of outside agitation; the Negroes—nigras—niggers (depending on the sophistication of the speaker) don't want 'all this' any more than we do. They're happy, things are getting better all the time—if we can be let alone!" A few may utter these words in callous cynicism, but there can be no doubt that for the most part these disturbed pleas are as sincere as they are unrealistic.

"Damn it all," one young Southerner tells you, as he tries to soothe some of the turbulence around him and within him with a third and fourth sample of bourbon-and-branch-water, "double-think has become a reality here. You know that Englishman, Orwell, and the double-think he predicts in 1984? We're ahead of the times—we've had double-talk, but now we've got the real double-think, too."

A taxi driver in Houston is almost a caricature of himself in the utter unconsciousness of his lack of variation on this theme of past tranquillity. "No—, we don't have any integration here. Everything's fine. We got a city full of niggers, they don't want these changes any more than we do. But we know how to handle them. Over in Beaumont a bus driver killed a nigger a few years ago. He got on the bus, sat down on the front seat, the driver told him to move. He said, no, he was from up there, used to riding on the front seat, and he drew a knife on the driver. The driver just pulled out his pistol and shot him. They fined the driver five dollars for shooting in the city limits."

Against the white protestations of mutual good will and lack of trouble, you hear again and again this counterpoint of veiled threat and tense unease. It is impossible to escape the fact that much of the unease builds from the Southerner's increasing awareness of his estrangement from the Negro. It is not mere cant on the part of many white people when they say they "know the Negro." For years they have had Negroes in their homes, on their farms—as one young plantation owner tells you, "I spend a lot more of my time with nigras than with white people; my wife even tells me I talk a lot more like they do than like the boys I knew in college . . ."—and it has not occurred to them until recently that the Negro might have a whole area of thought and experience that was blocked off to white knowledge.

Another Southerner says to you, "The most surprising thing to most of us, I suppose, is to discover that these people we'd prided ourselves on knowing so well, we didn't know at all. Oh, we had cooks and house-boys and we talked to them, but we didn't communicate with them. And now we find out that the Negro had ideas on everything, including his place in life—and he didn't like that place! It was we white people who were naïve in the whole thing."

A Negro professor in Atlanta smiles: "Some white people were really amazed recently when a poll was taken in one Southern city and the Negroes weren't for segregation."

If white people have begun to look at Negroes with somewhat sharper attentiveness, the reverse has also been true. Many Negroes had thought that it was the wool-hat people, the red-necks, the "po' buckra and hound-dog-walk-the-same-path" boys, who feared them, hated them, lynched them. They believed that the "quality," the folks in the big house, the people whose daily lives they often knew as intimately as their own, these people were really their friends, their advocates, who might advance the cause of Negro justice as rapidly as they could in the face of opposition from the ignorant masses. Then the showdown came, and these white folks joined other white folks they did not know against Negroes they had often known all their lives—and the latter felt bitter disappointment bordering on a sense of betrayal. Then an ironic thing happened: as the Negro saw the unified front the whites seemed to present—even with the individual apologetic denials which might be made to him secretly— he began to move toward more unity, too. A man who leaves his baby with the maid on the evenings he leads the local White Citizens' Council meetings, will tell you with sincere amazement: "I just found out yesterday that Lula Mae belongs to the NAACP! After all these years, when we thought she liked us so much, too! It just shows, you can't ever tell about them."

What is revealed by these experiences among both races is, of course, one of the basic misconceptions of our time, true not only of the South: we've built millions of miles of telephone lines, put tomorrow morning's newspaper on the street tonight, made radio and television household commonplaces—in short, we have improved communications and thought communication would inevitably follow. Reverence for life has too often given ground to reverence for gadgets, and hearing someone speak from another continent becomes more wonderful than understanding what someone says in the next room. While images on a vast network of screens talk incessantly at one another and at us, we stand dumb before each other and cannot share the secret knowledge locked within our hearts.

The complexity of our whole age may be epitomized in the complexity of this problem, involving racial tolerance and justice and good will, which has its sharpest focus for us in the South, but widens to include the nation and finally the world. We are learning to our dismay that as the world's boundaries shrink, man's horizons do not automatically expand; as desegregation becomes more legal, segregation itself becomes more real; as mass communications improve, individual communication is as halting and lame as ever. It is pertinent that the Southern reporter for one of the national news magazines should tell you, one warm morning in Alabama: "The more you know about all this, the less you know about it; that's the one thing I've really learned since I've been down here."

Thoughtful white people are saying ever more frequently, "There's no real conversation between our white and Negro people. A Negro choir used to come and sing at our church once in a while, but we don't even have that now." Or, "We used to be able to talk to the Professor—he was principal of the Negro high school here and a deacon in the church and a good businessman, knew who his friends were—but since he died last year there aren't any of these young ones we can talk to."

There are those who seem content with this lack of communication, like the Charlestonian who says with weary arrogance: "We used to have an interracial committee here, I think. It held mixed meetings once in a while. I think it's dissolved now and since all this unpleasant agitation, I'm not sure we'd do anything to revive it if we could. I doubt if we'd bother."

Of course there are the old communications mentioned by a taxi driver in Georgia: "We got the niggers pretty well in line here. They've talked about these boycotts, one thing and another, but we burned a few crosses around, they got the message and straightened out." When the regular channels of exchange break down, the old Southern smoke signal reappears.

Or, as Bonita Valien, an especially articulate young Negro woman who is also a sociologist at Fisk University in Nashville, tells you, "What is communication? White people want to talk to, beyond or for—but never with—the Negro, and of course that pattern's disappearing. But we think Montgomery, Alabama, and fifty thousand Negroes in protest, is communication, too. The difference is that the message isn't the same; just not what was being communicated before.

"Another thing I'd like to mention is this talk about voluntary integration. 'You can't legislate this!' Well, apparently you don't segregate voluntarily, because there are laws to enforce segregation. Why not laws to enforce integration? 'How can you legislate people's attitudes?' they ask. You can't, of course, but people do change their attitudes, all the time, and you can make it logical and comfortable for them to do so."

A Negro teacher in Louisville, Kentucky, points out: "Communication is a two-way street. In the past Negroes have worked for white people and in the process of survival have learned how to work on white people, now they must also learn how to work with white people."

This lack of communication exists not only between the races but between the regions trying to understand the problem, too. "Right now I'm not worried about the South as much as I am about the North," says one of the few old-line South Carolinians who dares to speak out, on his home soil, for integration. "Northerners can't comprehend the depth and violence of feeling down here on this school integration, and they're puzzled and irritated at the resistance. They had thought desegregation would be quick and easy, like something pulled out of a do-it-yourself kit, and now that they've discovered it's not, I'm afraid they're ready to throw up their hands on the whole thing."

In the 1860s much of the North thought, or hoped, that proclaiming emancipation would be synonymous with its achievement; in the 1950s the bulk of Northerners seem to have hoped again that by declaring for something, this time racial desegregation in the schools, it would be *ipso facto* brought into being. It is difficult to realize and wearisome to admit that the solution of one problem may often give rise to other, momentarily even more bothersome, ones. Legal slavery was wiped out in the South abruptly—but the problems it spawned remain with us today. Like thorn bushes in a Tennessee hillside pasture when they are hastily cut down year after year but are not grubbed out by the roots, so these issues, never squarely met and solved, sprout back to plague us again and again.

It requires tolerance to comprehend what one Southerner tells you: "The Civil War brought about the physical emancipation of the black man from the white. It's taken a century to get around to the struggle we're in now of the white man to emancipate himself spiritually from the black man."

A Negro leader in East Texas understands this. He phrases it in concrete terms for you. "Looking at this community you must realize you're moving on two levels: the laws, which we've struck down one by one, and traditions, which only time will strike down. We're ridden by tradition, Negro and white community alike. You'd think any man down here who was white and twenty-one was free, wouldn't you? He's not. In any court of law, white men have to believe white men against Negroes, even if they know a Negro is telling the truth. The white man isn't free to be honest."

Political scientist V. O. Key, Jr., has said that "Northerners, provincials that they are, regard the South as one large Mississippi." A Negro schoolteacher tells you: "The white folks who fight against us having equal rights paint us all as shiftless and lazy and full of disease and meanness. The ones who're on our side like to see us all as Marian Andersons or George Washington Carvers. Of course we're not all one or the other—and all we want is encouragement for the best to come out." The problems of life, or literature, are easy to solve if you can think of people involved as stereotypes rather than complex fellow creatures. We once heard an eminent drama critic say, "If you want true drama, simplify your action, complicate your people. Melodrama makes things black and white." The South is not involved today in a melodrama—and its people, all of them, deserve more than stereotyping by each other, by outsiders.

Even the words we use—North and South—mean such different things to different people that it sometimes seems we are not speaking the same language. A Tennessee labor leader who has had to meet many of these problems of prejudice and semantics tells you: "One place I think the greatest mistake was made was right at the first calling this 'integration.' Integration means mixing together, suggests all these intermarriage bugaboos, by its very nature stirs up deep-seated fears. But desegregation has to do with justice in our democracy; it should have been called 'anti-discrimination in the schools.' "

The majority of Southerners feel today that they are being pushed into social contacts they do not want. Their feeling is suggested by the elderly gentleman at a dinner party who turns suddenly and asks: "What right has the Supreme Court to rule on my associations, my children's associates? When that privilege is denied us, freedom will indeed be dead in America." It is summed up in the crude shout of a speaker who assures his motionless audience: "The key that opens the door of the schoolroom to niggers unlocks the door to the bedroom, too!"

Desegregation can take place as a legal necessity determined by a democratic society; integration can only take place as a moral conviction in the individual heart and mind. The people of the South must listen and realize the meaning of words such as those spoken by Dr. Benjamin Mays, president of Morehouse College in Atlanta: "It is false accusation to say that Negroes hail the May 17, 1954, Decision of the Supreme Court because they want to mingle socially with white people. Negroes want segregation abolished because they want the legal stigma of inferiority removed and because they do not believe that equality of educational opportunities can be completely achieved in a society where the law brands a group inferior."

Desegregation is a matter of equal facilities and freedom of association; integration is a matter of personal acceptance and mutual bonds of respect. But until a great many more people of both races on both sides of the Mason-Dixon line realize that they are not being coerced into any abridgement of their personal liberties but offered an expanded horizon for those liberties, we shall have bitterness and opposition.

A term which has come in for much criticism from Negro leaders, and which has caused wide misunderstanding, is "gradualism." Sometimes it almost seems that as much energy has been spent fighting gradualism as fighting discrimination itself. Its denunciation has become a stock in trade of some Negro leadership which has little constructive in the way of a program to offer its following. Certainly some of those white people who advocate a gradual approach to solution of race problems are—"well, not really for segregation; no, not really for integration either; just for 'gration,' I guess." But there are many others who seek, in their troubled knowledge of the situation, to use the word precisely and honestly. And too often, while the advocates of all-or-nothing are busy belaboring the term, the word, the label of gradualism—time is ticking away in a hundred little schoolrooms and courts and villages, making it a fact.

"Essentially I'm against the idea," one interracial leader explains, "but I'm also a pragmatist and I know that's the way it's coming: gradually—but surely. Two years ago I was on a panel discussion of school desegregation and one of the members kept hacking away at gradualism, that he'd never accept it. Well, he has accepted it—we all have. In the two years since that panel met, events have unfolded gradually—the steps forward, the pull back, the little but real gain—and that's reality. As Galileo murmured after he told his inquisitors the earth didn't revolve around the sun—'but it still moves.' It seems to me that we need to talk less vaguely about what ought to be and look more closely at what is possible."

Those who have tried to make gradualism a method rather than an excuse have often been caught in a cross fire from the two camps which say only "Never!" and "Now!"

There are the Negroes who reject any part of "gradualism." ("These are our rights now, and we're sick of all this stalling and pussyfooting." A very energetic and very bitter young man fairly spits out the words, and you know the price he has had to pay for segregation and why he would stamp it out now like a venomous rattlesnake.) There are the white people who refuse to consider desegregation. ("We're right up to that lick-log now." A Citizens' Council leader slams his sudden fist on the desk in his little office at the edge of the city. "We've got a court order to mix the schools come next fall. Far as we're concerned, it doesn't matter how many niggers, or how few, there are. A little desegregation to us is like a little polecat smell. They's no such thing, and if there was, a little would be too much.") Between these two unrealistic attitudes are a bulk of confused people who need nothing so much as some definitions and some logic.

But the South is a region of paradox, which sometimes makes the truth of a situation difficult to come by. If the South seems to exist by contradiction, any book about it will slide again and again into a quick-sand of contradictions, some more apparent than real. We are famed for our hospitality—and the highest homicide rate in the nation. We have garnered a reputation for good cooking—and a bad record of malnutrition. We are both Don Quixote and Sancho Panza in the same flesh. We are incurably romantic and instinctively shrewd and one of our voices cries, "Cover yourself with glory," while another voice warns, "Stay home and keep on your warm long underwear!"

Jonathan Daniels spoke recently of "the wonderful sadness of the South. We have so much humor because we're such a sad people." In our natural world we are blessed—in the mountains of North Carolina and Tennessee, Kentucky and Georgia and Virginia—with one of the most abundant rainfalls and some of the purest water in the United States; and we are cursed—in Texas and Oklahoma—with droughts which threaten to blow away the earth "clean down to the roof of hell," as a very old-timer said.

We formalized segregation but never observed it in many of its sub-tleties, while the North formalized integration but never practiced it in many of its practicalities. A well-educated leader in Mississippi can say: "The social, political, economic, and religious preferences of the Negro remain close to the caterpillar and the cockroach." And in nearby Mem-phis a newspaper editor can point out that "the Negro restraint matches white respect for law; Negroes meet justice with generosity, and the principle of justice, as Negroes identify it with integration, is important to all Negroes. But the practice of integration is important to few." And the voices of both men can be typical of the South today.

Our sharpest contradictions are foisted onto our minority, of course, which places it in a dilemma best described by a group of Alabama Presbyterians: "We encourage him [the Negro] to be clean but rent him houses with no bath facilities; to be healthy in moldy shacks on unpaved streets, in bottom lands; to dress properly on a pauper's income, to pay taxes when there is no property to own; to finish his schooling when he has to work to eat; to vote when registrars ask impossible questions; to love his country which shows little affection for him."

In Macon County, Alabama, 84 per cent Negro—largest proportion of Negro population in any county in the United States—you may dis-cover one of the most advanced and one of the most backward Negro populations in the South flourishing side by side. A young reporter tells you about Macon County: "First, you must go and talk with some of the farm workers yourself. Their ignorance, their dullness—it's incredible. Sam Englehardt, Jr., who's led the Alabama fight for segregation, is a legislator from up there. He has a big plantation, he'll tell you they're not ready for integration—and after you try to talk with some of the poor devils a minute, you know he's right, no matter what the cause, or where the blame. They wouldn't even know the word integration; the idea would scare them to death. But that county also has some of the most learned Negroes anywhere, and Englehardt forgets to mention them. Tuskegee Institute is there, and they have recently completed a medical center which will specialize in neuro-surgery. Think of that—all Negro, and working in the most advanced branch of medicine! In the space of a few miles it's like going from the witch doctors to the laboratories of tomorrow!

"Another interesting thing, the White Citizens' Councils haven't made any headway in Macon County, because of the large colored population. Sounds like a contradiction, doesn't it? Your small businessmen, who would normally make up a Citizens' Council in other places, know their bread and butter too well to belong to one there. They look out their store windows, see those Negroes in Cadillacs (or shoes without any soles), and that makes them stop and think about customers and cash registers."

Our contradictions permit us to denounce Negroes as a group in chilling words, while we extend warmth and even affection to individuals we know. We indulge in large generalizations—but we live on a very particularistic level. We frequently refuse to call a Negro Mr. or Mrs.—but in some towns we will occasionally substitute the titles of Madam or Colonel or Doctor.

John Marion, of the Virginia Council on Human Relations, sums up a deeper contradiction: "Our predicament roots in the fact that we Southerners, often without knowing it, have tried to mix two things that are as fundamentally unmixable as kerosene and Coca-Cola. With our right hand, as it were, we have tried to maintain a school system based on democratic principles, and with our left hand a pattern of segregation that is too much akin to India's age-old caste system to be at home in a real democracy."

In addition to this old contradiction, there is a newer one just a-borning. It is perhaps the saddest of all to contemplate. In a region which has been proud of its live-and-let-live individuality, cherishing its eccentrics the way some people collect pressed glass, conformity is now becoming a new measure of acceptance. Perhaps the South has always been a region of internal conforming to an outward nonconformity and we have only deluded ourselves all these years with our tolerance of crusty individualism. Be that as it may, this region which has deplored most audibly the "organization man" of the big cities and big business, is now busily organizing this man's cousin. Proud of being different from an "industrialized, mechanized" culture, suddenly we are demanding that our people all think alike, speak alike, act alike, on this Supreme Court decision, school desegregation, and the races in general. Deviation calls forth ostracism. The harshest anger is reserved for those native sons on the national scene who reject the regional dictates and make even a gesture toward the national, the global view. The 1956 Democratic convention in Chicago provided a startling spectacle of this, with Southern states casting their votes for the vice-presidential nomination to Massachusetts' Senator John Kennedy rather than Tennessee's Senator Estes Kefauver. That Kennedy was a Catholic (which has usually been lethal in Southern politics), that he was no less liberal on the matter of segregation than Kefauver, and that he had conducted a vocal campaign against the South's success in attracting some of the textile industry away from New England—all proved less important to Southern emotions than the fact that Kefauver was a Southerner who had spoken out for the Supreme Court decision.

The case of Supreme Court Justice Hugo Black is equally revealing. Born and reared in Alabama, his endorsement of the school segregation decision suddenly transformed him from a native son into a scalawag intruder. Following the decision and subsequent developments at the University of Alabama in Tuscaloosa, a former friend and associate in Augusta, Georgia, hung a piece of black crepe over Justice Black's photograph and sent him a message of mourning. A taxi driver in Montgomery slows his cab to a crawl as he tries to make clear to you the depth of Black's betrayal:

"The Supreme Court done made its ruling and there's none higher than them. But there's lots of folks don't agree with them. And what we don't like most is our own that's up there with them. Hugo Black. He's from right up here in Birmingham. I used to live there. And I can tell you exactly how Hugo Black got his start in politics. You couldn't get anywhere in them days unless you were a Ku Klucker. And he was one of them. Like I say, he's turned so square against anything he ever was. Said he had a change of heart, but I guess his heart got helped to change by some of that NAPC money. Now you take Warren, some of those others up there, that's different. They've got integration out in California, always had it, Warren and the rest of them men have never known nothing different. But Black has. He's lived down here with us and he knows!"

As the South meets another time of change and crisis and bolts the door against any difference of opinion and protest, we remember a young man in Virginia who said the South once took a great tradition and made it a hitching-post instead of a steppingstone.

Two of the hitching-posts which hold us fast today are fear and tension. Fear is not new to the South, especially fear between the races. Rumors of slave plots and uprisings ran always just below the easy surface, as the most casual reading of newspapers and other documents of the period will indicate, and when any sort of revolt in the quarters did break loose, it was quelled with a heavy hand that in itself betrayed terror and guilt. True, these were years of harsh self-survival everywhere: starving New England whalers sometimes ate their sailing mates, the cat-o'-nine-tails was familiar on both sides of the Atlantic, and a Negro convicted of arson was burned in New York City. But in the South the fierce retaliations represented more than individual punishments; they involved a social system which must survive by sheer force or perish. The secret meeting, the averted eye, the mumbled insubordination were all threats from underground which could portend the end of the master's existence. The religion and violence which came to be two of the indelible characteristics of the region both had deep feeder roots in fear. Their juxtaposition was sometimes reminiscent of Spain and Mexico, where the cathedral and bull ring rose side by side.

Today fear runs like a dark thread through an old pattern cut from new cloth. It appears in unexpected moments of reminiscence when the lynching seen in childhood, the shooting observed long ago, the death and degradation remembered, are briefly touched on an pushed back out of sight. Memories of race riots keep cropping up in the cities you visit, if you talk long enough: "Lord no, we don't ever again want anything like that riot down in the Delta at Elaine, back in 'twenty-one. After all, you might say Elaine's almost more Mississippi than it is Arkansas anyway. I don't know how the trouble began. But I know they shot the Negroes down like animals, just slaughtered them. It was awful! We won't see integration there in my lifetime!

"One of my earliest memories is going with my father, who had volunteered to defend the ten Negroes arrested in the race riot, to visit them up at the state prison. They hadn't finished the trial but the prisoners had already been put to work building their own coffins. I can remember seeing those ten boxes all lined up in a row, and those men in a row talking with my father."

There are the little daily fears of the white woman who lives on an isolated plantation far out in the country, surrounded by black people who are so familiar and yet so alien to her. As you talk together in the pretty sunlit living room, you slowly begin to feel that she is a prisoner here. The bonds of law and custom which hold the Negroes in "their place" hold her just as surely. "We sent our fifteen-year-old daughter away to boarding school this year. It broke my heart to have her leave home so young, but she would have been going in town to the high school this term and that would mean driving back and forth, all by herself, over this lonely road. You just can't tell what might happen—there are only Negroes between our farm here and the highway—and we couldn't take the risk." Her fingers unconsciously trace the carved pattern on the arm of the Victorian sofa where she is sitting. "Myself, I've only been really afraid once since I came here to live. Lawrence was very late coming home one night. I got frightened thinking about how sometimes in set-tling up accounts there will be disagreements, and sometimes a white man will be killed. But, of course, there was nothing to it. Lawrence had had to go and bail one of our workers out of jail." You remember all those waiting women, black and white, back through the years, waiting for the accounts to be settled, or never settled.

There is another fear we know in the South today, too. The tiny librarian with red-blonde hair wound in a braid around her head, who spoke publicly for school desegregation in her bitterly Deep South city, explains the feeling to you: "I know there are many people, many Southern-ers, who feel as I do. It's just when it comes to signing their name to something that they back down. I can sympathize with them. The cuts from old friends, the ringing telephone with anonymous voice—I know how it feels when the butterflies in your stomach start turning to buz-zards."

A man in north Florida tells you about a friend of his: "It's a small thing, really, but indicative, I think. Here at our county courthouse, one of the officials who handles some of the deed and property records comes in contact with quite a few Negroes in the course of a year. He's always been mildly liberal, used to always shake hands when any Negro came in to look at the records. Not long ago he told me that since this situation and all the local reaction, he doesn't shake hands with Negroes at the office anymore. He says he doesn't dare."

One of the few men presently in Mississippi who will talk about integration, although he cannot "speak out" for it, describes this current fear a degree more concretely. "It's these cold-eyed rural people we have to come to terms with down here. They're like the boys who marched off and fought for the Confederacy for two, three, four long dreary years.

Most of them didn't know what they were fighting for, but one thing they had—and these people have it too: physical bravery.

"I can't help but feel sorry for them. The smart ones know they're going to lose; but they're just caught, can't give this thing up. They're, lots of them, the goodhearted, everyday people you meet anywhere else and talk to—but on this they're demented.

"One of my associates and I went to the organizational meeting of the White Citizens' Council here. When the time came for everyone to speak, I made a few remarks, said I didn't see any need for a Citizens' Council here, and my friend and I were invited to leave. Before I left I walked down to the front—we were sitting on the back row—and shook hands with the big wheel from the state organization who was running this meeting. There were about two hundred people there, and I've lived here a good part of my life but I didn't know over three out of that number. They were farmers and country people from out in the county mostly, and I'll never forget walking back down that aisle past their faces. They were not inflamed, they made no gesture toward me—but their faces were utterly cold. Stony. I wouldn't want to meet them on a road at night. They're the ones who are going to kill over this. I'm pessimistic about the situation in Mississippi. I feel there will be bloodshed here. It's all coming."

One odd fact emerges as you travel over the South: none of the individuals you talk with are going to have a part in the violence they dread. "People" are going to bring it about if the Supreme Court decision is enforced. Where are these people? They exist, all right. They have appeared sporadically in our midst already. But if all the individuals with whom you talk combined themselves into some "people" against violence, the ones they profess to be afraid of would be emasculated. You are reminded again, in this time of racial crisis, of a President's statement in a time of economic crisis: the only thing we have to fear is fear itself. Fear creates a vacuum, and there are already far too many vacuums in the South.

If there is one word that has been used more than any other to describe the South since 1954, it is undoubtedly the adjective "tense," growing into the noun "tension." An alert young Negro professor discusses it with you. "All this talk about 'things will get worse,' and 'tension,' just immobilizes the situation. Tension is an umbrella term and it's being used now to cover everything anyone doesn't understand. Where is it? Who's tense? Down in Mississippi the old plantations are still there, the people are still working; Supreme Court decision or not, the plantation rocks on—it's a system of control. That's what Faulkner understands, and damn it he's so right about it. Oh, of course there's tenseness down here, but it's got to be put in perspective, seen for what it is.

"Segregationists use this word to work both sides of the street. On one side they say, 'Things are tense enough down here, you troublemakers from outside go home before you stir up more trouble. Let's leave everything alone.' Then a reporter comes visiting and they give him a desk between two local men, show him around a little, and he goes away writing: 'What's all the hollering about? There's no trouble down here, none of this tension.' "

A resident of Tallahassee tells you, "There's not been any all-pervading sense of tension here. We read in the newspapers about the bus troubles, saw the newscasts on TV, but actually it's hardly touched many of the white people. A funny thing happened during the boycott: a friend of ours here went to visit in Birmingham and from what we'd been reading about Birmingham we thought things were in a dreadful turmoil there. So when my friend got there he said, 'You've really had a tense time here in Birmingham, haven't you?' And his host said, 'No, but you folks down there have really been having it rugged, haven't you, with everything so tense?' And my friend had to admit that he hadn't noticed either."

If by tension we mean a triggered gun ready to go off any moment, it would seem that there are actually very few Southern places with such deadly poise; if, on the other hand, we mean the tautness resulting from two adamant attitudes facing each other, then most of the South is tense. But perhaps we have assumed too readily that tension is bad. In a report to the Attorney General of Florida concerning reactions of various localities to the Supreme Court decision, one investigator observed, "Progress in race relations is generally accompanied by a certain amount of tension."

In 1956, a statement of the World Council of Churches said, "If there is no tension between church and society, then either society is regenerated or the church is conformed." A slack violin string makes no music. A limp rubber band has no snap. Tensions are what we make them—signposts or stumbling blocks.

It is not surprising that a national craze for tranquillizer drugs should accompany our constant conversation about tension. In December, 1956, the Washington *Post* estimated that thirty-five million prescriptions for these drugs would be issued during the year, and it pointed out editorially that "they are invaluable in curing symptoms, but they cannot deal with the real underlying problems.

"Relaxation, within limits, is all very well; but it can be carried to a point at which the individuals are removed from participation in society, or at least made less aware than they ought to be of their surroundings.

"A community, most members of which were rendered wholly free from worry and tension, could become a complacent community readily susceptible to the manipulation of a dictator. Opium smoking relieves anxiety, too. But it removes the smoker from reality."

If the South can overcome its fears and misconceptions, survive its tension, and come to terms with its fundamental paradoxes and problems rather than the symptoms only—if, in short, it can develop a measure of self-knowledge rather than reliance on tranquillizers—then its ordeal will not have been in vain. It is confronting one of the oldest, deepest problems of the human race, a dilemma global in scope, embracing all mankind in its implications. The British political observer, Miss Barbara Ward, writing in *The New York Times* recently on "Race Relations as a World Issue," placed our own situation in fresh perspective: "At present, most Westerners think of the race problem as being primarily one of whether men and women of African stock—in Africa or the United States —can achieve full equality of status. But this definition is probably already outdated. The question is no longer whether Africans can achieve equality. It is becoming the wider query whether men and women of white color shall lose it. There is no certainty that mankind will, after three hundred years of white dominance, move safely to race equality."

It would seem that the reverence we mete out to life may soon be meted back to us in like measure. The South, perhaps more than any other region in our own country, has an opportunity at this moment to set a pattern by which the whole world of interracial conflict may meet a new day. We are the only part of the United States that has suffered war on our own soil—and defeat. We are the region that has most responsibility to reconcile publicly our traditions and our ideals and our expediencies.

Thoreau wrote by Walden Pond, "Only that day dawns to which we are awake." Over the South you hear today the voices of the few who are awake, the voices of the few who are deep in a Rip Van Winkle slumber, and the voices of the many in between who are stirring—eager, sluggish, bitter, hopeful, silly, cynical, brave, fearful. They are helping the dawn come up like thunder down South.

3 ░ You Have Heard Their Voices

He is a tall, white-haired doctor of divinity. His high, un-wrinkled forehead, keen eyes behind steel-rimmed glasses, and rigid collar encasing his thin, wrinkled neck, all seem in harmony. In fact, as he sits austerely on the antique sofa of the parsonage drawing room, he appears to be almost a portrait of reality rather than reality itself. Born in England, he has a peculiarly Southern background, having lived in many parts of the region from Kentucky to Miami and been married to a Carolinian, one of whose ancestors was a signer of the famous Mecklenburg Declaration. In many corners of the South you may encounter ladies and gentlemen still fighting the Civil War, but there are only a handful who deplore the Revolution. The doctor is one of them:

"I'm concerned about all this agitation and unrest stirring in our beloved Southland today." His talk is as courtly as his manner, with no sloppiness around the edges. "I am disturbed by the Supreme Court which has reached beyond the bounds of propriety and needlessly interfered in state and personal affairs. I look back at the beginning of this century and recall the peace and harmony which seemed to exist then, and I wonder where this dissatisfaction today is leading us. It was a shame that matters could not have been settled more amicably back in the 1860s, and the War averted, with all its bloodshed and bitterness reaching down into the present day. The whole world seems so unsettled and unhappy. I have often thought what a pity it was that the English-speaking peoples could not have stuck together back in the troubled times of the 1770s. If only more reasonable counsel might have prevailed then and that War been averted and the colonies remained a part of the Empire, who knows that the whole world could not have been united in a Christian spirit today?"

The veteran newspaper reporter tamps down the tobacco in his pipe slowly and firmly. "Well, this matter of prejudice, it's a long study.

If we live long enough, we'll all encounter it someday. I know something about it firsthand because I was born and brought up in Laurel, Mississippi, and my folks were Catholics! When I was in Boston and New York years ago, studying journalism, writing a little, I couldn't get over the prejudice there against the Jews. That was something new to me. And I discovered that that prejudice seemed to work from the top down, while our Negro prejudice down here seems to work strongest from below up. I believe that this is true because prejudice always seems to be greater wherever the economic threat is greatest. Down South the blue-collar whites and the Negroes are in closest competition; those are the only jobs Negroes can hold—and the economic fear is great. Up North there is a great deal of wealth centered in Jewish hands, in banking, clothing, entertainment, many fields, and it's at this economic level that the fear and competition enter there.

"Something happened here in the city this afternoon that I haven't quite gotten over yet. We have a neighborhood here where a Negro housing unit is on one block and whites live on the next block. A white woman on this street accused a Negro boy in the neighborhood of throwing his arms around her. The police went out there, drove into the Negro family's yard—they've got a nice house, brick, fifteen to twenty thousand dollars, nicely furnished—and sent a couple of kids playing nearby to get this boy. When he came, they took him down to a local station, didn't tell his mother or father they were taking him. Down there three or four of the policemen held him an hour or two, hit him over the head so hard with a flashlight that they broke it, hit him around the thighs with their night sticks, poked him in the sides with their elbows, making him entertain them, dance around singing, 'I'm a nigger, I'm a nigger. I'm a black-skinned nigger, I'll be a nigger till I die.' I did a little research on the boy, found out he's fifteen years old, a good student at school, goes to Sunday School and sings in the church choir, never arrested before for anything. He says the only thing he can think of that made the woman accuse him of such a thing was when he was delivering papers a couple of days ago, a car nearly hit his bike and he swerved it over to the sidewalk and one of the handle bars did touch some woman, maybe this woman, but he swears that was all. Anyway, he's still in jail; and no matter what he did, he doesn't have to be entertaining the police force. Actually, I think the boy's father has gotten to the heart of the matter: he says maybe this white woman was jealous because the Negroes in this neighborhood, and particularly his family, live better than some of the white families. They work out at one of the new plants that is integrated, get good pay, buy a nice home and car, and the whites don't like it."

More than two thousand listeners have gathered in a little suburban community to hear the prominent political speaker from the nearby city. He sums up the history of the Negro race by asserting that no civilization of any importance has been developed by other than white men. "The nigra occupied Africa for at least ten thousand years without realizing any of the continent's economic potential until the white man arrived. The nigra had remained content throughout that period to sleep all day, frolic all night, file his teeth, eat his fellow tribesmen and sell his brother into slavery."

The Negro insurance man is obviously prosperous and even more obviously eager to talk with any white person who will share concern in mutual problems. "We had a case about public beach segregation here in the courts recently. And the lawyer on the other side said to me one day, 'Aren't you fellows trying to rush this thing? You've got the white man down with this Supreme Court school decision, now you're trying to start on the parks. It's like stomping in his face." That made me sort of mad. I said, 'Let's look at a little history. Let's be factual. In 1863, Lincoln signed the Emancipation Proclamation. It's nearly a hundred years later. Is that rushing? Look, the Constitution of the United States was written by all white men, didn't have a single Negro signer. The Federal Court in South Carolina and the other states in the 1954 lawsuit were all white men. The nine men on the Supreme Court of the United States are all white, not a single Negro. We're just trying to get the white people to keep their own laws. We've not made any new ones or broken any old ones!"

In the green quiet village in southside Virginia, a filling-station operator changes tires for you. Big, friendly in a gruff, gross way, he talks and puffs as he works. "This school situation's in a bad twist. You can't trust anybody any more. Your vote don't mean nothing. Might as well stay home and watch the ball game on TV. We ain't got no privileges any more. Everything's done for the nigger. There ain't a lawyer or a judge that wouldn't sell his grandmother for a dime cash. White folks ain't got a chance.

"I tell you, you can't trust a nigger. I've worked 'em and I know. A nigger's ignorant and filthy and sassy and as full of disease as a dog is fleas. I don't want 'em around. If I had my way, and the way of most

folks I know, they'd be back in Africa tomorrow. That's the way I feel
about it. Maybe I oughtn't to, but I can't help it. We could just have
another Civil War over this thing, looks like that's what we're coming to.
I tell you, it's serious. It might come to more than they bargained for up
there. I don't know nobody who's civilized who's for mixing the races. The
law says so, and they've got the money. They also get the votes when they
need 'em. A poor man ain't got a chance, that's about what it boils down
to."

At the sleepy Sunday-morning town in Florida, you talk with the
awkward, overgrown seventeen-year-old who looks you in the eye across
the gas pumps. "Whatever they do in the schools down here won't bother
me. I'd as soon they brought the nigras in. They're just people like anybody else. They've got to live like everybody else. There aren't many
right here in town but several out in the county. I grew up about a
hundred miles from here and there were a lot more around there. I had
some good nigra friends there, played with them. And you go into the
service, you're with them, everybody all the same. We might as well be
getting used to it."

The woman's voice in Clay, Kentucky, was very loud as she called,
"We don't believe in mob violence, but this is one question, if they want
to push it, we'll be waitin' for 'em."

The university professor is very tired and very troubled. The green
lawn in front of his house is unusually well trimmed and neat, and the
desk in his little study where you talk is also neat and uncluttered.
"The most disappointing feature of the last few years in the South has
been, to me, the failure of our leadership. Those who should be making
themselves felt are simply not doing so." He offers you a cigarette and
looks around the room slowly, at his typewriter, shelves of books and the
window between the shelves. "The difficulty of trying to be a true moderate in the South today is almost insurmountable. If you speak, you're
often a traitor to one side and no good to the other. I think most of the
Southerners probably belong to this group, certainly a large number, but
they are not vocal. I've never minded standing up and being counted in a
cause if it will do some good. I have never seen any reason just to be
counted."

The mountain man with the round, open face and blue eyes full of
suspicion talks with you earnestly: "I tell you, it's the hardest thing in the

world to live a Christian life. I want to treat the nigger right, and I know I ought to, but there's just something about it all that worries me. You know there's something in the blood that's agin mixing. We can talk about it all we want to—justice, equality, all that sort of thing, talking—but when we come right down to it, that's what it's all about: a nigger a-marrying your sister or your daughter."

The elderly Negro man sits in his office and looks at you shrewdly. You know that, during a long lifetime of being known as a "fighter" and a "trouble shooter," he has had to make many such evaluations of white people. After a while, he chuckles and tells you a story. "About four weeks ago I went to town just north of here to make a talk. I had a little time before my appointment, and so I went into a restaurant I knew to get a cup of coffee. It's a bootleg joint, too, and there were three white men in there. It was Sunday morning, about eleven thirty. When I came in the Negro waiter repeated my name out good and loud a couple of times and after I sat down in one of the booths, one of the white men came over to me. 'I read something you said a while back on intermarriage. I don't believe I agree with what you advocate.' 'I'm not advocating anything,' I said. 'I was asked if I believed in intermarriage and I said yes. If I was asked if I believe in sunshine, I'd say yes. I know the sun's shining. That's a fact. I know my grandfather was a white man. There's nothing you can do about it, nothing I can do about it. Maybe neither one of us like it, but two human beings are mixed in me. And there are about two million you can identify who are white and Negro. And then there are about three million more you can't identify, unless they tell you. So that's an eternal verity, like the sun shining.' Well, the man went and got another drink and came back: 'But I'm a Southerner.' I said, 'Southerner's met Southerner then. Where you from?' 'Georgia.' 'Well, I'm from Virginia, and when's Georgia been more Southern than Virginia?' He got another drink, came back and leaned on my table: 'God Himself is against intermarriage.' 'Maybe so,' I said. 'You read the twelfth book of Numbers. Moses married an Ethiopian woman. Anyway, I'm sitting here looking at you, part white and part black, just like the sun is shining. The sun's a fact and I'm a fact.' "

The young Floridian, native of Georgia with both the University of Georgia and the University of Chicago in his schizophrenic educational background, mulls over a leisurely Saturday-morning omelet. His Bermuda shorts and plaid shirt are casual, as befits home life in Florida with two small children, but there is nothing casual about his conversation when he says, "One of the things that makes me maddest about this whole segregation-integration issue is that people seem to assume you aren't a Southerner if you're not wild for segregation. In everything else I think of myself as a true Southerner, born, reared, mostly educated in the South—but there are people who act like I'm somehow not Southern because I'm for integration. This is especially irritating in Northerners, who seem to expect all Southerners to be exactly alike, and think there's something wrong when they're not.

"We're just like people everywhere. Some of us change. I was brought up in the old South tradition, didn't change till I went to college, began to grow up, things gradually seeped in. I got a scholarship at college that required my research to be done in the field of race relations. I wasn't particularly interested in the field, but I was interested in the scholarship. So I went into the Negro community hat in hand, so to speak. And I found out when I went to call on Negro doctors and ministers and businessmen that I had to wait in their offices until they could see me. It was at their convenience. And I began to talk with them, and for the first time I came to know Negro people as people, and then as equal. After a while I did some special studies on domestic help, and I was shocked to discover what they earned. In my town, in Georgia, in 1940, the average cash wage for household help was two dollars and fifty cents a week. There were two families in town who paid as high as ten dollars. I guess I've been interested in segregation ever since."

As you walk down the street in Richmond, the air is fragrant with the biting sweetness of the smell of tobacco everywhere. The gentleman who walks with you, in his broad Panama hat, is as much a part of the past and present of Virginia as that tobacco. He puts his thoughts into words easily and well: "People are talking a great deal about the South. Just what is the South? Did you ever stop to consider how many different Souths there are? What makes it stand apart as a region then? Geography and climate didn't make the South. We vary from a rainfall of eighty-five inches in some parts to less than fifteen inches a year in others. Virginia and Texas are no more alike geographically than Virginia and the steppes of Asia. I'd say there were four things that have made the South.

"First, an indigenous people. We're nearly all North European. Take the Scotch-Irish. I'm interested in that because it's my background. My ancestors landed at the middle ports, up in Pennsylvania, spread out into the interior, down into Virginia.

"Second, practically all of us in the South are identical as to faith and religious beliefs. We're almost wholly Protestant.

"Third, we're rural. We're still all essentially people of the soil or only one generation removed.

"But fourth, and most important, and what really made the South, was the presence of this completely unassimilable people. If there had been a belt between Virginia and Montana, and Negroes had been there the way they've been down here—you'd have the same attitudes. That's always the way, no matter where you are, in South Africa or anywhere else. The white people are going to insist on complete segregation from the black people. The white people down here now are perfectly calm about this. They know some way is going to be found to educate the white children if the schools close. But what about the Negro children? Who's going to see about them?"

The troubled young man looks out of the car window at the rich Delta acres rolling along the miles. "We pulled all this down on ourselves. I sure inherited a lapful of problems and I'd just sorta like to see some of them solved. This business of buck-passing has gone on long enough. Grandpa didn't do anything; Pa didn't do anything; but I'd like to think my kid might live in a little peace. Somebody's got to get started owning up to trouble and facing it sometime, and I reckon it might as well be me."

4 **Black Earth and White Cotton**

From southside Virginia, down the coastal Carolinas, curving inward across central and south-central Georgia and Alabama, then bending up in the mighty sweep of the river between Mississippi and Louisiana to the northern tip of the Tennessee-Arkansas border: this is the fertile crescent of American earth in fact and fiction called the Black Belt. For over a century it has stamped its image on the popular imagination of the world as *the* South.

Its rich black soil gave birth to a basic white crop, and wherever there was cotton, there was black labor and white ownership and these became more than a crop and a system—they evolved into a "way of life." In this area were concentrated the fabulous plantation operations, and most of the more modest ones, of the antebellum period. Today, the Black Belt is generally made up of counties having more than 34 per cent non-white population, with a few scattered additions in north Florida and east Texas. (Neither Kentucky nor Oklahoma has a single county with as many as 30 per cent Negroes.)

This is the solar plexus of the South. Everything about it is designed to promote primary opposite colors in the eye and mind. White bolls fatten and burst in miles of long black fields; stocky black Angus and white-faced Herefords graze on bright green grass beneath pecan trees; black faces crowd the bright counters of small towns on Saturday afternoons and white faces confront them on the other side of the cash register. About a million dollars a year come to Mississippi's coffers from its legal black-market tax on illegal white lightning. The black robes of the Supreme Court have been defied here by the white robes of the Ku Klux Klan. It is easy, in this rich, broad sweep of land, for the eye and mind to escape the subtleties or even the possibility of a spectrum. But even here the spectrum exists, and especially here the people of all shades between ebony and albino must be, in any measure possible, understood. You cannot begin to know the South until you begin to know them.

43

Sometime during his life every good Moslem makes a journey to Mecca, every devout Catholic hopes to view the Vatican, and every devoted Southerner plans a pilgrimage to Natchez-on-the-Mississippi.

Natchez and its South are as far removed from the Great Smokies and the Blue Ridge as Smuggler's Notch and its Yankee hills are removed from Pittsburgh or Philadelphia. Each spring nostalgic Southerners and curious Northerners come to view the full-blown camellias and Spanish moss, the long galleries and swinging punkahs, and hear the legends—all part of the reconstructed mansions and unreconstructed memoirs of an era whose ghost resembles its original form only slightly. We visited Natchez during her annual invasion—not by boys in blue bearing arms this time, but by ladies in navy blue bearing fat pocketbooks. It was an experience of fear and friendliness enmeshed in fantasy, as we descended from the Border to the Delta, choosing the Natchez Trace as our route.

Long before that indefatigable sight-seer and scavenger, Hernando de Soto, took up his memorable march to the Mississippi River, this network of interlocking trails linked the towns and people of the great Natchez, Choctaw, Chickasaw, Creek and Cherokee Nations. It began on the banks of the lower Mississippi, turned northeast through the upland heart of the present state named for that river, cut across a northwest corner of what is now Alabama, and then ran almost due north through the middle of Tennessee. A United States official said in 1800 that it was "an Indian footpath very devious and narrow." It seems an accurate, even prophetic, description of a trail that was known among some of the Indian tribes as the Path of Peace.

Through the years, French traders, English settlers, Spanish conspirators, flatboatmen from Kentucky and adventurers from the seaboard —all in their turn made this part of the lower Mississippi one of the earliest melting pots of America.

The legend of the Natchez Trace is gaudy with greed and gore. The murderous Big Harpe and Little Harpe traveled it before they were finally beheaded for their crimes. (Law, as well as lawlessness, had often been a fierce repayment in kind along this road, throughout the South.) The Murrell gang and other land pirates turned it into a route of terror; Aaron Burr, conspirator against the United States, was captured in a home on the Trace. And melancholy Meriwether Lewis, having penetrated the unmapped wilderness of the Far West with his friend Clark, met a strange death, probably suicide, at a tavern beside this trail. His personal story seems meaningful today: a man who could conquer the physical fear and hardship of a rugged unknown land, and yet could not explore or reconcile the dark depths within himself. Looking at the broken shaft which marks his lonely grave beside the Trace, we wondered if this might not be a more fitting monument to much of the South than the military hero who adorns every courthouse lawn.

However, we traveled the restored intervals of the Natchez Trace not for its bloody past but because it was once the vital thread of communication between the plantation country and the upper South, between the old Southwest and the rest of the United States. And because once it was the Path of Peace—which we need again today: not peace at any price, or peace that is merely the absence of conflict, but the peace that comes from mutual understanding of problems and possibilities.

Near the northern beginning of the completed portion of the Natchez Trace Parkway which is being restored as a national park, we spent the night at our latter-day version of the tavern: a motel. The water came out of chromium taps instead of wooden buckets; the night noises were those of the air conditioner and television rather than the howling wolves and barking foxes earlier travelers mentioned. But there was one link with the past: the tavern-motel keeper.

Brown slacks and a short-sleeved sports shirt hung limply on his slight, almost scrawny frame. He fixed us with his small milky-blue eyes.

"I can tell you right now there'll never be a nigger in this town try to go to school with white children. We got a past for handling that kind of thing. You came through Lynchburg this afternoon, didn't you, where they make the Jack Daniel whiskey? Well, you know how it got that name, way back when? From lynchings. My grandfather remembered. There were three lynched at one time, six another, one was a white man they strung up for helping one of the niggers. There wasn't anything but a store there then, folks got to calling it Lynch, then when it got to be a town they just put the burg onto it. And let me tell you, the niggers up around there really know their place today. I don't reckon anybody knows whether they got the right ones ever' time or not, but them niggers up there got the right respect toward white folks now.

"We're just setting on a powder keg here today, and the niggers around here know better than to set it off. A few years back we had a few bad days in this town. Somebody found where some of the niggers had been storing up guns and ammunition—some of the Communists had got hold of them and it was a plot to overthrow just any kind of law and order we had—and boy, after that discovery I tell you, no niggers come out on the streets of this town for four, five days. About the sixth or seventh day this nigger woman got mighty independent, shoved this little white girl on the street. There was this redheaded boy standing there, he just went over and knocked that nigger down, knocked ever' tooth out of her head. There was some nigger men there thought they'd straighten things out, they got in it. Let me tell you a bunch of white men, businessmen, ever'body, went in there and beat them niggers up. Blackjacks, ever'thing they could get hold of. One got killed. And there wasn't never any investigation made about it. There's never been any more children pushed around since then neither. I just think, what if it had been my little niece that nigger shoved?"

He reached into his pocket and as he opened a fat, worn billfold, his small pointed face suddenly looked less harried and foxlike, more touched with human warmth. "I tell you I just love little children. This is a picture of my little niece. She's six years old there, cute as a speckled pup under a red wagon. And she's just crazy about me. She runs up and hugs me ever' time she sees me, no matter where. And she's so mannered, says 'sir' and 'ma'am' and ever'thing so nice. I think being mannered counts for as much as being pretty in children, don't you?" After we had looked at the dog-eared snapshot, he slipped it carefully back into his billfold. "I tell you it just makes me sick-mad when I think of what they're trying to put over on our poor helpless children in the schools."

After he had gone, we didn't say much. We went to bed and turned out the fluorescent light—and the night was very dark around us.

Going from the mountains south the sky widens out, the earth unrolls. Instead of patches of late spring snow on distant peaks there are clusters of brilliant azaleas and the sweet, light fragrance of spring sun on early leaf and bloom.

Across a corner of Alabama and down through Mississippi. In a deserted, weed-choked field, a giant japonica bush blazes in pink bloom. Into the filling station where Sunday-afternoon lethargy slows the big loose-jowled proprietor and even the three wild-eyed boys working on the entrails of their battered 'thirty-six Chevvie.

"Sure enough, you're in nigger country now. You passed a lot of their houses on the road in, a lot of them back off the road, too. We're about fifty-fifty black-white here. Never had much trouble except what was brought in. We'd never have no trouble a-tall if it wasn't for the agitators. That Till boy that was killed down here a while back, he was planted in here out of Chicago to stir up something. It's a fact, and when they come down and start something a-purpose like that, there's going to be hell to pay. But we got good niggers. They know their place. We know ours." His jowls shake a little and he takes off his spattered felt hat and resets it to his head as we drive away. The boys are still tampering with the motor of the broken car in a bored, listless way.

On the outskirts of Natchez we saw the first of the old mansions: a lofty mass of white behind great trees dripping with the graceful moss. Just below it, strung along a hard-packed dirt alley, clustered unpainted Negro cabins—like neglected children around an aged mistress. This first sight of Natchez was to persist and grow as we saw more—the "mansions" side by side with small dingy houses; there was no segregated housing here. As an editor from Massachusetts was to point out in his newspaper some months later, with an air of surprise: "In the cities, such as Natchez, [Negro] school facilities appeared to be superior, we found the homes of whites and blacks side by side on the same streets." This "marble caking," of course, merely bespeaks Natchez' age, for in the years before motorcars it was necessary for those who worked up at the big house to live nearby; as in the ancient lovely hill towns of Italy, the castle sat in the midst of the fiefs whose labor and loyalty kept it alive.

Visitors and natives alike were bemused by the Natchez of wishful hearsay rather than actual history, for in the legend everything was neatly separated and labeled, and in these troubled times that is a beguiling dream. The contrast was classic: Natchez-Under-the-Hill, the bawdy water front where squalor and violence spawned in the heavy sun-warmed mud of the river front and where all things evil were contemplated and undertaken. On the heights above, in Natchez proper, breezes cooled the leafy streets among spacious dwellings, and gentlefolk lived in leisurely elegance and purity. As one historian has pointed out, "The chief defects of this type of analysis in black and white are that, like many good stories, it lacks the pedestrian virtues of accuracy and completeness."

Natchez in its heyday might, in fact, be called the antebellum Houston. In some ways the temper of those times closely resembled our own, and the fever of the river town resembled the fever of the western metropolis now, except that white gold, rather than black gold, was its impetus. Natchez was the largest town in Mississippi and center of the boom which opened the land of an advancing Southwest to cotton and hence to slavery and hence to plantation life; a boom which reached its zenith in the 1850s. Then ten or twelve millionaires in this small area before the Civil War were the nouveaux riches of their day, and some of them frequently acted the part. Here was the frontier, not a homogeneous static group of aristocrats on one hand and laborers on the other, but a mixture of newcomers (over one fourth of the residents in 1850 had been born in foreign countries: Ireland, England, Germany, Italy, France), and Yankees and Free Negroes. Undergirding this large middle group and the powerful few at the top was, of course, the slave one third of the population.

When Frederick Law Olmsted visited Natchez in 1854, he found the country beautiful, the soil very rich and "the land almost all inclosed in plantations." The town itself was the prototype of a typical frontier town in his description of the shops as small and inelegant, the number of fine horses at the stables and tracks impressive, and "no recent publications of any sort at the bookseller's."

A few years previously, in 1833, when a native son, Governor George R. Gilmer of Georgia (then a Representative in Congress) visited some kinfolks at Montgomery in the heart of Alabama's Black Belt, he had been impressed with the same wealth and the same frontier appetite for more. He wrote: "I found the fertile lands of Montgomery settled up with active, intelligent, wealthy citizens, who had been drawn there from the old states, by the many great advantages which these afforded to those who desired to increase their riches. The rapid accumulation of wealth whetted the appetite for getting more money, until the people could not be satisfied with any quantity acquired.

"It was a subject of wondering cogitation for me, who had for many years been constantly taken up with the affairs of government, and the strife of party politics, to listen to my Montgomery friends talking without ceasing of cotton, Negroes, land and money."

Some of the results of this get-rich-quick fever of the place and period were foreshadowed in Olmsted's conversation with a resident of Natchez who told him that "old land, after a while, isn't worth bothering with" and that the planters generally had their money spent three and four crops ahead. In traveling through the more hilly country beyond Natchez, he observed during one day "four or five large plantations, the hillsides worn, cleft, and channelled like icebergs; stables and Negro quarters all abandoned, and everything given up to nature and decay."

There, in a capsule, was much of the economic, sociological, and agricultural past and future of the South: clear the land, use it up, move on. But because Olmsted was more concerned with fertile acres than French antiques, because he looked beneath the immediate wealth to the eventual loss, because he talked with anyone he met and did not merely puddle-jump from one big plantation to another, because he cared enough to see and hear and record for himself rather than accept the testimony of either friend or detractor—he has met the usual castigation of "biased intruder."

For the modern Olmsteds, the Natchez newspaper printed an editorial during their spring season: "When the Natchez Pilgrimage opens here tomorrow it will bring many visitors from north of the Mason-Dixon line who will have a chance to see for themselves that our way of life does not in any way correspond to the sordid picture which they have had painted for them of conditions in the Deep South and more especially in Mississippi. . . .

"Propaganda which has been directed against the Deep South by agencies with ulterior motives which seek to divide the nation, rather than betterment of any group, will be effectively refuted if those who come to enjoy the hospitality of our people will take time out to glimpse the life around them.

"We have some of the finest schools in the state for our white students, we have other schools equally fine for our Negro students and we invite visitors here to see those schools.

"Natchez prides itself on retaining the tradition of the old South while offering a good way of life to all."

It was a plump elderly Natchez lady with grey eyes behind her rimless spectacles and naïve bitterness behind her wounded tone, who asked us, "Why does everybody pick on Mississippi so much? I just can't understand it. Sending folks in to stir up our nigras, keeping everybody upset all the time. We're trying to help our nigras. We want them to go as fast as they can—or will. We built a fine school for them, it cost us a lot, and they don't pay five per cent of the taxes! We want them to win their spurs. We're trying to get this great unwashed to wash and become educated. But it's hard to help them when everybody keeps things so bitter. You know, Arkansas says thank God for Mississippi. We keep her from being forty-eighth on every national list. (Like I've heard North Carolina used to say thank God for South Carolina.) Not that we are any worse than they are, but they're no better than we are. That's what we don't like. Why does everybody try to tell Mississippi what to do?" This earnest woman, who would be so easily refuted by logic and then discounted, is not easily dismissed in the flesh, the disturbed, quivering flesh.

Hers was a cry we heard again and again. "Let do-gooders stay home and clean up their own mess. Drop a bomb on New York City, you wouldn't kill but two real Americans." Or, "Outsiders simply can't know what it's like here. They don't know our niggers—you go out in the fields with me tomorrow, talk to some of the ones I work, you'll soon know what we're facing down here. And no Supreme Court decision on God's green earth can change them—or us—overnight. A hundred years from

now, I don't know. Now, I do know. No black and white mixing in Mississippi."

We heard the voices and we saw the mansions of Natchez, some in
the town, many scattered through the countryside on the acres which
built them. We saw Richmond, where history had tacked on architecture
and three houses joined in one told the story of the region from its Spanish era through its days of commerce to antebellum boom; and Mon-
mouth, solid dwelling of General John Quitman who did two things the
South could respect and make them forget his Yankee birth: he won
fame as a fighter in the Mexican War, and built a handsome home in
their midst; comfortable Elgin Plantation, where the fireplaces had recently been used for fires and things seemed not so much lovingly preserved as lovingly used; and the mansions of the great cotton era:
D'Evereux, Monteigne, Melrose, Dunleith, Stanton Hall.

We went to Longwood last and alone. No one greeted us as we
walked through the deserted yard and around the unfinished octagonal
monstrosity known as "Nutt's Folly," after the doctor who was building
it when war came, and the carpenters laid down their hammers and the
painters their brushes and never picked them up again. A deep silence
hung about the empty window sockets of this ghost of something that
never was. It was the essence of gaudy grandeur never realized, romantic
and ridiculous, a monument of atrocious taste implemented by ample
funds, all frozen in incompleteness by sudden war and poverty—yet preserved and displayed today in the necessity to make the ghosts help pay
for upkeep on a legend they helped create.

We drove away from Longwood and from Natchez remembering the
houses—remembering more, however, the people who had subordinated
themselves, during these weeks, to the houses, as if sticks and stones somehow held firmer links with the past than flesh and bone. Yet it is out of
this blood and flesh that we have fashioned the chain which today binds us
to an irretrievable past.

We remembered the charming and handsome woman who said, "All
the old ways, the old lovely ways and things, are disappearing. There are
no manners any more, there is no culture—there are only hurrying machines and hurrying people. Not long ago, on a trip, I visited a big factory
for the first time, and when I saw those great wheels, pounding and pounding, and men working among them all day, I said, 'I hope to God we know
what we're doing to ourselves.' All this talk of integration of the races, it's
just part of the general breakdown.

"The people who are behind it say they're against discrimination.

Of course they are. They want everyone herded together, everything and everybody just alike; but there was a time when people thought it an asset to be discriminating—to have some personal taste, some set of values, and try to abide by them. We don't have values any more, we just have prices. And that's what the North will have to find out about us down here: there are a few things on which we just don't set a price. We're still paying for a war we lost a hundred years ago. But we only lost it on the battlefields, we didn't lose it in our drawing rooms. If we lose *this* struggle, we've lost the drawing rooms, too. And no one I know in Natchez, or Mississippi or the South, for that matter, has the slightest intention of going against every tradition and belief he holds dear."

There was the old Negro woman—who could guess how old, under the bent shoulders and guarded eyes and grey hair wrapped in a white bandana?—at one of the houses. She was properly uniformed in black with a dressy white apron, but the way she rocked the antique cradle which was her "setting" made the old pictures of "mammies" live again. Until we spoke with her. Quickly she abandoned the cradle and turned to speak, like a mannequin suddenly given a voice and a listener. "I rocked that a long time ago when it already had somebody in it. But I not been here always. I was to Chicago for a while. They're not as friendly up there but I wasn't up there to visit 'round nohow; I was up there to work, friendly didn't matter. Lordy, I made money up there! Ten dollar a day. That much as I get here a week. I'm old now, I can talk."

And the white man who said quietly, "Yes they can vote here. But they don't." And there was no more said.

The young Negro helper at a filling station taught us the realities of caution. He talked quietly in the beginning, then slowly his voice grew louder until he was making public testimonial. "Yessir, I been above Mason-Dixon. Been to Illinois. But I like it better here. Lots better here. Don't cost so much to live. My mother's here too, I come back to be with her. But up there when you outa work, you just outa work. Down here ever'thing all right. Schools all right, we got ever'thing all right." Two white men, one in a service-station suit, the other in faded khakis and a shapeless hat, had come from inside the station and were edging slowly toward us. Less watchful than our helper, we had not noticed them at first. They stood in the middle of the station driveway until we left, suspicious and alert as bloodhounds sniffing a strange scent.

We remembered the wide upstairs bedroom at one plantation and the twin pillow shams with the elaborate embroidery. On one: "I slept and dreamed that life was beauty." And the other: "I woke and found that life was duty." In the stereotype of the Old South, it was the dream that was beautiful. Perhaps in the process of awakening to the New South we shall discover that life is not so utterly joyless because we combine the grace of beauty which is life with a discipline of duty toward life.

And then there was the Natchez man we met in casual conversation one afternoon when the sun was especially warm and hinted of the drowsy summer heat to come, which could stifle and enervate. "You know how long it'll be before the niggers down here go to school with the whites? Well, if somebody was standing in the Panama Canal trying to mix half the Atlantic and half the Pacific together, dipping with a silver teaspoon, however long it'd take him to mix them up, that's how long it'll be before the blacks and whites mix up down here."

The truth is, of course, that much of Natchez today is poor and spending the money it does have to preserve the legends of its wealth; many of its people are genteel, burying under their gentility the push and drive and shrewdness which brought Natchez to its zenith. But to comprehend anything about this town or the rest of the Black Belt of which it is such an integral part, it is necessary to know a little about the crop it made and which made it. To know more than a little about cotton is a lifetime's work. The cotton economy may be dead, as industrialists and experts looking toward the future will tell you, but its influence and effects still live in the South to a depth and breadth it would be difficult to measure. Perhaps this is true in part because it was and is a crop with peculiar human involvements.

"No white man can tell a nigra how to grow cotton," one planter said to us. "Give a nigra a field and a plow and a mule and he'll turn it just so deep and side it, back and forth, turning and siding, and you can take all the tractors in the world and never make cotton so good."

But he, and all the other planters, have tractors now. And that is remaking the Black Belt. "We made a big discovery not long ago," a Delta man said. "We discovered that a white man fit on a tractor seat as good as a nigger."

Or, from another viewpoint, one Southerner told us, "If the white planters and farmers keep using black labor on their farms, they're going to have to see that the Negroes are educated. A man's a fool to turn a five-thousand-dollar tractor over to a man with a fifty-cent education."

The pendulum swings: changes in the cotton economy brought the Negroes to Mississippi in the first place—the increased demands for the raw product, the opening of new lands that made big plantations possible and the need for slave labor imperative; and changes in the cotton economy—increased mechanization, diversification of crops, growing urbanization—are now taking the Negroes away. If cotton was creator of many of the racial problems that grip the South today, perhaps eventually it will also be their alleviator.

When Eli Whitney invented a machine to separate the seed from the lint in cotton, a chain of events was set in motion whose significance has best been summarized by Mississippi's David Cohn, in his excellent recent study of *The Life and Times of King Cotton:* "The gin's direct and indirect effects at home and abroad were prodigious. Here it stopped the slow dying of Negro slavery and stimulated it anew on a huge scale, started a westward movement that is still in progress, founded a cotton plantation system that profoundly affected the culture and politics of a great region, fostered the controversy that ended in civil war, and fastened on the United States a massive race problem. It made possible great cotton exports from the United States to Europe and enormously advanced the industrialization first of England, and later of continental European states. . . . At the same time, cotton became a principal element in American economic relations with Europe, the most important item in the American trade balance, and it also affected European interests in the United States by becoming a factor in international politics and economics."

The interlocking nature of the cotton economy with the rest of the nation and the rest of the world should emphasize the interlocking responsibilities for the institutions it produced and nurtured, most potent of which was slavery. The slave was in bondage to the planter who bought him, the planter was in bondage to the cotton on which he staked everything, and cotton was under the rule of Nature's pleasures or disasters and the North's industrially determined prices. The North could drive cotton prices down—but the only thing the planters could drive in retaliation were the slaves.

"Boll weevil" and "ten-cent cotton" came, in the decades between Reconstruction and World War II, to be terrible phrases in the South, maiming planter or sharecropper, white or black, textile-mill worker or small farmer, giving birth to demagogues, deepening race fears. And gradually the growing of cotton began to move west—far west. Between 1930 and 1939 the West produced only 4.4 per cent of the total U.S. cotton crop. In 1956 it had 19 per cent of the crop. Income from cotton in eight key states of the Black Belt dropped $213 million in 1956—in the West the cotton income increased by about $80 million. Arizona produced more cotton per acre than any state in the Union—and put more than one third of her irrigated acreage into raising this crop. All of which spells at least one good word for the agricultural economy of the South: diversification.

If cotton has had its local, national, international problems in the past, it has them no less today. Long a victim of recurring overproduction, it is now facing the competition of synthetic fibers. While rayon, nylon, orlon and other such materials appear on the counters and racks of shops throughout the world, cotton suffers the inroads of their competition. In 1955 these synthetic fibers reached the equivalent of over 13 million bales of cotton which approximates the whole U.S. crop of cotton for 1956.

In concern over the sudden rise of textile imports from Japan, two Southern states, Alabama and South Carolina, passed laws in 1956 which required stores selling such goods to display signs stating in effect: "Japanese Textiles Sold Here." Early in 1957, when a resolution asking for Congressional investigation of Japan's recently adopted voluntary program for controlling its cotton-textile exports to the United States was introduced in the House of Representatives, a Southern Representative made this statement: "We in South Carolina are going to run our business whether or not it suits Japan, the State Department, the Supreme Court."

The Black Belt is not free from cotton—nor from the past economy of cotton which rested, as Hodding Carter has said, "on the backs of the Negroes, slave and free." The slavery it fostered, and finally demanded, was from the first seen by some within the region to be wasteful and self-destructive. In 1823, Dr. R. H. Helmes, in Johnston County at the edge of North Carolina's Black Belt, called slavery the dark spot in the South. He blamed it for keeping the region "for a long time behind our brethren of the North in agricultural improvements," and said that farming would always "flourish most successfully, and improvements go on more rapidly in a country where the manual labor is the work of freemen." With this protest, however, he followed the pattern of resignation to the seemingly inevitable and agreed that slavery was "an evil we all regret but cannot remedy."

A few slaveholders, during the years before the Civil War, liberated their Negroes. Such was the case of Captain Edward Brett Randolph of Columbus, Mississippi, a cousin of Thomas Jefferson, who, in 1830, freed all of the several hundred slaves he had brought from his Virginia home, and even hired a ship to transport those who wished to return to Liberia, their native land.

As today, the more remote Southerners were from the Black Belt, the more objective their view of slavery might be. (In fact, the more they might resent it, not always from humane principles but as unfair competition for the five million white people who lived in the South in 1860 and owned no slaves.) For them, a member of the Tennessee Manumission Society spoke in 1820: "Slavery is unfriendly to a genuine course of agriculture, turning in most cases the fair and fertile face of nature into barren sterility. It is the bane of manufacturing enterprise and internal improvements; injurious to mechanical prosperity; oppressive and degrading to the poor and laboring classes of the white population that live in its vicinity; the death of religion; and finally it is a volcano in disguise, and dangerous to the safety and happiness of any government on earth when it is tolerated."

Even some of the Black Belt dwellers who fought hardest during the Civil War did not overly lament the passing of slavery. Richard Taylor, son of Zachary Taylor, who had managed his father's plantation in Mississippi and bought a larger one in Louisiana before he went to the War, wrote in his later memoirs: "The extinction of slavery was expected by all and regretted by none."

This, of course, was an overstatement, but it does show that there were many deeply involved in the slave system who felt that its burdens might be greater than its benefits. As a Mississippi professor pointed out recently: "Slavery was not, as devotees imagined, decreed by God; nor was it, as abolitionists argued, devised by the devil; rather it was the invention of man." It was an economic system in which the sweat of the black man and the efficiency of the white man combined to keep the ledger out of the red. But because the key factor involved was human, it became, in addition, a social system, "a way of life." Those who would prove that slavery was a practical labor system have only to submit the dusty ledgers of the great plantations for examination (although whether it was profitable has been debated by historians). And those who would prove it was more than that have only to witness the turmoil in the South today, which stems in part from slavery as surely as textile mills stemmed from cotton.

Following the Supreme Court decision on school segregation, two of the strongest early statements of criticism came from newspapers in South Carolina and Mississippi. ("On the matter of slavery," one knowledgeable Southerner says, "South Carolina fell into sin, but Mississippi was conceived in sin.") South Carolina has been called the typical Reconstruction state. In 1860 it had 412,320 Negroes and 291,300 white people. Mississippi in 1860 had 437,404 Negroes and 353,899 whites. Those figures may be more helpful, at the present moment, in understanding the strength and bitterness of Deep South feeling, than the significant fact that in 1950 South Carolina had 822,077 Negroes and 1,293,405 whites and Mississippi had 986,494 Negroes and 1,188,632 white people.

The Charleston, South Carolina *News and Courier* said, in part: "In depriving the states of the right to administer public schools according to their own regional customs, the Supreme Court has cut deep into the sinews of the Republic.

"Though the court was unanimous, and though the full implications have not yet sunk in, we receive the decision with distaste and apprehension."

The Jackson, Mississippi *Daily News* wrote: "Human blood may stain southern soil in many places because of this decision, but the dark red stain of that blood will be on the marble steps of the United States Supreme Court Building. White and Negro children in the same schools will lead to miscegenation. It means racial strife of the bitterest sort. Mississippi cannot and will not try to abide by such a decision."

These were not as muscular as earlier denunciations of Reconstruction governments, but then the times have softened somewhat. The Fairfield, South Carolina *Herald* could speak against Reconstruction as the hell-born policy which has trampled the fairest and noblest States of our great sisterhood beneath the unholy hoofs of African savages and shoulder-strapped brigands—the policy which has given up millions of our free-born, high-souled brethren and sisters, countrymen and countrywomen of Washington, Rutledge, Marion, and Lee, to the rule of gibbering, louse-eaten, devil-worshiping barbarians, from the jungles of Dahomey, and peripatetic buccaneers from Cape Cod, Memphremagog, Hell, and Boston."

Over fifty years ago, when the century was just a-borning, a resident of one of the coastal Black Belt counties—whose population is now 56 per cent Negro—wrote: "The negro is unlike every other race. He lives for the present, while the Mongolian lives in the past, and the Caucasian or European lives in the future or for the future. He does not seek, nor expect, social recognition—they gang to themselves, and would not be contented otherwise; they have a contempt for the white man who puts himself on a level with them. . . . The negro can live on less than anyone among us—there are few or no strikes in the South—the negro don't strike. He has a monopoly of farm labor and the agriculturists have a monopoly of its employment—the one monopoly is entirely dependent on the other, and so long as that relation subsists and is maintained, there will be no friction, but harmony and good feeling will be maintained."

Today, a man in one of the inland Black Belt counties—71 per cent Negro—told us, in some of the harshest words we heard throughout the South, an echo from a half century ago, "Let me hear about a nigger trying to get in the school here, I'll take my shotgun and fix him so quick! I know a nigger ain't got no soul, at least not like we have. Why you take nigger younguns, they don't know who their fathers are. They're just like dogs or cats. You take the ones up North, they've got white blood, they're different from what we've got down here. The Bible or the Supreme Court or nothing else is going to make us take in the niggers.

"Now you take this restaurant I've got: here's the best nigger cook, she's just as clean and knows her place, but you know she's getting a little spoiled now. Folks come in, they get her to cook up some of that ham, and brag on her; like a feller from off somewhere the other day, he come in, got her to make some good biscuits and some of the best redeye gravy you ever sopped a biscuit in, and after he'd eat it he went back where she was and told her how good it was and give her fifty cents. Things like that got her acting a little spoiled lately, but I'm keeping my eye on her.

"You take out at our little country club here. I'm caddy-coach out there, and those nigger boys got to acting so uppity I couldn't take it any longer. 'Huh?' they'd say. And they decided they'd just carry the bags for who they wanted and all that. Well, one day I knocked one of them down and every time he got up I slapped him down again, and when another one started to run, I grabbed him by the collar and turned him across my knee. We've had mostly white caddies since. I pay them two dollars when they caddy eighteen holes, pay the nigger boys fifty cents. And let me tell you they say 'yessir' and 'nosir' and know a nigger's place.

"I pay my white help here forty dollars a week, and whenever I do get in a nigger I pay her twelve or fourteen dollars. Why, if I had my way I'd just as soon go out right now and shoot 'em down, run 'em out till there wasn't a nigger in this county. They want 'em up North, they can have 'em. There'll be an uprising against the niggers up North before there's one down here. I've just come back from a trip across the country. They hate the niggers up in Chicago and Detroit. They just let us alone down here, we'll keep everything peace and quiet. The niggers are happy, we'll be happy if they'll let us."

It is familiar and depressing—even the familiar chuckle over the

Negro's happiness and good humor. How necessary it has always been in the South to see the Negro being cheerful, on auction block or in segregated school; the first because it was economically sound for us (what sullen depressed slave brought a good price?), and the second because it was psychologically necessary for us (if the Negro children were laughing in their segregated schools how could we be mistreating them?). Always because it was necessary for *us*.

The voices of the past—the strident destructive voices, the confident constructive ones—always speak more plainly in time of crisis. And as it has been estimated that an oligarchy of some six to ten thousand ruled the five million white citizens and the four million black slaves in the antebellum South and stamped their economic interests and social habits most indelibly on the region's character, so it seems today that the Black Belt has arrogated to itself the right to speak for the whole South. More than the right, it realizes the desperate necessity to do so, for the South is no longer the old homogeneous rural region which could be counted on to man the walls at the sentry's shout of "nigger." There are cracks in the masonry, and they must be patched or camouflaged or discredited as soon as possible. Above all, they must be prevented from increasing.

To realize the well-organized attitude that has developed in the Black Belt during the three years since the Supreme Court decision, you have only to glance through a file of newspapers covering those years—or you can take the case of Mississippi as the most intransigent of all.

On July 19, 1955, a petition allegedly signed by 140 Negroes, asking that immediate steps be taken to reorganize the school system, was filed in Vicksburg. Vicksburg, which for over eighty years refused to celebrate national Independence Day on July fourth because that was the day in 1863 that it fell to the Union forces. The president of the state NAACP, which had helped file the petition, said it was not a petition but an ultimatum and that other ultimatums would be sent to Jackson and the Delta towns of Natchez, Yazoo City and Clarksdale (sometimes referred to as "the Golden Buckle on the Cotton Belt.")

The news soon recorded a significant sequence of events. The names of all signers of the Vicksburg petition were published in a daily Vicksburg newspaper. On July twenty-third, four days after the filing and subsequent publication of names, a Negro minister who was on the list as one of the petitioners issued a statement charging his name was a "forgery." He said he knew nothing about the petition until he saw it published in the newspaper.

Attorney-General J. P. Coleman, in the midst of a successful campaign for governor, conferred with the Board of Education and stated that the communication received through the mails failed to meet the requirements for a petition. "The public school system of Mississippi is in no danger whatever from the attempted attack at Vicksburg."

The Citizens' Councils, which had been organized up in Sunflower County almost exactly a year before, received a new impetus with the NAACP move at Vicksburg. New local chapters were born and memberships increased.

The integration petitions presented in five Mississippi towns by September, 1955, were filed away by the school boards without action, while U.S. Senator John Stennis called on Mississippi Negro leaders to "assure white leaders they plan no law suits to desegregate the public school system. . . . It took the Supreme Court seventy-five years to make up its mind, and I believe the court should give Mississippi at least seventy-five years to work out the problem of segregation." Newly elected Governor Coleman pledged that "there will be no necessity to abolish the public schools, nor will there be any mixing of the races in those schools."

With the creation, by the governor in early 1956, of a twelve-member commission to act as official "watch-dog," the Great Wall of Mississippi seemed to be complete. The commission was authorized "to do and perform any and all acts and things deemed necessary and proper to protect the sovereignty of the state of Mississippi and her sister states from encroachment thereon by the Federal government or any branch, department or agency thereof; and to resist the usurpation of the rights and powers reserved to this state and our sister states by the Federal government or any branch, department or agency thereof."

With a quarter of a million dollars at its disposal, the commission's duties were extended from those of watchdog to those of bird dog: it was to point and present "the South's side" in the segregation controversy to a nationwide audience. The fact which created most apprehension in some Mississippians' minds, however, was its decision to employ secret investigators and informants in its all-out efforts to maintain segregation. A newspaper in Nashville, Tennessee summed up the widespread Southern disapproval of this tactic when it wrote: "What this plainly means is police intimidation of those exercising their privileges as citizens, and it is in line with the program of White Citizens' Councils. The whole setup is patterned after the Gestapo and NKVD. And it is something that has never happened in this land before.

"In some quarters it is being said that this adoption of dictatorship methods is clearly illegal, but we are not sure of that. It carries, however, the implication of intolerable repression of personal liberties, and is a dark portent of what is coming about in this land of the free."

Throughout the Black Belt, the commitment to segregation at all costs seems complete. People throughout the South shake their heads and sigh, "But over in the Delta——"

A Negro in one of the Gulf Coast towns says, "I don't know where it's all heading. Look like everybody got theirself in a bind, all-or-nothing they say, and those Citizen Council up along the Delta, they gonna make sure it's nothing for the colored folks."

"To say that the perspective on the segregation problem is different if you're on the Hudson River from what it'll be if you're standing by the Mississippi, even if it's the same eyes looking—that's the understatement of the generation." The young newspaper reporter smiles at you and you know he is sorry for all the things you need to know and probably don't about this peculiar area he calls home. "Look, it's the tremendous migration of Negroes away from the Delta that's the big story here. Government regulations cut down on cotton, farmers turned more to rice and cattle which could mean more mechanized farming, didn't need the Negro labor as much. That's affected our lives in ways you wouldn't suspect.

"Take the Citizens' Councils. We didn't have a WCC here till the salesmen came back to the wholesalers here and said the little country towns wouldn't buy from people who didn't belong to the WCC. All the little crossroads stores around here were what formed the Council in this city."

A Negro schoolteacher from an eastern Mississippi county: "I tell you, Mississippi is just like every other place. Here we all get along fine. Over on the Delta, that's where it's bad, that's where everybody writes about when they come down, write up all those books and all about Mississippi. I tell you a little how it is over there: they all live on somebody big plantation, never know how much they are getting, go down the store, 'give me some flour, a sack of sugar, give me some Cokes,' go down get their clothes. End of the year come, The Man hand him ten dollar, fifteen dollar, that's it. He don't ever know. If he try to ask Man about it, He talk him right down. You can't tell them that live there about it though. They say, 'I get anything I need. Missus, she let me drive the Buick any time I want to, I getting along fine.' At school, when the children don't come, teacher send word home about it. Pretty soon Man come down, say to you, 'You know so-and-so lives on my place?' 'Yessir.'

'You know who I am?' 'Yessir.' 'Well, then, you let them children alone. If I want them to stay out school, they stay out school. You got your job here, you get your pay just the same if ten or thirty here.' "

And there are the Negroes who talked with us earnestly against integration. "Far as I can see, do more harm than good. Just put our kids where they be hurt. Even if they wasn't any trouble from the white folk, how we gonna get as good clothes for our children? They'd stay embarrassed all the time. And the teachers would all be white. Couldn't expect them to pay as much attention to a Negro child—ours all at the foot of the class, whites all at the top, we'd just have more trouble with everything." A Negro lawyer from Mississippi tells an NAACP conference that 99 per cent of the state's Negroes believe desegregation would be impossible there at this time.

The commitment seems complete, the wall solid—and yet—

One of the most persistent voices pleading for a "lowering of the barriers we have put up among ourselves against any intelligent discussion of the racial problem in the South" comes from Greenville, in the middle of the Delta. That voice belongs to Hodding Carter. As editor of the *Delta Democrat-Times*, in a town that has one fifth of the Negro voters in the entire state, he has fought a long battle for reason against violence, and kept his powder dry while his pen was wet. He has not advocated integration in the public schools in his part of the South, but he has tried to point out to fellow citizens that "it is unrealistic to try to stop the entire trend," and he has tried to bury the bugaboo of "mongrelization" and substitute rational co-operation where whites and Negroes can face a mutual task and seek a mutual solution together.

A man in Mississippi laughs (an unusual sound accompanying this subject down here): "There's a Georgia brag that in Stone Mountain they've got the biggest exposed body of solid granite anywhere in the world. I'm gonna call their hand on that: they've not seen the exposed heads of a lot of these white men we've got around here! They'd make granite look like foam rubber."

"Negroes in Mississippi are used to waiting," a young Negro man in one of the middle cities explains. "We'll wait on. We hadn't expected such a defiance against the Supreme Court of the United States—reaction and trouble, yes, but not this organizing. But the Negroes feel real sympathy for the white folks. We know this is the end of the world for many of them. And the Negroes know we're going to win, now or a little later—it's coming."

And most important of all, perhaps, in the Mississippi picture: in

1948, the average salary for Mississippi's white teachers was $1,731, and for Negro teachers it was $659. In 1956 the average classroom teacher's salary for whites was $2,609. For Negroes it was $2,010. (Actually these figures, these bare numbers, exposing what Mississippi has paid, does pay, can pay, its teachers both black and white, reveals the impossibility of defining its problem today as black and white. Much of it is grey, the drab grey look and smell and feel of poverty.)

During the past year, as Mississippi has launched on a school-expansion program, of the $9,653,000 estimated for new buildings, $7,227,000 has been earmarked for Negroes. Until 1952 there was practically no transportation for Negroes going to school. In 1956 Mississippi spent a little over $1,830,000 for Negro school transportation. Compared with 1952, this figure is progress. Compared with the $4,128,000 spent for white children's transportation, it is discrimination. But states, like individuals, crawl before they walk—the poorest state in the union must spend "some" before it spends "more." And when you realize that the cotton and slavery upon which this place was built demanded ignorance, and that now even the most rabid segregationist admits the necessity of improved Negro education (if it will only stay separate)—then you note the first faltering steps of progress.

Throughout the Black Belt you realize that it is not just the numbers of Negro-whites in the population that create the intensest problem, but the proportions of population. Georgia and North Carolina have more Negroes than any other Southern states, but Mississippi has more than any in proportion to her white population. (It is interesting to note that by the 1950 census Texas has more Negroes than either Louisiana or South Carolina—and that Illinois with more than 645,000 Negroes has almost as many as Virginia's 734,000, more than Florida's 603,000, Tennessee's 530,000—and far more than Arkansas, Kentucky or Oklahoma.)

As changes appear in agricultural patterns, it seems likely that amelioration of attitudes will come, too—not as quickly, not as obviously, but change, nevertheless. For instance, the soil-bank program, which will result in an estimated cotton acreage of not quite 1,400,000 acres for Mississippi in 1957, will be the smallest acreage planting since 1868. Reporter Kenneth Toler of Memphis points out that this may have particular impact on the rural communities throughout the state, for although the farmers will be paid over $17,600,000 for idling their land, this is not the same as money circulated throughout the community for seed, fertilizers, farm machinery and labor. Necessity for industrialization of one of the nation's most rural states will thus be intensified further.

And cotton growing concentrates ever more heavily in the Delta and part Delta counties.

Cotton growing on the big plantations of the Black Belt was, and is, indeed a way of life. Two such planters we came to know rather better than any others: one born before the Civil War near Natchez—at the end of the Path of Peace—who spoke to us from the unpublished dusty archives of Tennessee, where he had placed his memories of daily life as he had known it in the Deep South. Factual, detailed, revealing so much of the responsibility and irresponsibility, the savor and the waste, of a life that has disappeared, this man, who for thirty-one years was a professor of engineering at one of the Southern universities, set down his story.

"I was born in Adams County, Mississippi, but father's home plantation was in Carroll Parish, Louisiana. Of its 1400 acres, a thousand were in cultivation, two hundred in lawns and pastures, two hundred in woodland. There were more than 125 miles of ditches in the plantation. Father also owned more than 3,000 acres of uncleared land in Coahoma County, Mississippi, about 85 acres in Wisconsin, some lots in Chicago, about 75 horses and mules, 30 cattle, 200 sheep and more than 200 negroes. When the War Between the States began, the total value of my father's property was about $450,000.

"We lived on the plantation in a five acre lawn with ten acres of flower garden, poultry yard, etc. The main house consisted of seven rooms with four porches; then the school room also detached. The kitchen and laundry were in another building with a porch. There was a dairy too, and a wood and metal workshop for the boys.

"We, the boys, were in the school room five forenoons of the week, and we took music lessons of an hour each twice a week in the afternoons. At all other times we were free to hunt, fish, swim, row, ride on horseback, make traps and toys and other things to our taste in our shop, or do well nigh whatever we pleased. We did not do farm work.

"My father would sometimes help us to make toys or other devices in our shop, but generally his whole time was spent in looking after the plantation. He employed an overseer. My mother was somewhat of an invalid. She spent her time, in large measure, on a couch, but generally she would take one or two carriage drives a day. She gave directions as to household affairs, but did no part of the work herself. My father, mother and children spent a large part of each summer in Kentucky.

"The negroes cultivated the plantation, but some twenty to twenty-five, including several children, were detailed to wait upon the family as coachman, butler, cook, laundress, gardener, poultry keeper, dairy man. We had much company.

"There, as everywhere else as far as I have ever seen, money and education went far towards making an aristocracy. . . . But, as I look back at the situation after sixty years, the thing that impresses me is the singular lack of efficiency that attached to the institution of slavery. Neither master nor slave seems to have sought to economize in time or anything else. . . .

"Slaveholders were as human as any other class of people. Some were kind and philanthropic and some were not. As they generally possessed more or less of money they were generally more or less inclined to self indulgence. I do not know what others did, but I recall the fact that my father educated one poor young man. I also remember that my father employed a Presbyterian minister for his whole time to preach to his own negroes and to those of an estate for which he was the executor.

"For two or three years I attended a mixed public school in our neighborhood. After I was ten years old and until our home was broken up by the advent of the U.S. gunboats above Vicksburg, I was taught at home by private tutors.

"I enlisted in Carroll Parish, Louisiana, on June 27, 1863. In May, 1865, I went from Shreveport to my mother who was a refugee in Tyler, Texas, where my father had suddenly died in 1863 while trying to get his negroes to a place of safety. In 1862 the U.S. had seized our plantation and it rented it till January 1, 1866. I remained with the negroes in Texas till the crop they had planted was gathered, then we all went back to Louisiana. I left for college April 16, 1866.

"My father in early life wanted to free his negroes. In order that he might have a living after this he graduated as M.D. at the University of Pennsylvania. But he never practiced medicine, as he found the state law forbade any one to free the negroes without sending them out of the state, so he continued a cotton planter until his death."

Our second planter was very much alive, in a county where well over 60 per cent of the population was Negro. His more than one thousand acres are planted to cotton and peanuts; his home is a comfortable frame farmhouse with modern electrical servants and only a part-time Negro maid. His friendliness, and that of his wife and children, is warm and genuine; as you ride and walk with him over his acres, the feeling of a mutual ownership between this farm and the man grows stronger. If he possesses a deed to these acres, they and their people also possess invisible title to him.

"This land's been in my family far back as I know. My father didn't live on it, it got run-down, the farmers stole him out, before I moved down here. All the nigras here now have been born here for generations. Twenty families on this plantation, and they come to me for everything. I've only got three children but I've paid for more babies than any other man in the state. Nigra girl has an illegitimate baby, comes to me, I send for the doctor, then after a few months she goes off to Chicago or somewhere, the bill comes to me, I don't know who the daddy is any more than a billy goat, so I pay it.

"They're in fightings, cuttings, scrapes all the time. Sometimes I have to help settle it, sometimes not. I give them everything—house, food, wood to burn, mule to haul it, axe to cut it, everything—and then they get a money settlement at the end of the year. Spend it, make a down payment on a car, wreck the car by Christmas, never get it paid for, company comes and takes it back. No doubt about it, share-cropping is just not a good system.

"The nigras around here are full of superstition still. They won't admit it, but it's there. You can't get them to start planting a crop on Friday. They may drop just one row on Thursday, but that begins it, and damn if they haven't got me into it now, too.

"Up at their school here they had a big row a year or so ago: one of the teachers put a hex on the principal's wife. She was in love with the principal, got a conjurer in town to sell her some conjure powder, put it in the wife's stove. They found out about it, had to fire her from her job there was such a racket about it. That's going on up at their school.

"Now about their school, I'll admit it isn't right for those two hundred or more pupils to be up there in three rooms. Little wood stoves, two out-door privies. We ought to build them a good schoolhouse if that's what they want."

Down the rutted little roads between the spreading fields, past the two-room, three-room, four-room houses in all stages of repair and disrepair, you move between the level sky and level earth.

"I need to build some good roads all over this farm. I'm trying to replace all the houses, too, one at a time, as I can. They all have electricity now. I'm making the new ones of cinder block; they can't burn them down as easy then, and the upkeep is cheaper, too. There's a lot maybe ought to be done different about the farm, but I guess I'm just slow on the changing. We work from first light till first dark here in the summer and fall, just sort of let down in the winter. Do things as we can.

"You see that house over there? That's the sorriest house on my whole place, I'd be way better off with it torn down, but I can't because of Governor and Pearl. Governor is that little dried-up nigra in the big army overcoat we passed back there a ways, and Pearl's his wife. Governor Weatherbaugh—if you paid him just exactly what he was worth a day, he'd owe you a dollar. Oh, he'll do anything you tell him to: 'Governor, go out there and help dig those peanuts.' 'Yessuh.' 'Governor, go down and get that mule.' He'll do it. But when it's done, it's the worst-done job you ever saw. And if he works for you five minutes during the week, he's the first one there for his pay Saturday morning.

"He doesn't deserve Pearl. Pearl's a smart wife. She keeps Governor's dilapidated house, a lot more than he earns, the cleanest on the place. It's spick-and-span inside. During cotton picking, she works in the field. 'I may be gettin' along, but I sure can keep up with any of them on the picking, can't I, Mister Bill?' she's always asking me. She goes to church every Sunday, when I see her pass the house here I get out the car and carry her up to the church house lots of times. 'Good Lord, don't I look good today, Mister Bill?' 'Yessuh, Pearl, but not as good as you did last Sunday.' 'That's the truth, Mister Bill. I'm wearing my white dress today, wore my blue last Sunday.'

"Governor just lives in the house free, wood off the place, what food he makes. I can't tell him to move. Where would he go? He barbecues for the other nigras, digs graves, sinks wells. To sink a well you just use an augur and keep screwing on lengths of pipe. Anybody else could do it, and better, too; but we've just let Governor take it for his job here. He's sexton up at their church, too.

"When we first moved out to the farm here, seems like one of the things I remember best is meeting Governor all times of the day or night hunched up in that big army overcoat, sitting on a little wagon he had that looked as if it was about to fall to pieces, driving up and down the road. At night sometimes after I was in bed, way up in the night, I'd hear that old wagon creaking, turning off on the road right below our house that led down to Governor's and Pearl's. Poor old Governor took such poor care of the mule I let him use that I finally had to take it away from him. I guess he burned the wagon for firewood. Now Governor has to walk everywhere he goes. I guess he has wanderlust. But I don't hear his wagon creaking along the road any more, although I suppose he's still out there in the dark somewhere moving around."

There is an intricate insolubility about the relationship between Governor and Mister Bill. This planter might epitomize so much of the South's tolerance and intolerance: its intolerance of the Negro race, its tolerance of individual Negroes—where in other areas of the country a tolerance for the race might often be contrasted by intolerance for some of its individuals. Governor's and Mister Bill's lives, however, seem utterly remote from all abstractions. Theirs is a concrete daily existence in rain and mud, sun and dust, joy and dejection. Black and white they are bound together by the Black Belt of the land and the past.

5 ░ **Green Hills, Green Hopes**

There are many Souths. If you look you can see the Souths of camellias and collards, of live oaks and broom sedge, of mangrove swamps and mountain spruce. And beside and beyond the South of black loam and cotton and alluvial silt, stretch the green crop fields, the rolling uplands, and finally the mountain ranges. The feel of the earth, the look of the sky, is different in each of these geographies, and as the land differs so do the people. Only their interdependence remains constant.

If land is mistreated, if any segment of people is denied full respect, yes reverence, for life, then the region and all the people in it are diminished. The fields and gullies are eloquent today with both waste and fulfillment. For the South just now seems not so much a place of black and white, as of green. To understand the surface, you must seek what lies beneath: to try to know the people here, you must know their earth. A varied earth—harsh and worn, high and wooded, turned by a bull-tongue plow or an indefatigable tractor, or left in peace in countless hills and valleys—it has molded the recreation as well as the work, the manner of living as well as the means of livelihood, for all its people. There are many ways to know the land:

It is a late September morning just before dawn. Crouched in the chilly half-light surrounding a Georgia lespedeza field, or an abandoned wheat field, or the rustling stubble of a corn patch, you feel the fresh, astringent morning air full on your face, smell the autumnal blend of dry leaves and seed pods and dust, and hear the beat of wings out there in front of you. The birds are coming in to feed—and you are waiting with your rifle.

In October, the Kentucky hills ring with the night-music of deep-chested hounds on a fresh trail, while you lounge with the hunters beside a leaping orange campfire and listen to the distant chorus and swap stories and watch a shower of sparks rise in the darkness when someone drops another pine chunk on the blazing coals. "Old Blue" and "Thunder" and

"Big Tom" follow the scent across the ridge and their baying echoes in the distance.

By mid-November the rugged mountains between North Carolina and Tennessee are stripped of their foliage except for the stubborn oak leaves and the tangled undergrowth of evergreens. Stamping your boots and rubbing your hands, you wait in the icy morning air for the party to gather and start their difficult hunt for the wild boar which roam this wilderness. Only in such rare, remote spots are these vicious animals found today, and you wait with controlled tension when, after a long, hard stalk, the noise of a plunge through the dense laurel on the steep hillside comes closer. Suddenly, into your stand breaks a small-eyed, rangy tusker. You raise your rifle, ready for the charge.

The green fields and forests and waters of the South are filled with a marvelous variety of living things, and the nearest many visitors ever come to knowing the region is on the trail or in the blind or beside the stream. Southerners themselves know how to enjoy the hunt, and how to transmit that enjoyment to others. They endow it with leisure and ritual, center a large part of its comradeship around food (and drink!), and achieve a final blend of adventure and well-being which seems to suggest the best of both the frontier and the genteel in its tradition. Southern boys, white and Negro, grow up together in the little towns and the rural places, and many of the long, hazy blue Saturdays of autumn, or the drowsy, endless summer days, are spent roving the woods and pastures.

"I remember when I was a boy," one textile-mill manager tells you in mellow reminiscence, "we lived in a small town and there weren't any children my age close by. My father paid this nigra boy fifty cents a week just to come and play with me. He was about ten or twelve, I was seven or eight; from then on, for years, we were practically inseparable. We played, and then we went hunting and fishing together, and for a while he was just about as important to me as my father. We ate and slept and swam together. Then we grew up, like boys will, and went different ways, of course. I didn't hear from him again for a long time. Then, during the War, I had a letter from him while I was a private in the infantry in Europe. He was a captain in the air force."

It is the fields—sometimes tilted toward the sky, sometimes level out to the rim of the horizon, sometimes rolling like a gentle sea—the fields and woods, tall old stands of hardwood or green masses of young pine, which fill the eye of the traveler through the South and bind all its diversities together. For no matter how positively statistics may be used to prove that the South has recently climbed past the 50 per cent mark in its urbanization, it is still essentially a rural region. Changing? Yes, as inevitably as the seasons and as fitfully, with inward transfer from rural ways and habits slower than outward changes from hand-hewn boards to cinder-block veneer.

The land is old here. It has known the tread of many people. They have left their languages upon its towns and rivers, hills and valleys, and their variety sings and belies the narrow single image some would seek to stamp on this rich past, this diverse Southern realm: the Indian words on land and water, the Spanish names, the French terms, the firm English titles, and the names the Negroes made their own through living in the narrow backways. These are the South's amalgamated inheritance: the everyday words of extraordinary beauty and meaning. Alabama and Mississippi and Tennessee; Chattanooga and Shenandoah and Okeechobee from the proud red tribes of ancient lineage. St. Augustine and Florida and the Brazos River from the restless Spaniards. France's New Orleans and Louisiana and Mobile Bay; and Britain's Williamsburg, Prince Edward County, Charlestown and the Cumberlands, like a march. And the sad gaiety of black and brown and coffee-colored Catfish Row and Congo Avenue and old Beale Street.

"How'd we come here in the first place?" one angry young Southerner asks you, and answers himself. "What've we got to be so all-fired high and mighty about? All these highway markers they're putting up everywhere now—a Choctaw Council Place, Cherokee Round Up Fort, and on and on—all the hell they really mean is that here's where we broke another treaty and stole some more of the country from the Indians. When you get gunpowder on one end of the springs of justice, what've you got? Not justice, that's for sure."

The Western waters beckoned the early comers to Southern soil, and long hunters were followed by home builders. Fire and steel felled the forests, the bull-tongue plow turned the face of the earth, passenger pigeons that darkened the day with their migrations disappeared from the sky. The tall trees were snaked down the mountain sides and the rivers ran red to the sea. Men and women sweated and bled, killed and were killed, for parcels of this Southern earth they loved—and yet, as "all men kill the thing they love," they just as surely sucked the lifeblood of their land. The pattern was established early: clear, mine, abandon, then clear more; mine the topsoil deeper, abandon sooner. Thomas Jefferson, the Leonardo of Virginia, who combined a wide range of talents and interests in his career, was already aware of the waste inherent in the pattern during the early days of the republic, when he stated, "We can buy an acre of new land cheaper than we can manure an old one."

It is surely one of the South's most baffling paradoxes that we can love the "home place" with a fervor that often borders on the unreasonable—and yet let that "home place" go without care for year after year. We still love the land, the little pocket we know and hold, with such fierceness many people today might find it difficult to understand—yet we watched it wash away for decades before we moved to save it. The deep relationship between Southerners of all races, all ages, all conditions, and the soil that both fed and starved them, kept them at once bond and free, is part of the complexity infusing our racial problems today. With the land, as with the people, the more intricate the dilemma, the simpler we have tried to make the answers. The problems which plagued the Old South were once oversimplified in the national mind. As Vann Woodward has so aptly pointed out, "The evils of land monopoly, absentee ownership, soil mining, and the one-crop system, once associated with and blamed upon slavery, did not disappear with that institution but were, instead, aggravated, intensified and multiplied."

Slavery was a symptom as well as a cause, just as segregation today is not only a cause but a symptom, too, of deep disturbances in our national dream and our regional development. Irreverence for life in one form callouses our reverence for all other life. Poor land breeds poor people and poor people bring forth poor civilizations. That is why the greening fields of the South today must give us hope. That is why we try to balance what we see and hear with the facts and figures of analyses on what is happening in the South today between the land and its people. Once upon a time, talk of the marginal land could prove colorful for a traveler:

"This here Georgia upland's so no-count it ain't good for nothing but to hold the world together."

"I've heard say that some of this Arkansas ground is so pore it takes three seeds to make one cornstalk: one to push, one to pull, and one to grow."

"My Tennessee pasture here won't sprout nothing but rocks, but I figure at that it must be pretty strong ground or it couldn't hold all them rocks up."

Mississippi and Alabama and Arkansas, three of the nation's most rural states, also have the three lowest per-capita incomes of the forty-eight states. Their rural income per person is fantastically small. According to the 1950 census, North Carolina had more farm people than any other state in the Union, with Texas second, Mississippi third and Tennessee fourth. The Southerners are obviously winners on the rural lists. But between 1940 and 1950, North Carolina's urban and rural non-farm populations each increased 40 per cent, while the rural farm population decreased almost 17 per cent. The shift has not totally altered the state's appearance, however; it would be worth remembering that in 1950 thirty-seven of North Carolina's hundred counties still contained no urban centers, and although the percentage of tenant farmers (including sharecroppers) had decreased since 1930, there were still, in 1950, twenty-six counties where more than half of the farms were operated by tenants, and in ten counties more than two thirds of the farms were operated by tenants.

These are the figures you see made tangible as you drive down the country roads past weather-beaten barns and houses. ("It could rain paint for a year down South and still give everything just one prime coat it needs," a Piedmont farmer grins.) Tenancy grew out of the lien system, and that system was a curse, but it had been pointed out that it was "not a plot but a makeshift." Like the broken latch on the gate and the pasture fence temporarily mended with baling wire, and the wagon held together by loose bolts and bits of rope and the grace of God, it was a makeshift. It would have to do until something better, sturdier, came along. Meanwhile everyone became accustomed to the temporary substitute, until it seemed to be the traditional permanent order. Some years ago, a Southern governor summed up the evil chain reaction of tenant cultivation: "The Negro skins the land and the landlord skins the Negro."

"No doubt about it," a farmer tells you in troubled perplexity, looking over his peanut harvest and the several families who live in houses scattered over his place, "tenant farming's no good. I can't pay but half what I'd like to, they don't give me but about half as good work as they ought to; these peas will be harvested about half as clean as they could be before we turn the hogs in to forage. That's the way it goes. I can't figure how to get from under unless I let go everybody that's here now. Some have been on this land most of their lives, longer than I have. I can't run them off. Don't any of us know any different way of doing, and I guess they're as slow to change as I am."

Even as the exploitation which once characterized most tenancy and sharecropping diminishes, however, there is one group which does not share proportionately in improved wages or increased ownership of the land it tills: the Negro farmer. Between 1920 and 1950, surveys have concluded, Negro farmers as a group lost ground. Improved methods and machines and fertilizers, larger capital outlays, diversified crops and larger operations all have brought Southern farm production to a new high level—and have been of little benefit to most Negroes. (Illustrative of the growing tendency toward larger and more mechanized farms, Georgia, in the four-year period between 1950 and 1954, lost more than 32,000 individual farms and more than 111,000 horses and mules.)

With poor education, little credit and less capital, and small acreages, Negroes are crippled in efforts at improvement or extension of themselves or their farms. In 1954, the median money income of a white urban family in the Northeast was $4,837 and for a Negro family, $3,243. For a white farm family in the South the median income was $1,516. For a Southern Negro farm family the figure was $742. Small wonder that Negro farmers throughout the South have been leaving the land for the city until, at present, the approximate division of America's Negro population is one third in the rural South, one third in Southern cities, and the other one third scattered in clusters through the rest of the United States. (We must also not overlook the fact that the disparity beween Negro and white farm income in the South is almost in exact proportion to the disparity between Southern white farm family income and Negro urban family income in the Northeast.)

The poverty and inadequacies of the rural Negroes of the South are a drain on all the region and all the nation. James McBride Dabbs, a wise and witty farmer in South Carolina, a dedicated layman of the Presbyterian church, an outspoken foe of segregation in a Deep South county, stands on the wide veranda of his ancestral home and says, with a twinkle in his fine blue eyes, "Yesterday I told the Negro man who lives here on my place that I just couldn't afford segregation any longer. I took him out to the field there and showed him where his son had been plowing the day before. 'What do you think of that, Henry?' I asked him. 'Yessir, Mister Dabbs, that's mighty sorry plowing.' 'It's so sorry that we'll just have to do it over again today. That's what I mean, Henry, this segregation simply costs more than I can afford. If your boy had been able to go to school up here with my boys, maybe he'd have learned more about the right way to do things. Now he's learning at my expense and none of us are doing any good.' "

The people at the crossroads stores (Coca-Cola and snuff and headache tablets advertised on the sides of the square frame, or whitewashed cinder-block, building), the people down the farm roads, or in the little rural towns, these are probably the ones who will eventually determine the general tone of acceptance of desegregation. It is strange that although they are probably the smallest part of the real power structure of state or region, their provincialisms and fears, their desperate inferiorities and superiorities, have been used to determine the basic issues of segregation, and the people of power who often agree in essence with their country cousins—although for somewhat different reasons and to different ends—permit and encourage this partnership as a necessary demonstration of unanimity. A Deep South Senator famous for his racist views says in apparent candor, "Give me another issue I can run on and be sure of winning out in the counties, and I'll drop the nigger question."

Local politicians and ministers assure you, "You don't know the way these people around here feel. Even if we disagreed with segregation, if we spoke out our views we'd be done for. We could go to New York and preach integration—but what good would that do here? You don't know all the pressures a little community like this can bring to bear on anybody it doesn't accept."

"It's us that'll have to sit beside the niggers in the schools," one woman on a lonesome little farm in Alabama tells you. "The big rich folks, their younguns already go to separate schools from ours. They can pay for being educated private. This integration talk ain't nothing but words to them. It's a heap more than that to us."

And it is at the little crossroads, whether deep in the cotton country or in the upland of red gullies or slash pine or gradually healing hills of green cover crop, that most of the shocking racial violences so far have occurred: the dynamite explosion, the sudden shot, the body in the river.

There is in the South a current meeting and merging of rural and urban life that has long since taken place in certain other sections with somewhat different results. That this process should be going on at the same time the social upheaval of desegregation is being confronted, is significant and dramatic. Southern cities, expanded from the sea and river ports, the state and county capitals and the even-sized cotton-centered hamlets of an earlier period, stand at present in more equilibrium to rural influence. Although they are still unable to take over many of the functions of the old established metropolitian areas of the nation, they are bringing about a balance in the South which may eventually create an enviable situation. To those agrarians who dream only of a society living on and by the soil without any of the standardizations of the metropolis, the South's cities are already too many and too large. To those urbanites who despair of the problems and poverty of agriculture and envision an industrial utopia of two tiled bathrooms in every home and a television antenna as shade tree for the swimming pool, the rural areas of the South are still too many and too large. For all those in between, however, an ideal balance may be in the making—that between green money and green fields, which can eventually ameliorate the difficulties of black and white.

Most of the past problems of poverty in the South have been those of white men and black men living by the land. As black slavery made it possible for a few white men to own great boundaries of the richest soil, more and more white people were pushed into the country above, below and around the wealthy Black Belt. They varied from sturdy, prosperous farmers in the fertile little valleys and upland flats, to the "poor white trash" who scratched a bare existence from their "crawfish land." Bemused by the exotic folklore and obvious troubles of the Negro on one hand, and the colorful and often-envied individualism of the Southern elite on the other hand, this great middle-class group in the South has frequently been ignored by the scholar as well as the visitor. It is this group which contains most of the uncommitted majority confronting Southern racial issues today. On its attitudes and actions will depend the final adaptations to integration of all our citizens into full community participation.

It is often misleading, if not downright inaccurate, to generalize about so large and diverse a group. For instance, you are often told that in the counties where there are few Negroes, integration could take place without a ripple on the social surface. This is true in some cases, but in others, where economic or historic or leadership factors vary, it may be untrue.

A filling-station operator in one of North Carolina's most mountainous counties says, "No, the niggers won't try nothing here. Don't have over a hundred or a hundred-fifty in the whole county of ten thousand. They know their place. They's a town just across the mountain yonder, if a nigger passes through there and it's getting close to sundown, they'll jerk him out of his car and tell him he better get on through before night catches him. Ain't been any nigger spend any time there after dark since Civil War days. We won't have no trouble. They know the score around here."

And there is the variety within each state: in Richmond, a segregation leader tells you, "We've got everything in Virginia—three counties up in the southwest part of the state that don't have any nigras. That don't mean they like them. They're prejudiced against them or they'd have some. Then you have southside Virginia, where white people are outnumbered in some places. I don't believe any of these people will stand for integration." And a little later he makes a more revealing statement: "Our group knows once integration gets a toe hold anywhere in Virginia, it will weaken the whole state." Actually, Negroes make up only 24.8 per cent of Virginia's population and this is only 3 per cent more Negroes than in Maryland, where integration is well under way.

A Birmingham man describes his state: "Alabama, like Tennessee and all Gaul, is divided into three parts—only where it's east, middle and west Tennessee, it's north, central and south Alabama. Feeling here against integration is probably least strong in the Mobile area, where you have industrialized people and no cotton-belt influence. The last places to integrate, I suspect, will be the rural areas in north Alabama, and the cotton communities in the south-central part of the state. Some of these last ones may never really integrate—could start a guerilla delaying action that will go on for decades."

And a teacher in Coral Gables explains, "Florida is in an odd situation: you have to go south to find the north, and northern Florida is really little Georgia. Our attitudes are anything but homogeneous."

A resident of Little Rock, who has probably observed as widely and deeply as any person in the state on this particular issue, sums up: "In three or four of the eastern counties, where the Negro population is 50 per cent or more of the white population, you can't even discuss integration. But up in Heber Springs, north of here, there are no Negroes at all—and you can't discuss integration there either. In many counties without Negroes, throughout the South, there is stronger feeling against them than in other sections. I would say that the greatest difficulties of desegregation probably come where there are almost no Negroes or where there are a great many. The easiest places should be where there are 10 to 25, even 30 per cent, but where they are a recognized part of the community and there has been at least some semblance of communication between the Negroes and whites, or their leaders, anyway. Of course it's hazardous, making rules of thumb like this, but it's probably less dangerous than seeing this as an all-or-nothing, black-or-white proposition all the way down the line."

Southern farming is diversifying rather rapidly; Southern attitudes are diversifying more gradually. But there is diversity. In South Carolina, a stranger tells you in casual conversation, "Used to be all cotton around here, now we have a lot of cattle. Niggers have left out, headed North for jobs. From what I hear, the North don't like them any better than we do and is trying to send them back down here. We know how to handle them. Few years back, one got sassy with a white woman, a bunch of folks decided to save the county some money trying him with a lot of rascally lawyers. They tied some rocks to his feet and dumped him in the Congaree. Best for everybody to do it that way."

But a couple of days later another stranger in a drowsy little antebellum town in Georgia says, "We've gone to grass here in Wilkes County. Lots of the nigras have left. About half and half here now, used to be three to one nigra. I've got a farm myself, out about three miles, along with my business here in town. There's a nigra family on that place I love like my own family. Any time they want any food, clothes, I give it to them. They don't do that up North, just let them shift for themselves.

"We're building a six-hundred-thousand-dollar school out here for the nigras, and a three-hundred-thousand-dollar one for the whites. But I don't begrudge it. We've not had good enough schools for them. And lots of the farmers around here haven't paid them enough. If we all start doing right, I don't see why we'd have any trouble."

A woman in North Carolina confides, "It seems to me that one of the saddest things that's happened to us down here is the effort of the white supremacists to isolate any citizens who would like to voice their aspirations for the South in different terms. Outsiders are given the impression that no really conscientious, bona fide Southern citizen can possibly disagree with segregation. But many of us do disagree, and who's to say we're less Southern than someone who can shout louder and angrier?"

An outsider can sometimes see changes in the landscape and the people that escape a native of the region. A historian whose home happens to be in New England at the present, a man with an inquiring mind and a keenly perceptive eye, tells you during a brief visit South in the spring of 1957, "Ten years ago I made a trip through part of the South; I can see enormous changes and improvements everywhere since then. There are the big differences—all the green fields where I remember so much cotton and corn stubble before, and almost no cover crops then. I think this the first and probably most important change I've seen. Then there are the little things: in the banks now everyone stands in line together. I remember my amazement ten years ago when I was waiting before a bank window and a Negro in front of me got out of line and stepped back for me to go ahead of him. And I recall seeing a Negro man step completely off the sidewalk for a white woman to go by.

"So many of the men I talked with then, men of reputation and long residence here, were fearful of the trouble which might develop during the postwar period, when the Negro and white soldiers returned from Europe and the Pacific. Of course it never came.

"Oh, the change is enormous and apparent everywhere. The houses are better; there aren't as many of the shacks as I saw before. A few Negroes are driving nice cars; there are even some good-looking new schools. I'm aware the old wrongs of segregation are still here, but I'm aware there has been improvement. Over in the Delta, one of the planters I talked with was really very proud of the economic progress of the Negroes. Said he believed the Negro would have to be made economically equal before anything else, and I told him I couldn't agree with him more. Then he went on proudly to tell about the Johns-Manville plant and how Negroes and whites worked there. He told about the good Negro schools they were trying to build, told about courses they were giving in typing, secretarial work. I asked if eventually Negro girls could be integrated in the offices of companies down here. There the barrier went up. He could give in on all the rest and still hold the line there. But when you realize how far they've come in the last ten years, you know that people go forward a point at a time."

What harvests are growing in the green fields the New England visitor found in the South? There are the oldest crops—rice in Arkansas and Louisiana, sugar cane in Florida and Louisiana, and that first of the big four staples which gave rise to the plantations: tobacco. If cotton has been king in the South, tobacco has been crown prince, and has set its seal no less indelibly on the land and people who produced it.

The very existence and stability of the Virginia Colony (thirteen years older than the settlement at Plymouth Rock) was most uncertain until 1612, when John Rolfe introduced the cultivation of "the weed." Seven years later a Dutch man-of-war brought twenty Negroes to the colony, where the captain sold them to the Virginians. Tobacco became the staple export of the New World, and slaves became an increasing item of import in its economy. Tobacco was hard on soil—it wore out land in three successive years of planting—but there was always plenty more topsoil waiting to be cleared and used up; it was hard on labor, too ("'baccer's thirteen months a year work," growers say today), but there was always cheap labor—at first the slaves, and later the poor whites and Negroes, who always seemed to stand in most urgent need of a cash crop. Chewing plugs and snuff, pipes and cigars, and finally cigarettes, all became in turn part of America's national life. In 1955, 412 billion cigarettes were consumed, and one state, North Carolina, grew almost half of all the tobacco produced that year. The other Southern states, especially Kentucky, South

Carolina and Virginia, were responsible for the major portion of the other half of the crop.

Before the sharp bite of winter has left the hills of the upland South, in the burley-tobacco country, long white patches still appear every spring on the hillsides. Wrapped like giant cocoons, in their cheesecloth covering, tobacco beds nestle in new ground, protected against possible frost or damage. These are the farmers' tender plants for his year's allotted tobacco acreage.

In the mountains it is burley tobacco that will fill the fields with its broad, sticky leaves; in the piedmont, the bright leaf flourishes. Either type, it is the final auction of the great golden tiers of harvest that provides the crop's real excitement.

Corn, along with tobacco, is older to this country than the white man. From the earliest days of settlement, Indian maize was essential to American life. A half-dozen years before Iowa entered the Union, Tennessee was known as "the hog and hominy state." Her production of corn made markets necessary, and these were found in the towns and counties of the Lower South. Since there were no railroads connecting East Tennessee with Georgia and the Carolinas at this time and haulage on the poor roads was both hazardous and expensive, mountain farmers put the corn on the ribs of hogs and drove it to market for the big plantations. Pork and meal were the main items of diet for the slaves, but because most of the large planters were so completely wedded to one crop, and that cotton, they did not become, on their hundreds of acres, in any wise self-sufficient. An antebellum visitor in Mississippi saw that "the bacon is almost entirely imported from the Northern states, as well as a considerable quantity of Indian corn. This is reckoned bad management by intelligent planters."

Tennessee helped supply some of the plantations of South Carolina and Georgia. As Negro labor (slave before the War, tenant or sharecropper afterwards) increased, the market for hogs grew, too, and ever more land was cleared and planted to corn in Tennessee. Hillsides that bore a mighty crop of virgin hardwood or pine were slashed and brought into rich and temporary cultivation. Haste and ignorance and expediency all hid from upland farmer, lowland planter and laborer alike the fact that the poor Negro, munching a hunk of fat back at dinnertime in the long rows of cotton, was devouring a portion of the Southern earth it would require generations to replace. Perhaps in the growing and consumption of this one crop the web of interdependence between black man and white man, poverty of soil and poverty of cities, is woven most clearly. Cheap labor requires cheap food; cheap food demands farming based on "the most for the least"—and respect for the laws and necessities of nature is subjugated to the sterile criteria of immediate profits in the ledgers.

From the steep slopes of the Blue Ridge, where shocks stand on every small farm in the autumn, like tasseled Indian tepees, to the level lands where the Negro and white farms have at least a patch of "roastin' ears" and "fodder," corn is still one of the heavy feeders, and basic foods, on Southern soil.

"Goober" is one of the few words in our language which probably derives from the African. *Eating Goober Peas* was one of the popular army songs of the Civil War. Indeed, few crops have been so closely associated with the Negro in the South as peanuts. By his experiments with them, a man born in slavery brought freedom to many Southern acres which were under the bondage of a single crop. With an astonishing lack of personal interest in money, this foundling laid the foundations for a harvest now worth over $150 million a year. George Washington Carver and his achievements are a true story familiar throughout the world, yet in Georgia and Virginia today, the two top peanut-producing states of the Union, you can hear some white farmers say, as they watch the green vines and heavy-laden tentacles of roots come out of the ground, "What good will education do these niggers here but make them dissatisfied and unhappy? They'll never amount to nothing anyhow."

When Carver advised Coffee County, Alabama, to shift from cotton to peanuts, it did, and in 1934 held the world's record for peanut production. Carver told his students at Tuskegee Institute, "First you must get an idea about a given thing; then you must attempt to drift back to the cause; there is a life-study in the attempt to determine the first causes in any given thing." And there he enunciated a necessity, not only for agriculturists and scientists, but for all human beings struggling to understand their own dilemmas and the problems of others.

War and a Negro slave were, then, the two catalytic agents which thrust peanuts into the agriculture of the South. In 1842, a sea captain in Norfolk sold some peanuts to a Sussex County, Virginia, farmer. During the Civil War, many of the battles were fought on fields where peanuts had been grown, and Union soldiers acquired a taste for them and even sent some home. During the five years after the end of the War, peanut production increased 300 per cent. From Virginia peanut growing moved South. Then, in 1896, George Washington Carver came from Iowa State College to a little-known institute in Alabama and turned his attention to the depleted soil of Tuskegee's two thousand acres. He discovered the necessity for change and diversity and helped bring both about. He developed over two hundred and fifty products from the peanut alone, experimented with sweet potatoes, wild berries, common clay. The peanut began its rise to importance as a part of the Southern economy—and the spirits of Negroes everywhere (indeed of men of good will everywhere) rose a little higher at thought of one of the humblest of them, who had worked with care and wisdom to preserve and enrich the Southern earth.

If there is one item of food with which the South has become completely identified, it is fried chicken. Visitors to the old plantations often recorded watching a Negro boy, or the cook, chase a frying-size chicken around the kitchen yard and finally catch and pluck it while guests waited in the parlor. Supplying the appetites of preachers and politicians alone must have decimated great flocks of poultry through the years. But with the advent of broilers on the scene, and their growing popularity throughout the rest of the country, chicken raising took on a new dimension in the South. At present 16 per cent of all the broilers consumed in the United States are raised in one state, Georgia. Perhaps even more important, the major part of this $125 million gross business is centered in five northern counties of the state, in a section where the land and people have been, prior to this, traditionally poorer than in the Black Belt region. Only one of these counties has as high as a 10 per cent Negro population, two have no Negro population, and the other two have 4 or 5 per cent. Arkansas and Texas are the other big poultry producers of the nation, although poultry is North Carolina's second-ranking "cash crop," being outstripped only by tobacco.

Hogs and the enormous importance of pork in the Southern diet and economy have already been mentioned in connection with corn. Their genealogy in America reaches even farther back than those seemingly countless human ancestors who arrived in the *Mayflower*. The razorback hogs which the early settlers found here were descendants of swine de Soto had brought with him in his daring explorations of the New World. They were destined to become "meat" for generations of Southerners, black and white. Who, standing in the yards of one of the South's big livestock centers today, looking at the mass of moving, grunting flesh, can realize the poignance of the stricken cry of the Negro woman who calls a white friend one bleak morning in late autumn and weeps into the phone, "My hog's gone! Oh Lordamercy, somebody done come and stole my hog right out of the pen last night—and it just ready to kill, and Jonas and me a-counting on the meat. Lordamercy, they done come and took it in the night and what'll we ever do now?"

Even everyday talk needed the porkers to make comparison vivid. In some early South Carolina records one old Negro is remembered for his description of the plantation: "Massa, everybody work here; man work, woman work, child work, horse work, cow work, all work but hog; hog walk about and do nothing, just like a gentleman."

An old man on one of the photogenic little mountain farms in the Great Smokies tells you, "Law, the way things have changed around here! Farming ain't what it used to be. I can remember when a veal calf or a fattening hog, a little corn or tobacco, was all I could raise for cash money. Nowadays they pay for all kinds of garden truck."

Florida is where we must look for the truly golden harvest of fruit and vegetables, however. With the largest citrus industry in the world (244 million dollars' income in 1956), the world's largest food-freezing industry (citrus concentrate), this Southern promontory seems to belie the old adage that money doesn't grow on trees. Some also grows in the ground: vegetable crops returned 187 million dollars to Florida in 1956.

"Around Lake Okeechobee," a Floridian says, "Many farmers come down from the Midwest, harvest a winter crop here, then go back north and make their summer crop. They bring their tractors, machinery, with them. You can see them coming in all loaded up with that heavy equipment for a season's stay. We call them the high-style Okies; they're on the move but that's the only resemblance they bear to the Joads."

Every season more machines are being used in the fields; it is big industry when a farm can afford a mammoth harvester for celery alone, costing twenty thousand dollars and using forty or fifty Negro workers in its operation. Somehow that machine makes vivid and real the truisms you hear repeated with Coué optimism throughout the South: "We've waked up. We're improving our land and our crops together now. We'll come out of our agricultural lag.

"And look at our cattle!"

Increase in beef and dairy herds throughout the South in the past decade seems to exemplify, at least in some cases, a new relationship to the land. Dr. Howard Odum and others pointed out, years ago, the South's heavy importation of fertilizers; during and after the depression years, people with excellent motives but tactless strategy brought the underprivileged backwardness of much of the region to national attention. Concern over being the poor cousin was nothing compared to the resentment at being informed of that condition. But Federal government agencies forged ahead and much was done to equalize the South with the rest of the nation. A new self-consciousness was stirring; now not just a few visionary leaders, but whole communities began the slow process of accumulating buried treasure—the fertility of their soil. And cattle were an important part of that "new look" in farming.

Tourists in Florida often do not realize that the state which appears to be built only for play has its share of hard work, too, including Texas-style ranches which are making it a beef-producing region of no negligible proportions. Over a million and a half cattle graze in the wide pasture-lands converted from palmetto wilderness. Citrus pulp developed from the wastes of the canning and freezing industry has solved an important part of the feed problem. It required importation of a "furrin" breed to overcome the two big drawbacks which had generally plagued attempts at cattle raising in the Deep South: heat and ticks. The great humpbacked Brahmans which you see scattered throughout the pastures of the South today have an advantageous ability to sweat, and therefore they can withstand the intense heat of Southern summers and still adjust to cold spells in winter; they also withstand attacks of the cattle tick. Crossing the Brahmans with native range breeds, or specializing in herds of white-faced Herefords or Black Angus, beef-cattle production is on the rise in Dixie. (For this particular subject we are not considering Texas or Oklahoma part of the South, as their cattle industry is really Western in all its orientation. Dallas and Fort Worth are excellent examples of the dividing line. Residents will tell you, "Dallas is where the South ends and Fort Worth is where the West begins. Dallas is a trade town; Fort Worth, a cattle town. We're only a few miles apart in space, but we're a continent apart in spirit!")

Of the remaining eleven Southern states, Mississippi, at present, has more cattle than any other, with Louisiana second. Even during the antebellum days of her great cotton boom, many of the piney-woods non-slaveholding farmers of Mississippi raised thousands of cattle for market, letting them range on luxuriant grasses that often grew three feet high, and on the tender cane that flourished in the swamps.

The face of the South is changing. The gullies are gradually healing, the slashed hillsides are slowly greening. Roots are holding the earth together and less topsoil is washing into the rivers. The tragedy is that while the potential of the land is being realized more fully all the time, the potential of one segment of Southern people should remain unfulfilled.

"When'll folks ever learn," a Negro undertaker asks you with a patient sort of impatience, "that the ground makes everybody one color? On top living by it, or underneath dead in it, old ground don't know nothing about color."

There are the individual Negroes who have proved how well they can live on the land, given a shred of opportunity. Near Bennetsville, South Carolina, there are a thirty-eight-year-old poultry man and his wife who have built the largest Negro enterprise of its kind in the United States. Their turkey farm, begun in 1942, now grosses some ninety thousand dollars a year. In Oklahoma, a Negro who had been a sharecropper and renter for nearly half his life before finally buying an eighty-acre farm some sixteen years ago, was acclaimed state-champion conservation farmer. Collin Johnson has followed careful water and soil practices and made it pay. He says, "Conservation farming is like having a good pocket to put your money in, instead of a pocket with a hole in it." And not far from Houston, one of the most successful small-crop enterprises in East Texas is a Negro farmer's hybrid-seed-corn farm.

Late in November, 1956, a ninety-seven-year-old man near Shreveport, Louisiana, died. Born in slavery, reared in ignorance of how to read or write, when he began farming in 1885 he had to borrow enough money from the son of his former white owner to buy two oxen. At his death his estate was worth more than one third of a million dollars. From the two oxen his capital had grown to include two mules, then forty acres of land, then a hundred mules doing various hauling and clearing jobs, and finally two thousand acres of top-grade cotton land. Most of the value of his estate was in this earth.

In a Georgia county near the Alabama line, there is a young Negro man who, with his brother, has a farm of about four hundred acres. When you talk with him, his countenance livens and his enthusiasm is apparent as he tells about his land. "We've got about a hundred and twenty-five acres in peanuts, some beef cattle, a little cotton, a little corn, pastures. You know, I'm discouraged over lots that's happening in the South now and I'm worried over lots that's happening in Georgia, but I'm proud of my county. There are a good many Negroes here who own their farms; we've always had pretty good feeling between my folks and white folks. And I think a lot of it goes back before the Civil War. There were better relations between the slaves and masters than in most places, and then there was this fine family, a white doctor and his many children who lived here and always set the way for good treatment of the Negroes. After the War, Negroes were encouraged to buy land and be farmers here. The doctor and his family always kept the way open for talk. My father couldn't have ridden on a bus beside the old doctor maybe, but he could eat with him. All those little things add up to the difference here—and me being able to have this farm today."

He walks with easy independence and talks soberly but hopefully about the future. What a distance he has come from the people one minister describes to you a little while later, "I heard a report by an NAACP field man here who had tried to go out in rural areas and find out what the working Negroes were thinking. He found out they weren't. He was a Negro, too, but he learned that the issues of the day were so far removed from their everyday problems of sheer existence that they don't even consider them. When you're wrestling to get the next meal's food, you don't worry about next month's vote, or next year's social security."

"Keep Virginia Green!" the signs along her highways read. For true prosperity of the state or region or nation, hope in the people living on the land must be kept no less green than the fields themselves.

Of all things growing in the South, probably the most important for today and tomorrow are the pine trees. At a recent conference of Southern Industrial Management, two outstanding speakers—one from Georgia and one from Alabama—who differed on almost every other point, agreed on the pre-eminence of the pine in the Southern economy. "The pine tree is the most important renewable resource in the South today. It's the big and coming thing down here. Before long, all our fields may be at least partly planted to pine."

The cycle runs its course and man returns to nature's pattern—with poorer land but wiser practices, perhaps. Before the settlement of America, the virgin pineries of the South covered 130 million acres. Like shadowy cathedrals they stood with the silence of centuries under their green domes and the rich fertility of centuries under their web of roots.

After the first great onslaughts against the forests, the idea began to germinate in the Southern (as well as the national) mind that in terms of an economy trees are not a mine but a crop. It is this concept which is at present reforesting hills and valleys from the Savannah River to the Arkansas. In this area at present is nearly half of the nation's growing sawtimber, and pine exceeds all the other softwoods combined. Logically then, the United States Forest Service predicts that the nation's lumber industry will ultimately be concentrated in the South.

Already it is a more important crop than cotton. The Southern Pine Association reported that in 1955 in the ten states which make up the heart of the Southern pine-producing area, timber income totaled four and a quarter billion dollars: 44 per cent of their production was for lumber, 39 per cent was for the pulp and paper industry, and 17 per cent was for miscellaneous other industries.

Growth of paper manufacturing in the South has been an important factor in increased pine plantings. More than half of approximately thirty paper mills built during the last five years in this country were located below the Mason-Dixon line, bringing the total number of mills in the South to sixty-nine. It is somehow ironic that the long-desired arrival of industry has had as one of its effects the return of forests at least resembling those which existed in the earliest days before civilization began its onward march.

Because of the longer growing season, warmer climate and ample rainfall, pine trees grow twice as fast in the South as in most other regions of the country. And the profits from its forests will be more than the cash received from progressive thinnings for pulp and its eventual harvesting as lumber: there will be the benefits accruing as it holds the earth back from destructive erosion, restores some of the natural mulch to the hard, bleached topsoil, and regulates once more the natural runoff of rainwater.

Of the men who work on the twelve to fifteen thousand little sawmills scattered through the South, or on the fifteen hundred big mills which produce over half of the region's lumber, many are Negro. Of those who work in the turpentine orchards, most are Negro. From the day he is born, perhaps beside the warmth of a rich-pine fire, to the day he dies and is laid away in a pine box, the life of many a Georgia black man is surrounded and determined by this most Southern of all trees. The pungent smell of pine logs lying in a hot noon sun, the bright cleanliness of its rough boards stacked foursquare in a lumber yard, the lonely pyramids of its sawdust abandoned through numerous fields and woods: all these are memories no Southerner of any color will ever quite forget.

As the new forests march across the states—not great old heavy-limbed trees in random places, but orderly new ones arranged in rows as neat as broccoli and tobacco—they are welcome. They will restore the green color of life and growth and promise to areas too long made barren by men's shortsightedness. As one Negro small farmer in Tennessee said, "We're planting now, but it's our children will take in the harvest."

6 ▓ Alphabet Stew

"We gotta all join up together."

Throughout the South you hear the words like a thematic melody running through a variety of discords. You hear them in the harsh light of sixty-watt bulbs dangling from electric cords in a bare-benched one-room Negro church, or in the fluorescent glow of a deep-cushioned club-room whose chief excellence seems to be its exclusiveness among whites, or in the tense atmosphere of the ball park or a hired hall or the impromptu field—anywhere that Negro or white may be holding "a rally"—anywhere you go and wait and listen you can hear this message.

Many have heeded, and joined. "I got a duty to stick with my own kind," one tall old man confides, a little uneasily, a little defiantly. "Like I told my preacher a while back. He asked me if I didn't think we're all brothers under the skin. 'Maybe,' I said, 'but right now we're shore-to-God brothers under each other's skin.'"

He waits for your smile or nod, some recognition. "And I got a right to join up with others who feel like I do. The nigras, they got NAPC or whatever it is. Well, we got the WCCs. Regular alphabet stew we've brewed up for ourselves down here—ever since Franklin Roosevelt came along with all his NRAs and WPAs."

He is right. It is indeed an alphabet stew—but it began brewing a long time ago.

In April, 1865, the war of arms between the South and the North of the nation came to an end. In December of that year the formal organization of a second struggle commenced. The undergrowth of the secret societies, the clubs, the committees, frequently active prior to this but unable to capture the imagination of great groups, now came into poison-ous flower with the night-blooming Ku Klux Klan.

> The wolf is in the desert,
> And the panther in the brake.
> The fox is on his rambles,
> And the owl is wide awake;

For now 'tis noon of darkness,
And the world is all asleep;
And some shall wake to glory,
And some shall wake to weep.
                    Ku Klux

Thrice hath the lone owl hooted,
And thrice the panther cried;
And swifter through the darkness,
The Pale Brigade shall ride.
No trumpet sounds its coming,
And no drum-beat stirs the air;
But noiseless in their vengeance,
They wreak it everywhere.
                    Ku Klux

Thus, with a rhythm as definite as "Annabel Lee" and the brooding mystery of "The Fall of the House of Usher," the early KKK inaugurated its notice, in code, of meetings and intents.

Born, like so many other things in the South, of frustration and boredom, the rise and decline of the Invisible Empire is perhaps more significant than many historians have realized or some sociologists cared to admit. As one courageous young attorney in the mid-South will tell you, "It's too bad most of us don't understand that the Klan was the illegitimate grandfather of today's more 'respectable' outlaws—or, as I call some of my fellow workers—outlawyers."

The paradoxes of the KKK were inherent in the region: lofty statements of intent, justifying lowly intimidations of the helpless; romantic new furbelows of synthetic chivalry decorating the old homespun fabric of economic power and social superiority. Its vitality, which shaped it into one of the symbolic movements of our national history, derived chiefly from the fact that it offered the cloak of companionship and anonymity to the ugly gnawing fears and hates, the brutal reprisals and vindications, which are locked within a society and a man alike. When the first Klansman crawled into the first white robe and pulled the hooded mask over his face, the way had been won for cowardice to masquerade as courage, and know-nothingness to pose as the knowledgeable voice of a people. The KKK is the midnight prank that has lasted for almost a century, the small-town joke that has become a national disaster. Its birth has been called accidental. Unpremeditated would be a more accurate term. It was too inevitable to have been a historic accident.

Pride and despair and suspicion, intensified a thousandfold by the hardships of Reconstruction that often seemed more like Redestruction, had fastened on the Southern spirit during the defeat of a major war and the disorder of an ill-planned peace. That these intangible forces would find some form of expression was no less sure than that the battle-scarred land would grow green again at the coming of spring with either jimson weed or nourishing crops.

In December, the "Dying Month," 1865, a half-dozen young men in the little village of Pulaski, Tennessee, gathered in the ruins of a house wrecked by a cyclone. Confederate veterans, their world, too, had been wrecked by a man-made cyclone, and now that the excitement of war had passed and only the thorny problems of peace remained, with daily drudgery, they came together to concoct some fun and excitement. Of course, their group must have a high-flown name, preferably derived from the Greek (*kuklos*—circle), even if meaningless in its final form. As winter wore on and spring and summer passed, as they carried on secret rites and made nocturnal rides, news of the mysterious cabal filtered through the rural countryside and stories of the ghosts of Confederate dead increased. Fear was the reaction to their antics and not only the little Pulaski coterie but other groups as well began to comprehend the potential power of these mysterious methods. They were ideal weapons to turn against the poor, groping, uneducated freedman whose vote had become such a threat to White Supremacy.

By spring of 1867 there were sufficient Dens of the KKK, both in Tennessee and her sister Southern states, to allow a gathering of delegates in Nashville (probably in the new Maxwell House which was later to lend its name to a locally born brand of coffee). Although secrecy shrouded the gathering, it has been generally agreed that it was here the KKK elected as its first leader General Nathan Bedford Forrest.

Of all Confederate cavalrymen (and how the South did idolize her men who wore spurs!) few were more romanticized than this tall, bearded general. Yet he was the very epitome of many of the things the Bourbon Southerners loved to accuse the Yankees of being: unlettered, uncultured, aggressive in business, a "self-made" man. Before the war, Forrest had become a millionaire as a trader in land and slaves—his slave market was one of the best-known in the South—and after the war, among other things he eventually sold insurance. In short, he was a successful tradesman, who had been transformed by the fable of an unsuccessful war into a legendary aristocrat. And the Wizard of the Saddle became the Grand Wizard of the KKK. Many of the hierarchy, the Dragons, the Furies, the

Goblins and Night-Hawks, were politicians and businessmen and planters as shrewd and alert and careless of means-to-their-end as Forrest himself. The bulk of the Klan, known as Ghouls, were the lower-income
whites, who had always been in closest competition with the Negroes
and were easily rallied against them.

Rituals and membership were well-guarded secrets—but much of
the effectiveness of the organization's mysteriousness would be lost if
it remained altogether secret. Besides, it needed a wide membership so
that it might present a solid front to the forces it opposed: the Republican
state governments, the carpetbaggers and scalawags, and—most of all—
the Negroes who must at all cost be "kept in their place." As Southern
control of the Negroes was forced to shift from the slavery system to the
caste system, organizations for control changed, too. The Slave Code and
other controls were destroyed in the Civil War—and the KKK arose.
Following through into our own day, as approval of the KKK waned,
lessening its control through superstitious terror and physical violence,
new organizations with subtler controls have appeared. But their shame-
faced secrecy, on one hand, even among many of the latter-day groups,
has always needed to be balanced with at least the appearance of solid
public approval, or at least acquiescence.

So there were parades and demonstrations to win the faint-hearted
and convince the recalcitrant. Through the breathless midsummer streets
of dozens of swarming little towns, around the courthouse squares, past
the old galleried homes and the shacks huddled in back of them, out into
the lonely country lanes and highways, they passed in solemn, white-
sheeted procession. On chilly autumn evenings, when the hunter's moon
was full and the land lay bleached and barren, the Klan rode high. They
had embraced other vigilante groups whose ends were similar but whose
methods were less spectacular: Men of Justice, the Palefaces, the Constitutional Union Guards, the White Brotherhood and the Order of the
White Rose. The Knights of the White Camellias blossomed, as one
might expect, in the more formal gardens of the Lower South. They had,
by reputation, as many or more members than the Klan, but could never
bring themselves to either join with their country cousins or completely
adopt their heathenish ways.

The Klan's vague threat without vivid example was like war without
ammunition, however, and so the pretenses at being ghosts of the Confederate dead soon gave way to leather and hemp and kerosene. Terror
of the unknown gave way to horror of the well-known, and the original
Klan cried long and furiously that it was being degraded by imitators, by

men twisting it for their own purposes and using similar costumes and methods to wreak death and destruction and throw the blame on the KKK.

In August, 1868, General Forrest gave one of the rare interviews ever recorded on the subject of the Klan, and perhaps his main purpose was to dissociate the Klan he envisioned from the Klan as it was in reality. When the reporter said to Forrest, "Why, General, we people up North have regarded the Ku Klux Klan as an organization which existed only in the frightened imaginations of a few politicians," the General is reported to have replied, "Well, there is such an organization not only in Tennessee, but all over the South, and its numbers have not been exaggerated."

"What are its numbers, General?"

"In Tennessee there are over forty thousand and in all the Southern States they number about five hundred and fifty thousand men."

"What is the character of the organization, may I enquire?"

"Yes, sir. It is a protective, political, military organization. I am willing to show any man the constitution of the society. The members are sworn to recognize the Government of the United States. It does not say anything at all about the Government of the State of Tennessee. Its objects originally were protection against the Loyal Leagues and the Grand Army of the Republic, but after it became general, it was found that political matters and interests could best be promoted within it, and it was then made a political organization, giving its support, of course, to the Democratic party."

Allegedly organized for physical protection of the weak (white) and the return of power to "responsible" (white) hands, testimony concerning the early days of the Klan, during the lengthy Congressional investigation of 1871, stressed the fact it was made up of "the best people." Forrest himself, evasive as to his sources of knowledge and disclaiming any direct connection with the KKK, said his "information was that they admitted no man who was not a gentleman and a man who could be relied upon to act discreetly . . . worthy men who belonged to the Southern army; the others are not to be trusted; they would not fight when the war was on them, and of course they would not do anything when it was over."

The fact was, the Klan was from the first foredoomed to failure of its professed ideals. In disgust and despair, Grand Wizard Forrest disbanded it, probably in 1869. But a weapon so potent, combining the paradoxical features of the Old South's vision of the Crusades with a sadistic practicality of control, was not so easily set aside by decree. In creating the Ku Klux Klan, those six young men in Pulaski and Nathan Bedford Forrest and all their fellow workers had brought into being something they could neither control nor recall. It was cursed with the twin vices of secrecy and lawlessness.

While most Southerners were still readily accepting its help in re-establishing their old supremacy, a North Carolina judge, Thomas Ruffin, warned his son in July, 1869, of this great pitfall of the KKK: "To do evil that good may come of it, is a horrible heresy in Religion, morals and public polity, even if the good hoped for really resulted. But, in truth, it hardly ever does, but evil almost certainly follows evil. . . . It is wrong—all wrong . . . and I beg you to have nothing to do with it. . . . At best it is committing one crime, to prevent or punish another."

But the Klan had already been born, and there were not enough Judge Ruffins to destroy the Hydra-headed monster it was becoming. Those Northerners and Midwesterners who chose to ignore it as only another manifestation of Southern decadence, filling a momentary vacancy in Southern life, were to be rudely jolted in the new century when the KKK began to emerge as one part of the whole national pattern. In 1915 a second Klan was formed, at Stone Mountain, Georgia, ready to seize on the situation following World War I, when a wave of anti-Semitic, anti-Catholic, anti-immigrant feeling swept a large part of the United States. The old KKK opened new headquarters in Atlanta and drew its membership from many points far beyond the South. Indiana was one of its firmest strongholds, as were Oregon, Oklahoma and Maine. The Negro received slightly less attention as the Klan extended its guardianship of community and national morals. By October, 1921, its membership throughout the United States was revealed to be one hundred thousand, and before the decade was out it had reached an estimated four million; it controlled politics in many sections, electing state officials and congressmen; Klan bribery and corruption ruined at least one mayor and governor in a Midwestern state. As the old brutalities persisted, however, public revulsion against the Klan grew until many states passed laws aimed directly at its expulsion. Among these were some of the Southern states. It is an ironic sidelight that some of these very laws have recently been resurrected by various Southern states groping for ways of banning the NAACP in their domain.

So the KKK went into another deep-freeze of disfavor and its activities wilted to the inconspicuousness of Bermuda grass in winter. But like 'moody grass,' its roots are tough and deep; a little favorable weather stirs them to flourishing life again.

"The Supreme Court decision on school integration was what the Klan needed," the earnest young mid-South lawyer tell you, drawing deeply on a cigarette and expelling the smoke slowly as he tries to explain what he believes about this group.

"They're trying to make it into Reconstruction and Radical Rule all over again. Actually, of course, they don't give a whoop-in-hell for the schools or anything else but their own sickly peeves and starved-out appetite for some kind of power. They're trying to turn the South back to 1865 and make us think the only difference is that the brief case has taken the place of the carpetbag." He laughs and crushes out his cigarette on a glass ash tray. "Poor fools. They don't know, or won't admit, that some of those brief cases are carrying the contracts for the mills that manufacture the sheets they're wearing."

It would seem, then, that the Klan is being revived—more by the artificial respiration of its hangers-on who have no place else to go than by any vigorous influx of new recruits. But as the KKK reappears in Louisiana after an absence of over thirty years and asks for a state charter in Baton Rouge, as the towns in Piedmont North Carolina and Eastern Texas hear the old cries raised against Jew and Catholic and "nigger," as Low Country and Up Country South Carolina and the cities of Northern Florida and Western Tennessee feel the tensions of secret memberships and anonymous threats, as Georgia's metropolis and villages and Alabama's capital listen to the swish of the long robes once more walking their streets, the old specters of bloodshed and violence return. There is also a dim awareness that here is a symbol of the anachronisms burdening the South today.

This is sensed by the alert young matron with whom you eat the Chef's salad bowl in the coffee shop of the chain hotel in which centers the commercial and men's-club life of one medium-sized Southern city. In her green tweed suit and cloche to match, with her lizard spectator pumps and handbag, she might be in town for the day from Westchester County, or Lark Forest, or Grosse Pointe. But it happens she's come from a small Southern town nearby.

"We had the weirdest experience the other night. Did I tell you about Bill and me, on the way to the dance? Well, it was simply the darndest thing. A couple of Saturdays ago, we'd been in for the football game as usual and gone back home to change for the party out at the club that night. After we'd dressed and started back, as we passed this old field at the edge of town I saw some people. I told Bill to slow down. Over at the edge of the lot I could see three crosses set up and a half-dozen men standing around and they were dressed in full Klan regalia. If you've never seen it before, I tell you it's spooky—not sheets but regular white robes of some sort with tall, pointed caps. We came on, and about halfway to the city limits we met a whole caravan of them. I'd judge there were a hundred cars, and four or five men in every car, all in KKK robes. The inside ceiling lights were turned on so you could get the full effect of all those white hoods in each car. And the lead car had a cross, all lit up, standing on the top—and there was another cross on one of the cars about midway in the caravan. Somehow it was hard for me to believe; I'd never seen any Klan doings before. We didn't want to stay around there for fear there might be trouble. Bill and I came on to the country club. After the dance, when we went home that night, we could see where they'd held their meeting. The three crosses were still smoking."

Thus, on a Saturday night in autumn, suburbia and the frontier meet.

You watch a Klan meeting on a still summer night or under a chilly autumn wind, as it is directed from the bed of a battered truck backed up into a sedge field on the city's outskirts. There is an opening prayer and the light of a kerosene-soaked cross aflame; there is a closing collection of funds and a call for memberships. In between, the faithful few hear the ill-organized, defiant, familiar messages of impotent anger.

"The Knights of Columbus can go back to Rome, the Jews to Jerusalem and the niggers to Africa. And our Communist-inspired Supreme Court can go to Moscow." There are not so many to hear his message as the Kleagle had hoped for.

The drab crowd breaks up. Under several of the hoods you detect women's faces—wrinkled, weathered, dumbly resentful faces. The charred cross lies where it fell an hour before. A man winds up the cord leading to the loud-speaker on the truck-bed while another takes down the American flag. They drive away in the truck and only the debris of a few stray membership applications rustles in the night wind. The robes of the Ku Klux Klan, which once served as weapons, now seem only to be the wearers' own shrouds.

It is no accident that a state law, invoked by Louisiana in its present effort to outlaw the NAACP, was originally passed in 1924 against the KKK. It is no accident that a Miami minister, president of his state

NAACP group, should contemplate asking the Florida governor and legislature to investigate the resurgence of the KKK. Historically and psychologically it would appear inevitable that the KKK and the atmosphere in which it was kept alive should eventually give birth to the NAACP, somewhat as a drunkard may have the strictest of teetotalers for a son. And to say that the later organization came into being as a counteraction against the earlier group is not to equate or polarize the two. It is to understand that fear, like all destructive weapons, seems to arrive after a while at a point of diminishing efficiency—and when that point has been reached, through KKK or more subtle tactics, there is bound to be change. With the change may come, not a gradual incline but a sudden upsurge in the opposite direction of release. Thus fear, once experienced and overcome, may turn into the truest fearlessness of all. As one Southerner has put it, "In the Deep South of 1956, the white man fears the Negro; the Jew fears other white men; and the Negro, the focal point of this entire embroglio, fears no one."

Although this may overstate matters somewhat, it is nevertheless true that in traveling over the South today you sense among increasing numbers of Negroes a new and widespread confidence. Insofar as their courage is individual, it may have several sources; but insofar as that courage is collective, much of it must be attributed to the National Association for the Advancement of Colored People.

Perhaps no organization in our time has incurred such concentrated wrath as the NAACP. As one Virginian said, "I think the people here, and all over the South, hate the N double-A C P more than integration itself."

And in state after state the words are repeated until they become a regular theme song among the white Southerners: "We were getting along fine, everything would be all right—if the outsiders would just leave us alone—if the NAACP wouldn't come and stir up trouble!"

A young Negro executive in one of the state offices of the Association shakes his head at the familiar words and smiles with a sad mixture of tolerance and frustration. "When a man cuts out a cancer growing inside him he may be stirring up trouble, sure—or he may be trying to cure a worse trouble." He gets up from his desk suddenly and walks around the room, slapping the back of his hand against several of the enlarged photographs hanging there. They show some of the Negro schools in his state with dilapidated outside toilets, potbellied stoves for heat of the one-room buildings; and some of the hovels the Negro pupils call home. "Would you call this 'getting along fine'? Would you call this 'separate but equal'? Would you call going into the court to ask for some of the liberty, equality and justice we're always hearing about 'stirring up trouble'?"

He sits down again, as suddenly as he stood. "You know what a white man here said to me yesterday? Over the phone, of course. He said he guessed the South could thank God they had the NAACP instead of the Mau Maus."

The National Association for the Advancement of Colored People was, in fact, born of a bloodletting, to forestall, if possible, its recurrence in the future. In the summer of 1908, Springfield, Illinois, home of Abraham Lincoln, was torn by a race riot. The death and havoc wrought by prejudice on the rampage caused a Kentucky writer, a feminine social worker, a New York editor and a leader of immigrant groups—all white— to come together and issue a call for a national conference on the racial problems facing the United States. Of the fifty-three eminent signers of this appeal, only six were Negroes. The call was successful. A year later this active, liberal, white committee merged with an active, liberal Negro organization called the Niagara Movement, and the NAACP was formed. Its ultimate objective is short and simple to state, long and tedious to achieve: full equality for the Negro as an American citizen.

As one white Southerner, a young Quaker trying to make a life as well as a living on the anemic acres of the family farm where he and his wife have settled in the rolling Piedmont country, says: "They're asking for so little, when you come to think about it. A chance for equal education in the schools they help support; a chance to vote for the officials who will govern them; a chance to work for the livelihood we now blame them for not earning; a chance to ride or stand or sit in any public place and not feel singled out for separation from the rest of the human species. Are those such radical requests? We'd despise them if they asked for less.

"You know, I've thought about it a lot: in our American preoccupation with manliness and aggressiveness and all the folklore that goes with combat, maybe we've come to low-rate the Negroes among us because they haven't been overly aggressive and bold before this. I don't know that it's right in the long-range view of the human situation, but I believe it's accurate in this case to say many Southerners who wouldn't admit it with their dying breath are feeling right now their first twinges of respect for the Negro. They may hate his leaders, and most of them do. They may try to punish, in all the ways they know, any individual who shows this new-found confidence. But underneath they know that Sam and Wash and Slick and the Reverend are trading in a new-model, chrome-plated slavery for old-fashioned sterling citizenship. And subconsciously they respect him for it."

Perhaps this probing young farmer-philosopher has also suggested one of the deepest causes for Southern hatred of the NAACP. It is re-echoed in the cry of scattered housewives and storekeepers and farmers, who tell you over and over, "Our Negroes are going to be all right. They'll find out that it's their white friends who live here who'll do something for them. Not outsiders with big offices up in New York who come in and tell them what the NAACP says do."

The mind of the South is accustomed to doing things for the Negro; the subject of rights is embarrassing in the stifling atmosphere of "noblesse oblige." The best part of the Southern mind is not against the Negro—it is for him: doing for him, in fits and starts of conscience and caprice. But now, suddenly, here is an organization interposing itself between the white giver and the waiting black, saying the gift is no gift at all when it is composed of those rights guaranteed everyone by the Constitution. The NAACP has made the Southerner stop and look at the Negro as an American citizen.

A Negro woman tells you, "These white folks here were gettin' ready to try to work up to givin' us something we already had a claim to: schoolin' as good as the best. And while they were still studyin' about it, along came the NAACP and nudged the Supreme Court into lettin' the cat out of the bag. That's what makes them so boiling mad: that even our Uncle Toms and ole handkerchief heads aren't going to bend their knees in thank-yous for something we got privileges to, but not permission."

In courts of law—where Negro cases were, in the white man's folklore, traditionally concerned with Saturday-night fights, or whiskey-making, or petty thievery, or rape—the NAACP initiated and won a long series of legal contests. Slowly but very surely they undermined the very foundations of white supremacy. From the first case NAACP lawyers took to the Supreme Court in 1915—which resulted in the so-called grandfather clause being declared unconstitutional in its efforts to keep the Negro from voting—through more than forty victorious decisions it won before this highest tribunal, until the May, 1954, declaration on school desegregation, the Association has moved unswervingly in the area it defined for itself. That was the area of equality established through law.

NAACP workers hear the complaint rising from the South: "They're going too fast. Slow down . . . too fast. . . ." And they smile wearily and ask, "Have you ever tried to get a case through the courts?" And they add, "Autherine Lucy applied for admission to the University of Alabama in 1952. It was spring of 1956 before she went to register. Is almost four years too fast? Virgil Hawkins began trying to enter the University of Florida in 1949. He was ordered admitted in March, 1956. Is seven years too fast?" One may even say to you, "Can you spell 'slow' s-t-o-p? How many people are spelling 'gradual' n-e-v-e-r? It's not what the gradualists say but what they mean that keeps the NAACP working. We've been deliberate, but in this business of timing if we get any more gradual, we'll be backing up."

Perhaps the greatest irony that has befallen the organization is in the development that after some forty years of being denounced by many of its followers as too conservative and too cautious in its effort to construct a new world, it is now damned as being too radical, too rapid, in its attacks on an old world.

"*The Daily Worker* assaults us as a servant of bourgeois interests betraying the lower-class Negro. The segregationists label us a Communist front betraying everyone. Looks like we're the only really middle-of-the road organization there is because we're being hit from both sides."

Attacks by the Communists and the segregationists seem not to have hurt its growth. Seven hundred of its eleven hundred branch offices are in the South, and about 45 per cent of its membership. Its president has always been a white man, and there is a bewhiskered joke that some people used to call the group the National Association for the Advancement of Certain People. But in recent years the Association has broadened its base considerably. In 1944, Gunnar Myrdal noted that the Association should have a much larger popular support if it was to fight most successfully. In that year the total membership of NAACP was only eighty-five thousand. Today it has three hundred thousand members in forty-four states, and the greater number of these are Negroes in the middle and lower income groups. Criticism of NAACP, when it is justified, would seem to have constructive results; when it is unjustified, it would seem merely to strengthen the members' allegiance.

Loss of jobs, threats, actual bodily harm: these have been the experiences of many of the Negroes whose NAACP membership became known. Gus Courts, who was president of the branch in a little Mississippi town, related some of the pressures in his area: "Some workers made the year's crops and when time came to pay, the boss told those who belonged to the NACCP, 'Let the NAACP pay you.' The NAACP distributed clothing and helped get work on other plantations and in other states." Himself the victim of a shotgun blast after he refused to remove his name from the voting register, Courts says, "The colored people have been intimidated. They killed Rev. George Lee and tried to kill me to keep us from voting."

In a land where "credit at the bank" makes possible the whole intricate pattern of farm existence from year to year, its withdrawal is one of the deadliest weapons turned against the shoestring grower whose ideas are "uppity." And the sharecropper or tenant farmer who will sign his name to an NAACP-sponsored petition must have arrived at the desperate conclusion that the thousand harrying uncertainties of his precarious existence would be just as well resolved in the one big certainty that his contract for the coming year will not be renewed. With his wagon or truckload of wordly possessions and his frightened family, he can start down that lonesome road, looking for new acres to tend.

When a South Carolina state representative explained why he would introduce a bill in the General Assembly forbidding any state, county or municipal employee from belonging to the NAACP, he summarized the climate of opinion segregationists are seeking to establish throughout the South: "The bill . . . is designed to protect our Negro citizens and colored public employees, most of whom are not members of the organization, from the intimidation and coercion of the NAACP as well as to limit its activities against the best interests of our white citizens. . . . There is no more place in our state for the NAACP, as presently constituted and with its present policies and aims, than there is for the Ku Klux Klan. The people, whites and Negroes alike, are in need of some form of protection."

To counteract this effort at winning the public mind, many NAACP leaders now point out that abstract legal victories must not be confused with concrete community action.

"The school segregation problems can't be worked out in our offices in New York," Thurgood Marshall told one group. "They must be worked out in each little town and each little county. When the Supreme Court decision came, the average man said one of two things: 'Fine! Segregation's gone. Hallelujah! I can sit down.' The other said, 'It'll never work! Nothing I can do about it. I'll sit down.' When you get two halves sitting down, you're out of business. Immobilized. Well, we've got to mobilize them again."

If the NAACP has furnished its foes a target on which to concentrate their old cry of "carpetbagger" and their new cry of "Communist," it has also provided a rallying point for its followers. ("If Senator Eastland would just make one more hell-fire-and-brimstone speech against us," they joke, "our membership files would burst at the seams.") And even some of those who have no affiliation with the group have artfully turned that fact to their own advantage.

"We've said for generations we understood the Negro," a middle-aged North Carolina man tells you, "when all the time it was really the Negro who understood us. Half the time he knew what we were thinking and most of the time he knew how we'd react to a situation before we knew ourselves. You take this business of the NAACP. I know one or two Negroes in this town who are making better livings than they've ever made before because they're so good at dropping hints to their white friends that 'that ole NACP has been after me again to join up with 'em but I jus' stan' right up to 'em and say no siree, you ain't seein' the color of my money as long as I got my white folks to back me up. No siree.' And the white man gets the message, he's afraid not to, and then he likes to think that he's got some 'inside' information as to how the Negroes feel."

The veterinarian chairman of one Alabama White Citizens' Council chapter probably did not realize how much he was revealing when he reported, "One nigra went to one of our banks and asked for a one-hundred-dollar loan. The nigra said that he wasn't a member of the NAPC, that they'd been trying to get him to join but he wouldn't have anything to do with them. He got the loan!"

Those who would turn the fact that they do not belong to the NAACP to their own advantage would seem to be surprisingly few in number, considering the incentives involved. For those who do, the Negroes themselves have a new term: no longer Uncle Toms, they now join the new professors and ministers and leaders who would still play end man to the white's straight role, and are Uncle Thomases.

In the living room of one Southern white woman who has sought to understand the forces shaping her time and place you may suddenly confront the two current and divergent Southern attitudes toward the NAACP. "Here"—your hostess hands you a typed envelope—"is an anonymous letter I received from Arkansas recently."

You read: "The NAAPC, a communistic inspired hate organization, has authorized all black preachers to encourage all black females to bear all the children possible, legitimately or illegitimately, to eventually outnumber the white population and to ultimately uprise and massacre the white race in much the manner as the Indians did to General Custer and his soldiers at Big Bend. The NAAPC has publicly admitted that more than 50% of the blacks in this country are genuine bastards. No parents or relatives to speak of. . . . How much is that niggardly NAACP paying you?"

Then the woman herself tells you, "It's too bad that people here in the South don't know the NAAPC, or won't even try to. The greater your familiarity with the organization, the greater your respect for it. Again and again I've heard from their speakers a stream of expression which even a casual student of pre-Revolution history would recognize as the molten iron ore which fashioned the steel structure of our nation."

In 1951, when the NAACP held its national convention in Atlanta, it was given a cordial greeting by that city's mayor. In 1957 there seems little doubt that this public official would hardly extend the same welcome. And probably the strongest and most widely circulated denunciation came from Georgia's attorney general, Eugene Cook, in an address and subsequent pamphlet called "The Ugly Truth About the NAACP." This all might seem to indicate a deterioration in public relationship, which would be only part of a complex truth. One labor leader in a large Southern city tells you, "The NAACP helped bring some of its present trouble on itself. After the first victories, they grew a little elated. You can't blame them. Take a person out of a strait jacket he's been in for generations and he might stretch around some. I don't blame them at all. I'd have done more. But it did help bring some of their present difficulties, I believe. People suddenly saw that here was a group working for Negro rights and they were effective!"

To be effective *and* elated could only add up to effrontery, as far as many Southerners are concerned. They are ready to believe anything they hear about this new face of the enemy. Many a filling-station attendant, in any part of the South, will tell you with utter confidence, "You know what NAACP stands for, don't you? National Association for the Advancement of the Communist Party."

And so—much of our confusion and animosity is compounded by our concern for labels. Labels dehumanize; they let us attack an organization as if it were something apart from the people who make it. That is why the states who have sought to outlaw the NAACP appear to have been utterly unrealistic. When Alabama state courts slapped on an injunction against the Association's doing business, an organization called the Alabama Christian Movement for Human Rights came into being. It is the South's own tragedy that we have been more willing to grasp a label and blame all our disturbances on it than to grasp the meaning behind the label and search out the roots of unrest.

Perhaps wise and witty Harry Golden, of Charlotte, North Carolina, with the dark hair and round belly and ready humor, points out most clearly the deep urges behind the NAACP when he tells you, "Where is this group the strongest? Not in those rural counties having the most Negroes, but in the places where there are comparatively few. That's proof that mass integration won't come this year. You see, it's when the Negro gets half that he wants the whole. When anyone tastes half of democracy, he wants democracy all the way. That's what makes it so wonderful.

"You know, the most satisfying relationship in the world is probably the aristocracy and the peasantry. One on top, one on the bottom. Everything settled. It's when you get a big middle class, anywhere in history, that you get people who are unhappy. Who's on the move in America today? The middle-class man has a good home, a fine car, maybe a swimming pool in the back yard—and he's unhappy, unhappy, unhappy. It's when the Negro joins the middle class that he wants the whole loaf. He's got a car, now he wants to vote, too. When you're in Egypt making bricks you tip your hat, you grovel. It's when you're on Mt. Nebo you want the Promised Land."

"Here, you take this-here paper with you and read it and then hand it on to a friend."

You look at the man holding the printed stapled sheets toward you. He stands at one side of the county courtroom where a White Citizens' Council meeting is just breaking up. His face is lean, clean-shaven, his blue eyes glittering and deep-set under shaggy dark eyebrows that match his black, slightly greying hair. The brown coat which covers his hunched, thin shoulders, and does not match his khaki wash-trousers, is threadbare from years of wearing to church meetings and courtrooms and Saturdays-in-town. The hands which press the leaflet into yours are hard and cracked as trampled earth. You are suddenly moved by his earnestness and you look at him more carefully.

This man, at home, would probably share his last crumb of hot cornbread, his last glass of churned buttermilk, with you. He would be embarrassed at weddings, stoic at funerals and a little sheepish at births. He laughs at heavy-handed country jokes; his wife has "high blood," and he endures toothache and rheumatic joints and uncertainty about next week's payroll with a sort of dumb desperation. He is at once friendly and suspicious, eager and resentful.

"Look at the NAPC picture of those little childern there on that sheet," he points out. "All mixed up, black and white playing together, pore little things." His eyes grow bluer, more intense. "That-there's what we're going to put a stop to!"

You take the paper and walk away from him. The pitiful and proud! How easily he separates a segment of humanity under a label; how easily he in turn is set apart and dehumanized. This man is one of the sincere ones in the Councils—between the leaders who know where they are going and how, and the lawless fringe who seize on any cause for dissatisfaction and strike out blindly. Most bitterly would this man resent your honest pity, for his false pride is what he fights this desperate rearguard action to preserve. You read the hate-sheet he has given you, and grief for all the hated and the haters overwhelms you.

Just as the lawlessness of the KKK helped bring the lawfulness of the NAACP into being, so the successes of the NAACP brought about the White Citizens' Councils. The date and place of the Councils' birth is evidence enough of this: in 1954, a few months after the Supreme Court decision, at the small town of Indianola, Mississippi.

At first they were only one among many groups which mushroomed in many parts of the South following that historic May seventeenth. As the old man said, a regular alphabet stew brewing. Naturally there was an NAAWP (National Association for the Advancement of White People), which reached its peak of publicity during the difficulties at Milford, Delaware, and seems to have been in steady decline ever since. There were those groups which stressed color in their titles: the White Brotherhood in Florida; White Men, Inc. in North Carolina; and Knights of the White Christians in Louisiana; a few who emphasized region: the Pro-Southerners and the Minute Women of Houston, which was active as early as 1951; and some which invoked religion: the Christian Civic League in Georgia, the Association of Catholic Laymen in Louisiana. True to the Southern need to localize its allegiances ever more closely, several of the groups were designated as to particular state: Patriots of North Carolina, Inc.; South Carolina Committee of 52; Tennessee Society to Maintain Segregation. And in keeping with the need to formalize and outwardly stabilize structures having their deepest base in emotions, many titles mentioned the issue of states' rights: The American States Rights Association, States Rights Council of Georgia, Tennessee Federation for Constitutional Government, States Rights League of South Carolina, Society for Preservation of State Government and Racial Integrity, and—with the slightly more elevated language we might expect from Virginia—the Virginia Defenders of State Sovereignty and Individual Liberties. For implied delineation of membership and purpose, however, for pure arrogance of definition and appeal, no group has equalled the simple title: Southern Gentlemen. If the title "Southern Gentlemen" was the epitome of the image these groups hoped to stamp on the public mind, the organization itself also epitomized the chasm which often gapes between these titles and the reality behind them, when one of the more vocal Southern Gentlemen recently admitted that he had served two prison terms for writing bogus checks. Of all the organizations resisting desegregation, by far the most important are the White Citizens' Councils.

Ancient fears have stirred once more in the South as the strident daily cries and the hushed night-time atmosphere of these new vigilantes spread again around the synagogues and cathedrals and the new brick churches and the one-room piney-woods meeting places. Unanimously these new groups reject the KKK, with its old terrorizations and rebel yells, but the closer one studies them the more apparent it must become that, in varying degree, these organizations differ from the Klan more in idiom than in idea. Sartorially alien, they are spiritually akin.

Within their pattern, the groups vary widely, of course. The founder and leader of one of the less flourishing reveals a deep wound of personal malice and bitterness as you talk with him. A man between fifty-five and sixty years old, whose medium-sized body is not quite in proportion to his large head, his square-shaped face is dominated by a cast in one grey-blue eye. He wears no coat, his white shirt is wrinkled and soiled and open at the thick neck. When he smiles, it is without humor; his lips merely draw back and reveal yellowed teeth. His conversation is an odd mixture of illiteracy and labored reading in his cause.

"I'm from one of the oldest families in this county—but I've traveled around some, worked on the water front in Seattle for a while, been to sea. But I tell you the best relations ever existed in the world between two races has existed here in the South. Till Barney Baruch, the king of the Jews, got behind the NAACP and they come down here to mess things up. I'll tell you what it's all working up to: a hardware man came through the other day, said he had sold sixteen guns the past ten days, all to niggers. Oh, they're arming, but we're ready for 'em. Let 'em start something, they'll never live to see the finish. Or let a white man try to force my little granddaughter to go to school with niggers. I'd as soon kill a white man as a nigger—had rather, if he'd be for a thing like that! He's lower than a nigger. A nigger can't help what he is."

The corruption of the word "Negro" seems to give him some inner satisfaction as he spits it out between the yellow teeth. He has warmed to his subject, you can feel the anger bubbling in him. "Oh, it's the Jews are behind it all—the Jews and the Yankees would like to make over the South. International, interracial, atheistic: that's their tripod, and they're working through two organizations to overthrow everything else: the NAACP and the World Council of Churches. They'd like to see the blacks and whites in a battle so they could send Federal troops down and have Reconstruction all over again. Want to change it all, even the way we talk. They tell us now to say Negro. I've known 'em all my life and they're not Negroes. They're niggers, and that's all they'll ever be. Oh, the dictionary says 'nigger' is a term of contempt, but tell me this: did you ever hear a nigger call another nigger anything but 'nigger'?"

He shakes his shaggy head like a wounded buffalo. "The North'll believe anything it reads about the South. Now there's some good people up there—in the small towns, on farms—but that lot in the cities are all Johnny-come-latelys from God-knows-where. They're the ones believe in all this freedom and mixing. They don't know nothing about what America stands for."

On the other hand there is the educated, successful Virginian, who has played a vital role in the organization of his state's Defenders. He talks with you coolly and easily, yet very firmly, drawing deliberately on his pipe as he pauses now and then for the right word, the exact thought.

"When the first Supreme Court decision was rendered, I would say the people of Virginia were in a state of stunned shock. There did not seem to be anything for them to do but submit to this thing. This brought about a monumental apathy. But I thought I knew how at least some of the people of Virginia thought on this, and a few of us tried to determine if there was opposition and if it was theoretical or real.

"Then this suit was brought and tried down in Prince Edward County, and I think that did as much as anything to stir public opinion. When the integration verdict was handed down there, that began to bring the thing home to people. And a strange thing began to happen down there: people began to say they wouldn't do it, they'd close the schools. They formed the Prince Edward Educational Corporation.

"Now Prince Edward is almost altogether an agricultural county; not a single really wealthy man in it probably. Oh, there are many in very comfortable circumstances, but mostly it's a fairly average county. Yet at their first meeting that Corporation raised seventy-five thousand dollars in pledges to go toward paying for private schools if the public schools were closed. They never solicited, but I got calls from people all around asking how they could contribute. I had some twenty-five thousand dollars pledged. They raised around one hundred and fifty thousand, I think. Of course, they've never needed it yet, but that showed the rest of Virginia something could be done. Here was one area that wasn't going to submit lying down. I've said before, Napoleon had his Tenth Legion, Lee had his Stonewall Brigade, and Virginia has its Prince Edward County!

"What we've done has been purely a process of awakening public opinion. I don't believe we've changed any public opinion in Virginia. The Defenders have given people a medium through which they could express their opinion. To me, Virginia has been the perfect example—not of influencing people but of giving them a medium.

"Of course it was right that this should have occurred in Virginia, home of so many of our founding fathers, who have been so deliberately misunderstood recently. Now anybody knows—and Thomas Jefferson was one of the wisest men America ever had and he certainly knew—that men are not created equal. What Jefferson meant, of course, was that they were all equal before the law. And certainly no one would quarrel with that. I believe everyone ought to have equal justice. If Thomas Jefferson were living today and lived in Vermont or South Dakota, I think he'd be for integration. If he lived in Virginia, I think he'd believe like we do—he'd see the problem. One thing I know, if he lived in South Dakota or Virginia, he'd be concerned about the Supreme Court rewriting the Constitution. That's what they've done, and that's really the important thing behind this whole question.

"Most of the reporters and writers refuse to include that in their stories. I've found most of them who come and talk to me already have their own ideas about it all. They listen well, go back and write whatever they want to. What they're looking for is not information but confirmation.

"For instance, they want to think our group is making this resistance feeling here in Virginia. As I said, we haven't changed anything, especially any opinions. Take all the great movements in history, Patrick Henry, George Mason, George Washington, those great leaders of the Revolution. They didn't make public opinion. It was there and they simply arose to the occasion. Or Hitler. He didn't change the Germans—those feelings were lying there dormant in them all the time. He opened a way for them."

This man's thinking and talk have brought him to a crucial point, which he does not pursue to its conclusion. In all societies there are latent forces yearning toward the enlightenment of Jefferson or prodding toward the primitivism of Hitler. It has perhaps come as a shock to realize that these urges are forever struggling not only "there" and "yesterday" but "here" and "today." And although the material of leadership may rise from opinion and emotion already existing in the public mind and viscera, the morality of leadership consists in determining which emotion it shall appeal to, which opinion it shall lead.

The dilemma of all the resistance groups eventually boils down to this decision. And the more "respectable" the organization, the more acute its problem. It capsules so neatly many of the South's paradoxes: How to keep lawlessness within lawful bounds? How to camouflage condemnation of a race so that it will appear to be commendation? How bend illogic until it will be accepted logically?

Over half the states in the Union, about twenty-five in fact, have some sort of organized resistance to the Supreme Court integration decision. Only eleven of these form the hard core, however, from which somewhat more than three hundred thousand members of the half million the movement claims are drawn. Of these eleven states, Tennessee and Florida are less dominated by their Citizens' Councils than the other states. There are many reasons for this, including the distinctive political situation in each state, but one important one may be Tennessee's reaching for respectability and *status quo* based on her past, and Florida's reaching for respectability and *status quo* based on her future.

"We're the most middle-class, respectable state in the Union," a Florida resident tells you. "One reason Florida has been, on the whole, better than adjacent states on this race issue, is that we're strictly a 'nice' state. And it's making us the most monotonous state in the Union. We're the typical Jaycee personality. This composite of real-estate-insurance-luxury-agriculture-type economy (citrus, winter vegetables, cattle raisers who are also half realtors) has made Florida the greatest middle-class state in the nation. As a result we're the least interesting socially. We want to be liked, and we don't want any loud groups stirring up trouble. That's meant the Citizens' Councils has had a hard time convincing us they were really 'nice enough' for Florida."

There are, then, nine key states of organized associations. Among these, only the North Carolina group, called the Patriots, The Virginia Defenders, and the States Rights Council of Georgia, do not bear the name Citizens' Councils. It is no doubt significant, as part of their claim to responsible leadership, that most of these groups have dropped the word "White" which was in the early name of the Councils, and are now merely Citizens' Councils. In the popular mind and local conversation, however, they are still WCCs.

By far the largest and most unanimous support of the Citizens' Councils exists in Mississippi, where the WCC was born and nurtured, and in Alabama. Each of these has eighty thousand, or more, members, mostly in the central and southern portions of each state. This is twice the number of the next ranking state, Louisiana, with approximately forty thousand members, and South Carolina with thirty thousand. Texas and Arkansas have some twenty-five thousand and twenty thousand respectively.

With dues ranging from one to five dollars, usually the latter, approximately one million dollars annually in membership money alone is at the WCCs' disposal, and it has been estimated that another million might be received from contributions, fund-raising drives and other sources. With two million dollars involved, the Councils are, from the standpoint of cash assets, one of the most powerful opinion-making groups in the South. As a side light on their income, the variance in their membership is reflected in frequent discussions of dues:

"We found, over in our branch, that five dollars was just too high for our folks. We had only a handful of members. Then we lowered to three dollars and got a smattering more. But when we dropped to one dollar they poured in like rosin running in spring, and we've had a right peart chapter ever since."

"Well, I'm opposed to lowering our membership fees of five dollars for this group, no matter what experience our neighbor here has had. I say if our white way of life isn't worth ten cents a week to us, then we don't deserve to keep it."

In the beginning the WCCs sprang from the old plantation South of the traditional "Black Belt." Here many of its members were the "leading" people—planters, businessmen, lawyers, merchants—whose vested economic and emotional commitments to segregation were now threatened as those same investments in slavery had once been threatened and destroyed.

"Segregation's the cornerstone of our way of life," one of these elderly, courtly Delta men will explain to you patiently, a trifle wearily perhaps, as if spelling out an obvious fact for a child who is either a little backward or a little perverse; he is uncertain just which. "Take away that cornerstone, or even shake it hard enough, and the whole structure we've built here will tumble down around us. Not around us, upon us. Upon us all. Black and white."

He fixes you with a steady gaze. You know he has turned this concentration upon many a one before you: a white foreman who has miscalculated the cotton planting or picking, a Negro accused of pilfering a ham or a tank of gas out of the tractor. Behind the gaze is an authority assumed by so many generations of ancestors that now this man accepts it as unconsciously and incontrovertibly as the once divine right of kings.

"You take this county we're in: 74 to 75 per cent nigra. It's what we're all used to—but what would happen to us, all of us, if suddenly everything was shifted? That's why we've got the Council here: to keep things stable." When you nod, he permits himself a brief twinkle. "Like my father used to say about the Southern cavalry during that other War Against the South: we've been outnumbered but we've yet to be outmaneuvered."

Eventually, however, the WCCs had to appeal to the grass roots. And here their schism in leadership and method was exposed. As one astute observer says, "It's hard to get a crowd worked up over abstractions like states' rights; it's hard to weld them together with careful explanations of interposition. One or two of the dullest meetings I've ever attended were some of the early WCC rallies. You could hear people muttering and grumbling: 'Too much talking, not enough doing.' That sort of thing. Lately they've picked up some. When the going gets tough they've learned to holler 'Intermarriage!' "

Of course, some of the Councils divided early over this very issue. In Alabama, Sam Englehardt, Jr., and Asa ["Ace"] Carter parted company over Ace's more inflammatory methods. Ace's North Alabama Citizens' Council now centers around Birmingham, while State Senator Englehardt's Council has headquarters, properly enough, in Montgomery, the state capital. The fact that Englehardt's group now has much the major power, both numerically and politically, may indicate that the Councils are going to maintain at least an outward propriety as long as possible. Yet among some of this group you can detect a certain envy when they say, "Ace's gang up in Birmingham won't put up with what we have down here during these bus boycotts. Those boys up there are tough; they mean business!" (That the boys are tough was illustrated when Ace was arrested on a charge of assault with intent to commit murder in a January, 1957, KKK fracas in Birmingham.)

The achievement wherein WCCs have been most successful is in the creation of a climate where agreement with them is taken as natural and loyal, disagreement is made to appear either churlish or downright treacherous. To paraphrase the great English phrasemaker: Seldom have so few been accepted by so many as the voice of all. North and South, the WCCs' defiant pronouncements have been heeded as "the" voice of "the" South.

Particularly in the small towns of some of the more adamant states has this come to be almost altogether true. There are several reasons why this should be so. One is that old, but very important, reality that almost every phase of Southern life is still of a highly personal nature, and the smaller the town the more this is so. Others may read this and yet not have the vaguest comprehension what it means in terms of daily living. A Northern person seldom considers himself the embodiment of every Northerner, yet a Southerner somehow feels that he is every other Southerner. Despite the rich variety of the lives, each segment feels it is a special incarnation of the whole. That is why a Southerner feels so deeply betrayed and why the region is so united in hatred of its own who disagree or—as its people say—"turn against us."

Open disagreement is intolerable to the Councils and neutrality is unthinkable. South Carolina editor Jack O'Dowd discussed the problem in a speech before the Rotary Club of Hartsville, S.C. He told of men who did not belong to the Citizens' Council, and wanted nothing to do with it, but when their names were published as participants they did not move to have the error corrected. "These men who would not disclaim— even conditionally—affiliation with the Citizens' Council were intimidated. The negative philosophy pervading much of the South deals in absolutes. These men were afraid that, by saying they had not given their blessing to this unknown organization, they would be thought of as saying they were in favor of integration. Guilt through disassociation!" (Editor O'Dowd himself left South Carolina a few months after this speech.)

The need for uniformity which infuses the entire WCC movement has given rise to one of the sharpest of ironies. These groups predicate their appeal on the fact that they are against "outside" interference, against Federal law which would supersede state law or custom. In their turn, however, the Councils have opposed leaving the decision of desegregation up to the individual communities in these states. The situation is comparable to that which existed during the Civil War: the Southern states denounced the heavy hand of central authority from Washington when it impinged on liberties they claimed for themselves; but the Confederacy into which they joined themselves was in turn denounced by certain members for its own heavy hand of central authority from Richmond when it denied them liberties they also claimed as their own to be administered only from their own capitals. Governor Zeb Vance of North Carolina continually struggled with President Jefferson Davis and other C.S.A. officials over this matter of his state's rights—under the Confederacy which was supposedly based on that very premise. Today those who speak up loudest for the liberty of the state, as opposed to the "authoritarianism" of Washington, seem to oppose just as rigidly the liberty of the community if it is opposed to the dictates of the state. One

Southern state official summed up the situation and all the talk on rights with revealing succinctness when he said, "We'll never get solid segregation if we leave it up to each little locality." In short, the one right the Councils and their fellow groups defend most valiantly is the right of everyone to agree with them.

For dissenters, or even those who are still uncommitted to any definite position, they have not shown quite the same democratic concern. When the rector of a fashionable Episcopal church in the Deep South can say to you, "Sometimes during the past year I have felt as if I might be living in Nazi Germany—that's how strong these groups are here, that's how intensely the vocal people feel," then you begin to comprehend the meaning of the "watchdog" atmosphere which has been the WCCs' main achievement.

Two other points should be made in connection with the Councils: One is their alliance with groups who have their own specific grudges, other than integration, against the government or society in general. These may advocate abolition of the United Nations or the income tax, return to Prohibition, curtailment of labor-union activity, or a variety of other social changes—but they are ready and willing to use the much more emotion-charged issue of race relations to further these various purposes.

Second, although each state group distributes much the same literature, although there is some exchange of speakers and, in the case of newly organized units, frequently a sharing of leadership, and even though there is now a co-ordinating headquarters in Greenwood, Mississippi, called "Citizens' Councils of America," these are still fairly localized groups, operating independently of one another. In fact, they sometimes seem rather less than eager to recognize one another officially. This is understandable when the disparity between the various groups is recognized. While certain chapters are composed of leading politicians and members of the business and professional community, others are made up almost altogether of marginal farmers and factory workers and the generally dissatisfied loungers who fringe every town. The goals of these two groups, aside from the race issue, are seldom the same, not to mention their methods. And their attitude toward each other is a little like that of the amateur genealogist who hesitates to accept fully certain members of the family tree until he can be sure they will not prove embarrassing.

The big problem facing the WCCs is obvious: How are the ladies with white gloves and the gentlemen with scholarly addresses going to generate anger among their fellow workers and yet keep the boys in the plaid jackets and the men in denims from translating that anger into action? By creating a highly charged atmosphere they have arranged for an explosion, and the guilt of who strikes the match is one of degree only.

The uncertainties aroused by WCC interference in daily routines are not confined only to the Negro community. They have gripped white relations, too. One Negro man in South Carolina, having observed the white situation in his town, tells you:

"Some men who are strong members of the Council got in a cross section between themselves. One particular white farmer, I must tell you about him. He drove the people off his place. He had some families there that had six or seven children that could help on the farm, large families, and he rented a whole lot of land and had people tend it. He ran everybody off. And I happened to be in the bank when he went in there. He was trying to get a loan for about three thousand dollars to run his farm another year. And the banker told him, 'We can't let you have money when you have nobody to farm the land. If you don't farm the land, how will you make the money to pay us back? You have to get somebody to farm the land and then come back and we will see what we can do for you.' 'Well,' he said, 'now isn't that the devil? The Citizens' Council told me to run them all off and get rid of them.' The banker said, 'Well, you go to the Citizens' Council then and borrow your money.' He was going out the door just as I was going out. He said to me, 'Uncle, isn't that hell?' I said, 'How's that?' He said, 'The Citizens' Council told me to run them off and I could get help, and now the bank tells me to go to the Citizens' Council to borrow money, that they aren't going to lend me any.' I said, 'That's pretty bad. I am sorry for you.' "

It is possible that the WCCs and their fellow groups stand this moment at the peak of their power. Their membership already exceeds that of the NAACP. They have found a serviceable weapon in fear—fear of economic reprisals and social ostracism. They have the frequent backing of local political power and in some states their influence is decisive in legislative halls and public offices. And they are vocal. They have managed to have their voice accepted as official for the "Solid South," an illusion they have revived and re-established in the public mind. They are prolific and prosperous and powerful.

Yet, like Harry Golden's middle-class man with the two-car garage and the barbecue pit, they are fearful, fearful, fearful. Their hatred of the NAACP borders on the pathological. In the same Southern city you may go from the newly decorated, fluorescent-lighted, centrally located offices of the segregation organization across town to the second-floor, shabby state NAACP headquarters—and you wonder at the power of these two groups and the pressures they have imposed on each other. Then you realize that their strength does not lie in these offices nor even in the leaders with whom you talk. The strength of all the groups is out there—in the churches, little and large, the credit books of crossroads stores and village banks, in the country-club chatter and the men's-club bull sessions and the ladies' auxilliaries. All the statistics of membership and finances are simple: it is what men believe behind the statistics that makes them complex. What its members believe, or fail to believe, plants the seeds of death or life in every organization's birth. In busywork of pamphlets and reprints, speeches and membership campaigns, these obvious, fundamental generalizations are frequently forgotten by the hierarchy. But not by their following.

"We won't be integrated here in the South," a WCC man assures you flatly. "We'll fight it out in the streets, if that's what it takes to prove to the black-nigras and the white-nigras, too, that we won't ever give in. Before we mix our blood, we'll spill it."

And across town an NAACP member says, "We're American citizens. All we want is our citizenship. We're working against generations of wrongs for next generation's rights. We can't help but win!"

Talking with the leaders and some members of all these groups who have chosen sides in an historic tug of war, men impelled by urges as powerful as blood-fear and blood-pride (black and white and brown), motives as venal as self-pity and self-aggrandizement, as worthy as human dignity—talking with the men and women driven by a simple or complex combination of these forces, you are moved to cry: "What a waste is here! What a waste of energy and organization spent in fighting against a reality as sure as tomorrow morning's sun, or spent in fighting for a certainty which needs implementation but not justification. What a distortion of fraternal instinct, which abounds so lavishly in the South and yet is put on a leash and told 'Thus far and no farther'; brotherhood including 'us,' excluding 'them.' "

And what a waste of wonder is here, dissipating man's natural awe and fear on petty fascimiles of pain and destruction when one clear night in the high peaks of the Great Smokies, or on the wide lonely mesas of Texas, will dwarf him with the majestic beauty and terror of his universe, and one moment's thought at Oak Ridge or Aiken on the present possibility of human annihilation will free him from the arrogance of prejudice by clique. The unknown reaches of space and the mind:

these are subjects worthy of our terror and investigation. But not men in bed sheets, not nameless voices at the other end of a telephone wire, not trivial annoyances and malicious injuries without purpose or meaning.

Between the blackness of the night behind us and the whiteness of the day ahead, revealed in one atomic flash, our common humanity stands poised, neither black nor white, but only blood and bone and spirit. When we betray it, alone or collectively, we admit we have let the prattle of our neighbors deafen us to the thunder of Jehovah.

7   Look Down That Lonesome Road

The hard-baked, barren yards under the chinaberry trees, the long, rutted lanes between the cotton fields, the winding roads through the piney-woods flats, are layered more thickly each year with the dust of their one-time dwellers who are pulling stakes and leaving the South. A people close to the cycle of earth and the seasons has suddenly taken to concrete; a region whose most persistent myth has been one of static aimlessness is presently being recognized as a crossroads with a purpose. The old road that used to stretch out so long and lonesome in the distance is all at once a crowded thoroughfare with the more than one million Southerners who leave Dixie for other sections of the nation each year, and the two and three-quarters million who move their homes inside the region. The highways lead out, and they also lead in, and they are busy now with traffic in both directions.

"Lord, the comin' and the goin'!" an old man at a one-pump filling station beside one of the new superhighways sighs as he fills up your gas tank. "Niggers pull in here in big fine cars; white boys sixteen, seventeen years old that ought to be out behind a mule are sittin' behind a steerin' wheel. Everybody touristin' around. Everybody lookin' for something besides what they already got. Looks like gasoline and rubber's turned the world upside down."

There have been roads leading out of the South for a long time, and some of them have not told a happy story. Two, indeed, bear heavy loads of injustice: the Trail of Tears and the Underground Railroad. The first came into being in 1838 after gold was discovered in the hills of Georgia, and government troops of the United States forcibly removed the unwilling Cherokee Indians from their homes in the mountains of Tennessee, North Carolina and Georgia to the territory of Oklahoma. The issue of Cherokee removal brought one of the sharpest and most obvious clashes between Federal authority and states' rights

115

that preceded the Civil War—and it, too, centered around the question of justice to a minority race. When President Van Buren, in May, 1838, submitted a compromise which would at least permit the Indians two more years to complete their removal, the language used by Georgia's Governor Gilmer in reply seems not altogether unfamiliar today. He asserted: "I can give it no sanction whatever. The proposal could not be carried into effect but in violation of the rights of the state. It is necessary that I should know whether the President intends that the Indians shall be maintained in their occupancy by armed force in opposition to the right of the owners of the soil. [Governor Gilmer obviously believed that might established right in the matter of ownership!] If such be the intentions, a direct collision between the authorities of the state and the general Government must ensue. My duty will require that I shall prevent any interference whatever by the troops with the rights of the state and its citizens. I shall not fail to perform it."

The states won their rights, and gold, on this occasion, and the Cherokees began their weary march westward. Before their journey was finished, four thousand, or approximately one fourth of the men, women and children who had begun the hegira, were dead on the trail. Small wonder they remembered it by their tears. Some white Americans, witnessing this expulsion of red Americans from their homes, shared their grief. One said, "When I passed the last detachment of these suffering exiles . . . I turned from the sight with feelings which language cannot express, and wept like childhood. I felt that I would not encounter the secret prayers of one of those sufferers, if there be a God who avenges the wrongs of the injured, for all the lands in Georgia."

Hardened soldiers were moved by the plight of their helpless victims. General Winfield Scott, in command of the removal, finally allowed a remnant to remain behind in its native Southern mountains, after he had secured the surrender of the rebel Tsali, his brother and son, and had them executed before a firing squad. Descendants of these home-lovers live there today, in the valleys and coves of the Great Smokies, and beside one of the swift mountain streams lives the mother of one young Cherokee who received the nation's Congressional Medal of Honor for courage in action, fighting for his country in World War II. So white men have come in and red men have gone forth on the interweaving trails of history and imperfect justice.

As for the Underground Railroad, we shall never know how many black men used its unmarked route to escape from bondage. Its story has been eloquently told in many other places. It set the Negroes' sight on the distant North as a sort of Sweet Beulah Land where freedom and equality spelled success. Some of that same dream lures both Negro and white down that un-lonesome road today.

People on the move like to get their history in capsule form. Southerners and their visitors have enjoyed for the past couple of years this concentrate of a decade: "Yankees coming South, Negroes going North, cattle coming East, cotton going West, money coming in." It has all been true: people from other regions have come in *almost* as fast as natives left (roughly three quarters of a million arriving every year for the past three years); the Deep South has grown whiter as every train for Los Angeles, Chicago, Detroit and New York carried off some of its Negro population (although now a counter-trend of white migration seems to be altering this somewhat); Florida has ranches that are more than reasonable facsimiles of Texas, and Wisconsin no longer has to provide most of the milk for the land of Coca-Cola; California grows more cotton than any other state in the Union; the Southern per capita income is still the lowest for any region in the United States, but it's still a long way from the days of the Black Patch War and fatback on credit.

Harry Ashmore, casual in tweeds, cordial and attentive in his modern office as editor of the *Arkansas Gazette*, is himself an example of the New South he discusses. He is as far removed from the old stereotype of the Southern editor as a Martini is different from a fruit jar of moonshine. He tells you, "The key to the whole mind of the South now, it seems to me, is change. It's changing so rapidly you can't really peg it anywhere and say, 'This is it.' Look at the breakup of the one-party political picture in the South—at least on the national level, if not yet on the state-legislature level. It's very important. Politics will never be the same in the South again, and because of that lots of other things will never be the same either. Then there are the migrations, from country to town, from town to city, from South to North, and all that means deep and lasting change."

The roads of the South and the travelers who followed them have always played a vital part in the region's story. There are few today, however, who would state one viewpoint as candidly as a planter in the Alabama Black Belt, who tells you, "It wasn't Sherman marching through the South that spelled the end of our way of life. The real end came with asphalt. When we brought in all these highways, we let in the rest of the country. Our nigras learned about different ways from what they'd always known. Neither the nigras nor anything else has been the same since."

Following the Civil War, the ten thousand miles of railroads which the Southern states had had prior to war's destruction were in sad condition, but it has been asserted that by 1880 the South possessed a modern railroad system twice as great as that of 1860. And highways began to give the iron tracks competition. As the automobile came to accelerate the highway programs, North Carolina led the way among Southern states in road building, and was only superseded when Louisiana's Huey Long decided to make every man a king and pave his way to the palace.

Generations before big-time demagogues and six-lane boulevards, however, the region had had to meet the "problem" of its visitors. Following the Civil War, travelers came South to see this strange land. Some, like John Trowbridge, Boston novelist and journalist, found the Desolate South, a victim of the past, and returned home to write about it. Others found the New South, a challenge to the future, and stayed to become part of it. Birmingham and Chattanooga and other villages began to grow into cities. The forces which would inevitably challenge the racial patterns of the region were being wooed and won to the South by some of the very people who would most resist that eventual challenge—which has come in our day. After the war, when Southern pride was still raw but its purses were still flat, the pantomime was begun which persists today. Its essence is paradox: the stranger is invited to stay home and mind his own business—he is invited to come and live among us and bring his business. But that is a matter to discuss a little later; our concern now is the coming and the going.

"One thing about it," a man in middle Georgia says, "the niggers are pulling out. Like the balding man's hair, they're going a batch at a time. Enough of them leave, they'll take this race trouble with them and dump it in the laps of them fellers up North that know all the answers."

Recent statistics show that since 1910 about five million Negroes have left the Southern states. Half of the Negroes living outside the region today were born in the South. While the number of Negroes in the North increased by 52 per cent during the decade 1940 to 1950, the Negro population in the West increased by 234 per cent—and the Negro population in the South showed a 3 per cent increase! Contrary to many popular ideas, no Southern state has as many Negroes as it does whites—and instead of increasing, as alarmed whites often intimate, the actual proportions of Negro to white have decreased steadily. For instance, in Mississippi in 1940, Negroes made up 49 per cent of the population, in 1950 only 45 per cent. In South Carolina the decrease for the same period was from 42 to 38 per cent, in Louisiana from 35 to 32 per cent, and in Georgia from 34 to 30 per cent. Taking a longer-range view, a University of Virginia News Letter early in 1955 set forth some facts which would indicate fairly accurately the general population pattern in the South. In Virginia in 1790, 43 per cent of the people were Negro. In 1830, 47 per cent; in 1860, 43 per cent. By 1900 only 35 per cent of the Virginians were Negro; in 1930, 26 per cent; and in 1950, 22 per cent. "The colored race traditionally has a much higher birth rate than the white," the News Letter concluded. "Ordinarily it is emphasis on this fact, without due consideration of the high colored death rate and the net outward migration pattern, which has led to the misconception that the colored population of the state is increasing at a rapid rate."

Chicago, one of the main points of destination for emigrants from the Deep South, has, at latest estimates, a population nearly 20 per cent Negro. That is practically kissing kin to Virginia's percentage. And of course Harlem has more Negroes than any city in the South, and New York has a larger Negro population than any Southern state except North Carolina and Georgia.

From 1940 to 1950, nearly four times as many Negroes as whites left North Carolina, and this trend held true through most of the South. From statistical analysts to bitter segregationists, the consensus of opinion seems generally to have been one of relief at this "natural solution to a problem of numbers," or "let 'em go!" There can be no doubt that smaller concentrations of Negroes in some areas of the South would lessen tension. But in recent months we have suddenly discovered that, at least in certain parts of the South, this trend of a decade—or longer, or half a century—is being reversed and, at least in Mississippi and Tennessee, more whites are now leaving the state than are Negroes.

When the United States Census Bureau issued reports in November, 1956, showing that nine of the thirteen Southern States we are considering here either lost population or gained less than the national average, many Southerners who bothered to be concerned about this loss still said, "It's the Negroes who are leaving. And that'll help solve our race problem." One voice which suggested that the South's loss of Negro citizens could not be reckoned as all gain for the region was that of a former dean of Mississippi State College's School of Business. He said that the Negro migration, of which he had made a study, might lessen the state's social problems, but he added that it would be "very difficult to point to it as an economic asset."

Now we discover that some of the factors influencing Negro migration also affect white people: the push of mechanization, the pull of industrialization. Dr. Harald A. Pedersen, of the Mississippi Agricultural Experiment Station, reports that between April, 1950, and July, 1956, Mississippi lost over 51,000 white residents but only 28,800 Negroes. Census studies made by the University of Tennessee indicate that recent migration from rural West Tennessee has been practically all white. In one area, including two counties of approximately two-to-one Negro population, there has been a loss of 4,209 whites with an actual gain of 941 Negroes! In another area, including all the Middle Tennessee counties along the Tennessee River, the loss has been 5,567 whites and one Negro!

Whether this is a trend of only local and temporary importance, or whether it suggests a significant change along the South's high road of emigration, remains to be seen. It may imply, even now, however, that some of the handicaps to the Negro's full enjoyment of citizenship in the South may also become handicaps for white people, too. "You can't keep a man in the ditch unless you get down there with him," is a favorite saying of Negroes throughout the South today. Perhaps some of the poorer Southerners of both colors will climb out of the ditch together.

Many factors influence such changes, however. Dr. Preston Valien of Fisk University says, "It is entirely possible that the difference in job opportunities at the other end of the line has slowed the Negro movement and speeded the white movement." If this is the case, then the hopes of Negroes for better opportunities through emigration are lessened. But balancing this may be the fact that in-state shifts of Negro population are painting a new picture.

In Mississippi, a fact of almost equal interest to the discovery of the growth of white migration is the decisive movement of Negroes out of the Delta into the predominantly white section of Northeastern Mississippi. Dr. Pedersen explains this situation: "I think you will find the Negro population rising in any area where you have a high proportion of Negro home ownership, and especially where they own small to medium-sized farms. They're going where they can expect a reasonably stable economy for their families, something to eat, enough money to pay taxes and maybe a little extra."

There are, of course, no hard-and-fast rules which will explain why a man packs his little worldly accumulations into a secondhand car or third-hand truck or battered suitcase, and starts on the long road "up North." But they are arriving every day to knock on the battered door of opportunity in one metropolis or another. Dismayed, exhilarated, bewildered, stubborn, they come from the country to the concrete, and the cords of family, church and community are cut behind them. In this situation, the worst aspect of our modern industrial age is revealed in all its impersonal shortcomings. The individual, black or white, who has been accustomed to the leisurely personal life of the land suddenly becomes part of an impersonal mass whose days are measured and implemented by machines of incredible complexness. Disillusionment and insecurity follow naturally.

Under these conditions, it is small wonder that underprivileged people react in pretty much the same way. When a Chicago reporter asserted early in March, 1957, that "hillbillies" who had come to the city from some of the Southern states "have the lowest moral code, if any, of any [group], the biggest capacity for liquor and the most savage and vicious tactics when drunk, which is most of the time," and went on to say that police estimated it would take two thousand extra officers to cope with these displaced Anglo-Saxons' crimes, the words were curiously reminiscent of allegations against the Negroes in similar circumstances.

For instance, Francis Butler Simkins, in *A History of the South*, had written, "The most appalling fact about the Negro crime record was that the forces of progress to which the race was heir did not reduce it. . . . Not even education had turned the trick; indeed, the cynics asserted that it merely widened the criminal opportunities of the blacks. If such a claim seems like arrant anti-Negroism, there is sound statistical evidence that migrations had an evil effect. . . . Negro migrants to the North got in the clutches of the law more often than those who remained in the South. . . . An example of the high crime rate of those who moved North is the fact that, in 1945, 74 per cent of the adults arrested in the District of Columbia were Negroes, although Negroes constituted only one third of the population."

Anglo-Saxon or Negro, Chicago still seeks to attract one hundred thousand new workers each year to keep its tremendous industries alive, and the large majority of these are from the South. The city offers them congestion where they have often been accustomed to space, hard reality where they have built naïve hopes, and if they frequently react with a fierceness born of frustration, surely their behavior cannot be laid only to original sin and the innate mischief of a particular race.

A Negro leader in Chicago, a man called a "social statesman" by those who know his work among the city's newcomers, gives you a classic pattern of Negro migration in his own life: "I was born in Memphis. My father was a D.P. from a small town in Middle Tennessee. It was a little place where gentlemen in white sheets would ride around and when Negro boys came to adolescence, the gentlemen would spank them just to remind them to stay in their place. My father didn't like to be spanked so he moved to Memphis.

"My mother had come with her family from Mississippi. Her father had a disagreement with his white employer and so he took his children under a load of hay in a wagon out of the state to Memphis.

"When I was about grown and my turn came to move on, I went to Chicago. Chicago is the only city in America I ever heard of whose first settler was a Negro. Now they call it a melting pot, but the different people don't melt much in Chicago. More often they coagulate. And the places where the newcomers have to coagulate are the poorest, dirtiest, most rundown and congested of all. Negroes seek escape in song, liquor and flight. One third of the name-brand liquor consumed in Chicago, so I've been told, is consumed by Negroes. Flight means not only the flight of Southern Negroes to Northern cities—but flight of the long-time Negro residents there away from the newcomers.

"There's a battle on now between the North and South concerning Negro migration. Mississippi wants as many Negroes as will to leave so they can keep the voting power safe. Chicago and other cities don't want them to come because of politics again—we now have five aldermen instead of two. [The pursuit of happiness mustn't interfere with party politics!]

"You know, the promised land can be a weary land! Sometimes it takes Negroes twenty years to celebrate getting there before they settle down to being responsible citizens. That's what some of us are working on now: for our people to be shorter on the celebration and longer on the citizenship. We've always got to remember that Negroes become statistics quicker than white folks do. It helps prejudice. Not the why or the wherefore, just the neat round figures.

"I want to spread this problem all over the North and West so that it will be easier to solve. We have to go where our talents can be made known, where they can be used!"

Dr. Charles Johnson once called the liquor store the poor man's psychiatrist. "Psychiatrists are pretty expensive," he smiled sadly, "but there's always temporary treatment at a neighborhood liquor counter.

"Of course," he added, "there are the many Negroes who find what they are looking for in the cities. Let me tell you a story I heard a few weeks ago. A young fellow went to Detroit and stayed a couple of years. After a while his parents got lonesome and they wrote to him. 'It's time to come on home now,' they said. 'Your cot is waiting out in the side shed, we've got a ham all cured ready to eat and your old mule is waiting out in the field ready for you to say "Get up." ' Well, the boy got the letter, waited a few weeks, and finally wrote back to his family: 'I'm not coming home. I wouldn't tell another mule to "Get up" if one was sitting on my lap!' "

The sad feature of Negro migration, as far as the South as a whole is concerned, is suggested in our Chicagoan's remark that Negroes "have to go where our talents can be used." For if the South has been wasteful of its fish and fowl, its woods and waters, it is being no less shortsighted in its squandering of human resources today. Again, in Little Rock, Harry Ashmore tells you, "One thing that's occurring to many of the powerful men who can look into the future at all is that one of our chief assets here for many years has been cheap labor. When immigration laws blocked European labor from streaming in, the South was the next big source.

"We've been exporting labor to all the big centers for years now, not only Detroit and Cleveland and Chicago, but California and the Far West, too. Of course we've been aware of the Negro migrations, but perhaps not so much of the white Southerners who make up large colonies in some centers.

"Well, our labor reservoir is going to run dry one of these days. And when the white labor supply is all used up we'll have to depend on the Negroes, and we'll find that we have been frittering away an asset as valuable as our water or timber or any other resource."

And fellow editor Jonathan Daniels, over in Raleigh, North Carolina, wrote on the same theme in an article for *The Virginia Quarterly Review*, in spring, 1955: "Next year the 'New South' of Henry Grady's adored and durable phrase will be seventy years old. Nothing has happened in that time to change the fact that, whatever courts may say and people may plan, the South can only fulfill itself if it uses the capacities, the strong backs, the talents, and the energy of all the people in it. The Negro sometimes seems to count on desegregation as a miracle in that business as simple as a decision. The whites have sometimes seemed to carry segregation to the point of insisting upon carrying the Negro as a load.

"Not even now can the South spare the labor of its Negroes.

"And the Negro knows, standing on a corner or hitting the road to uncertain distant places, that the only basis of dignity is a man's right to earn his bread.

"The fulfilled South and not merely the aging 'New South' depends upon those facts. So does the real meaning of America."

But not all editors and fellow Southerners agree that it is loss when a Negro leaves the South.

In February, 1957, the secretary of the Association of Citizens' Councils wrote from Greenwood, Mississippi, to President Eisenhower. He said, in part: "Here is a proposal that is so simple no federal government agency could consider it. Let the state governments of those states whose representatives and press advocate integration for the South, make available accommodations for the number of Negro citizens necessary to bring their Negro population up to the national average of 10 per cent. This includes housing and jobs, as well as school and church facilities. Of course, the migration would be voluntary, and we could give the message wide publicity throughout the South. . . . The only thing wrong with this plan is that it is too simple and too logical. The alternative is continued chaos, confusion and further destruction of national unity."

One North Carolinian sighs as he talks with you about some of the facts of Negro migration from the South. " 'Oh, the Negroes are leaving by the wholesale,' some people tell you and they're glad. They've never noticed that it's the boy with the engineering degree who's leaving, and it's his idiot brother who's staying."

In more formal language, buttressed by statistics, Eli Ginsberg in his study, *The Negro Potential*, says, "The very poorly educated are less mobile than the better educated. The low percentage of illiterates among Northern Negroes confirms the conclusion that the functionally illiterate Southern Negro generally remains in the South." And he is the very one least equipped to man the machines of new industry and new farming techniques.

Most of the Southern states are becoming alarmed over their loss of young people. According to one study, over 60 per cent of the migrants from Mississippi are between fifteen and thirty-four years old. After rearing and educating these boys and girls, Mississippi loses the benefits of their most productive years. In Tennessee, the Nashville *Tennessean* warned, in April, 1957: "One of the most shocking and challenging problems to the state of Tennessee is the continuing and costly loss of its young people.

"In a survey conducted by a reporter for this newspaper, it was found that the state is losing an estimated 20,000 young persons a year, and wasting an estimated $200 million invested in them because of inability to provide jobs for them."

Dr. Horace Hamilton of North Carolina State College, observing that his state lost some 261,000 people by migration during the decade of 1940 to 1950, says that this "represents a transfer of real economic wealth—directly and indirectly." He estimates the indirect loss at $15,000 per person, the cost of his rearing and education, and arrives at the staggering total loss of $3,900,000,000. It is well that this deficit is indirect—otherwise the state debt of North Carolina would soon equal that of the Federal government.

Fortunately, all the people going down those crowded roads are not leaving the South. Many of them are simply going to town. The South went to town later than the North—in fact, started just in time to meet the North halfway on the move back to the country: in suburbia. So the South has jumped from the country to the suburbs and in many ways bypassed the metropolitan experience. As illustration of this jump, consider the differences between the rustic Ku Klux Klan and the streamlined White Citizens' Councils.

There are also the small industries scattered over the South whose workers live on their own small farms and consider employment at the mill simply as their cash crop. A Georgia educator says: "I was talking with one of our county agents recently and he told me that he couldn't think of one rural family in his whole county who lived solely from the income of its farm. If the father farmed steadily, then the mother, or maybe a daughter, worked at some plant or business nearby, and earned supplemental income. That's the important story in the South today. Don't fall into this intellectual trap of how fast we're growing. The Pacific Northwest, California, Indiana, Ohio—they're all growing more. Nowadays the South has got to run to stand still! But what we can talk about is this shift from country to town."

The fact that partial decentralization of industry and partial desegregation of schools should be taking place at the same time, and simultaneously affecting the very roots—as well as the future flowering—of the South, will be recognized several times throughout this book, for this situation has many aspects. Two widely different frames of reference have suddenly been brought to bear on an emotion-laden issue: these might be called the rural and the Jaycee views. The differences between them, in the matter of race, are more often those of method than basic belief. However, these disagreements over method are creating a real schism in the present segregation front of the South. Perhaps this schism has been demonstrated most clearly in the case of a traveling salesman of hate, who followed the roads running South to trouble and crisis—and, as he hoped, to fame and fortune.

A Southern segregation leader shakes his head ruefully and confides,

"The day John Kasper crossed the Mason-Dixon line, it set the cause of white supremacy back twenty years." Yet white (Protestant) supremacy was precisely what the tall young zealot from New Jersey, via Washington, D.C., came down to sell the South. Of course, this was a luxury it already had plenty of, but with a true pitchman's optimism he was confident he could whet the appetite for more. He used all the right words: "mongrelization," "opposed to placing the fair white bodies of our children in the schools beside niggers," "Communist agitation," "blood will flow in the streets," "we will have to have our martyr . . . the Federal government means death to all of us." Why, then, was his career meteoric? Why—after only seven months (from August 1956 until March 1957), during which he was credited with organizing, practically singlehanded, one riot, several branches of his Seaboard Citizens' Councils, and many cross-burnings—was he so suddenly dropped?

The itinerary of Mr. Kasper's travels may indicate the foundation of both his failure and success in refurbishing old prejudices for new crises. More important, it may reveal some changing realities about the current situation in the South.

After brief scouting trips into Delaware and Maryland, John Kasper began the more public phase of his career with forays into Virginia, using his Washington bookshop as home base. When Charlottesville, in the summer of 1956, was ordered to desegregate its schools during the coming term, Kasper really went to work. Your reporters first encountered the resistance to his "super-sell" in Charlottesville in mid-August. A pro-segregation leader sat on the lawn of the old county courthouse there and told us, early in the soft summer morning, of the lawyers, business-men, professional men, who were members of his organization, the Defenders of State Sovereignty and Individual Liberties. "We're the home of Thomas Jefferson and we're proud of that. We're the home of the University of Virginia and we have a gentleman's reputation, you know. Nobody can make us desegregate the schools in Charlottesville, but we're going to fight this tyranny with law. Over last weekend this Seaboard Citizens' Council group appeared here, a fellow named Kasper from out of Washington with a lot of handbills and a mass meeting. They had a talk with the mayor and police chief, but they didn't get any encouragement from our officials. They passed out this inflammatory material, white girls kissing niggers, all that sort of thing—we don't want any part of that."

A few days later Kasper added a last touch to his Virginia sales campaign: he and a handful of friends broke up an interracial church meeting of the Charlottesville chapter of the Virginia Council on Human Relations. A cross was subsequently burned on the lawn of a widely respected Council leader, Sarah Patton Boyle.

By now, word reached the traveling salesman that new territory was opening up. At Clinton, Tennessee, twelve Negro children had been ordered admitted to a white high school with some eight hundred students. On Tuesday, August twenty-eighth, three days after John Kasper's arrival in Clinton, we sat in the Clinton courtroom and studied him—the narrow face, the slouchy clothes, his contrived disdain of the lawyers and his frequent and searching looks into the audience. These were hard, desperate, work-bitten people in the courtroom, shrewd and yet with a kind of innocence which left them gullible to any medicine man. Essentially rural, they look with suspicion on urban devices for coping with difficult situations. As the mystery writers say, "had we but known" that within a few days Clinton would be a new word in the growing vocabulary of desegregation history, we would have looked with greater alarm on this young fellow who was so obviously an opportunist, a second-rate-go-getter, whose incentive was not so much money as notoriety.

"We need all the rabble rousers we can get. We want trouble and we want it everywhere. We need a band of roving patriots. A collapse of law and order is near at hand." Yet in the town of Clinton, the handful of leaders—from school principal to lawyer to editor to preacher to mayor—who held firm in a shifting quagmire, had finally brought failure even here, at the site of his greatest triumph, to Kasper's sales campaign.

When Florida's Governor, LeRoy Collins, in his inaugural speech on January 8, 1957, said that the Supreme Court was the highest tribunal in the land (although, he added, schools in Florida would not integrate in the foreseeable future), a few segregationists felt that their cause had been struck a body blow. John Kasper thought he sensed another soft spot in the South's solid front for segregation. "Looks like Collins is trying to out-nigger Chandler of Kentucky and Clement of Tennessee." He arrived in Florida's watermelon-growing belt and began hawking race—and now, stronger than ever, religious—hate. In Miami an attempted cross-burning, reports of a dynamite cache waiting for "John's" signal, and bitter denunciation of the Jews, aroused the state to action. "Damn all race-mixers . . . Roose, Harry & Ike . . . alien, unclean, unchristian . . . hang the nine swine." Kasper was summoned to Tallahassee and questioned by a legislative committee. At the hearing, and in a series of well-timed newspaper articles in the *Miami Herald*, accounts of the friendship between Kasper and certain Negroes during his Greenwich Village bookshop days reached even his strongest supporters. Suddenly he saw his customers melting away. The Citizens' Council of Clinton, Tennessee, which Kasper had formed, was dissolved. Even his staunch side-kick, "Ace" Carter of Birmingham, said, "That will about fix Kasper in the South." Said a former dragon of the Florida Ku Klux Klan who is now a private detective in Tampa: "We have had enough. . . . To encourage a race riot or to start a revolution is worse than integration."

Actually, it had already become popular to be against Kasper in most of the South. "Why does Kasper talk that way?" many puzzled Southerners asked. "He's smart, educated, went to Columbia University. He's had advantages. How can he believe all those things?" The answer is, obviously, that he does not believe many of the statements he makes. He "talks that way" because he thinks that is what the South wants to hear. In New York and Washington he had formed a stereotype of the South so strong in his mind that he hardly recognized the reality when it faced him—and rejected him.

And this brings us to two facts which seem to emerge from John Kasper's failure—whether temporary or final—as a traveling salesman of the old fire-eating white supremacy. The first is inability of many people outside the region to really comprehend that the old stereotypes are fading in the South. In Arthur Miller's memorable play, *Death of a Salesman*, Willie Loman was battered to defeat because he could not adapt his old techniques of personal salesmanship to a more streamlined impersonal era. What John Kasper found in Virginia was the Old South which wanted to keep its reputation clean, and in Florida the Chamber of Commerce New South which wanted to keep its coffers full. He could comprehend or cope with neither. Clinton lies in between; it fits the stereotype just enough to mislead Kasper and others—both within and outside the South—into thinking the days of Vardaman and Bilbo still exist and that the unashamed yokel-racist reigns supreme. Certainly he still exists, but he no longer reigns. Lynching is old-fashioned and the country-club crowd does not relish talk of blood in the streets when an economic boycott will be just as effective. Although many Northerners do not seem to realize it, Tobacco Road and Main Street have heard of Madison Avenue. There is a "new sell" on in the South.

The majority of Southerners have come to see themselves in a new light, and this is fact number two which is borne out by Kasper's adventures. "We're a pure 'public-relations' mentality now in most of Florida," a resident told us a few weeks before John Kasper's arrival. "The majority of us don't want anything to do with the KKK, and we're even suspicious of the White Citizens' Councils. Their agitation might hurt property values or disturb our tourist trade. We're just too busy making money and we're too damned set on being popular."

From Virginia to Florida, the image the New South has managed to sell itself is that of genteel lawlessness. In South Carolina, where the Councils flourish, one man told us: "I think some of the councils are perfectly sincere when they say they do not advocate violence. They think they can get what they want without it." Time and again, from the Atlantic to the Mississippi, you hear these contradictory words: "We won't obey the Supreme Court—but we're going to do what we have to legally."

Herman Talmadge has discarded Old Gene's galluses, although he still wears the same pants, and in Alabama, council leader Sam Englehardt, Jr., state legislator who has adopted the grey-flannel techniques, has proved far more effective than "Ace" Carter, with his overalls-and-blue-jeans approach. (They don't build a Federal government big enough," "Ace" has said, "to integrate my daughter with niggers . . . we'll settle it like white men ought to settle it.") And when John Kasper holds up the mirror to this nonconforming conformity, and reminds white supremacists of what they must do when their legalities fail, they slap him down in fear and anger. When it also develops that the stranger they momentarily trusted has flagrantly violated those social taboos the South observes most rigidly, at least on the surface, chagrin is added to deep unease—and bitter denunciation provides the easiest catharsis.

"Ace" Carter has taken an inventory of Kasper's salesmanship: "If we have a fire in our house—and in some ways you can say we are having a fire in the South—we are interested in saving our families. There are some who just like to see a fire and who might help throw the furniture out. I believe John Kasper is more like that. . . . Some people like excitement and to be in the public eye. . . . I told Kasper we didn't want him back in Alabama."

After Kasper's attack on the Jews, it is possible that some white Southerners turned on him out of a deep subconscious guilt: steeped in Hebrew legend and history by generations of Baptist and Methodist preachers, the question may arise within them: "How can Jesus of Nazareth be my Savior unless, in some inscrutable way—and the ways of the Lord are mysterious—he is also my social equal?" Southerners are gradually growing up; always an intensely patriotic people, their enthusiasm for Kasper cooled when they learned of his close friendship with Ezra Pound, the anti-Semitic poet indicted for treason. Who knows? In a few more years Southern white Christians may come to realize that it would be impossible for Martin Luther King, Jr., to show them the path to justice and peace—to save their souls—unless he were also their equal socially.

John Kasper had an old and popular product—but he forgot that this is an age of packaging. His successor to the Southern Territory may not be so naïve—he may wrap white supremacy in triple foil to keep it fresh and shiny and double the sales. That is why it is imperative that people of good will, on both sides of the Mason-Dixon line, try to comprehend as clearly as possible the realities of the New South. Lincoln said, "The dogmas of the quiet past are inadequate to the stormy present. The occasion is piled high with difficulty, and we must rise with the occasion. As our case is new, we must think anew, and act anew. We must disenthrall ourselves, and then we shall save our country."

So the roads run North and South and West, and they are no longer lonesome. Roots are being displaced by wheels, the city of the stranger reaches out to overwhelm the village where everyone is cousin to his neighbor. As the asphalt miles lengthen and concrete suburbs expand, there is something lost and something gained down South. Other countries, other regions of our own country, have experienced this transition long since. Is it possible for the South to acquire, for once, some measure of detachment, and profit by these previous experiences so that some of the best features of both the rural and industrial, the traditional and the new, may be merged in a more ideal society? It is possible—but only when all the different Souths which exist today have faced up to the acute and peculiar challenge of the Negro in their midst.

As a small, but meaningful, example, the larger problems will be closer to solution when freedom for a very ordinary Negro can find a larger symbol than daydreams before the used-car lot. It is difficult to realize that after Abraham Lincoln's Emancipation Proclamation had freed black slaves from their formal bondage, the second great emancipation—that from Jim Crow—was brought about by Henry Ford. An automobile became power and mobility and a measure of freedom to many people who were long denied all three.

There are the Negroes who come back South to visit the homefolks, and a glossy car is quickest, most tangible evidence of their transformed life "up there."

"Pearla Mae, she used to cook for me, you know, came by to see me yesterday," an elderly white woman tells you with a knowing little smile. "She had just come in, as they say, from Detroit and you know what she was driving? A secondhand Cadillac, of course. I walked out to the driveway and looked at it with her, as she was leaving. Somehow I couldn't help saying to her, 'Well, it's certainly been a long time since those depression days, hasn't it?' It was all Pearla Mae could do to get shoes to walk then, and now all God's chillun got Cads!"

But a man in Birmingham gives you the closest analysis of this matter of cars and skin color and homes and their relationships to each other. "You know there's been competition between real-estate men and automobile salesmen for the Negro's dollar. A Negro who could afford a twenty-five-thousand-dollar home will have a big Buick or Cadillac, and live in a hovel. I've wondered about this many times. The explanation is simple but it had never occurred to me until recently when a Negro pointed it out to me: when a Negro goes in to buy a Ford or a Chrysler, no one asks what color he is, where he is going to drive it, next to whom he'll be parking it. When he goes to buy a house, on the other hand, the first thing he's asked is what color he is, where the house he wants is located—and he's simply not able to buy the good houses he wants.

"We had a public discussion on civic problems a while back and I was a member of the panel. I pointed these facts out to a real-estate man on our round table and asked him if this didn't seem to call for some real-estate developments. He said, 'Yes, my friend, do you have any simple solutions?' You see, the same credit is not available for Negro houses as for white houses, because the risks are greater. There are many causes, some subtle, some more apparent, for this, but the largest one is the fact that their employment security is less—'last hired, first fired,' you know." Thus the vicious circle is perpetuated: poor job prospects, poor credit, poor housing, defeatist attitudes and more careless spending leading to poorer job prospects . . . and round and round. . . .

It need hardly be pointed out, of course, that the majority of Negroes in the South do not have any vehicle but the ankle express—and such public facilities as are available. The struggle to bar Jim Crow from this public transportation has added a new experience to Negro history in America and has brought a fresh awareness of Negro rights and dignity to many white Southerners: its symbol was labeled "Montgomery." A little later we will look more closely at the Montgomery, Alabama, story, but it must be said here that from the year-long boycott of its buses by fifty thousand Negro residents came the Supreme Court ruling which declared invalid a state law and a city ordinance requiring segregation of the races on intrastate buses. This, as *New York Times* correspondent Luther A. Huston said, "was thought to have placed a headstone at the grave of Plessy v. Ferguson," that being the case in 1896 which had established for the first time the "separate but equal" doctrine.

Some of the earliest Jim Crow legislation was that assuring the separation of the races on railway trains. Tennessee passed a law in 1881 which is sometimes called the first Jim Crow law. It directed that first-class Negro passengers on trains should be provided separate cars or portions of cars, instead of the customary second-class accommodations. But Virginia, the last Southern state to pass such laws, did not complete this phase of the segregation process until 1900. And one of the first people to defy segregation on streetcars was none other than the daughter of General Robert E. Lee. A history, *The Negro In Virginia*, published by the Works Progress Administration under sponsorship of the Virginia State Conservation Commission, says that "Mary Custis Lee . . . deliberately flouted the law. . . . Taking a seat on the Alexandria car in Washington, she refused to move forward when the car crossed the Potomac River into Virginia. At Alexandria she was arrested and conducted to police headquarters, where testimony revealed that she had been guilty of violating the same law before."

In January, 1957, the Southern Regional Council released the results of a spot survey it had made and disclosed that twenty-one Southern cities had ended compulsory segregation on local buses. These ranged from Little Rock, Arkansas, to Norfolk, Virginia; from San Antonio, Texas, to Knoxville, Tennessee, and in each case the desegregation took place without court action, without any organized protest, and without difficulty.

A good example of how simply desegregation could take place in public vehicles was the case of Richmond, Virginia. The first day of Jim Crow's disappearance from the buses there, one bus driver said, "I expected a real mess." At the end of the day, which had been orderly and peaceful, he said, "It worked out nice. Much better than I expected."

In contrast to this experience, and that of the twenty other quiet, law-abiding cities which desegregated and went on about their business, has been the violence in Montgomery and Tallahassee, Atlanta and Birmingham. But everywhere it becomes more and more apparent that, on the public conveyances traveling the roads and streets of the South, Jim Crow is dead. One bitter man says, "All that's left is to drag his rotting carcass out of the way."

The court decisions have marched one after the other, inevitable as the seasons: the Mitchell case outlawed Pullman segregation on trains in 1941; the Henderson case outlawed dining-car segregation. In November, 1952, the decision in the Chance case made it illegal for an interstate railroad to practice segregation on coaches. Furthermore, it established that such segregation is unlawful even if the separate facilities are equal in every respect! The school decision of 1954 should hardly have been the surprise many of its opponents claimed—if they had bothered to examine the sequence of events taking place in other areas of segregation.

Senator Harry Byrd of Virginia has said, "At the rate the Federal government is spending money, we're going to hell in a Cadillac." There's a saying in their state that Mississippians ride to the poorhouse on the best roads in the country. To hell or the poorhouse or simply to town, Southerners are certainly on their way. Suddenly they are bound to the rest of the nation by Dairi-Kreme and DeLuxe Motels and "regular or hi-test?"

But behind them is the memory of all the Negroes and Irishmen and Indians and Englishmen who blasted out the railroads and carved out the highways and were buried nameless and unremembered in the sweat and muck and blood of Southern earth. Theirs is the tradition—older than Jim Crow. Theirs is the tradition of men working together rather than riding separately. Between these, black and white and red and olive, and their children's children, stretches the road, lonesome and crowded: the road out and the road in, the road back—the road forward.

8 Sugar and Spice and Plenty of Backbone

"It's hell to be a Southern lady," the blonde girl under the dripping Spanish moss tells you. Except for the Bermuda shorts where crinolines used to be and her short wind-blown hair, she might be the epitome of chivalry's dream. "Oh, I suppose there's been a crack in the old mold, but we're still supposed to know more about Great-grandma's tester and Great-aunt Jessica's sillabub set than about the history of World War I. And if we're interested in anything like politics—well, we're looked on as cute little ole aberrations. When we go up East it's even worse. We're supposed to be beautiful and brainless, with a fan in one hand to ply our witchery and a lynch-rope in the other to hand our menfolks in case they're called out to protect our honor. Sugar and spice and everything nice— that's what little belles are made of. We're just not that good, or bad, and we're certainly not all that insipid, and we never have been!"

Remembering some of the women you've seen, some of the things you've learned, from the stately old homes on the Tidewater to the ranch-style houses on the St. Johns, from the mountain cabins perched beside patches of burley tobacco to the unpainted shacks in sprawling fields of cotton, you understand this girl's vehemence against a legend. Sugar and spice aplenty Southern women have had, but not always everything nice. Instead, many seem to have had an extra portion of backbone. White and black, the backbone to endure indentured servitude and slavery, to withstand and conquer the loneliness and hardships of wilderness and war; to withstand, almost, the legend of which they were not so much the beneficiary as the prisoner. The legend and reality of Southern womanhood was, is, inextricably interwoven with the legend and reality of the Negro.

Both were shaped, to a degree difficult to measure but certainly large, by the tyranny of cotton. One of the unique features of cotton culture has been its demand for hand labor. Like dry land soaking up

134

summer rain, cotton absorbs the days and weeks and months of a man's life; since it is also seasonal, it sucks in the hours and years of labor of his wife and children, too. In fact, if Black Belt loam is the planter's main capital in this realm of cotton, the tenant's, the small farmer's capital is his family—a ready reservoir of labor receiving no pay in the long lapses between work.

The importance of this single fact—cotton's requirement of intensive manual labor—shaped the family life of Negro and poor white in the Deep South for generations. To begin with, it demanded slavery— the formal bondage of the black race at first, and then the slightly more subtle peonage of the sharecropper, white or black, who barely subsisted from one year to the next, one crop's harvest to the next one's planting. The hopelessness and brutality of such an existence was reflected in a wretched home life. With none of the conveniences and too few of the physical necessities, how much less were the psychological niceties, even the affectionate needs of children and parents alike fulfilled.

It has been said that cotton is a by-product of large families. This was certainly one of the reasons why antebellum plantation owners encouraged their slaves to have children and, in some cases, set a select few aside mainly for breeding purposes. For proof of this, as for many other facts of slavery, one of the best sources to heed is the very voice of the time and place itself—the newspapers. In a Charleston, South Carolina *Gazette* of 1796, an advertisement referring to women who were on sale said, in part: ". . . [these] are not Negroes selected out of a larger gang for the purpose of a sale, but are prime, their present Owner, with great trouble and expence, selected them out of many for several years past. They were purchased for stock and breeding Negroes, and to any Planter who particularly wanted them for that purpose, they are a very choice and desirable gang."

The truth of the Southern black woman's life is in dark shadow compared to the halo of the Southern white woman's legend. And part of the tragedy of it all was the inability of the latter, even when so inclined, to materially alter the plight of her fellow creature. One of the most moving documents we have on the everyday workings of the slave system was written by a white woman. Fanny Kemble, the attractive, lively and articulate actress of the English stage, married a Georgia planter, Pierce Butler, in 1834, and kept a Journal of her experiences on his plantation. It is only to be expected that many of her observations are even today discounted as "a woman's" dramatic emotionalism. She was never able to fit her intimate knowledge of slavery into the columns of a ledger—especially when she recorded some of the facts of the slave mothers' lives around her, and their requests to her:

"Fanny has had six children; all dead but one. She came to beg to have her work in the field lightened.

"Nanny has had three children; two of them dead. She came to implore that the rule of sending them into the field three weeks after their confinement might be altered.

"Sarah, Stephen's wife . . . has had four miscarriages, had brought seven children into the world; five of whom were dead, and was again with child. She complained of dreadful pains in the back, and an internal tumor which swells with the exertion of working in the fields; probably, I think, she is ruptured."

Cotton demanded toil in the field from female and male alike—and went right on demanding it after slavery, as before. At the close of the war, the big planters of the South had their land and little else, the Negroes had the strength of their muscles and nothing else, and neither had any money; so the sharecropping system came into being. Born of bitter necessity, all too soon it became the implement for a new servitude. There was no emancipation proclamation which could loosen its grip— and once again the South wasted its most precious resource in a staggering irreverence for life.

In the early 1920's a distinguished South Carolina planter, David R. Coker, told an interviewer, "Perhaps we haven't all realized how wretched an existence the small cotton grower has been forced to lead. Since the Civil War, whether white or colored, he has been the equivalent of slave labor." And the interviewer added, "Whenever and wherever I travel through the Cotton Belt east of the Mississippi the things that haunt me most are the ragged tenants, wrinkled wives, half-fed, anemic children, and the wretched hovels in which they live, whether white or Negro . . . for the past fifty years cotton has been produced out of the very life blood of the South."

Dr. Rupert Vance tells us that in "the 1920 Census of Occupations, 1,084,128 women in the United States were listed as engaged in agriculture and kindred pursuits. Of these, 869,416, or 80 per cent, were in the ten chief cotton growing states." White tenant or Negro 'cropper, the wife and the children above the age of six that he could put into the field were the keys to Southern cotton economy. When a study was made in 1934 of 612 Negro families in Macon County, Alabama, only 31 of the women were listed mainly as housewives and mothers. Only 20 were in domestic service. But 470 women were farmer-housekeepers!

The pressure of the need for this family labor is brought up to the minute as you visit one cotton plantation and the owner tells about his various families. As you pass one neat two-room house he says, "Frazier lives there—the stout, hearty nigra you met back in the field a little bit ago—he's about the best worker I got but I reckon I'll let him go next season. He's not enough good to me on the crop." Answering your surprise, he explains, "No children. His wife's all right in the house, but she don't like the fields. Most of them do. The nigra women will quit almost any job they have to pick cotton: it's something they know how to do, they like the socializing all working along together, and then it's pretty good pay for as long as it lasts. But when you need a big team in a hurry, it hurts when somebody like Frazier doesn't have any younguns and only half a wife."

Against the bare subsistence level of the Negro on the big plantation, the upland white farmer of a few acres pitted the sweat of himself, his wife and children—and was doomed to lose the contest. No matter how little he lived on, it seemed that the Negro had learned to live on less. When he moved to the mill villages and there put to work his wife and such children as were permitted to labor, he was determined to be free of the Negro's competition. Many times he refused, with a ferocity bordering on panic, to work beside a "nigger"—and although he might not realize or admit it even to himself, his immediate concern was often more to keep his payroll than his pigmentation intact.

Other industries came, new farming crops and methods developed, the face of the South began to change, but the scars of the old struggles, not yet altogether old or dead, either, remain. Their lines may still be seen carved in the unflinching faces of the women who picket a school where a dozen Negro children have applied for admission, bearing crude signs which say: "We Don't Want Niggers Here." They may be revealed by the harshness with which a scrawny, freckle-armed woman in North Carolina's Piedmont tells you: "I seen that big buck talking over television last night and I'm telling you I never wanted to do anything so bad in my life as be where I could just pick up a board and bash him in the mouth till the blood spurted!"

The complexity of the whole Southern dilemma—if you care as much about *why* as about *how* people are—is nowhere more baffling or poignant than in this realm of the Southern woman and her life and meaning. What has been done, through the generations, to the Negro woman, slave and free (she who has somehow been excluded from the vision conjured up by the phrase, "flower of Southern womanhood"), to the white woman, "po' trash" or aristocrat? And what have they done to themselves? What will they, can they, do for their region now in this moment of crisis? To ask the questions is to experience the frustration of half-truth, knowing that neither the historian, the social scientist, the economist, the psychologist, nor even the Professional Southerner, can provide the whole answer. You can only try to know and reveal with as much breadth and depth as possible this most complex feature of a tormenting situation.

Pondering it—the whole meshed fabric of Southern life—you remember:

The tall, keen-eyed, sardonic industrialist, who stood of a late afternoon looking over the tremendous throbbing plant he had built, telling you its story, and the reminiscence slipped in: "That was the year we had a woman minor executive in our office, and I always said she'd have owned the business if she'd been a man; and we had a nigra working down in the boiler rooms who'd have been the plant manager if he'd been white."

Or: the small, determined minister who sat in his study and said, "One of the experiences of my life I'll never forget occurred in New Orleans. I had just come into the city limits and I saw five boys who had a child backed up against the wall. As I came closer I could see the boys were in their early teens and their victim was a Negro girl about eleven or twelve years old. They were throwing stones at her. She had her arms up over her face and head, trying to protect herself. Anger flew all over me. I stopped the car right in the street and jumped out. I grabbed one of the boys by the collar. 'Stop it!' I yelled. 'Stop stoning that little girl this minute or I'll mop up the street with you!' They were so surprised that while they turned their attention to me the child escaped. But it was what one of the bullies said to me then that really made me shudder. 'That's not a little girl, mister,' he said, 'that's a nigger.' "

You remember: a long, warm, silent Sunday in the Florida Everglades, and the magical sight of a white bird sitting atop a tall grey tree, suddenly lifting great graceful wings and disappearing in the distance like a ghost. It might have been the ghost of itself, it might be the symbol of all the South's beauty and loss and greed and destruction, as your boatman tells briefly the story. At one time egret plumes brought sixty-four dollars an ounce on the American market. That was twice the going price for gold, and these rare feathers might have been called white gold. Their use: trimming for the hats that adorned the ladies of fashion from New Orleans to New York to San Francisco. The great rush was on. But the plumes that were so lacy and so valuable appeared only in the mating season and this was when the tall snowy birds were sought out and clubbed to death in their nests. Laws passed to protect the rookeries were disregarded as so much Federal interference in private enterprise. The slaughter continued, the plumes were bootlegged—and the nests of America's most beautiful birds were disgracefully diminished year after year. Then Warden Guy Bradley, trying to arrest a plume hunter, was deliberately shot and killed. His murderer was never even punished. But national attention was focused on the plight of the egret and a law was passed forbidding the wearing of egret plumes. Bradley died—and one of America's natural beauties survived. Little wonder that some of the "mystique" of the South's legendary lady surrounds the flight of the egret you watch. It embodies the blasphemy against life in all its rich variety which can eventually extend to the destruction of human life, as well.

You remember: the meticulously ordered house in the beautiful residential area, and the long, cool drinks in the long, cool sitting room above the sound of children's voices on the lawn and tennis court outside. "There's one"—your host nods toward his wife—"who was born and reared a California prune picker and when she came to Louisiana she used to say, 'Look at those cute little pickaninnies,' and now she's the biggest damn nigger hater south of Chicago!"

His perfectly groomed wife smiles indulgently. "Understatement isn't one of Tom's virtues. But I suppose part of what he says is true. Out in California I was in school with Negroes. I taught them, substituted in a music class for a Negro teacher. I had classes at the university with them and never thought a thing about it. But when I moved here, I found an altogether different type of Negro. I saw the lower-class ones; they were dirty and shiftless. I've just never had any patience with shiftlessness. I suppose the difference in them has made the difference in me."

Or: a round table of church women from various towns in East Texas discussing their schools and desegregation problems. One young woman reports: "We're not having any trouble with the children but a lot with the parents." And a calm middle-aged lady adds, "We're not having much trouble with the parents but a lot with the grandparents." A wrinkled woman whose face and hands have known the feel of Texas sun and wind for many seasons pulls her sailor-style hat more firmly over her grey hair and announces cheerfully, "We've just got to remember that progress is made by the death of folks."

And you remember the hard-packed clay lawns of the little houses in backwoods Georgia and South Carolina, Alabama and Mississippi, beaten by the rains, baked by sun, so bare that when the housewife, black or white, wants to clean the yard, she doesn't need a rake but a broom. And especially the grey winter day hanging heavy over waterlogged cotton fields and the absolute desolation of the shacks studding those acres in Western Tennessee and Eastern Arkansas. In one stretch along the highway, a rusty pump stands midway between every two houses. The houses are far enough apart so that the pumps appear abandoned— but at one you see a Negro woman and two children drawing a galvanized washtub full of water. They are bareheaded, barefooted, bare-armed, in the chilly drizzle of rain, as they lift the handle slowly up and down in the middle of the brown fields.

And: the grandmother at the Negro mass meeting in Montgomery, Alabama, who stands up and replies to the question whether they shall keep on trudging in their boycott of Jim Crow buses. "Keep on! We're not walking for ourselves; we're walking for our grandchildren!"

The warm sun of late spring slants pleasantly across the terrace of the country club. The French doors from the dining room have been folded back so that the ladies at the luncheon may wander freely from the smoky interior to the edge of the fat green golf course outside. On the terrace a very black waiter wearing a very white coat stands behind a flower-decked table and dispenses iced champagne for the ladies.

This is a debtor's luncheon, cancelling out dozens of cocktail parties, bridge foursomes, quarterly trips to federated club gatherings, committee meetings, all the social debits except the formal dinners which are repayable only in kind here—and as a consequence it is large and at slightly loose ends. There are young matrons in severe grey flannel suits belied by frothy blouses trimmed in lace; there are blue-haired older matrons in lavender silk suits with furs and flowered hats.

At the table for six, where you sit, a woman with wrinkled face and hands, accented by scarlet lips and fingernails, brings up The Subject. "Well, our house is hereby declared a disaster zone again. Mattie May quit yesterday and——"

"No!"

"Isn't it disgusting, the way they just up and leave nowadays?"

"She stayed longer than most of them do."

". . . and Son's children are visiting us too, you know."

"Oh, no! Whatever did you do?"

"What could I do with a five-year-old and ten-year-old? I got a day-girl in for this morning and afternoon, and tomorrow I'll start beating the bushes for another maid. I just hope the one today will leave the kitchen sink. Well, I've learned to lock up my jewelry and trinkets anyway, just to be on the safe side."

Two or three of the ladies obviously wince at this uncouth admission to a practice many of them follow. None of them realizes how sharply it points up the illogic of one of the fundamental relationships in the South: the white women who lock their rhinestones away from the Negro maids at the same time they give those maids their children for safekeeping.

At luncheons such as this, on the golf courses, at charity bazaars and the neighborhood supermarkets, you can hear the old muttered complaints of some of the women: the dirt and disease and dishonesty of their cooks' home environment; their sullenness, the untrustworthiness, the stupidity. Yet they cannot, or will not, do without their help—and at the moment of these complaints they are leaving these women they label "inferiors" in charge of their homes and the most important minutes and years of their children's lives. Their ancestral counterpart is the half-fictional woman of the "big house" who was raised by Mammy-Lou and has never recovered from those pampered, effortless years. She would be horrified at the thought of eating with a Negro at her country club and yet she remembers, "Mama used to tell me that when I was little Mammy would chew up a little bitty piece of meat for me sometimes and take it from her own mouth and poke it in mine." This is part of the pattern of the South—but only part.

The day after the luncheon you may be in another city in an adjoining state, even more Deep South in allegiance, talking with a gracious widow in her early fifties. Her dark hair is threaded with grey that accentuates the black and grey texture of her tweed suit, and her voice is as soft as her cashmere sweater.

"Since my husband died and my children married I've devoted more and more of my time to work through my church, through interracial committees, to try and bring individuals together. Segregation, integration, they're words. It's easy for people to be against words. Sometimes it's harder to be against flesh and blood, especially if the person is sitting across the table from you."

How had she come to care?

She smiles. "Why it was such a little thing, really, and yet so big. I'd lived in Alabama and Georgia all my life. My family and friends, we were always 'good to the Negroes,' as we say. I never saw any actual physical harm done to them. Everyone seemed to think they were happy so I thought they were happy, too. It was easiest that way.

"Then I went to Chicago for a year. My husband was an educator here in the state; he took a leave of absence and spent a year at the University of Chicago. For the first time in my life I saw educated Negroes. That opened a while new realm of thought to me. Then I remember being on a bus one day—it was very crowded and I had to stand. As I held onto the metal bar, or strap, or whatever it was, I suddenly noticed my hand was touching a Negro man's. I had all the normal reactions of a person with my background: to jerk my hand away instantly. But somehow I didn't. I moved it over gradually.

"Being, I hope, fundamentally decent, I began to analyze what I had done. From then on, while we were in Chicago, I made myself sit down by a Negro whenever possible, not just when necessary. And as I began not to notice and finally realized that I was beyond paying attention to color, a wonderful freedom came to me. I don't think anyone can appreciate what a real liberation it is to be free of that constant consciousness of color unless he's been a Southerner and lived through it, do you? When I came back down here I looked at Negroes and their life through different eyes."

The ancestral counterpart of this woman, and the others like her, is the plantation mistress who ignored the fact that it was long a misdemeanor to teach Negroes to read and write and did her best to bootleg to them what little learning she could. On a chilly midwinter afternoon before the flashing blaze of a pine fire to ward off the chill of her second-story drawing room, a Charleston lady tells you, "I think my mother would have understood this situation today. She had a great deal of imagination."

Then, pensively, gazing into the fire: "I remember her concern for the Negroes we always had around us—even when, because of circumstances over which she had no authority at all, she could do so little. Of course in her day she felt the need of looking after them—and while that's obsolete now, immoral I think, to consider doing for them when they only want to do for themselves—still, I think that old, kind attitude of concern was parent to the present liberal attitude some of us strive for."

The fact is, of course, that the Southern woman was long assigned a role only slightly less strict and abject than that of the Negro—and the two were curiously intertwined. In a variety of ways, important and unimportant, their separateness from the public mainstream of life was made manifest. As one Negro man says, "There was once the tradition that an authentic Southern lady had her name in the newspaper but three times:

when she was born, when she was married, and when she died. There was also the unwritten agreement that a Negro's picture never appeared in the newspaper but three times: when he was arrested, when he confessed, and when he died—in the electric chair."

And he goes on to point out: "Southern white women ought to know better than anybody else the falseness of this double-standard business. They lived for generations on the little end of double standard. They ought to know it's wrong when it's set up black and white, too."

Crinolines-among-the-camellias or calicos-in-the-cotton-patch, Southern women have been in part overwhelmed by their romantic idealization. It is another of the ironies of history that during those decades when our foremothers were supposed to be occupying their proudest pedestals many of them were, in reality, pushing the family plow. Recent historians who have studied the census records and other documents of the period assure us that there were many more yeomen than aristocrats in the confines of the old Confederacy, and there was still much of the frontier in the South of the 1860's. There was also the sharing of hard work and responsibility on the part of the women which characterizes such a society.

That an aristocratic type did come into existence, a lady of languid helplessness and beautiful hopelessness, goes without saying. And it was no doubt inevitable that she should be focused in the limelight while her less pampered sisters were ignored. It is also probable that she was created less by her own wishes than by the high-flown language of aspiring politicians with a poverty of platform and perspiring orators with a poverty of thought.

In the early frontier days of the South, during the War, in times of crisis, Southern women seized the plow handles and worked alongside their men with equal determination toward a common goal. But in times of leisure when, as an early British traveler observed, land was too cheap to create adequate social distinction, their wives' backs became one of the few places where the men could display—or at least indicate—their wealth. They made their wives into puppets whose indolence would serve to highlight their own successes, whose adornments would reflect their own accumulations.

Perhaps one of the reasons Southern women took Scarlett O'Hara so enthusiastically to their hearts was that they were relieved to find one heroine of fiction's Old South who at last combined coyness with courage, sex appeal with shrewdness, a hard head and hard work in some of the natural proportions they had always suspected in their grandmothers and great-grandmothers. Of course, Margaret Mitchell did not completely discard the pedestal—but she set Melanie on it; and, like John Milton in his creation of Lucifer, made imperfect Scarlett the more interesting character.

Southern women have always been so much less than their protectors would admit, so much more than their protectors would permit. For generations, like the Negroes, they had "their place," and they were kept in that place by many devices. The Negro's place was in the muck beneath the white man's, the woman's was in the ethereal realms above—but both positions served the same purpose of keeping them out of the marketplace. The claim, of course, was that the black man was too bad, or ignorant, the white woman too good, or spiritual, to have any voice in the laws and customs that bound their lives. This left the white man with the burden of standard-making, which he assumed with almost embarrassing alacrity; soon he even accepted the need to be standard-bearer of his own superiority.

Some women not only acquiesced in being set apart from one whole realm of life—they advocated it. A few still do, just as a few Negroes still advocate segregation and profit by the irresponsibility of their fellow citizens. In 1955 a woman editor in Texas announced that that state would now have women on its juries. Her opinion followed:

"The matter has been agitated for years by a small minority of frustrated females who, for some reason, felt the sex was being discriminated against because women were not compelled to hang around the court house bull-pen awaiting their chance to pass sentence on criminals.

"The argument which seemed to prove most effective in the campaign was the claim that Texas was one of only a few states which did not compel women to serve in this capacity. To us this was no argument at all and was additional reason why the state should retain its originality and continue to protect its womanhood from this often humiliating experience."

In 1956, when opening jury service to women was proposed in Mississippi, a women's leader from the state capital opposed it roundly. Tying the measure in with racial integration, she said, "We don't want to mix the races on juries at this time. . . . You see what the NAACP has done with Autherine Lucy, and they'll try to do the same with jury service in Mississippi if this bill is passed. . . . The men are supposed to take care of juries, not women. They say women are allowed to serve on juries in other states. But we of the South and Mississippi are different from people elsewhere. We shouldn't care what they do."

So in jury duty as in schools and jobs: one separate and superior, by sex, the other separate and inferior, by race. The important part is to be sure they're separate. For those who seem to have the most invested, psychologically or economically, in segregation, have discovered that, like selling soap flakes or refrigerators, it takes sex to sell White Supremacy, too.

The one word more hateful to Southerners than "Sherman," more degrading than "carpetbagger," and more terrifying than "boll weevil," is the word "intermarriage." "Miscegenation" is the intellectual term, "mixing" is the folk expression, and although each has its own different and precise meaning in the dictionary, each stirs the same subterranean abyss in the Southerner's emotions. "The flower of Southern womanhood" has elected many a sheriff and state legislator and governor to easy Southern office—even long before that womanhood could vote. "The flower of Southern womanhood" has swayed many a bewildered and benighted jury to its final decision of life or death—even when that womanhood could not serve on a jury. Southern women have had many burdens to bear, but none more wearisome than being used as a buffer between the Negro and justice. In their name, black people have been cheated and lynched. In their name much of the battle of segregation is being waged today.

"Would you want your sister to marry a Negro?" The Southern university instructor spreads his hands wearily. "If we had a nickel for every time that question had been asked down here in the past three years, we'd have funds enough to overcome all our education deficits. Anyone asks me this, I always answer, 'She can say no, can't she?' "

Perhaps one of the reasons why it is difficult for non-Southerners to understand the preoccupation with marriage resulting from mixed classrooms is their lack of understanding of the clublike nature of Southern life. A man who has lived many years of his life in North Carolina tells you the story succinctly:

"The South was settled by the English and the Scotch-Irish. There were a few Germans and Huguenots scattered around, but no East Europeans, no Orientals, no Mexicans or Puerto Ricans. Everybody just alike. Every time anyone looked around he saw other people just like himself. So what happened? It all became one big club. Social life carried over from the homes into school and business, everything in the community was on a social basis. So now it's got to stop being a club. We've got to separate the social from the education and the business.

"When I was in school in New York, we had Irish and Jews and Italians and Negroes. We all went in the same classroom, the bell rang, the teacher said, 'The lesson today is on page nine.' We studied our lesson. When school was over, we left the classroom, went home with the kids from our group. There was no socializing with these others. At dances, parties, we all had private groups, went to our own parties. Athletics was the only other place we were together except in the classroom. But the difference between New York and here was when the teacher said, 'Page 9,' not 'How's your Aunt Minnie today, Johnny?' Down here the school's not just school, it's part of the club, too. And it's too exclusive. We've got to make way for the school, separate the education from the social."

Being, then, predominantly rural and small-town and homogeneous, except for this one race of different color in its midst—the South's family ties and rifts, its personal flaws and collective virtues, its generations-old knowledge of everyone's life are all carried by the children into classrooms and home again, and marriages not made in heaven are frequently made in the science lab or lunchroom because these are the boys and girls who would marry each other anyway!

A minister in Southern Texas makes an interesting point. "I talked to a woman's group last week on the injustices of segregation and when I finished, someone immediately asked about intermarriage. Of course that was irrelevant to all I had tried to say, but I knew it would be foolish to point that out. They would merely say I was evading the question. So I replied by asking them about the Mexicans. Had there been much marriage of the Mexicans and other citizens? Oh yes! In their vicinity, had it been more between those who had gone to school together or between the Mexican girls and the men at the big air force base? Mostly the air force men, from other parts of the country. Well, maybe then going to school together brings out differences as well as similarities in people. Maybe it shows difficulties that arise in marriage between people of widely different backgrounds. And these difficulties need to be realized at their daily level—not set apart like some forbidden but exotic fruit. The same would apply to desegregation of Negro and white schools and the possibilities of intermarriage that would result. . . . Of course," he smiles, "anyone really concerned about miscegenation should have begun to shout long before May, 1954."

And he has brought us to the heart of the matter. As a Negro newspaper editor says, "There are today six million brown Americans. I want to know, did they get here by immaculate conception or moonlight conception? There was nothing 'separate but equal' about that deal."

It has been convenient to forget that these past generations of miscegenation have occurred under segregation—and in large part because of it. In the 1870's New Orleans author George Washington Cable, who could write with the knowledge of a native son, observed, "Just in proportion to the rigor, the fierceness, and the injustice with which excommunication from the common rights of man has fallen upon the darker race, has amalgamation taken place."

By placing one race at the mercy of another, social, economic, psychological factors of tremendous importance were brought to bear on relationships between the sexes. The white aristocrat could keep his wife on a pedestal in the parlor because he had a black woman in the kitchen and backroom, and the individual exceptions only made the rule more respectable. That such an arrangement degraded everyone concerned was no topic for polite conversation. As for the Negro woman, one white Southerner stated the situation thus: "She lived under the stigma of segregation, usually as unequal as it was separate, and sometimes a half-white baby gave her a little status. But if she were freed of the stigma of segregation, certainly she'd have a chance for more pride in her race. Now a Negro girl has a baby, she looks at him, knows he can't ever be anything but a janitor in the town where she lives, what the hell—go out and sleep with anybody. It's a desperation, a sort of revenge, too, on her part. I believe this: with segregation you've got miscegenation and lots of it; with integration you'd have intermarriage and less of it. One is inequality and hypocrisy; the other is equality and honesty."

One of the most important features of the Southern white woman's pedestal was its loneliness. When her husband, brothers, sons, had children by Negro women, she might be hurt or angry, filled with despair or contempt or pity—but whatever the emotion, it was impotent against the rigid absurdity of mind and custom which is reflected in one of the truly revealing folk anecdotes of our present scene: Two South Carolina planters went down to Miami for a gay weekend but when they made a visit to one of the better-known houses of pleasure, the hostess greeted them by apologizing, "I'm afraid we don't have anyone to entertain you gentlemen. It's been a busy Saturday. All I have left are two Negro girls, and I know you're Southerners——" At which her callers interrupted. "Oh, that's all right. We just want to sleep with them, not go to school with them."

A plump Negro schoolteacher with a quick, frank face and a quick, frank tongue turns a pencil slowly between her long fingers as she talks with you. "I was discussing Negro people—what we want, what we've been told is ours because we're Americans—with one of our state's big politicians, and all the time he kept talking about Negro men marrying white women. I told him, 'If we wanted to mix with the white folks, we wouldn't have to go to your race to find color. We've got a rainbow ourselves. Somebody saw to that. The fear Negroes have is so plain you won't admit it: that our children won't fare right.' But he didn't pay any attention to me. Kept on talking about keeping the races pure. Finally I said. 'That's not our problem. Can't keep something that hasn't been. The races haven't been pure for a long time. Who did this to me?'" She sweeps her hand up beside her light golden-brown face. "I asked him who gave me my skin this color. Then I tried to tell him, 'When the folks in this state vote for segregation, they're working against some of their own grandchildren and cousins and blood-kin going to decent schools.' You know, that man got a sudden appointment. He had to leave that meeting so fast—sorry, but he had to go. No more talk that day!"

The pale brown eyes reflecting bluish lights from the blue suit she is wearing are suddenly bright with laughter. "I'll tell you something that happened in one big city in East Texas recently. Some of the leaders of one of the civic boys' club organizations met to discuss whether or not they should integrate the various branches of their club. In the office where they happened to be meeting a Negro boy was working. He was not in the discussion, no business there at all as far as these men were concerned, but he overheard all the argument. Didn't speak a word until after a while one of the white men said: 'Well, one thing we're not going to have nigras marrying our daughters!' Then the boy said, 'Now wait a minute, mister. You mean Negroes aren't going to be marrying your wife's daughters. We've been marrying your daughters for a long time.'"

He is right. Studies have told us recently that between 70 and 90 per cent of the Negroes in the United States have at least one known white ancestor. Perhaps nothing touching on the whole question of segregation is as illogical as continued pledges of allegiance to a purity that doesn't exist and hasn't for several generations.

In the midst of this, sometimes at its periphery, the Negro woman has gone on working. As the South becomes more urbanized she has shifted somewhat from field to house and even from household work to other service jobs. Between 1940 and 1950 the proportion of Negro women working as operatives nearly doubled. But, as a recent study indicated, "these occupations still accounted for only one-tenth of all Negro working women. Moreover, more than half of the operatives worked in laundries." As job opportunities improve in the South, it is still apparent that the Negro woman's salary and working conditions are slowest to shift for the better. As a side light on the individual difficulties and personal blocks to change, there is the highly articulate Alabama woman who tells you, "I lived in the North for a half-dozen years after I was married and when I came home, I began to realize how incompetent the whole help level is here. Since maids were only getting three dollars a day, I thought perhaps an improvement in their pay would bring about an improvement in their performance, too. So when I hired this Negro woman to help me, I told her I would pay her three dollars for a half day. She became very suspicious. 'Don't want no three dollars a half day. Just want my three dollars a whole day.' I tried to explain to her I didn't think that was enough for her work but since I couldn't afford to pay more just then she could go and work somewhere else for the rest of the day and earn that much more money. Well, when she came back to work the first day, I took her money in at noon. 'Don't want it. Haven't finished my ironing.' 'But I told you——' 'You just wanting to rush me up, like all them fast Northern ways. Can't do this-here ironing in no half day.' Well, she'd turned the tables on me all right. I thought I was trying to help her and she made me appear to be a real old slave driver. I just gave up! She gets her three dollars and lunch now, and I get a seven- or eight-hour day. I guess it just takes more than a few seconds' conversation to wipe out a suspicion bred by generations."

The Negro woman has gone on having children, too—and gone on watching them die twice as fast as white infants. In Louisiana, Florida and North Carolina during 1953, in every 1,000 live births from 22 to 24 white infants died—and 48 non-whites. Since Negroes comprise well over 90 per cent of the non-whites in Southern states, we know that most of these infant mortalities were among Negroes. But it was in childbirth itself that non-white women all over the United States paid for their inferior status. In 1955, over four times as many non-whites as whites died during pregnancy and childbirth. In the South, pregnancy was particularly hazardous. In 1953, 37 white mothers out of each 100,000 died in childbirth, but 189 Negro mothers in the South died!

And the Southern Negro girls, following in the tradition of the harsh-and-tender old grandmothers who played such a major role in the matriarchy of Negro life, went to school, too. There are in the South today twice as many illiterates among Negro boys as girls, and one third more Negro women than men who graduate from college. And yet—compared with white girls, just half as many Negro girls graduate from high school, enter college, graduate from college. The fertile acres we leave untended, the reaches of mind we leave unawakened, in the region that can least afford this waste!

There are the individual portraits of many women and many places—all separate in fine, etched lines, all joined in one panoramic design. Each fits its own meaningful bit into the pattern of the plight faced by the South:

A woman in the Cradle of the Confederacy tells of a wonderful sort of ritual staged at her house during the days of the bus boycott. "My mother, who's eighty-two years old and lives in our ancestral home here, is just pure Old South. Katie Sue, the old Negro woman who works for Mother, is a past master at keeping up the old myths, too. On the walk outside, if I meet her in the mornings on her way around to the kitchen, she'll stop and whisper to me, 'Miss Caroline, what's happening on the boycott today?' Inside, to Mother, she'll say, 'Ain't it awful the way them niggers carrying on?' When Mother quizzes her on the boycott, she shakes her head and explains, 'Naw, ma'am, we don't none of us at my house have nothing to do with it. My brother he works down at that filling station, he just drives hisself down. My boy, he rides with two or three more out to his work; my sister and me we just walks to work. We ain't having nothing to do with that boycott or any trouble.' And Mother believes what Katie Sue says rather than what she tells her with her own tongue she's doing! You'd have to hear it to believe it.

"When I quiz Katie Sue about it, she just drops that blank, innocent look like a mask and she tells me, 'Miss Caroline, when you got your hand in the lion's mouth, might as well pat him on the head now and then.' "

There is the more poignant account one woman in the Deep South gives you of an experience with a Negro friend named Mrs. Johns and some white friends who were witnessing for God. "I came to know Mrs. Johns because our daughters met at a Quaker camp up East. The Johnses had lived here about two years, were originally from North Carolina but had lived in New Jersey for about fifteen years before they moved down here. Mrs. Johns had been active in women's church groups and when she called me one morning and said our interdenominational council here had invited her to come to their all-day meeting and talk, I could tell she was pleased. The day she was supposed to go, Martha Madision, a great church lady here, phoned me and said she'd just learned that the women weren't going to serve Mrs. Johns lunch. They'd invited her to speak to them, but they weren't going to let her eat with them. Martha had packed a basket lunch and was going to take it and since she couldn't drive, I was to go and drive the three of us out together. Well, Martha's the sort of person you can't refuse when she's made up her mind, so she and Mrs. Johns and I went out to the meeting hall. The morning was spent with the ladies witnessing for Christ. Finally Mrs. Johns witnessed. She told what the women's organizations had meant to her, that she hoped their influence would spread and have meaning in all our lives, made a real good churchly talk.

"When she sat down, the ladies began to get up. 'Now Mrs. Johns, you're from New Jersey, and we're your friends and would like to help you. We think you should know that you're going to be working with entirely different people here than you were up North.' 'Now we're talking about your own people. They're not as advanced down here, they're not as accustomed to certain things as they are up in New Jersey.' Or, 'Now Mrs. Johns, I know the Negroes as well as anyone could. We've always had twenty or thirty Negroes on our plantation. And I like them. They're our friends. But you've got to realize things are different here. They wouldn't want to come to our churches, they like their own sort of worship. It's more emotional. And we all think we'll be happiest with our own churches.' Well, after some more of this witnessing, Mrs. Johns told them that she had been born and lived in North Carolina most of her life, but they said North Carolina was different, too; not really Deep South. Then it was lunchtime. Mrs. Johns asked me, 'Do you suppose I could go to the rest room? Whenever I get nervous I always have to go to the rest room.' And I said, 'Well, I think so. Just come with me and we'll go ahead and go and that will be that.'

"As we came out of the rest room, I could see Martha Madison talking with the woman in charge and I could see Martha was looking very firm. So she came over and said to Mrs. Johns, 'Some of us are going to eat out on the lawn. Wouldn't you like to come and eat with us out there?' Trying to keep from telling her, of course, that she wasn't welcome inside with the others. Mrs. Johns said she was tired and she believed she'd just stay inside and eat. Then, to make matters worse, this Witness who was in charge came over and said, 'Mrs. Johns, you should know there's a rule here and we can't serve mixed groups.' We started outside and she delivered the final blow, 'And you can't eat mixed on the grounds, either.' So we had to take our basket out to the edge of the road, off of the grounds, in the dust on the state right-of-way, and eat.

"I must say, some of the other women took their lunches off the table inside and came out with us. Well, finally Mrs. Johns just broke down and cried. But after lunch she said she'd been invited for the afternoon meeting and she'd stay. She stayed till the end. When we got home that evening, I told her I was just sick about what had happened. She put her arm around my shoulder and said, 'I'm sorrier for you than I am for myself. You expect your people to act nice. We don't expect them to and then we can't be disappointed.' "

There is the bright-eyed sparrow of a woman who sat beside you at a lunch counter one day and said, as she cooled her cup of scalding coffee, "Yes, this is a right good place for working folks like me to eat. They don't charge so high. No they don't serve niggers here, standing or not. Where you from, anyway? Some of the bigwigs in the state may think they can get the children to school with niggers. They'll find out! You know it's half nigger here in our county. What the high-ups are really worried about is all their votes if them folks ever do get a hand in the elections. The nigger preachers down here are the ones stirring everything up: if they don't watch out, they're going to get whupped off of the map before they're through! And I'd help do it!"

A pretty, witty rector's wife pours tea in the beige-and-aqua sitting room of her brick home in the fashionable residential area of the state capital. "One of the worst things that has happened here in the past year is the ever-hardening fact that you can't discuss anything about the race question with even your closest friends. I used to be able to sit down and share views with almost all the women here—but not now. It's gone beyond that point. And Moore and I are both native Southerners! Isn't it dreadful when you can't really talk things over, share what you think with one another? When any of the women come to call, we talk about everything else, and know that we're skirting the whole subject that's really on our minds and hearts.

"It's so difficult to explain to anyone just how it is. You go to a party and the people you know always seem to be just ahead of you, and you never quite overtake them. Or they're looking the other way and you never quite catch their eye.

"We've had a noticeable decrease in dinner invitations these last eight or ten months. We didn't get invited to the Holiday Ball this year, that's our big social function here. I think some of this ostracism is not always because people don't agree with us, some of them may to some extent; but they know that everyone talks about this so much, and Moore, being a minister, would bring up their conscience and principles, and they're afraid it might be uncomfortable for everyone concerned if we were there."

One of the most significant facts of the segregation conflict in the South is this: many, perhaps a majority, of the crosses which have been burned in the revival of intimidation and coercion, have been for white people. And many of these white people have been women. They range from Charlottesville, Virginia, to Houston, Texas; from school-board members whose allegiances are not so much with integration as with the law, to church women dedicated to perfecting as much of the present world as possible; from the wealthy and well-known to the modest and obscure. One who seems to typify so many of the conflicts and challenges facing thoughtful people is a gentle-mannered, reserved lady in her early forties whose black hair and large brown eyes, behind tortoise-rim glasses, accentuate the milky whiteness of her skin. She speaks slowly but with the certainty which you suspect sustained many an earlier Southern woman, white and black, in her search toward the right.

"My father died when I was young. My mother, grandmother and two sisters and I lived on grandfather's estate. At nineteen I was given power of attorney to manage his estate. This experience in a masculine field may have given me a broader outlook. I had never thought of it before, but I suspect that was the case. Now on the matter of segregation I believe that it must go. I believe that way first because I'm a Christian and I can't reconcile anything else with Christianity. And then my father was a lawyer and I've always been reared with great respect for the law and the Supreme Court as the highest authority in the land. You know, in early days Christians were Christians if they said so because it meant death to say you were a Christian. Now it's socially acceptable—indeed, often necessary—to say you're a Christian. And it's all those who are in the church but aren't really committed to Christianity who are hurting the church today.

"I've been interested in mental health, too, the terrible illness and waste of many of our people. I've heard some of the most respected psychiatrists speak on the mental troubles caused by segregation, poverty, and all the related problems. That also helped make me aware of the race question.

"But I didn't get stirred up till I went to the segregationists' mass meeting here. Then I saw the rest of us would have to do something. I wrote a letter and took it down to the paper here. The editor had a long talk with me. Said the only hope in the South was for white people to put up a solid front. Pointed out how much harm my letter could do me. He tried to scare me, and he did. I went home. Then on Sunday our minister preached on this matter. He said the question now was not only what you believed but were you ready to stand and be counted. I thought about it and decided I was.

"That Sunday afternoon I mailed my letter with a note attached: 'Please Publish Letter.' I sent it to our local weekly and to the daily at our state capital. As soon as it appeared, I began to get phone calls. All the anonymous ones were vindictive. A few callers were in agreement. A neighbor I had known for eight years refused to speak to me. Then, of course, someone burned a cross on my lawn. Only my daughter and I were home, but after we got over the first surprise it didn't disturb us.

"I kept thinking all along that our leaders would take care of this. Someone would speak up and clarify issues and make some sense out of the nonsense. No one did. So some of the rest of us are doing what we can."

Like the Negro, the Southern woman today is both sowing the seeds and harvesting the fruits of transition. Her realm of influence is both ambiguous and challenging. Like the Minute Women of Houston, she may be organized to defend Americanism as she has defined it in her own limited terms; like the United Church Women, she may meet to extend Christianity as she has defined it in her own expansive terms.

Or she may not be in any organization at all, but a girl you meet casually at a party, a petite girl in red velvet with a sequin-splattered veil over her short black hair and bangs and round black eyes. A very real girl we'll call Polly—because that name combines the alertness and the quaintness which make her as deceptive as the first soft day in March. As you talk with her, meet her again on subsequent occasions, Polly becomes the perfect symbol of the Southern sweetheart with a steel-trap mind. She discusses historical trends with astounded elderly gentlemen of the teaching profession, and in addition to homemaking carries a full-time office career as lightly as a fan. She tells of facing down a belligerent White Citizens' Council leader at a public rally, of struggling in almost every daily contact for an atmosphere at least open to expression of all shades of opinion on segregation-integration.

"I'm Southern as far back as every ancestor I know," she smiles, "so I can say, 'You-all don't understand us,' to anyone outside the pale, but I can also say, 'We don't understand us.' "

Whatever there is of yesterday and today in the New South, Polly has combined it. She calls on all the wily means of her blue-blooded, iron-veined great-grandmother, but to far different ends. With that earlier lady, helplessness was often a camouflage for her concrete helpfulness; with this girl, helplessness is a camouflage for determined hopefulness. If there was a man around, she wouldn't open a door for herself—but she's waging an internecine war to open closed doors of tradition.

"A couple of months ago Bill called me at the office one morning and asked if he could bring a visiting professor from up North home for lunch. They wanted to talk about the segregation situation and lots of other phases of the modern South. Of course I told Bill to bring him, and I arranged an extra hour off for lunch. I got home and thawed a pot of Brunswick stew from the freezer—my real homemade brand, I make it on my days off and freeze it for just such emergencies. While Bill was giving the professor a drink I popped some biscuits in the oven and fixed a big juicy fresh-fruit salad. Then I went and put on my high-heeled shoes and frilly blouse and talked with them a few minutes and we went in to a leisurely lunch. After we'd eaten and he'd had three helpings of my stew and a half dozen of my biscuits, and I'd told him about the statistics of the sample surveys I'd helped make on our community problems, you know what he said: 'Well, to me this is the New South: a delicious meal—without a single servant; a pretty girl—without a dull moment!' It was about the nicest compliment I ever had!"

Polly smiles. "If you dress right, keep your eyes wide, don't deviate too much in the little things, you can get away with a lot of big ideas—and maybe even get a few of them across down here where it really counts!"

Polly's counterpart among the young Negro women might be the editor of a weekly newspaper several states distant. Trim, friendly, wearing an embroidered sweater over her tailored dress and a black pillbox hat to match her black pumps, she talks with animation about her work in building up the paper her husband owns and she edits, her work as an officer in the NAACP. Then she touches on a problem which worries her deeply: "We don't know one another—folks in this state, this town, don't try to know each other enough. Those hoodlums that burned a cross on my lawn last month, the ones that threw a Molotov cocktail in my carport, they didn't know me. I wasn't a person to them. I was just something called NAACP, called Negro. But not long ago I saw how people can learn to know each other. A white woman and I became acquainted on a mayor's committee. I'm sure she had never worked with a Negro before; she was very aloof at first. But not long ago she called me up one day and asked me to come out to her house. I did, and I imagine that's the first time a Negro has ever entered her front door and sat in her living room as an equal. She said to me, 'You've done a lot for me. You've opened my eyes to a lot of things. Now tell me, why can't I get a good maid and keep her?'

"Maybe I was a little disappointed that she'd wanted my friendship for that same old 'problem'—but I've learned that we have to start where we are and go on. So I asked how much she was paying. She told me, and I told her she couldn't expect anyone good for that. Then I told her I knew she demanded respect from anyone who helped her and she should pay them that same respect, as well as more money. We just had a good talk about a lot of things. In a few days she called me. 'I've got the best maid ever,' and as far as I know she's still got her. And on our committee work that woman and I are pretty good friends now. We've talked together.

"Of course it's not only the two races who have to try to know each other—it's the people of our own race, too. I know why some of our grassroots NAACP memberships fall off every now and then. The people in the big house have been talking to their 'help.' And I know lots of the cooks have been talking right with them, saying what they think their white folks want to hear. Well, now I'm about convinced that somewhere along the way we're all going to have to stand and be counted, high or low, cooks or professors. And we might as well be getting ready to plant our feet good and firm on one side or the other."

Sometimes it may be hell to be a Southern lady, as the girl in Bermuda shorts said. But finding the sugar and spice and plenty of backbone is a stirring adventure—separating the legend from the reality without ever forgetting that the legend of the Southern woman had enough reality to keep it alive for over a century and the reality of Southern woman had enough legend to thrust her into history. It was in the realms where her greatest resource, capacity to love, was wasted that the South and humanity suffered a grievous loss.

A Negro leader says to you, "The women down here are strongest. They're our hope. They hate worst against us or they work hardest for us. The Negro women—they'll suffer a lot more a lot longer then the men, if they get with something."

Perhaps Southern women have served to prove George Bernard Shaw's dictum: "The worst sin towards our fellow creatures is not to hate them, but to be indifferent to them; that's the essence of inhumanity. If you watch people carefully you'll be surprised to find how like hate is to love."

⑨ The Blue, the Grey and the Khaki

On a hot Saturday morning in one of the large old Southern cities, a stranger talks with you briefly, candidly. "We'll not see mixing of the schools in this town during my day. That's just not the way we've been brought up to do things down here. We believe in white folks and black folks staying separate, and it's not likely any ruling set down on a piece of paper up in Washington somewhere is going to change our ways."

He mops his red face with a white handkerchief before he looks at you again. "And if they're aiming to use something stronger than ink to carry out their rules, they'd better remember you don't change people with guns and you can't change their habits overnight."

In less than an hour, and less than twenty-five miles away, in the same heat and on the same soil, you are eating dinner at a table next to a party of two Negro couples and two white couples. Your host is a boy who was born, you happen to know, on a cotton plantation at the edge of the Black Belt, reared in the country where Negroes were considered most often in terms of overhead and underfoot.

He tells you, "Sure, Negroes come here any time they want to. Go anywhere, sit anywhere, do anything they want to. Far as I know, nobody even notices any more. You saw that duplex next to ours, back on the street where we live? Negro couple and their two little kids live there. Housing, schools, clubs, churches—everything is integrated here. Nobody ever says much about it unless they're visiting, like you. Sure we got Southern boys, place as big as this we got plenty from everywhere and some of all kinds. They have to get on the ball. I guess they find out pretty quick that if the world's not going to change to suit their fancy, then they'll have to change. I know I did."

This, of course, is one of the big army camps in the South. And when people tell you how hard it is and how long it takes to change, they forget these camps.

157

Only a few years ago a spokesman for the War Department could say that views on racial segregation would not be changed by "military order, fiat or dicta . . . the Army is not a sociological laboratory." Subsequent events soon rendered that statement inaccurate, as a glance at the past soon belies many of the doleful comments on the Negro's ability as a fighting man.

It was a Negro citizen who was America's first casualty in her War for Independence. On the cold, snowy evening of March 5, 1770, in the city of Boston, trouble which had been brewing for many weeks between the citizens of Massachusetts and the British soldiers broke into open conflict. Leading an angry crowd armed with sticks and hard-packed snowballs was a giant Negro who worked on a whaling ship. Crispus Attucks was his name, and when the British soldiers opened fire on the people, he was the first to fall. His was the first life claimed in the American Revolution. And when, in 1888, a monument was erected on Boston Common, a poem for the occasion by one John Boyle O'Reilly included these words, addressed to a fellow countryman:

"Has he learned through affliction's teaching what our
Crispus Attucks knew—
When Right is stricken, the white and black are counted as
one, not two?"

Since many of the state rolls did not carry any designation of race at the time of the Revolutionary War, there is no really accurate figure on the number of Negro soldiers who served during those years of the nation's delivery. The most widely accepted estimate seems to be five thousand. A few states, North Carolina for example, promised freedom to slaves who would serve in the army—if they joined under the impression that they were to receive freedom—and as late as 1849 an Edenton, North Carolina, newspaper would record the death of a free Negro soldier, 101 years old, who had "served under Washington at Yorktown at the close of the war."

During the War of 1812, some three thousand Negroes fought for America; there are several dispatches recording that white and black seamen were messmates aboard their ships with a seeming absence of prejudice.

The Civil War brought Negro troops to the tragedy of Fort Pillow, the assaults on Port Hudson and New Market Heights and the defense of

Charleston, among other encounters. Approximately two hundred thousand Negroes bore arms at some time during the conflict.

And the war posed the same old problem for the South: dare she use all her resources, or must she waste some of the manpower willing to aid her because it was black? The dilemma was stated when the Confederacy was faced with the decision of whether or not to enlist Negro troops. Howell Cobb, of Georgia, said, "The day you make soldiers of them is the beginning of revolution. If slaves will make good soldiers, our whole theory of slavery is wrong." And so once again, a theory of inferiority won out over the logic of necessity, and Negroes were not enlisted in the Confederate Army until the winter before Appomattox.

Following the end of that conflict, crack Negro cavalry units became some of the best Indian fighters on the frontier. In the Spanish-American War, the Tenth [colored] Cavalry joined with the famous Rough Riders to determine the outcome of the battle at San Juan Hill. But all the time he was fighting, hardening molds of segregation in other areas of activity affected the military, and the Negro was becoming more firmly segregated in his combat. Then came World War I.

With this war, the first mental testing of troops in really large numbers took place and seemed to prove everything that had been said about the inherent inferiority of Negroes. The relatively poor showing of the colored 92nd Division seemed to substantiate all that had been predicted about the Negro's inadequacy as a fighter. Upon closer examination it was discovered that uneducated rural white boys from the South had often scored lower on the mental tests than Negroes reared in the North, however, and the 369th colored Infantry Regiment held the line under fire for 191 consecutive days. But people preferred the old stereotype, even when contrary evidence should have prodded them to some probing beneath the surface.

The war to preserve democracy had brought its moments of evaluation on the home front, too. A Negro tells you this story: "During World War I, one of these overnight colonels—they made every big plantation man up and down the Mississippi a colonel, you know, and sent them out to bring in recruits—this man was on one of his speaking tours. About the second night he was rushed onto the train, given the name of a little town out in the country a ways, and told he was expected to make a speech out there that night. About halfway along, it occurred to him that nobody but niggers lived around this place where he was going! He got panicky! 'What can I say to niggers?' he asked himself. 'I don't have any speech for niggers. What'll I say to them?' And all the way on the train he kept tormenting himself with the same question and no answer.

"Finally the train pulled in, and sure enough there was a crowd of Negroes to meet him at the train. They took him to the church where the meeting was to be held, and he got up on the stage and a sea of black faces confronted him. Black psychology just engulfed him sure enough. He stood up to speak.

" 'Fellow citizens——' Well, that was some admission for this old colonel to make, but he'd got so in the habit of saying it at his other meetings, he didn't know how else to begin.

" 'This is your country——' That was a really big step! He didn't know what to say, and he didn't know what not to say.

" 'And this is your flag——' When he'd said that his mind was really paralyzed. He'd never admitted so much in his life before. So he started over again:

" 'Fellow citizens . . .

" 'This is your country . . .

" 'And this is your flag. . . . '

"About the third time he said this an old man in back stood up and said, 'Colonel, us niggers been knowing that all the time. Now when you white folks going to find it out?' "

The war intensified changes which were taking place in the Negroes' way of thinking. The large colored migrations out of the South were under way, and more Negroes began to identify themselves with the national rather than solely the regional scene.

An elderly Negro in the border South, an educated, traveled man, tells of one of those Negro soldiers he remembers from the first World War:

"You talk about downtrodden, depressed, spiritually downcast people—I can remember a trip I took through Alabama and Mississippi around the time of World War I. I began to notice it in Arkansas, grew more in the edge of Tennessee, around Memphis, and then when I got to Mississippi and Alabama: how all the Negroes just stood or sat and looked down. Never looked up. The train would come in a station, stand five or ten minutes, all the while you were there they'd just sit, maybe stirring the sand a little with the toe of their shoes, but always looking down.

"To show you what that daily stifling and looking down can do to a person, I remember a little later, in 1918, when I went to Camp Dodge, there was a Negro boy there from Alabama. He was as white as any white man you almost ever saw, must have had just that one drop it takes to make you of Negro blood. But he'd go around just holding the top of his head, pacing back and forth, looking, looking, looking. And one of the sergeants said to me one day, 'See that fellow? He's from way down South, and he just walks around like that all the time saying, "I didn't know the world was like this."' He'd gotten off the plantation for the first time, and I guess he thought the top of his head might blow off. I know it sounds crazy, but then this whole thing is crazy and always has been. I've seen a lot of things in my time, but I'll never forget the sight of that boy in the army camp nearly forty years ago."

Half of the four hundred thousand Negroes drafted to defeat the Kaiser were sent to France, and perhaps a song that became popular among the doughboys, concerning the relative attractions of the farm and gay Paree, had special significance for these particular soldiers catching sight of the big world.

Concern over this question of the Negro keeping or returning to "his place" bred unrest among both whites and Negroes following the war, and as tensions mounted, there was violence and death. The South resorted to the old brutalities of lynching and in the North an even older practice was revived: the race riot, which brought still greater bloodshed. The nation began to see that even as the war just concluded had demonstrated that democracy's problems were involved with those in the rest of the world, so the South was involved in the rest of the nation and its problems were not isolated. Unrest grew among Negroes and was shared by some white people who felt both guilt and challenge in their fellow Americans' plight; a ground swell of protest gathered, along with demands which even years of the Great Depression could not completely blight.

At the beginning of World War II, the Regular Army had four authorized Negro regiments and the number of Negro officers was three line officers and three chaplains. By the end of the war, 923,000 Negroes had been called to active duty as enlisted men. These included some cowards, some winners of the Silver Star and Navy Cross and many other citations for valor. They included men of skill and tenacity and many who were barely beyond illiteracy—but not therefore necessarily doomed to a role of idiocy. Most important, they included men who had been told since childhood that they were inferior humans, and now they were set apart in separate groups to serve and fight under that sign of inferiority. If the term "psychological warfare" has any meaning whatsoever, surely segregation in the armed forces could come under the heading of "psychological demolition."

But by the end of the war against the Fuehrer and The Son of Heaven, the attitudes of white fighting men had shown some small signs of altering. Army researchers, examining soldiers who had served in the European Theater, made the following discoveries: a large majority of the men "had rejected the idea of serving in mixed Negro-white units," until they had shared combat duty with Negroes. Then "86 per cent of the officers and 92 per cent of the GIs had come to feel that, with identical training, Negro soldiers would make out just as well as white ones."

Indeed, it was the returning GI, of every color and from every region, who often seemed to bring most tolerance to bear on the postwar tensions. You hear their voices during the present disorders. It was a former company commander in Korea, who has a Silver Star and five bullet wounds, Leo Grant, Jr., who organized a home guard during the September, 1956, riots in Clinton, Tennessee, and held the mob at bay until the state troopers could arrive. It was an ex-GI who engaged a barber in conversation at a neighboring town during the Clinton trouble.

Barber: "What does that National Guard mean, over in Clinton, fighting for the niggers?"

Customer: "Can't do nothing else, man. Law's on their side."

Barber: "Supreme Court can't make no law. I say the Guard oughten to take up for the nigger."

Customer: "I was overseas during the war, and they took up for everybody against anybody that made trouble. Man, them MPs were tough!"

Barber: "Well, I say they'll have to stay in Clinton till the snow flies and then the trouble won't blow over. Folks ain't going to stand for mixing in the schools."

Customer: "Well, I don't know about that, but I do know I'm not hankering to look down the mouth of one of them carbines. I'd rather go to school than have my head blown off!"

A young superintendent of schools in a rural county says, in his soft Southern accent, "My own attitude toward the whole race question has changed completely, and I know just when it happened. I'd been born and grown up here, never known or thought anything different from what everyone else did; it was the same way when I went to the state university.

"Then during the war, I joined the navy. At first I stayed away from the two or three Negroes we had on shipboard. I argued with a lot of the Northern boys about race—they always bring it up when a Southerner's around. I just didn't get near the Negroes if I could help it. I don't know what I'd have done if one had been assigned to bunk with me right there at the first.

"Well, there was one boy on board from Massachusetts who agreed with me on the Negroes, I remember. Maybe he even felt a little stronger than I did about the whole thing. Then one day another Massachusetts boy gave me a book to read. It was Richard Wright's *Black Boy*. Reading that book opened my eyes. I'd never thought before about what a Negro feels like growing up in the South. I looked at those Negroes on ship-board closer after that; even got to know them pretty well. And through the years since I've come to look at Negroes as people, one, two, three. That's all it takes."

One of the subjects of endless debate, attack and counterattack, growing out of World War II, concerned the relative merits and demerits of Negro soldiers. As late as April 27, 1956, General Mark Clark, former Chief of Army Field Forces, and now president of The Citadel, a military academy in South Carolina, said that after the war he had "opposed indiscriminate integration in the army." But by then "indiscriminate integration" had already been effected, and many people found it difficult to understand why General Clark had revived as a public issue his earlier opposition.

The crux of the debate over Negro performance in battle seems to have centered on the question of whether certain Negro units had made a poorer showing because they were Negro or because they were segregated. Here as elsewhere, obviously, what a person wants to believe seems largely to determine what he does believe. But a Negro ex-GI presents one phase of the problem when he tells you, with a puzzled frown, "The trouble as I see it is this: the army is supposed to try to keep all the divisions balanced up—some tiptop men, some low, some bright men, some slow, all kinds in all the groups. But what if you took all the Scotch-Irish boys out of the mountains and put just them together, or all the Mexican-descent boys from out West, or all the Brooklyn boys—and put them together, separate from everyone else—maybe you'd have some special traits develop, because of where they'd been born, or the way they'd lived, just as much as what group they belonged to. That's the way with the Negroes, and our troops we used to have. Only we're always easier to single out because we've always got this badge of color to wear."

On July 26, 1948, President Harry S. Truman signed Executive Order 9981 which called for "equality of treatment and opportunity for all persons in the armed forces without regard to race, color, or national origin," and to implement the words he appointed a committee headed by a native of Georgia. But the tone for this group, and the final processes of desegregation, were set when the President told the committee at its opening session, "I want concrete results and not publicity. I want the job done and I want to get it done in a way so everybody will be happy to co-operate."

It was during the war in Korea, when General Matthew Ridgway requested and received permission to integrate all the troops under his command, that real integration in the armed forces took place. The old bugaboos—violence, lower standards, social problems—faded, and the "long processes of adjustment" predicted by gloomy forecasters sometimes required only two hours, the amount of time one officer said it took Negro and white soldiers in his company to begin "treating one another exactly as they would treat anyone else."

In a report issued by the Office of the Assistant Secretary of Defense early in 1955, results of the effort to create an army that is neither black nor white, but American, were summarized:

"Combat effectiveness is increased as individual capabilities rather than racial designations determine assignments and promotions.

"Throughout the Army, Navy, Air Force, and Marine Corps, fully integrated units have replaced the all-Negro units which, until recent years, formed the only channel of military service for Negro enlistees and draftees since Colonial times.

"Economies in manpower, material, and money have resulted from the elimination of racially duplicated facilities and operations.

"The program has advanced more rapidly than had been considered possible in some quarters, and there have been no untoward incidents."

This does not mean that the process of integration in the armed forces has reached a point of perfection. There are many areas in which discrimination may still be practiced. For example, in February, 1957, Tennessee's Senator Albert Gore was threatened with "political retaliation" by a group of States' Righters when he named two Negro boys from Memphis as candidates for appointment to the Air Force Academy. To this, the Senator replied, "It is my understanding that it is not the practice of the local selective service boards to apply either racial preference or racial discrimination in the administration of the draft program. It had not occurred to me that I should do so in the case of those who voluntarily apply for training and service in the air force."

Although Senator Gore did not yield his position, it is hardly necessary to point out that human institutions are vulnerable to human pressures and weaknesses. Some branches of the service lag behind in implementing certain phases of the integration process; camps may vary slightly in their customs from place to place. But all over the nation—and the South—at this moment, are scattered these islands of integration.

Often surrounded by a rigidly segregated society, incorporating in its own make-up many who are from homes and communities where even the term "integration" is a dirty word, these installations of our national defense are on the offense against racial intolerance and inequality.

"I was in the Pacific two years," a young white officer at one of these camps says, "and I can tell you, I don't know about there not being any atheists in foxholes, but I know damned well there weren't any segregationists in the ones I saw. When you're looking forward to being blown to bits any minute, you're so glad to have anybody stick beside you I guess it makes you plumb color blind. I figure if we can get along together when we're in trouble, we ought to be able to do as well here on the post."

In these Federal military installations, school integration has also been effected. In some of the clubs, like the Enlisted Men's Wives' Club at Whiting Field, near Pensacola, Florida, a Negro can be elected president, even with some of the club members from the Deep South. Perhaps, as one woman says, "People do pretty much what's expected of them. Here, they're expected not to show any distinctions but those of rank in the service. And they don't, for the most part. At home, a lot of them are not supposed to admit a Negro can ever associate with a white person, and most of them don't. I guess we're all part chameleon!"

The difficulties of moving between a completely integrated military post and a completely segregated community nearby, create humorous, ridiculous, sometimes humiliating experiences. It seems likely that most of the Negroes follow the example of the young Negro private first class from Pennsylvania, who says, "I've never seen any discrimination here on this post, and I try to keep out of the town as much as I can. When I do go in, I just try to blot out all feeling about it as much as I can. I tell myself there's nothing I can do about this town here and I make up my mind to enjoy what I can as much as I can."

One young white officer says, "I've noticed most of the Negroes in my command seem to get together at mess, particularly. I think it's because they have to be together off the post and so they tend to remain together on the post, too."

Southern cities and states do not seem to have let the integrated military arrangements in their midst upset them unduly. A filling station man in Columbus, Georgia, grumbles: "Naw, I don't never go around Fort Benning none. I ain't wanting to associate with niggers that bad. But if that's what they want out there, let them go ahead, long as they keep coming in here, buying my gas."

When the Negro bus boycott was under way in Montgomery, a

woman from nearby Maxwell Air Base said, "Oh, the city people here tell those of us who are interested in trying to help solve the trouble that we're outsiders, not to meddle. Well, they've got their states' rights, but if the Federal government ever started to pull out of Maxwell, there'd be some hollering. With that million-dollar-a-week payroll we're mighty welcome. They don't want our outside meddling, just our outside money."

Money is certainly one reason why the South likes to have the armed services installations in its midst, but it is not the sole reason. Most Southerners have always cherished a high regard for the military. They like to boast that their university ROTC's now have more cadets in their ranks than West Point. At least one Southern state (Georgia) was founded in large part because of England's need for a military colony, and the nickname of another Southern state (Tennessee), The Volunteers, came into being because of the great numbers in which they flocked to enlist in the army in any time of war. Fighting, formally or informally, with or without reasonable cause, seems to be part of the region's deepest tradition. As John Hope Franklin recently pointed out in his excellent book, *The Militant South:* "Violence was inextricably woven into the most fundamental aspects of life in the South and constituted an important phase of the total experience of its people. Far from loathing violence, the man of the South was the product of his experiences as a frontiersman, Indian fighter, slaveholder, self-sufficient yeoman, poor white and Negro. He gladly fought, even if only to preserve his reputation as a fighter."

With white and Negro alike, then, violence was, and is, a past tradition and a present release. (In white people it was often attributed to high spirits; in Negroes, to low morals.) And war was the one definitive experience which set the South apart from the rest of the nation, which gave it a line of demarcation in time, separating forever the antebellum from the postbellum world.

War was, for generations of Southerners, more than a musty word in a history book. It was the reminiscences of a bright-eyed grandmother walking between the box hedges or propped on a chaise longue before an open window; it was the living word of an old man on Saturday at the general store with an audience of whittlers around his tilted chair, or at the family reunion on Sunday afternoon with the table spread in the yard. It was the old man remembering the long bivouac, the bloody encounter, the incredible heroes. At the beginning of World War I, the first American to shoot down an enemy plane was a young Southerner, Kiffin Yates Rockwell, who had gone to France and helped found the famous Lafayette

Escadrille. His brother, Paul, writing of Kiffin's early life, has provided a memorable picture of this transmission of military romanticism from the older to the younger generations in the South:

"Best of all for Kiffin was his grandfather, a Southerner of the old school, who had fought through the Confederate War from the beginning until the end. With Lee at Appomattox, in April, 1865, 'Marse Enoch,' as the Negroes called him, had mounted upon his horse when news of the surrender spread through the ragged little army, and had ridden away to his South Carolina home without waiting to be paroled. It was his boast that he had never surrendered to the 'Yankees,' had never taken the oath of allegiance to the Federal Government, and that he was 'unreconstructed. . . .'

"From his grandfather Kiffin heard stories of war, in camp and in battle. The little boy would listen for hours to his grandfather, his great-uncle 'Tommie,' and other elderly men of the neighborhood recounting their battles, their marches, their sufferings from hunger and cold, and their disappointment and grief over the 'Lost Cause,' and their struggles after. His imagination and his ambition were constantly fired with desire to shine upon the battlefield for a worthy purpose."

And so the South has marched off, one generation after another, to fight under the banner of liberty, equality, fraternity. "My great-grandfather on my mother's side wore the grey," a boy in the Bluegrass country says, "and one grandfather wore the blue. That's the way it was here in Kentucky. But my father and me both took our turn in plain old khaki. And I hope we got things settled down for a while now. Folks down in Georgia talking about fighting another civil war, they can get shot before they let nigra younguns go to school with theirs if they want to, but they can count me out!"

But in Georgia, in one of the really small rural towns, a boy you meet casually in a restaurant tells you, "We've got mostly cotton and cattle here, some pecans and peanuts and pines—a lot of colored folks, about half, I guess. Most people talk like there'll be a lot of trouble if any mixing comes. Myself, I don't think so. I been in the Marines three years with colored boys, nobody paid any attention one way or the other, got along fine. I think it'd be the same around here if everybody would let it work out."

The boys have gone out, and often come home changed—and just as often found their corner of the South unchanged. You remember a lieutenant in a small-town barbershop two years after he had returned from the war in the Pacific. Six feet, one hundred sixty pounds, with clean-cut features and a skin more bronze than black, in the prime years of his life at thirty: shining shoes.

"I got to get out of here, mister," he told you. "I got to leave. I'm going up to Mansfield, Ohio, next week, be close to my sister Daisy. Daisy, she says she can get me a good job up there making a dollar and a half an hour. That's more'n I can make shining shoes here a day.

"All this medal business during war, don't mean a thing. Don't buy a bite of meat or flour when the chips are down. It's shine, boy, or starve. I hate to leave my folks here, but I'll be glad to get my wife and kids out of this. I've got to get a man's work to do."

And a week later, on the way to Ohio, the lieutenant was killed in an automobile wreck. "His folks" brought him back to the small town and buried him with his medals and his uniform.

You remember a newspaperman who sat in his office one warm spring afternoon and told you about an encounter. "Couple of years ago I was waiting on a bus one night, had a bad cough. There was a young nigger about twenty-eight or twenty-nine standing nearby. He listened to me cough awhile, finally pulled out a bottle of gin and said, 'Sounds like you got a bad cough, mister. Take a drink of this.' He was already two-thirds drunk himself. I said, friendly as I could, 'Thank you kindly, sir, but I wouldn't care for any.' And you know, I thought that fellow was going to cry. Saddest look I ever saw came on his face. 'Over in Korea I used to drink after the white boys, they'd drink after me, nobody think nothing about it. Ever since I been back home, I can't get a single white man to drink after me.' Well, I knew it would look sillier than ever to take it then, so I thanked him again. But I'd have given a lot if I'd taken that drink the first time he offered it."

And there is the lawyer who tells you the incident summarizing the whole long procession of the South's struggles with its enemies—and with itself. "One of the hardest, most trying things I've ever seen"—the young attorney looks at you keenly, turning the silver letter opener on his desk—"was our state Congressman trying to explain to a conference of Negro ministers here in the state capital, why he signed the Southern Manifesto up in Washington. He told them it was one of the hardest decisions he'd ever had to make. He'd agonized over it. Finally he had signed the Manifesto to keep it from being any worse. The ministers all listened very quietly and very attentively, and then one eloquent old Negro man stood up near the end of the meeting and tossed him one he couldn't answer: 'Mister Congressman, I have seven children. One of my boys was killed in World War II. One of my boys was killed in Korea. Two of the others have been in the armed forces. Now how long are we going to have to fight for our country on foreign soil before our country will give us our civil rights here at home?"

There were years when the only uniform some white people would admit belonged on a Negro was a bellhop's uniform. There were years when it seemed that the only weapons of war the American army would freely share with the Negro were the paring knife and the scrub brush. But indeed, times and people do change. At last we have made it possible for Negroes to fight and die in equality—to the full extent of their capabilities—for America. Now it remains for all of us to live in equality—to the full extent of our abilities—for America.

10   The Embattled Ivory Towers

The people of the South are on the move. The armed forces have taken them out to the four corners of the earth and have brought huge encampments into their midst. The highways that lead south and north are also crowded with the exodus from farm to town to suburb. And at the apex of these crosscurrents and crossroads stand the schools.

The little red schoolhouse, that irreproachable shrine invoked by every candidate for public office; the college and university, that slightly suspect but gleaming citadel of progress: these are the institutions which have become a battleground for the current crisis in the South. This was probably inevitable. The school touches everyone's life; sometimes it seems to be everyone's business and no one's responsibility, but public education is still a keystone of democracy.

The Supreme Court recognized this when they declared segregation in the schools illegal. The citizens of the United States have recognized it with increasing awareness as they confronted their own inadequacies in cities and counties scattered across the nation, and as the struggle over desegregation of the schools in the South erupted into public violence and private soul searching. You travel over the South and you hear hundreds of voices shouting, whispering, threatening, pleading, wondering about their schools. As the voices grow familiar, you can remember those which are most frequent:

"Let ever who wants to, send their kids to school with niggers. Mine are gonna lay out and learn howsomever they can first. There's things more important than learning out of books." The man who tells you this is perhaps thirty-five years old. He looks more like fifty; those fifteen years have been added by the rocky land he's clearing of sassafras sprouts when you stop to talk with him. His earnestness, his needs, are not to be discounted.

A teacher who is also three times a mother, standing on the play-

170

ground of a new streamlined city school (white), says slowly, at the end of a long conversation, "A child, white or black, growing up in the South— maybe in some parts of the North and West, too, I don't know, but I do know down here—simply does not have the same education in democracy most other children have. You've heard the question asked by some Negro parent, 'How do you explain segregation to a four-year-old Negro child?' Well, I'd like to ask, 'Have you ever tried to explain segregation to a white child?' "

"I've got three children," a White Citizens' Council member confides. "One out of high school, one in, and one a-coming. If this resistance falls through and integration does start, they're coming out of school. It'll toll the death knell of the public school system in America. There'll just be private schools all over. Then where'll the nigras be?"

A distinguished newcomer, only five years' resident in the South, says, "Out in California no one can conceive of doing away with the public schools. They, along with most of the rest of the people in the country, don't realize that some of the Southerners are perfectly serious in their threat to abolish the schools."

"The basic need now is for the Negro himself to condition his own mind toward achieving integration," a Negro leader in one of the South's largest cities says. "Then he must get the best education he can. The lawsuits are about won—now we've got to participate where we can. And the sad truth is that Negroes aren't ready for many of the opportunities. Negroes who've gone on with any higher education—and they've been few enough, God knows, with good reason—have trained mostly to be teachers or preachers. We've got to think in terms of chemists and engineers. We've got to help make this integration palatable for the whites, too. It's a two-way street we're on."

You hear of two rhymes school children have made. The first, a teacher in one of the northern border counties of Tennessee tells you, was written ten years ago as part of a civic pride contest:

> "In our county we've been lucky,
> We don't have niggers like they do in Kentucky."

The other, current in at least one section of Mississippi, puts the old message to a rock and roll beat:

> "See you later, integrator;
> After while, choc'late chile."

A puzzled man, working in one of the new suburbs springing up through the South, says, "In one way I'm against this going to school together and in another way I'm not. You take our government, it's bringing in every kind of a foreigner, letting them get the best jobs, taking them into our schools, letting them do like everybody else—and then it's keeping native-born nigras out. That don't seem right. The nigras pay taxes and fight in our wars and they're part of our country, they been here as long as any of us, I reckon, and seems like they ought to be able to go to school where they want to if everybody else can. Mind you, I'm not really for the mixing. I'd rather everything stayed just like it is, but when you think about it, it don't seem right, and if they start this integration here, they won't have no trouble from me."

A member of the school board in a Border South city says, "On this business of 'choice of schools' by the students, I know of no other field where people may choose whether or not they will obey the Federal law. Perhaps pretty soon we'll let children have 'freedom of choice' as to whether or not they want to go to school at all!

"But prejudice will be eradicated only as people come together. 'We're not quite ready. We've got to understand each other.' We can't understand till we come together. We can look at a picture of George Washington and a picture of Booker T. Washington till we're blue, but we won't know each other until we come face to face."

A boy from Arizona, spending three months at a Southern university on a student-exchange program, has just attended a Ku Klux Klan rally at a small town about a hundred miles distant. Although he seems to consider this activity something typical for a boy in Dixie, it is doubtful if many of his fellow students have ever seen a KKK gathering. But he has listened and observed well, and he tells in excited detail of the various speeches and ceremonies which marked the Saturday night klanbake. Especially significant is the statement he remembers one robed member of the hierarchy making: "They're talking about building all these big fine schools for nigger younguns. I'm agin it. We didn't have things fancy or easy when I was growing up. Why, you should have saw where I went to school!"

If the boy from Arizona could understand all that lay behind that declaration, he would be well on his way toward a more knowledgeable grasp of both white and Negro troubles below the Mason-Dixon line.

Historically, the basic struggle here as in many other places has been between those who believe in tax-supported, free, universal education, and those who do not. Before the Civil War, a system of private tutors, the "old field" schools, and a far-flung fad for academies, provided education for some of the white people. In a region particularly allergic to taxes, the problem of education was how to make it public without requiring state taxation. A system of endowments and aid by the Federal government finally made it possible, before the Civil War, for every Southern state, with the exception of South Carolina, to establish permanent school funds. These, of course, were for whites only. Except for training in some special craft, and the occasional tutoring of an indulgent planter or his wife, education among the Negroes was rare. Following some of the slave uprisings and rumors of plots, it was, in fact, forbidden by law. ("I've heard my family tell about Grandmother," a middle-aged lady in Georgia tells you, "and how she would work with the slaves on her father's and, later, her husband's farm, teaching them to read and write. The men in the family told her that what she was doing was against the law, but she'd only laugh and say, 'Fiddle dee dee, too many horse thieves for the law to bother with me.' ")

Completely bypassing the Negro, the struggle for public education in the South went slowly forward. As a group of five Southern educators pointed out in *White and Negro Schools in the South*, in 1955: "The evolution of the public schools continued to be seriously hampered by the institution of slavery with its inherent class distinctions, by persistent aristocratic conceptions favoring private or religious schools, and by the tenacious conviction that state-supported education should be provided only to the poor."

Following the war and during that traumatic decade between 1867, when the United States Congress passed the Reconstruction Acts, and 1877, when the last Federal troops were withdrawn from the South, free public education was established—and the question of mixed Negro and white schools was raised. At this time, South Carolina, Mississippi, Florida and Alabama made mixed schools legal, but it was a legality more of theory than practice. As soon as the South was "redeemed" and Southern whites were returned to power, separate education for the two races came into being. Here, also, was born the attitude toward Negro education which considered it "more a function of the Federal government and of private philanthropy than as a local responsibility—which none of the ruined Southern states was in a position to discharge anyway." In addition to this was the fact that the activities of the Freedmen's Bureau, which organized some four thousand separate elementary schools, and the Northern philanthropic and church groups, which were sending money South, favored Negro school improvements, and so fostered segregation by the very nature of their benevolences.

Considering the state of affairs in the South at this time—the bitterness of defeat, the almost equal impoverishment of states and their citizens, the heightened antagonisms between black and white, and the feebleness of the white public-school system—the position of Negro education in the South seemed precarious indeed. As Dr. Frank P. Graham, former President of the University of North Carolina and once United States Senator from that state, has pointed out, "The question was not whether the Negroes would receive an equal education in an integrated system but whether they would receive any at all in a segregated system." In this connection, the Swedish social scientist, Myrdal, has made one of his most revealing insights into the Southern character: he concludes that this inability of the Southerners to renounce then, when they might have, the Negroes' right to public education, arose from the strength of the American Creed with its inclusion of the sacred principle of public education, and the fact that Southerners "are also good Americans with all the standardized American ideals about education." Whatever the reasons, and no matter how multitudinous the motives, when the South accepted the principle of tax-supported education for all its white people and the possibility of schooling—inferior and separate though it might be—for its Negroes, it set in motion a chain reaction which was destined to result with irresistible logic in the Supreme Court decision of May, 1954.

By the turn of the century, the Populist movement had demonstrated that there was discrimination and dissatisfaction among white people, too, in much of the South; some of the roots of antagonism might be seen in a simple set of figures. In Mississippi in 1907, an upland county with a small Negro population spent $5.65 per year for the education of each white child and $3.50 for each Negro child; while one of the Black Belt counties, with a preponderant Negro population, spent $80 per white and $2.50 for each Negro child.

Disparity between the education given white rural and urban children was almost as great as that between Negro and white schooling in most Southern states. When the country people considered the inequalities, however, their resentment usually focused on the Negroes for receiving any part of the tax money. (This resentment is still alive today. "Look at all the schools we're building for them, and they don't pay one per cent of the taxes around here." The Negro's answer to this criticism has become classic, of course: "Criticizing us for not paying taxes on money we can't earn and land we can't own is like the man out in Texas who shot his father and mother and then threw himself on the mercy of the court because he was an orphan.")

These differences of opportunity created a fertile soil for demagoguery, and it was no accident that many a Southern practitioner of the art who was known outside the region only for his flamboyant denunciations of the Negro also had a firm plank in his local platform assuring more and better education—at least for whites. ("It was funny to see one of the old stem-winders hollering for education," an elderly Southern gentlemen tells you. "I always felt like asking them if they didn't know they'd be running themselves out of a job if they ever got good education for our people. Like the feller said to the man who'd come to open a Baptist academy back in the mountains: 'What you want to teach them for? Don't you know that as soon as they're educated they'll stop being Baptists?' ")

As Southern education was making its greatest strides, the gulf between white and Negro schools remained, but Negro education did improve. Outside philanthropy still provided both its priming and power, however. Ashmore says that in the dozen years between 1916 and 1928, the number of Negro high schools rose from 67 to 1,860, and at the beginning of the 1930s, Negro school attendance was proportionately as great as that of the whites, for the first time.

Then came the years of the Depression. School revenues declined while school attendance increased. "The South found itself in the impossible position of trying to educate one third of the nation's children in a dual school system supported by only one-sixth of the nation's school revenue." Under such conditions, everyone was the loser. As a result, "of the twenty-one million dollars spent directly to meet the rural school emergency between 1933 and 1935, eighty per cent went to the South." The rural Negro schools, never anywhere near adequate, remained on the lowest educational level in the United States and struggled to stay in existence.

With the advent of World War II, the Negro began to take a new look at the country and world around him; activity of Negro organizations increased both in scope and effectiveness; as already suggested, the South faced a new Reconstruction—but one in which it, and all its people, could be the winner.

The development of the South, combined with those innate qualities which would not permit it to deny the Negroes in its midst participation in public education—even though it kept that education crippled and set apart—paved a straight and certain path from Plessy vs. Ferguson to May, 1954, to today. For it would seem that free men, given a nibble of democracy, will be content with nothing less than the whole loaf; most men given a little learning will always insist on the chance for more, to the extent of their capabilities.

We have, then, in education in the South at this time, a swift-running historical and social tide of events. Those who think only in terms of momentary delay, or those who hope that if they look the other way long enough the problem will disappear, are rendering themselves and their region a disservice.

"The Negro has been integrated geographically, politically and socio-economically into the national economy," two sociologists at Tulane University in New Orleans point out. "Segregation is no longer a natural social order as it was in 1896. Educational integration is a major social movement, and one cannot turn such movements on or off."

Efforts to sidetrack the inevitable are consuming much time and energy and money in many parts of the South. "Oh, we're taking advantage of the Court's allowing us 'deliberate speed,' " one man tells you. "We're building a high school for 'them' here; the last county court set aside the money for it. We don't have as many colored folks as some places and the ones around here have always sent their high school students over to the next county. Just have enough for one little bus. But now we're building them a school. Never had any trouble out of them, don't want any."

States with the lowest per capita income in the nation are now spending larger comparative proportions of that income on education—some of it in a desperate effort to make equal a system they hope to keep separate. Allocation of funds for Negro schools has soared in many Southern states during the past few years.

"They got deathbed religion." One Negro man shakes his head. "They want to bribe us with new buildings outside and the same old education inside. Of course we'll take it now, we'll take whatever we can get—but we won't stop moving toward what's right."

"Bribery," another man, a white man this time, repeats slowly, "bribery is a hard word for what lots of folks think is a just and generous thing they're doing. What most people don't seem to realize is how poor the South is. In cash, I mean. We need more money for practically everything. We've stepped up our school building programs but we're still making less headway than any other section in catching up with our shortages. White schools stand in need, too, especially some of the ones out in the country. So it's a heavy burden for some of these states to even try to equalize. And then to tell them they're wrong in doing that is bearing down pretty hard.

"Now the thing I really don't like is the threat. Men in high places are making it, legislatures are hollering it, governors are repeating it: 'Stop your fuss or we'll shut down the schools.' Now that's no answer a-tall, and a man with a pea-podful of sense knows it!"

A high-school principal in a small town tells you passionately, "Close the schools? Can you imagine such a catastrophe here in a time like this when we need more, not less, learning, when what little we have now is so inadequate to our needs? Jonathan Daniels, over in North Carolina, said it all a few months ago. I read about it in the newspapers and I hope every other person in the South did, too. He was making a speech to some group and he said, best as I remember it, that we got all bothered once and we seceded from the union, but this time we're getting ready to secede from civilization."

While the school segregation issue was still under consideration by the Supreme Court, however, James F. Byrnes, Governor of South Carolina and himself a former associate justice of that court, had already put into words the attitude which would soon dominate at least one segment of the South: "Should the Supreme Court decide this case against our position," he told a meeting of his state's Education Association, "we will face a serious problem. Of only one thing can we be certain. South Carolina will not now, nor for some years to come, mix white and colored children in our schools. . . . If the Court changes what is now the law of the land, we will, if it is possible, live within the law, preserve the public-school system, and at the same time maintain segregation. If that is not possible, reluctantly we will abandon the public-school system."

Soon after the Supreme Court handed down its decision, South Carolina, Georgia and Mississippi adopted legislation permitting closing of the schools as an alternate to desegregation. Several of the other Southern states have since followed suit, usually with elaborate tuition-grant, private-school substitute plans. Georgia made it a felony for a school official to spend public funds on a desegregated school.

When North Carolina's legislature was in session in July, 1956, considering the Pearsall Committee's plan of local option with provision for closing the schools and providing tuition funds for private schools, one elderly man remarked: "Well, it's been a day of fine progress backward. When I remember how hard we worked to get good schools during those years back yonder when I was coming on, I wonder if folks today know what they're doing." But on September eighth, North Carolina voters adopted the Pearsall Plan amendments to the Constitution by a vote of four to one.

Along with moves to close the schools as a last-ditch measure against integration, many of the states took steps to insure conformity among the teachers. Contracts were put on a year to year basis, questionnaires delving into past affiliations and present memberships in organizations were circulated, and personal advocacy of integration was made suffcient grounds for dismissal. NAACP members frequently found themselves out of work. One of the many Negro teachers who has been fired tells you, "They let me go because my brother is a state official in the NAACP. Here I am, nothing to do, no other job I can get unless I leave the state. I guess that's what I'll have to do, but I hate to leave my family. You wonder sometimes how folks can be so mean. It's not like we were doing anything subversive, but they investigate us like we were spies or something, and here we are, out of a job."

Then a Negro leader in another Deep South state describes the situation there: "Teachers now have to fill out a long question blank stating what organizations they've belonged to, contributed to, now or in the past. When seven or eight teachers in our schools at the state capital were threatened with firing, they went to the Superintendent of Schools and had a closed meeting with him. Some people get chilly feet very easy. They told him that they had belonged to the NAACP three or four years before, had contributed a little to it once or twice, years ago, but they weren't having anything to do with it now. They're still teaching." He rubs his forehead slowly with his thumb and forefinger. "And who's to blame them?"

White teachers have faced "tests of loyalty," too. There was, for instance, the case of the young seventh-grade teacher in a rural county in Georgia. When her class pressed her, one day in May, as to whether or not she would object to teaching white and colored pupils, she said she would not. She also tried to make it clear that this was her personal answer and not part of her teaching program. By September about a hundred people in the community were reported to have signed a petition asking for her removal from the school. The county board refused to dismiss the young woman despite what it termed were probably "unwise or indiscreet expressions." The state Board of Education cut off the 90 per cent of her pay which came from the state, although the county presumably made up the difference since the teacher continued to receive her full salary. The struggle was finally resolved late in November when, expecting a baby and doubtless weary of the turmoil, she resigned.

It seems to be in those areas where equalization of teachers' pay—between white and Negro, and town and country as well—has been slowest, that pressures for conformity in opposition to integration are strongest. When you consider the average annual wage of the teachers in some of these districts, the wonder is that there are any schools at all. And the differences within the region, and within the states themselves, are astonishing. Negro teachers in every other Southern state have, for instance, a higher income than the white teachers in Mississippi. Two states, Oklahoma and Kentucky, now have systems under which the Negro teacher averages a higher salary than the white teacher. But the rural areas pay the teachers the poorest; they are the sections which—under antiquated political systems—often control the balance of power in the state government, and they generally contain the deepest reservoir of violent resistance to any possibility of change in racial customs.

Politics and education have always been uneasy bedfellows, but the stresses and strains of their recent shotgun marriage, precipitated by the Supreme Court, have been demoralizing for everyone concerned. Investigations of textbooks, questionings on subject matter taught in the classrooms, examinations of private opinion privately expressed: these have been some of the unhealthy results of an ill-fated alliance. It is no news that some of the demagogues of the past who paid loudest lip service to the schools often did most to destroy those principles and values upon which the school system was founded. But their attacks seem, in retrospect, to spring less from a hatred of education as such than from their personal ignorance of the nature of the educational process. They increased physical equipment in the classrooms and playgrounds, secured appropriations for bigger and better buildings—and diminished the freedom of questioning and expression which went on behind the brick and mortar. Their legacy to the present politicians has probably been a heightened awareness of that next election when they will come face to face with "the people" in a decisive situation, and an envy and suspicion of the professors in their state's "ivory towers," who have to undergo no such gruelling test.

"Professors are frequently criticized for being 'out of this world,' " a young instructor at a small college says, "but let one of us venture any leadership or opinion on this integration question, and we're 'sticking our nose into something that's none of our business.' Of course," he grins, "I guess the legislators are scared we're going to turn our ivory towers into ebony towers."

The tax-supported universities of those states most bitterly resisting the Supreme Court decision have paid a heavy price in loss of faculty for their insistence upon complete conformity to political opinion. On August 2, 1955, Dr. Chester C. Travelstead, Dean of the School of Education at the University of South Carolina, made a speech before approximately four hundred summer-school students and faculty. He noted that the education profession in South Carolina had made no public statement on integration, perhaps because of fear of embarrassment, ridicule or reprisal. Then he went on to say, "It is my firm conviction that enforced segregation of the races in our public schools can no longer be justified on any basis—and should, therefore, be abolished as soon as practicable. Even though, as a white Southerner, I have, since early childhood, taken for granted the practice of segregation, I can find now no justification for it.

"The fact that we have practiced segregation on the assumption that it is right and just does not make it right and just."

Shortly thereafter he received a note from the executive committee of the Board of Trustees, informing him of his dismissal from the university. One South Carolina newspaper, *The Cheraw Chronicle*, summarized the events and their consequences thus:

"The real problem involved in the firing of Dr. Chester C. Travelstead has nothing whatever to do with the question of segregation in our schools. Academic freedom and the right of a teacher or an administrator to self-expression is at stake. We believe that the action by the trustees in discharging Dr. Travelstead will do the university far more harm than any speech by the educator could possibly achieve.

"It will be very difficult to get or keep a first-class faculty so long as intellectual freedom is so threatened. The progress and well-being of our people depend upon good education. . . . Topnotch educators will not be inclinded to come to a school where there is a climate of fear, repression, censorship and reprisal. . . . This is a tragic and costly blunder. . . ."

While Dr. Travelstead was packing his bags in South Carolina, next door in Georgia, the State Board of Regents, which runs the University System of Georgia, and the Board of Education, were acting to strip Dr. Guy H. Wells of both a title and pension he had received as a result of long service in his state's schools. As executive director of the Georgia Committee on Interracial Cooperation (its members were called "dupes" by the state attorney general), Dr. Wells had incurred the displeasure of the political leaders. After announcement in a local political weekly that he was "seeking to sell the white people on mixing with the Negroes," the State Regents took back from Wells the title they had given him two years earlier as president emeritus of Georgia State College for Women, where he had served as president for nineteen years, before he resigned to work for the Federal government. The Board of Education also recommended unanimously that Wells' $518-a-month retirement pay be cut off.

Dr. Wells estimated that he had paid about $450 a year into the teacher retirement fund for ten years. He also answered, "I have advocated Negro and white leaders coming together in good will to resolve differences and work for agreement.

"I have nothing to retract or apologize for, and I am confident that the good people of Georgia will sustain my position.

"Neither desegregation nor integration, which most good men know will come in time, but freedom of speech and thought is the fundamental issue. If this attack on me will advance and help keep these rights for Georgians, the sacrifice will not be too great a price."

Once more it was a newspaper, this time the *Macon Telegraph*, which gave voice to the events and issues involved: "Dr. Wells was accused, tried and convicted without a single member of either group even doing him the courtesy of informing him directly about the charges.

"Indeed, he was given no hearing, he was given no opportunity to explain his position, he was never asked to verify or deny the charges.

"Further, not a single member of either board was present to hear first hand Dr. Wells' speeches for which he has been so bitterly criticized.

"In other words the Board of Regents and the Board of Education accepted second-hand information to bring action against a reputable citizen without ever consulting him on the truth of the charges. This seems to be a rather unusual circumstance."

Dr. Wells, a plump, pleasant, white-haired man with a keen eye and tongue, talks with you calmly about the storms he has weathered. "Well, I guess you could call me a native Georgian—my family goes back ten generations in the state. When all this trouble came up, I contested the loss of pay—they discovered they had no legal right to cut off those benefits—but not the loss of title. With men like that bestowing it, a title wouldn't have much meaning anyway. The healing would hurt worse than the wounds."

That same spring, in Mississippi, a university invitation to the Reverend Alvin Kershaw, of Oxford, Ohio, to take part in a Religious

Emphasis Week program on the campus, was withdrawn. The reason behind this revoked hospitality was the rector's announcement that he intended to give part of the money he had won on a recent television quiz show to the National Association for the Advancement of Colored People. Six other guest speakers who were scheduled to appear at the university withdrew from the program. Seventy-three per cent of the students polled by the campus newspaper and senate said that the Reverend Kershaw should have been allowed to appear.

Religious Emphasis Week was canceled. The chairman of the University of Mississippi department of sociology resigned. Dr. Morton King, a native of Tennessee and a member of the University of Mississippi faculty for ten years, said his resignation was based on a professional principle involving academic freedom—not segregation. He had come to feel that "Ole Miss is no longer a place where I can be happy or be a productive scholar and teacher." He considered Mississippi colleges weak "in the freedom of thought, inquiry and speech which are essential for higher education to flourish." In another part of the state, Dr. William Buchanan resigned from the faculty of Mississippi State College in protest over the "screening processes" which had been involved in the curfew on Kershaw.

These protests and losses of faculty did not dismay the legislature of Mississippi, however. They commended the university chancellor and the state college president for accepting the resignations and "safeguarding our culture and traditions from vicious attacks and influences . . . our state-supported institutions of higher learning should reflect the thinking of our people and, of right, should be the primary exponent and protectors of our culture and traditions."

It was at the University of Alabama, however, that the ivory towers were really assaulted, and for students and faculty, trustees and townspeople, it seemed, during February, 1956, that there was truly "no hiding place down there." Tuscaloosa and Autherine—one a strange musical name from the red man's language, and the other an unusual name borne by a twenty-six-year-old Negro girl—these were words that would long be remembered in the history of desegregation.

Visiting the campus almost a year after its troubling three days of mob violence and conquest, you walk under the sprawling limbs of the tall old trees, stand with book-laden students in the shelter of a doorway until a momentary shower passes over and the sun comes out again, and sit with some of the professors in their quiet offices insulated by tiers of books and the tree limbs beyond the windows. You wonder how the violence surged in here, and what flotsam, physical or spiritual, it has left on this campus in its wake. There are the sharply conflicting opinions on how it even began.

"She'd been fighting lawsuits for three years trying to get in our school," a man downtown in Tuscaloosa tells you, "and when that Federal Court finally told the university people they'd have to take her in, I reckon it went to her head. She come down here with five or six big high-powered Birmingham niggers, driving a Cadillac, flashing hundred-dollar bills, and the people in charge come rushing out to greet her and took her in like she was something special. I reckon the other students and folks around town just weren't ready to take all such as that. It stuck in our craw."

But one of the Negro men in Birmingham who aided and advised Autherine Lucy denies flatly the charges of deliberate conspicuousness. "It was like this: we'd been helping her all we could, and we didn't know how she was going to be greeted when she first came to the university. Besides, she was a little nervous, I guess, and wanted someone to go with her. A friend of ours drove her down that first day, and we went in his Pontiac. When we got there, the admissions people took her in and registered her right away. I guess they were afraid of embarrassment or trouble if she waited in the regular line a long time. Then about the hundred-dollar bills: we knew they probably wouldn't take any check of ours down at the university, and we thought we'd better have all we needed on hand so there wouldn't be any excuse for a delay in her registration. If we'd taken all dollar bills and counted them out in payment, people who wanted to would have still said we were trying to show off.

"The second or third day she went down to school, somebody different took her and they did go in a Cadillac. But that wasn't what started the trouble. It was white people who were determined that that Federal Court order would never be carried out."

Undercurrents which helped shape the whole event are suggested by both the white man's and the Negro's conversation, so that you feel one of the people you talk with who has tried to bring some measure of objectivity to the events he witnessed, at least in part, has a toe hold on the truth when he says, "Looking back, the whole trouble here seems to have been the result of a tragedy of errors. Everybody did the wrong thing at the wrong time. First, remember the bare outlines of what happened.

"After three years of litigation a Negro girl was ordered admitted to the University. She came and registered on Wednesday, February first. Friday, the third, she went to classes, with no incidents. That night there was a student demonstration; its main activities were popping off some firecrackers and shouting around, things like 'Keep Bama White!' Saturday the girl went to classes again without any trouble, but that night the demonstration was different. There were more people and lots of them weren't university students. They were from the town and country around. They marched downtown and back, shook up some cars, and ended up at President Carmichael's house where they booed him when he tried to talk to them.

"Monday morning, when Autherine Lucy came down from Birmingham, there was already a crowd of maybe fifty or so people outside the building where her first class was to meet. When she got ready to go to her second class, the Dean of Women and the Assistant to the President took her out the rear door, but they got a shower of rocks and eggs anyway, as they drove to the next classroom building. Now there seemed to be lots more outsiders in the mob of about a thousand, and things were pretty ugly. Some of the crowd were obscene. Some hollered, 'Kill her! Kill her!'

"Finally, with the help of highway patrolmen, they got her away. That night the university Board of Trustees met and 'excluded,' as they put it, Miss Lucy until further notice. That broke up the mob, of course, since that's what they'd wanted anyway.

"But look at it from the beginning: nobody was well enough prepared for the possibility of violence. There'd been, I guess, more hoping and poll-taking than good sound spadework, although I'd be the first to admit I don't know for sure just what that should have been. Then the Negroes; they were a little too triumphant about the whole registration, I think. Whether it was understandable or not isn't the point here—what mattered was their effect on the white people around them. And that was disastrous.

"If the whole thing had been planned, it couldn't have gone more solidly wrong. Even the people helping with the registration did their bit: you know how long it takes to enroll hundreds and hundreds of students. There's always a long line and hours and hours of waiting, and there's going to be resentment of anybody, no matter what color he is, who gets a short cut. When they took her in ahead of all the line that had been standing there, that just helped kindle feeling against Autherine Lucy. And the big-denomination bills didn't soften feelings any—I don't care why she had them—nor the expensive car, nor the squad of friends. Everything pyramided.

"And on the white side, just about everybody that had any authority lost his backbone. There were individual acts of courage—Dean Healy and Presidential Assistant Bennett risked rocks and eggs and the Dean got the windows of her car broken out when they took the girl from one class to another, and Episcopalian chaplain, Robert Gribben, Jr., helped devise the plan which made it possible for her to escape with her life— but for the most part, everyone was just frozen. The mob should never have been allowed to grow as it did—and even then it shouldn't have been allowed to carry the day.

"On top of all that, of course, the NAACP pulled a real boner. The girl accused university authorities of conspiring with the mob for her ouster. She had no proof of such a thing, and the school promptly ex- pelled her. So she's married to somebody out in Texas now—and the folks here have got a lot of good hindsight. I just hope it'll help a few other places have some foresight."

A professor at the university tells you, "I think all of us were sur- prised by the violence. These feelings had existed in circles among which I do not seem to move. But I will venture this opinion: if Autherine Lucy had won her case before the Supreme Court decision in 1954, I think it very probable she'd be in the university today and there would have been no turmoil. As it was, following the Court's decision on all schools, when she made such a point of entering the university people thought this would lead directly to integration of the secondary schools, too."

You remember a filling station man near the Alabama-Tennessee border who told you soon after the riots, "That Lucy gal! She's the damnd- est determindest you-know-what I ever heard of. I'll take my hat off to her, she's got guts, but I'd sure like to see her go back to that university. I've got friends around that place; I know what we'd like to do to her."

With all these disturbing echoes of what happened, you walk around the campus, as Dr. Carmichael may have done before he resigned as president of the university. He, perhaps more than any other, had been caught in the crossfire of criticism so familiar today, between those who said he could have done more and those who said he should have done less.

Editorials in two Southern papers lamented his dilemma and de- parture especially well. The Chattanooga Times said, "We are sorry indeed to learn of the resignation of Dr. O. C. Carmichael as president of the

University of Alabama. The South loses another fine educator at a time when it can ill afford it.

"Dr. Carmichael, a native of Clay County, Alabama, is a graduate of the university he now heads, a Rhodes scholar and a former chancellor of Vanderbilt University in Nashville. Now 65, he came back to Tuscaloosa from his post as head of the Carnegie Foundation for the Advancement of Teaching and an already distinguished career . . .

"Dr. Carmichael will continue, through the Fund for the Advancement of Education, his devotion to the cause he has served well. Education, together with the economic advancement to which it is so closely related, is the bright hope the South has in meeting justly this heavy problem."

And the *Montgomery Advertiser* explained, "Dr. Carmichael had ended his famous career to return to Alabama to give his last prime years to the service of his native state. In this return of the native he found the deepest satisfaction. But what he had logically visualized as a twilight labor of academic revival and expansion of the University became a turbulent situation in which he and his wife were assailed by a mob and he himself was racked by an inner conflict of principle and the granite reality of Alabama custom."

President Carmichael was not the only one to leave Tuscaloosa. Harry Shaffer, as associate professor of economics, was among the first to go, in a direct protest over the handling of Autherine Lucy's registration, the violence and her final expulsion. Shaffer says that of some twenty-one professors who resigned from the faculty, he knows of fifteen who said the Lucy affair was their main reason. Even as some teachers were leaving, one student told Professor Shaffer that while he was in the navy he had learned that Negroes were human beings, and he wished that everyone in the South might have his opportunity to know them. "Education is what we need down here, education."

The storm which centered about Autherine Lucy's attendance at the University of Alabama had many repercussions. Memberships in White Citizens' Councils, both in Alabama and adjoining states, reportedly skyrocketed. "That trouble just showed people in the South what they were up against," one Council member says, "and it put all the white people to thinking and banding together."

"In the past year attitudes have hardened." A professor nods slowly. "You can feel it everywhere."

One Alabama legislator proposed a resolution which would cut off the state appropriation to Tuskegee Institute, in Macon County, if any

Negro should be allowed to attend a white tax-supported college any-where in the state. The representative pointed out that the reason the state first appropriated funds to Booker T. Washington's famous institute anyway was to be sure Negroes and whites would not have to go to school together.

But despite the anxiety and fear and enormous waste which had resulted from Tuscaloosa's experience and indelibly engraved the name Autherine in many a memory, it was the exception and not the rule. Many people, reading of the riots here and the reprisals against professors else-where, jumped to the conclusion that Southern universities are all em-battled sanctuaries of white supremacy. Quite the opposite. Only five Southern state universities still refuse—in 1957—to admit Negroes. They are the Universities of Georgia, Alabama, Florida, South Carolina and Mississippi. And all of these states except one (South Carolina) has at least one private college which is integrated.

In none of the other eight states did the admission of Negroes create violence, or tension of serious consequence. When Professor Guy B. Johnson, of the University of North Carolina, made studies of seven-teen of the 122 integrated campuses in the South in 1953, he made an interesting discovery: "In almost every instance," he says, "when a state institution was faced with the fact that it might actually have to admit Negroes, there were serious predictions of violence and bloodshed if this thing came to pass. To the best of our knowledge, the first drop of blood is yet to be shed."

The case of the University of Arkansas is particularly interesting because it acted first of all the Southern states, it acted voluntarily, and it did so without undue publicity. While neighboring Oklahoma and Texas were embroiled in legal encounters testing the validity of their segregation laws at the university level, the Board of Trustees at the University of Arkansas, not threatened at the moment with legal action but wise enough to foresee the possibility—yes, inevitability—of such a challenge, ruled that qualified Negro students who could not secure the courses they wanted at the state-supported Negro college would be ad-mitted to the university. The Negro student who enrolled at the school of law early in 1948 was the first of his race "to enter a public university in any of the former Confederate states since Reconstruction." At present, all eight of the state colleges are open to Negroes at the graduate and undergraduate levels.

Of the five Deep South states whose official attitude toward the Supreme Court decision might be termed defiant, only Louisiana admits Negroes to its state university. This was a result of court action. In the summer of 1956, it was reported that fifteen per cent of the graduate students at Louisiana State University were Negro. Here, as elsewhere, once the barrier is broken legally, fair treatment toward Negroes seems to be the rule of fellow students and faculty.

At the University of Oklahoma in Norman, on the flat, sprawling campus, where a Western buoyance in the wind meets the warmer air from adjoining Southern states and the nearby "Little Dixie" corner of Oklahoma itself, you feel the presence of American frontiers. In 1946, Ada Lois Sipuel began a suit against the university here to gain admission to its school of law. In 1949, after having had the brief distinction of being the only student in a three-faculty law school conducted especially for her benefit in the state capitol building, she was finally admitted to the university. The attitude and activity of the university itself seems to have been, from available evidence, an example of what is meant by "deliberate speed:" not speed without necessary deliberation, or deliberation without movement.

"What we tried to do in this whole thing," one official says, "was move ahead as fast as we could and carry the people along with us. Sometimes that's faster than you think, sometimes slower, but you have to keep trying."

Another man says, "We went along with a lot of ridiculous things they set up—but we kept pushing toward the goal. For instance, when the legislature set up the separate law school, for one student, the administration could have come out with a statement of derision or protest, but they waited, and it was of course ruled in no way equitable or adequate. Then when the Supreme Court ordered us to admit the Negro student and the legislature said we'd have to provide separate facilities, we just roped off one little corner of the classrooms and would call them Room 112-A or 225-B, or something like that. Of course in a couple of days the students had cut the ropes up for souvenirs, and we didn't put them back. We put a card on one of the library study tables: For Negroes. And the next day the youngsters had taken it home, and we never replaced it."

In the office of the president you meet Dr. George Cross, the man who has guided the university through recent years of change and readjustment and growth. The room is spacious; it is dignified but not somber. Like the man who occupies it, it wears an easy, innate dignity. Dr. Cross, a man of medium height and fair, direct countenance, greets you with a firm handshake.

"On the whole I think this has been a revealing experience for the university. I'm convinced we could have had mass action several different times during our desegregation process. I got many letters from all over, particularly the Deep South. But we tried to keep things on an even keel as much as we could. One morning when I was opening my mail, I found two letters from two different sides of the controversy and from totally different areas of the country. One was for immediate integration, one was for complete segregation—and each called me 'a dirty dog.' I remember the term because each of them used the same words, 'dirty dog.' I had had to adopt some policy, by the law, which didn't suit the Negro cause, and then I had tried to counterbalance that somewhat by acting for the Negro students in another direction, and that didn't suit the segregationists. One thing almost all of the letters of rebuke I received had in common: they all seemed to be written by uneducated people.

"The university students themselves have been wonderful about this. A few come from the 'Little Dixie' region, but they don't feel as strongly as their parents on the race question. All our criticism came from older people, many of whom had no one in the university.

"Of all the experiences I have had during fourteen years of administration, I think the one which has been most satisfying inwardly, and the most rewarding, is that dealing with the university's desegregation."

In December, 1956, when Dr. Cross was honored in Dallas, Texas, at a dinner and award given him by the Anti-Defamation League of B'nai B'rith, Vice President Richard Nixon sent the following message:

"One of Oklahoma's first citizens," he said in part, "and an outstanding scientist, Dr. Cross has made a notable contribution in successfully promoting the American ideal of equality of educational opportunities for members of minority groups. To men like Dr. Cross, Americans of good will everywhere owe a great debt."

In carrying forth the desegregation of public schools in Louisville, Kentucky, Dr. Omer Carmichael, city Superintendent of Schools, won similar praise from President Eisenhower, and the fellow citizens of his city, state and nation. With foresight, sincerity, intelligence and hard work, Dr. Carmichael and leaders in his school system and town met the challenge of desegregation. After formulating a twelve-point plan, Louisville was entirely redistricted. Two vital points of the over-all plan called for "free choice," permitting pupils and parents to ask for transfers to schools outside the districts in which they lived if they so desired, and yet the redistricting was to be carried out "without gerrymandering and without regard to race."

Education and preparation for the new experience, on both the individual and community levels, was an important forerunner of the opening of school. On September 5, 1956, while demonstrations by unruly crowds were taking place in one town in Tennessee and two other towns in Kentucky, Louisville began desegregating classes without incident. More than fifty-four thousand white and twelve thousand Negro students were affected. The result of the "free choice" plan, by the end of the first month, was that 79 per cent of the pupils were in mixed schools, twenty per cent were in one all-Negro high school, and none were in all-white schools.

Late in October, Superintendent Carmichael said, "We all expected the desegregation program to start successfully, but it has begun more smoothly than we had supposed possible. This is a tribute to the excellent planning and preparation by all school groups and the splendid co-operation of the parent-teacher associations. I feel, also, that it is a tribute to the fundamental respect of our people for law."

When Dr. Carmichael was called to Washington, D.C., to confer with President Eisenhower on the Louisville success story, he also had several press and television interviews. Points he stressed repeatedly were that no one plan would work for every place—each locality must adopt techniques to suit its unique needs, although there would be certain factors held in common almost everywhere—and that permission to transfer would appear to be "basic anywhere in the beginning of desegregation."

"Louisville, of course, isn't a typical Southern city," you hear again and again, since September, 1956.

"Any city that desegregates successfully immediately ceases to be a 'Southern city' as far as some people are concerned," a Southern worker with the Friends' Service Committee says. "When Louisville desegregated, it became a Northern city; Washington—the same thing; if Birmingham integrated its schools tomorrow it would suddenly somehow cease to be a Southern city."

"What we need, I suppose," one woman in New Orleans explains, "is a course charted somewhere between easy hope and despair. Wasn't it John Calhoun who was supposed to have said something about 'the South, the poor South'? Well, sometimes I feel like saying, 'the schools, the poor schools!' We've saddled them with all sorts of ridiculous burdens all these years, now we're making them the battleground for our deepest prejudices and beliefs."

In the middle of this dilemma are the teachers, white and Negro, many underpaid, some overworked, compelled to bring their ideas and those of the institution they love and respect into some degree of compatibility, and both into harmony with the society they serve. Open to investigations of politicians, daily examination by the community, and the needs and threats of numerous individuals and groups, with them rests the fate of learning in the South for today and tomorrow.

"Industry looks at three things," a prominent chemical scientist in Alabama tell you. "They are salaries, equipment, buildings. Education seems to do just the opposite—it looks at buildings first, equipment second and salaries last. The research building where I work is efficient but quite unostentatious, not an inch of marble in the whole thing. But our men get top pay. The schools have been getting better buildings, at some of the universities even hunks of marble. But there's inadequately paid personnel inside.

"Yet from these schools must come the leaders for industry as well as everything else; the citizens of the future. Somewhere, somehow, we're going to have to re-examine the whole situation."

The head of a department at one of the outstanding Southern universities comments to you on the increasing difficulty some institutions are having in finding professors of high caliber. "In any of our departments here, if you have a vacancy, you can always get somebody from one of the Deep South universities. And nobody will go there. I don't believe I have one graduate student this year who would take a position at a college in the Deep South. Even the ones whose homes are there. Just the other day I asked a man from the capital city of one of those states, who'll be looking for a place next spring, what his stipulations were and he said first, nothing in his home state. Any man worth his salt wants to be able to think and speak and work with some degree of inquiry and freedom; he doesn't want to be involved in constant friction and turmoil."

The dilemma of the ivory towers grows from the innermost depths of the South's troubled conscience today. A professor at the University of Alabama, where the struggle has been displayed most forcefully, has given it eloquent voice in an article which appeared in *The Yale Review*. Dr. Iredell Jenkins said: "Universities are magnificently equipped to discover the truth and make it available to minds that have been prepared to appreciate it. But they are extremely ill equipped to mobilize and direct popular sentiment. The subtlety and caution, the detachment and balance, that are necessary to the first task disarm them for the second. . . .

"Universities are institutions. . . . Now the morality of institutions differs from that of individuals in several notable respects, and especially in this, that institutions must have a high regard for expedience. . . . The reason for this is simply that institutions are infinitely less expendable than individuals: they are, in fact, literally indispensable. When an institution is seriously weakened, it takes a long time to recover; and in the meantime it leaves a vacuum in which its functions go unperformed and its values unserved. So a university is justified, and even obligated, to bow to the expedient and to cultivate prudence in a manner that would be clearly immoral in an individual.

"Professors, as members of a university, inherit this obligation. And with this recognition the character of the dilemma that professors confront is exposed in all of its stark and unrelenting harshness. As individual moral agents they feel obliged to serve the right as they see it. As members of an institution they feel obliged to consider its judgment of what is expedient and practicable in the light of its vital interests.

"Given this conflict, it is inevitable that different men will resolve it in different ways. Furthermore, it should be evident that there is no single right solution to the problem. . . ."

On the tree-shaded campuses, in the shadows of aged brick buildings, under the sound of chimes at evening, ringing the hour, the issue will be met and resolved. On hot square strips of grammar-grade playgrounds, inside streamlined brick-and-glass high-school walls, under the blackboards carrying white-chalked formulas for problems of chemistry and physics, the issue will be met and resolved. Not the issues of black and white people and our future only—but of education, of what learning itself is and what it means, and the issue of democracy.

11 :::: Pressure on the Press

"The thrown stone makes news; the troubled heart does not." The Southern newspaper editor who tells you this summarizes well the problem of daily publishing in a place where stones are an easy release for hearts with a heavy burden.

His statement also suggests the related problem of how much the news makes the papers, and how much the papers make the news. The past few years have seen a heightened awareness in the South of this old question.

"Our paper here in Montgomery has covered the story of the bus boycott well," a reporter says, "but many people dislike us because we've done our job. They're mad at the paper, think because we report what's happening we create it."

The people holding the bastions of segregation and those manning the march of integration have each accused the press of hindering or misinterpreting their cause.

The tradition of Southern journalism is one of personal and heated individualism. H. C. Nixon in *Possum Trot*, his story of a "Rural Community, South," says that Southerners like "their editorials and their coffee strong." Small wonder then that one man can say, with a smile, "There's been a story that the real winner of the Civil War was the ABA—the American Bookseller's Association. Well, I believe the only people who won the Supreme Court segregation decision were the newspapermen."

It is true that some papers which had sunk into a rut of more or less provincial oblivion have been revived to national attention again by their handling of this explosive and fundamental issue. There are also those few which achieved and still try to maintain a measure of sobriety in their reporting of racial news and a degree of reasonableness in their editorials. Then there are the weeklies, semi-weeklies, fortnightlies, which have come into being for the sole purpose of propaganda on the integration question pro or con. In addition to all these there is the Negro press, of whose existence many white people are not even now aware;

these papers have recognized the integration issue as one of their very reasons for existence.

In a report issued by nine Nieman Fellows (newspapermen with special grants for study at Harvard University), they summarized the colored news in the white press this way: "As pictured in many newspapers, the Negro is either an entertaining fool, a dangerous animal, or (on the comparatively rare occasions when a Negro's achievements are applauded) a prodigy of astonishing attainments, considering his race."

Partly to meet the everyday need of the Negro to be an ordinary social part of a community, rather than an aberration of either evil or excellence, as well as to give him a voice of protest, the Negro newspapers came into being. Since the first one was founded in 1827 in New York City, the field has grown to include approximately 180 presently published in the United States. Most of these are weeklies, and they are paradoxical in intent and achievement. Their pattern of group protest sets them apart from the usual United States newspapers—they are inflammatory by nature and specialize in over-all news coverage by design—but they also provide the opportunity for individuals to "belong." In a way not otherwise possible, they permit Negroes to see themselves as part of the small town or city world of clubs and lodges, weddings and luncheons, dinners and receptions. Thus, while they are showing the Negro the division between his life and the mainstream of American existence, they are also unifying him to the activities of that mainstream.

The Negro newspapers and the necessities which have brought them into existence make, on the whole, small impression on most white communities. It is easy to remember nearly a dozen years back when a traveled, small-town Southern lady of your acquaintance saw, for the first time, the *Pittsburgh Courier*. All her life she had known Negroes, and she could call the first names of most of those in the town where she lived. Yet, except for special programs at the colored school and "white" services at the A.M.E. Church, she had been totally unaware of any of their social life. The newspaper was a revelation, at first humorous, then gradually more disturbing.

"Well, Minnie," she told a fourth cousin over the telephone the next morning, "you'll never guess how I spent the evening: reading a nigra newspaper! . . . Yes, they do, they have them everywhere—mostly up North, I guess—that's where this one was published—but there's one in Atlanta, I understand, and lots of other Southern cities, too. . . . No, they don't have any of our news, or much what you would call world news, but there's a lot about them you don't see in other papers. And on the inside are pages and pages of 'society.' Yes, ma'am, 'society,' with them all dressed up like us, little fur stoles and orchid corsages and everything— and having teas and debuts and all just like us. There's something kind of pitiful about it, poor things. . . . Oh, I'm saving it for you to see, too."

Perhaps the most striking feature of a visit with some of the Negro newspaper editors of the South is the disparity, in almost every instance, between them and the things you have been told about them by many in the white community.

"You needn't talk with him if you're looking for any sort of objectivity at all. It's his job to be biased, of course—and he does a damned good job."

"That one's a real demagogue. We ought to be thankful, I suppose, that he's a publisher and not a politician."

"Oh, he's bitter. Wild and bitter on this subject!"

"Why, the editor of that sheet they call a paper wouldn't write the truth if he could. I wouldn't believe him if he told me the time of day under oath."

"I really never read 'their' paper. Just glance at the front page once or twice—pretty sensational stuff. They have to make their living on dissatisfaction, I suppose. Some who know him say the editor's a crackpot, a rabble-rouser."

Then you meet the brown, smallish, elderly man with the alert eyes, and the tall, reticent, very dark man with an inquiring look in which trust and distrust balance carefully, and the eager younger man whose coat is slightly frayed around the edges, and the chic young woman who wears her hat—in the best lady-executive *Harper's Bazaar* fashion—behind a desk piled high with papers in a cubbyhole of an office. And they are so willing to talk, so eager to discuss, so anxious to communicate. You cannot escape the feeling that any move of the white majority toward mediation would transform their "wildness" into civic pride; any recognition on the part of the white community of common problems equally shared would reduce their "rabble-rousing" to the staunchest conformity.

In Texas, the very tall, very thin, slightly crippled editor, wearing a banker's-grey flannel suit with a beautifully tailored white shirt and grey tie, talks fluently, for he was trained as a lawyer. "What's the status of the schools here?" A wry smile. "The *status quo*. We had a good many liberals here before the Supreme Court decision. But the Minute People scare the whites to death with phone calls and threats and letters and that sort of thing. The Negroes are used to it, I guess.

"Most of these white supremacy organizations, their menace is so much greater than their potentiality for harm. If people would stand up and defy them a few times, they'd die. But those people in this community who would normally be liberal, if vocal, are not vocal. The traditions, in both Negro and white groups, are still strong. In looking at this city, and I should think the whole South, you must recognize that you are moving on two levels: there are the laws, which have been struck down, one by one, and there is the other level, of tradition, which takes time. I'm considered very militant, and yet I repeat this all the way along: it takes time and individuals to change tradition.

"I have all sorts of experiences editing this paper, of course. The most common is accusation that I'm causing trouble. A few years ago a Negro soldier was found dead at a town east of here. A little later another one was found dead, too. I wrote this up, asked for a thorough investigation, all the usual things in one of these cases of violence. Well, one of the top men in that county called me to see him. When we met, he said, 'We've always had good relations here.'

" 'That's a good thing,' I said.

" 'We've always had these good relations, and this is the sort of thing that disturbs race relations.'

" 'What sort of thing?' I asked him.

" 'This story you've printed in your paper,' he answered.

" 'I agree. When a couple of soldiers are killed that does disturb good feelings.'

"Then some man who was with this big shot stood up. He's mad and he's red. 'You know what we mean. We're talking about your putting that story in your paper!' "

The editor smiles and shrugs. He taps a cigarette slowly on his desk. "Of course one of the interesting things that's happened since the 1954 segregation decision is our reclassification of the Southern liberals. I suppose it's hard to keep writing in the Northern publications with one hand and keep circulation up on your Southern paper with the other. The thing that's difficult for these, and lots of others, to remember is that the old liberal guy may be ready to give you something, but in the old segregated pattern. What we want is an end to the segregation and then we won't need so many 'gifts.'

"I think it's time now for everybody to stand up and be counted. You can't get across the river if you don't plunge into the water."

In Alabama you sit in the offices of another newspaper, and the editor talks about Autherine Lucy, and the differences between Atlanta and Birmingham, and the segregation which is so much more a part of his life than most whites can even imagine. You especially remember random sentences:

"Our editorial policy during the Miss Lucy troubles was this: the University of Alabama is a great institution and if it is to keep company with other great institutions, it must keep conduct with them, too.

"Atlanta and Birmingham are two of the South's most interesting cities—maybe because of their differences. Atlanta is pre-Civil War, Birmingham is post-Civil War. Atlanta is a commercial city and Birmingham is industrial. Until about 1926 Birmingham had no racial zoning laws. It's always had a more or less fluid population. Atlanta has been calmer on the race question. In Atlanta the white-collar worker gets more for his work; in Birmingham the blue-collar worker gets more. So you see, the Negro question isn't at all the same from one state, or even from one city to another in the South.

"Another field that's been tragically misunderstood is the purpose the NAACP has in lawsuits. For years the NAACP engaged in defense only, down here in the South, and many of the cases were cases of morals, and some were murder cases of Negro vs. white man. People thought the NAACP was only interested in winning acquittals for accused Negroes; what it really wanted was to be sure that due process of the law was followed. That was the fundamental, and that was what was frequently violated in any case involving a Negro against a white person.

"Times and strategies and needs change. Today I see a type of alignment among all the segregation groups that supplement one another. A thief does not commit bloodshed, but he commits a crime. The Ten Commandments say, 'Thou shalt not steal,' and 'Thou shalt not kill.' Both are equally violations of the law of God. The White Citizens' Councils say, 'We're for violations but not for bloodshed.' The Councils say they're an improvement over the KKK. Well, they're an improvement the same way a 1957 Ford is an improvement over a 1926 Ford: the function is the same, it's only the ride that's different."

In Oklahoma, you follow the square upright back of Roscoe Dunjee into a little back office of the building which houses his newspaper. Seventy-four years old, seeming more like fifty-four, harboring bright eyes behind his rimless spectacles, he wears a brown business suit and vest with a yellow and brown tie—and old-fashioned, slightly dusty, high black shoes. His iron-grey hair is short in a crew cut.

"Things are changing in the world I've known.   Things are improving. I was born in the horse-and-buggy days and now I'm in the atomic age. I can remember when there used to be a hundred and two hundred lynchings a year in the South. Now we make admiration over it if there's one.

"My father was born a slave. His master was related to old Governor Wise of Virginia, and he allowed Father to be a houseboy in Governor Wise's family, and it was while he was working in Richmond that father escaped. He was twenty-seven years old and he went to Canada by way of the Underground Railroad. When he was about thirty he came back to the states and went to school in Maine and then to Oberlin College, in Ohio. He went to Harpers Ferry, West Virginia, to be a Baptist minister and publish a newspaper. I was born there.

"In 1892 the American Baptist Missionary Society sent father to Oklahoma to organize Baptist work in the Territory. Ten years later he died. I was left with a mother, sister and brother to look after, an old broken-down farm with an eleven-hundred-dollar mortgage, and one priceless treasure. That was my father's collection of more than fifteen hundred books. Whatever intellectual development I obtained came from that library.

"I lived and worked on the farm until I was thirty-two years old. Then I had an opportunity to buy a little job printing plant. My newspaper came from that; it was launched in November, 1915. Now we have circulation into every state in the Union. The reason for this, I think, is our editorial policy. I've been involved in some of the most famous legal fights in Oklahoma, or the United States: the one declaring the right of Negroes to sit on Oklahoma juries, rulings against disfranchisement, the case outlawing residential segregation in Oklahoma. I've been at two lynching scenes, one in Texas, the other in a small town in Oklahoma where a Negro halfwit was killed. And I helped Ada Lois Sipuel in the fight for Negroes to attend the University of Oklahoma.

"To show you how reality doesn't match men's fears: when I took that girl down to the university for the first time, some folks said to me, 'Blood will flow in the streets.' When we started pressing for the public schools here to desegregate, some more said, 'Blood will flow in the streets.' Like I told someone only yesterday, both things have come about and no blood's flowing in the streets yet. It's not in the gutters yet, just in everybody's veins, where it ought to be."

Outside the office, the rhythmic pumping of an oil well is loud and steady, like a heartbeat. The rich odor of the oil fills the room where you sit.

"You know, I'm inspired with the thought that the whole solution to this problem of integration lies with the young people—of both races.

Many white Southerners don't realize we Negro Southerners have our troublesome inheritances from the past, too. There was my mother. I looked after her, and honored her and loved her until she died a few years ago, but my mother was a victim of the slave period. I remember the times when my mother would come from our home up town here, walk into my office and sit down.

" 'Now, Roscoe,' she'd say, 'I read your paper today. We mustn't talk about the white people that way. We know our metes and bounds. We know our place.'

"Well, I knew she had a sweet tooth and I'd go buy her a soda and carry her home. After mother's death I was sad, but I was released.

"Then there's another solution for the Negro: he must learn to depend upon some type of resource within his own racial structure to plant the mass of Negroes physically at the polling place on election day. You can see that Negro leaders like Martin Luther King in Montgomery are responsible for dynamiting the sensibilities and urging Negroes to claim and embrace their larger duties as citizens. Something must be done to get rid of the idea that a Negro who does nothing more than urge the everyday acceptance of his responsibilities is a dangerous individual.

"There's not a sheriff in a single political subdivision in Dixie who would for one minute protect a mob or a White Citizens' Council if he knew half the Negroes in his county voted, and that their votes were counted by the election officials when determination was made in selecting a sheriff."

All Negro editors are not as outspoken as these, of course. One in Mississippi recently suggested that "more Uncle Toms are the greatest need of the Southern Negro." He said that the new leadership of his race considers "any Negro is an 'Uncle Tom' who . . . seeks to maintain a friendly and respectful attitude toward the responsible white people of the community."

But although the debate over Uncle Tom and Booker T. Washington may flare from time to time, the common cause of all their newspapers is the Negro's forward surge.

There is no equally unifying theme binding the Southern white press together, unless it be intense awareness of the region as such. Groping forward or clutching at the past, editors and columnists and reporters have discovered that there is little so-called neutrality in the segregation controversy: "middle ground" seems in reality to be "no man's land."

Most striking proof of this is the fact that the no man's land often appears to be occupied today mainly by those who were once considered the advance trumpets of Southern change; troubled hearts now seem frequently gripped and frozen by the present situation. Listening to some of these people, the ones who have not completely altered their earlier views, the ones time has not bypassed, you feel that the message which burdens them most now is the one of communication between the South and the rest of the country.

"People up North just don't realize the depth of feeling down here on this question. Plenty of our folks are willing to close down the public schools tomorrow before they'll permit integration. And that would be the most unthinkable calamity that could befall the South—for everyone. They can't realize the brink of violence we're teetering on.

"And the Southerners don't understand yet that the Supreme Court isn't regulating their whole personal life when it says that discrimination in schools can't be legalized any longer. They don't know that the Court didn't say all Negroes suddenly have to go to white schools. It's almost unbelievable how little most of the ones who're doing the most talking have tried to comprehend what the Court said or meant.

"Both sections of this country misunderstand and are misunderstood, but it's a devil of a job trying to say so to either one. Up North you're a reactionary Dixiecrat and down here you're an outside agitator."

One of the most curious outgrowths of the lack of understanding lamented by this man is the recurrence of a familiar type of journalism. George Mitchell, former executive director of the Southern Regional Council in Atlanta, says, "My father used to tell me there were two types of Southern literature: first, tombstone literature. That was the genealogy we all love so well. Second, calling the North 'you're another.' "

In this time of dilemma, when any local criticism will probably be denounced as gross disloyalty, one way of proving that loyalty is to analyze other sections even more sharply. And for those who have no inclination toward self-criticism in the first place, the North's shortcomings provide a convenient scapegoat for editorial wrath.

The man who has executed the neatest, most acid and most widely publicized reporting on what he calls the "self-righteous North," is undoubtedly Grover C. Hall, Jr., editor of the Montgomery, Alabama, Advertiser. Piqued by Northern newsmen who flocked to his city and offices to cover the bus boycott, he needled them with some questions about racial affairs in their own cities and then launched a series of articles headlined, "Tell It Not in Gath, Publish It Not in the Streets of Askelon." (The quotation, of course, referred to David's efforts to keep the death of King Saul and Jonathan secret from the enemy Philistines.)

The theme of this series of reports and editorials was simple: "The race issue is not a Southern dilemma but a national problem. Discrimination is discrimination everywhere, not just when it happens under a Southern magnolia." The material was plentiful. "Only once in 125 years has *The New York Times* published a picture of a Negro bride on its society page, although a million Negroes live in the city."

Or, moving from New York out to Michigan, editor Hall made this comment: "*The Jackson Citizen-Patriot* is another of those long-range experts on Southern race difficulties.

"It has emitted a bleat about the report on Washington schools since the races were mixed. . . . It comes with poor grace that a Michigan newspaper should speak with such pompous dogmatism about remote conditions when Michigan is one of the more conspicuously prejudiced states. For example, its fourth largest city, Dearborn, permits not one single colored citizen to reside within its limits and virtually doubled its mayor's salary in a referendum some months ago for his success in excluding Negroes. Wyandotte, Royal Oak and Owosso have distinguished themselves by their devious, effective methods of excluding the Negro. Why does *The Citizen-Patriot* not first deal with these situations, all more conveniently located, before going into its pietistical shimmy over Southern conditions?"

In recognition of Hall's success in "putting the spotlight on the Yanks," as the Alabama legislature phrased it, that body awarded his newspaper an official commendation. Other papers throughout the South reprinted and praised his editorials.

Grover C. Hall, Sr., won a Pulitzer Prize for his fight against the Ku Klux Klan. His son started out to fight the Citizens' Councils—but since they have "eschewed violence" and are "out in the open" he finds "nothing to criticize." He is typical of several Deep South editors who have been fearless in their admissions that segregation is eventually doomed, and fearful in their assertions that the region is a monolithic mass unalterably opposed to integration.

The question posed by this seemingly incompatible combination concerns, of course, a newspaper's responsibility. If it believes that integration is inevitable, is the task then to labor for a transition where regional, racial and other animosities have been minimized rather than magnified? Is the surface unity of any group made more solid by being frequently told it is so? A twofold necessity seems to emerge: to convey to the North the tensions and resistances which must be recognized and dealt with in the South, and to help the South see that what the North has in racial relations that the South does not is a legal and generally official sanction of equality which it feels must be universal, even if imperfectly practiced, in a democracy.

The dislike of the "foreign" or "outside" press, which undergirds the "you're another" campaign is, of course, both widespread and well rooted in the past. Avery Craven, in *The Coming of the Civil War*, quotes from antebellum journals to demonstrate the bitter complaints against dependence on Northern books and magazines. " 'Why should Southern men patronize these mammoth literary journals in the North, whose tendency in abolitionism and morals [is] so often detestable, to the exclusion of their own excellent editorials?' The only answer any one could give was that the North had 'more business enterprise in everything from a rocking chair to a review.' That certainly was a poor excuse for the South to accept 'intellectual vassalage.' "

Today "The Paper Curtain" has come to be a familiar term among columnists and writers who feel that Northern presses are in a conspiracy not to publish their viewpoints favoring segregation. Yet many of the major periodicals have printed pro-segregation articles and statements by some of the leading men who hold these views, among them such magazines as *Atlantic*, *Harper's* and, on numerous occasions, *U.S. News and World Report*.

When critics of some of the large-circulation papers and magazines say, "Those editors ought to come down here and see what it's like, they don't know what they're talking about . . ." such critics assume that entire staffs are composed only of people from north of the Mason-Dixon line. They forget that many of the professionals in this, as in all other fields, are from the South and have had a personal contact with the region since birth. A suggestion of this was unwittingly revealed by a columnist in a Jackson, Mississippi, paper several months ago: "In close to a million miles traveled up and down and across these United States in the last fifteen years, I have met thousands of native Mississippians who are contributing their talents to the progress of their adopted states.

". . . In the field of journalism I have met Turner Catledge, managing editor of *The New York Times*; Charles Schneider, editor of the *San Francisco News*, and Donald Ferguson, editor of the *Milwaukee Journal*, all native-born Mississippians. Everywhere I go I meet former Mississippians, and if we could get them all back into our state, I believe the other forty-seven states would dry up for lack of brain power." It is interesting to speculate on just how many of those so-called "outsiders" writing about the South are really "insiders" who simply have a different perspective.

The role of the outside press in the South today is as important as it is difficult to define. The turmoil which occurred in midsummer 1955 in Hoxie, Arkansas, has been laid by many responsible people directly at the door of Life. It was after that magazine's picture story of "Integration at Work in Hoxie" that protest became loud and active.

"Of course Life didn't cause the protest," one Arkansas lawyer says, "but it triggered it. That's something difficult for lots of news people to admit—that the wrong story (or even the right story) at the wrong time can create situations within situations, like the boxes in a Chinese puzzle."

At one town in Texas the superintendent of schools said, "We're doing so well on our integration program this year that I believe we'll have it made at the end of the term. I hold my breath for fear the newspapers will hear about how well it's going and ruin everything by writing a story about it."

Outside papers and magazines, as well as those in the region, obviously bear a heavy burden of responsibility for many of the attitudes and actions in the South. When the assertion was made recently that some of the more notorious demagogues of the past had been aided in their rise to power by the region's press, someone quickly pointed out that many of the demagogues had been opposed by the region's editors. Indeed they were, but while the demagogues were denied the editorials they received the headlines. The situation seems much the same today with regard to Southern violence and defiance: it may be condemned on the inner pages but its story is on the front page.

"Of course," an editor replies. "We have to tell the news as it happens. And if it's big news it gets big headlines. That's why we're in business." The decisive point is: Who decides the relative "bigness" of the news?

A prominent Tennessee attorney summarizes: "Newspapers are commercial enterprises. They cater to human nature at its most obvious. Calamity makes news. Something constructive happens, it's buried back in local or religious events. But let a couple of kids get in a hassle in a marble game in a parochial school, and if one of them's colored and the other's white, it's a race riot."

These are the subtleties of handling issues and events which are not always apparent to casual readers. How are headlines and leading paragraphs phrased? How many Letters to the Editor are printed and which ones? And, at a moment when group action is ever more widely urged, when is a mass meeting a mass?

A woman visiting in Alabama gives you some insight on this. "When I first came here, I read in the paper about a big mass meeting the

Citizens' Council was going to have. So I went along to see what it was about. Well, their 'crowd' consisted of about fifty people, and I suspect some of them were like me, present more because of curiosity than sympathy."

In Texas a minister relates this incident: "Newspapers can cause a lot of trouble, the way they handle things. The trouble down at Mansfield, when they tried to integrate the school and the state troopers came in, got a big play every day, of course. But at the same time, the little town of Buda was integrating without any trouble. There was no news on that.

"In one city, a rock was thrown through the window of a white church recently, and it's interesting how that occurred. A woman called the newspaper and said the church was having an interracial meeting. 'Oh?' the editor said.

" 'Yes'—the woman was quite excited—'aren't you going to put it in the paper?'

" 'We're going to put that the Synod of the Presbyterian church is having its meeting.'

" 'Well, if you don't think an interracial meeting is news, what does it take? Would a fight over there make news?'

" 'Now, Madam, that's unfair. If there was a big fracas, of course——'
And the next night the stone was thrown through the church window."

These problems of objectivity in reporting do not, however, plague some of the new publications that have appeared in the South in the past few years. Citizens' Councils have sponsored their own booklets, newspapers and reprints, and the quality of paper and printing, and the sophistication of approach, have grown steadily more slick.

Representative of the crudest approach used by some branches of the Citizens' Councils was the four-page newspaper founded in Clinton and Knoxville, Tennessee, by John Kasper, after his successful efforts to stir up turmoil there. Vol. 1, No. 1, of *The Stars and Bars* carried headlines on these subjects: "Tennessee Stays Segregated, White Citizens' Councils' Proposals Save State from Twentieth Century Carpetbaggers"; "Spider-Web of Race Mongrelizers Are Spread Throughout Knoxville"; "Three Jews"; "Clare Booth Luce"; "Clinton Water Now Has Rat Poison (Fluorine)"; a list of recommended reading, including *Protocols of the Learned Elders of Zion*, *You and Segregation* by Herman Talmadge, and *Cult of Equality*; and a Chinese poem as translated by Ezra Pound.

The inflammatory photographs in much of the printed matter circulated through the South include numerous scenes of Negroes and whites dancing, eating or embracing. The combination is usually a white woman with a Negro man or men and the quality of the pictures is almost uniformly so poor that it is difficult to detect the features—only a blur of black or white. The writing is crude and repetitious and always comes back to the single overriding theme, usually termed "mongrelization."

"Our movement arises from a deep-seated belief in the diverse natures of animals and plants as established by the Creator. To blot one single distinction is to defy the highest plan of Providence. Nigras were not meant to be WHITE. The white race was not intended to be anything but white. We damn all race-mixers. We believe the race-mongrelizer is degenerate. . . . We are organized to root out every degenerate preacher, civic leader, P.T.A. mongrelizer, school board official, Commissioner, pinko professor, lawyer, or politician who uses his honorable office to destroy our people," says one Council's publication.

In February, 1957, the Citizens' Councils of America, with branches in ten states and headquarters in Greenwood, Mississippi, published in its official newspaper "A Manual for Southerners." This "Manual" was aimed at third- and fourth-graders. Written in the simple language of a textbook, there is a striking difference between this streamlined approach and the ruder fringe efforts. Its main points were:

"Negroes and white people do not go to the same places together. We live in different parts of town. And we are kind to each other. This is called our Southern Way of Life.

"Do you know that some people in our country want the Negroes to live with the white people? These people want us to be unhappy. . . . They want to make our country weak.

"God put the white people off by themselves. He put the yellow, red and black people by themselves. God wanted the white people to live alone. . . . White men built America. The Negro came to our country after the white man did. The white man has always been kind to the Negro. But the white and black people do not live together in the South. . . . Did you know our country will grow weak if we mix our races? It will."

Largely in response to the White Citizens' Councils and their publications, an amazing weekly newspaper came into existence in the town of Petal and its larger neighbor, Hattiesburg, Mississippi. Called *The Petal Paper*, this unpretentious one-man operation wields the weapon least used and most necessary in the South just now: a sense of humor.

At a time when loyalty has become loud and grim, religion has become safe and easy, and conformity is the key to success and a locker room at the country club, P. D. East refuses to be blind in his loyalty to the state and region he loves or comfortable in his religion. Above all, he will not conform to the codes of conduct set forth by most of his fellow Mississippians on the most explosive issue in that state: race.

"I'm a Mississippian born and bred. I'm white, Anglo-Saxon, male, over twenty-one—in fact, a proper candidate for the KKK—but somewhere, somehow, in the days while attending the free public schools, I got the notion that the Bill of Rights was about the greatest thing yet conceived by mankind."

A tall, husky, deep-voiced man of thirty-five, East's dark eyes and frequently troubled expression belie the humor of what he says and writes.

When he learned that a Council might be formed in his own county, he ran a full-page ad, decorated by a braying donkey: "Suh, here's sweet music! Yes, you too, can be Superior. Join the glorious Citizens Clan next Thursday night!

"Be Super-Superior. Compare These 10 Freedoms with other Old Fashioned Offers: Freedom to interpret the Constitution of the United States to your own personal advantage!

"Freedom to hunt 'Blackbirds' with no bag limit, and without fear of prosecution!

"Freedom to sit on a jury in behalf of your fellow members!

"Freedom from worry and fear if you happen to sit before a jury!

"Freedom to exercise a great Southern privilege: To Exert Economic Pressure!

"Freedom from fear of having economic pressure exerted against you!

"Freedom to yell 'Nigger' as much as you please without your conscience bothering you!

"Freedom to wonder who is pocketing the five dollars you pay to join!

"Freedom to take a profitable part in the South's fastest growing business: Bigotry!

"Freedom to be superior without Brain, Character, or Principle!

. . . "Remember: Not to join could mean you're a Nigger Lover! Remember! The Clan needs YOU—But most of all, YOU may need the Clan!"

After this, East was in full swing. As subscriptions fell off, he took on his state's Senator Jim Eastland ("'Our Gem'—a real gone, a real cool cat!"), various officers of the Mississippi Councils, and incidents of local harassment of Negroes by hoodlums. His *Petal Paper* carried photographs of two school buildings 3.6 miles apart—one built of brick with spacious windows, the other a little frame building of perhaps three rooms set on cinder blocks. "We have no prizes to offer if you guess which is for white and which is for colored. . . . This is a good example of 'Separate But Equal,' Mississippi style, that is."

He ran a "For Sale" advertisement offering "Quantity of used lumber desirable for making crosses. Kerosene furnished with orders of half dozen or more. . . . 'How to Build Your Own Cross Kit' free with all orders. Act today—or tonight!"

In the early days of the paper, East suggested that Mississippi should replace the Magnolia with the Crawfish as the state symbol. His reason? ". . . the crawfish is synonymous with our progress. Here in the State of Mississippi we are making progress, progress such as no state heretofore has known. Our sagacious leaders are showing us how; they are leading the way. Their aim is to protect us from those crawfish who haven't the intelligence to move backward.

". . . This state is on the threshold of its greatest movement—and, as we have said, there are some who want to travel uphill, straight ahead—and, of course, they must be dealt with before we can hoist the crawfish symbol."

As a member with poor standing and abundant confusion in the order of Magnolia-becoming-Crawfish, East asked for some advice from dues-paying Councilmen: "If you will bear with one who has betrayed the Magnolia, gentlemen, I would like to make a suggestion to the Council. It would be advantageous to all Southerners if we had a manual by which we could be governed while traveling out of state.

"It happened on Saturday, May 26th, leaving Memphis, Tennessee in an airplane. I was sitting on my side of the plane, reading a book, minding my own business, and I looked up and across the aisle from me sat a nigger in a sailor's uniform. I looked around me and saw two more. Naturally, this was a perplexing problem, being a born Mississippian. And here, gentlemen, I failed the cause of the Magnolia, and for that I am ashamed and humiliated. I knew what to do, of course, and that was to get up and get off that machine on which I was riding. I knew to do it, but I failed. I just couldn't being myself to take that first step, gentlemen—you see, it was 11,000 feet."

Obviously, local advertisements for a newspaper with such views and comments aren't a large problem because they are almost nonexistent. Finances nag at the edges but do not dominate the center of East's life. He is able to laugh about his own problems. "A fiscal year? I run on a fiscal week!"

When an important advertiser canceled his ads in The Petal Paper, East said, ". . . With the help of God, as long as we can keep our head above water, we will print what we please in this paper, in so long as we believe it to be right, fair, or true. And if the time should come that to keep our head above water means to submit to pressure of any kind, then we will go under without hesitation, and at least with a clear conscience.

"In the meantime, however, we have only six words to say to those who would attempt to put economic pressure on us: the words are:

"Go To Hell In a Bucket!"

Sociable, with a wife and a daughter five years old, East is particularly sad about the breakdown in some of the South's neighborliness during the present push, at least in his corner of the region, for complete conformity. "Down here in Mississippi, we're like the old Chinese custom: tie a stone around a suspect and throw him in the river. If he sinks he's innocent, if he rises he's guilty."

Hodding Carter, Pulitzer Prize-winning newspaperman located a couple of hundred miles across the state, and Mark Ethridge, eminent editor of The Louisville Courier-Journal, have both called portions of East's barrage "a masterpiece." William Faulkner, at Oxford, north of East's home in Hattiesburg, invited The Petal editor on an outing in his boat, and after more than two hours of silence under a blistering sun, asked, "Well, East, anybody put any dead cats on your front porch lately?"

A professor in Mississippi, who knows P. D. East, says, "No one here can quite understand him. I think that's why he hasn't been lynched or shut up yet. 'What's he getting out of this?' they ask. Not a thing they can see. Of course, what he's 'got' is his conscience and his independence. Right now they're pretty scarce items around here—the cost is too high for most people."

In Texas, the editor of a small weekly in the state capital of Austin has wielded influence much larger than his paper's small (less than ten thousand) circulation would suggest. "With subscribers in all the 254 counties of the state, thirty-three other states, and a number of foreign countries, we have been advised by the Texas Press Association that we have the third largest circulation of the state's several hundred weeklies," Ronnie Dugger says. Young and energetic, Dugger is enthusiastic about his work.

The Texas Observer follows its name. It observes closely the activities of lobbyists in the government, the growth of slums in the cities, and the powerful loan-shark business in various parts of the state. It has kept a particularly sharp eye on the progress of integration in Texas. During the spring, 1957, session of the Texas legislature, one of Dugger's editorials on pro-segregation legislation commented:

"We are now edified by a declaration from the august Texas House of Representatives in favor of local option on the American Constitution. The Sadler bill prohibiting integration unless local school district voters adopt it proceeds on the theory that if a township doesn't like the constitutional rule against cruel and unusual punishments, it can have an election and reinstate the stocks and the lash; if it doesn't like the constitutional guarantee of free speech, it can adopt an ordinance by public vote prohibiting criticism of the local Birdbrain Lovers' Society; if it doesn't like the constitutional rule that segregation deprives Negro students of equal opportunity, it can maintain segregation by local vote. This is so absurd that the only plausible explanation for its passage by almost 100 mentally coherent men and women is that they thought it was a pretty good joke."

In April, 1957, when a jury in East Texas released a white boy who had confessed to the wanton killing of a Negro two years earlier, Dugger's paper carried a full account of the trial, interviews with the relatives of the killer and the boy who was killed, and some hard-hitting words of anger concerning responsibility for crime and miscarriage of justice.

"Here was a hopped-up, senseless murder. . . . Here was the killer, a callow, prejudice-nursed white boy of 20. Here was the victim, a poorly-educated, hurting-nobody Negro boy of 16 who wrote down the four freedoms before he could spell 'freedom.' Here was East Texas, left anchor of the Deep South.

"So twelve solid, respectable, income-earning white East Texans, knowing the killer was the killer (admitting that), and knowing the victim was innocent of any provocation, turned the white boy loose, turned him free, an example to his buddies of how you can get away with murder. . . .

"Who was really guilty? The boy who pulled the trigger, but also the men who loaded his mind. The boy who handed him the rifle, but also the women who handed him a heritage of hate and oppression.

". . . Has the Longview press no moral responsibility for the incredible frame of mind of twelve East Texas jurors which condones such totally malicious offenses gainst Negro citizens? . . .

"Texas is half South, half Not South. Are you one or the other? You may put off deciding for a few years, but decide you must."

Writing of the decisions which faced the Texas legislature, as well as the press and citizenry of his state, Ronnie Dugger said, in reference to the accumulation of segregation bills:

"There rise and fall in this nation tides of fear. When they are high each man who believes in the heritage of his country must help defend it. First he must defend free speech, ever on the principle that 'error of opinion may be tolerated where reason is left free to combat it.' Then he must defend equal opportunity, ever on the principle that every man and woman and child in the nation is equal under it with every other. Now in Texas is such a time."

A friend in Austin says of boyish-looking Ronnie Dugger: "He's brought something necessary back to state politics: the gadfly sting. And he's brought something healthy to our Southern journalism: a voice to reassure us that there still is a minority people who have not succumbed to the majority who shout so loud on this race question."

The minority and the papers who speak for them reach from Texas to South Carolina. In increasing measure their aim seems to be to make their fellow newspapermen and their next-door neighbors realize their responsibilities as citizens of this country.

In upper South Carolina, after acts of terror and intimidation in neighboring towns and states, the editor of The Cheraw Chronicle wrote an epitaph for 1956 and a challenge for 1957. Both the epitaph and challenge bid fair to remain pertinent for several seasons to come.

"There is nothing the South needs so much on this last day of the dying year as to drink a cup of kindness for the auld lang syne of Southern hospitality, courtesy, and good humor, all of which have been endangered by the growing controversy over civil rights and desegregation." After recounting various incidents of terrorism, he went on to say, "Surely we are not so naïve as to believe all the blame is to be leveled against the thugs who actually perform the dirty work. Every state always has had and always will have hoodlums and fringe lunatics who are ready, willing and able to break the law. They in themselves are not significant.

"The really responsible elements are: (1) breakdown of law enforcement, especially in rural areas; (2) abdication by the average, law-abiding, good citizen of his social responsibilities; (3) irresponsible journalism by some segments of the press which inflame hatred and encourage criminal elements to believe they can commit their excesses without punishment— indeed with secret approval; (4) demagogic political leadership which has stirred public hysteria and then been content to follow it, rather than to lead courageously and wisely; (5) formation of organizations which, while decrying violence, create an atmosphere which spawns it.

". . . The question has been reduced to an absurd contest of wills—a matter of false pride and a misguided sense of 'independence.' What is lacking in the contest is a spirit of humility, forgiveness, consideration and human understanding. These are the qualities which responsible citizens must supply if we are to be freed from the pit of social anarchy which grows deeper every passing day."

Surely the most unique, witty and erudite newspaper on the Southern scene today is a bi-monthly, Charlotte, North Carolina publication bearing the improbable name of *The Carolina Israelite*. Its editor, Harry Golden, has lived in Charlotte for fifteen years. His vivid personal accounts of growing up on the East Side of New York City have added a new experience to the lives of his Southern readers, and his observations on his present life in the rapidly changing South have added new insights to his readers in New York and all parts of the country.

In fact, Golden's paper is strictly a one-man show. It carries no news, has no regular features, boasts no photographs—but it comments from a wide background of knowledge and experience on the news others have reported. Its unflagging characteristics are breadth of interest and depth of insight.

Typical subjects for discussion by Editor Golden include "The Dead Sea Scrolls," "Our Great Love for Mother" (ranging from Philip Wylie on "Mom" to Isis and Ishtar), Thomas Wolfe ("the very essence of the Jewish spirit . . . alienation . . . ambivalence . . . spiritual rebirth"), "Professor Toynbee—the Rich Man's Tom Watson," "Soup Greens and Caruso" (a rich memoir of some of the minutiae of life on the East Side); and Shakespeare and other favorite authors.

The Carolina Israelite can even carry a fresh discussion of cross-burning, and its editor's triumph, here as elsewhere, is in combining light with heat and generous portions of each.

"Recently there have been a dozen or more cross-burnings in the Carolinas and Georgia. Now let us analyze this for a moment. Here are five or six men who hold various positions in the community—clerk, salesman, truck driver. Average guys. Nice fellows. If you met any one of them in the smoking car, you would discuss the usual things—politics, your home town, your grandchildren. Then at night these same five or six men put on white robes, go into some field, or to the street where a Negro lives, or to the lawn of a high school principal, and they light up a cross and run away.

"Now, what is this all about? The principle, of course, is intimidation. You'd better watch your step on that Supreme Court decision, the burning cross seems to say to the white school principal, or you'd better stop your 'agitating,' it seems to say to the Negro on whose street the cross has been fired. But why the cross? Why the burning cross?

"This goes back thousands of years, long before the dawn of Christianity. The burning of the wheel or an effigy before Christianity was an attempt to express hate, and is known to historians as 'fire-hate.' Usually the fire was lit up during a plague or some disaster. The burning of an effigy was in effect the burning of the witch, the evil spirits. The burning of the cross in our times has been known as the 'need-fire . . .'

"The use of a religious symbol for a burning was roundly condemned by all Christian authorities since it was recognized that the burning of the cross was the same 'need-fire' of pre-Christian days. The burning of the cross is really a symbol of the burning of Jesus. Jesus spoke for Brotherhood and the revolt against this idea would be to burn him. Thus the clerk or the white collar worker sitting in the smoking car and who will burn a cross later that night is motivated by instincts which go far back into his origins, —the 'Need-fire,' the burning of God. The man has become ill at ease under the moral restraints imposed upon him by the Father, and so—he burns Him."

Harry Golden has been called "the most interesting example of personal journalism today," and "one of the most valuable citizens of this state" (by North Carolina's Governor Luther Hodges). Short and heavyset, with a face slightly resembling an owl and a flow of words and wisdom very much like a geyser, his views and columns are enjoyed by political men as different as Adlai Stevenson and Thomas Dewey, and literary men as different as Carl Sandburg and James Street (before his death).

But Golden's fertile brain and pen not only comment on news—they sometimes make it, too. During the summer of 1956, when the Governor of North Carolina, his special committee appointed to study the school integration question, and the state legislature were all meeting to pass a plan of maximum legality and minimum compliance with the Supreme Court decision on schools, Harry Golden appeared in the huge auditorium where the legislature was in session and in the clear light of a warm July morning in Raleigh presented a plan for desegregation in North Carolina.

"Those who love North Carolina will jump at the chance to share in the great responsibility now confronting our Governor and the members of the Special Session of the State Legislature, which will be asked to pass a series of Amendments to the State Constitution. The proposals submitted by Governor Hodges and his Advisory Education Committee, include the following: (A) The elimination of the compulsory attendance statute 'to prevent any child from being forced to attend a school with a child of another race.' (B) The establishment of Education Expense Grants 'for education in a private school in the case of a child assigned to a school attended by a child of another race,' and (C) A 'uniform system of local option whereby a majority vote of the folks in a school district may suspend or close a school if a situation becomes intolerable.'

"But suppose a Negro child applies for an Education Expense Grant and says he wants to go to the private school too? There are fourteen recent decisions of the Supreme Court involving the use of public funds, whereas there are only two recent decisions affecting the public schools.

"The Governor has said that critics of these proposals have not offered constructive advice or alternatives. Permit me therefore to offer a proposal for the consideration of the Special Session.

"The white and Negro races stand at the same grocery and supermarket counters, deposit money at the same bank-teller's window, pay taxes, light and phone bills to the same clerks, walk through the same dime and department stores, and stand at the same drugstore counter. It is only when the Negro sits down that the folks become panicky. Now since the South is not even thinking of restoring vertical racial segregation, I think my plan would fulfill our three requirements of the moment, (a) Comply with the Supreme Court decisions, (b) save our public schools and (c) maintain sitting-down segregation. Now here is the Golden Vertical Negro Plan. Instead of all these complicated and costly proposals, all the Special Session needs do is pass one small amendment to provide only desks in all our public schools, no seats.

"The desks should be the stand-up type, like the old-fashioned bookkeeping desk. Since no one in the South pays the slightest attention to a Vertical Negro, this would solve our problem completely. And it should be no great inconvenience for young people to stand up in their classrooms. In fact this may be a blessing in disguise. They are not learning to read, sitting down, anyway, perhaps standing up will help. . . . In every direction the Golden Vertical Negro Plan will save millions of dollars, and forever eliminate any danger to our public education system, upon which rests the destiny, the hopes, and the happiness of this society."

Naturally the legislature felt that taking the comfortable seats out of the school rooms was too great a step backward from progress, although they would adopt a plan which could put the public schools themselves out of commission. But many throughout the South and the nation enjoyed the tonic effect of Golden's wit and logic.

Not to be daunted by lack of political sanction, this editor presented another plan to the public in the spring of 1957, in the pages of his *Carolina Israelite.*

"While I still have faith in the Golden Vertical Negro Plan, . . . I have found it difficult to get a School Board to try it. . . . Now, however, I am on much firmer ground. This time I submitted my plan to a successful test, and I am ready to formally announce—the Golden Out-of-Order Plan.

"I tried my Plan in a city of North Carolina where the Negroes represent thirty-nine per cent of the population.

"I prevailed upon the manager of a department store to shut the water off in his 'white' water fountain and put up a sign, 'Out-of-Order.' For the first day or two the 'whites' were hesitant, but little by little they began to drink out of the water fountain belonging to the 'coloreds';—and by the end of the third week everybody was drinking the 'segregated' water; with not a single, solitary complaint to date.

"I believe the test is of such sociological significance that the Governor should appoint a special committee of two members of the House and two Senators to investigate the Golden Out-of-Order Plan. We kept daily reports on the use of the unsegregated water fountain which should be of great value to this committee. This may be the answer to the necessary uplifting of the 'white morale.' It is possible that the 'whites' may accept desegregation if they were assured that the segregated facilities still exist, albeit, 'Out-of-Order.'

"As I see it now the key to my plan is to keep the 'Out-of-Order' sign up for at least two years. We must do this thing gradually."

Just as there is no one South, so there is certainly no one editorial voice which speaks for the many Souths today. But in traveling over the region, reading and talking and listening, you experience a growing conviction that the little dailies, along with the big ones, the little local weeklies, must eventually provide some of the leadership where it counts most in the long haul out of crisis: at the local level.

An example comes readily to mind: Buford Boone, young publisher of the *Tuscaloosa* [Alabama] *News.* When he was awarded a Pulitzer Prize in the spring of 1957, the citation noted his "fearless and reasoned editorials in a community inflamed by a segregation issue."

A co-worker on his paper tells you: "Buford Boone is quite a man. I've known him several years now, worked for him and with him, and he's about the bravest person I ever met. He'll stick by what he believes in. He came from Georgia. When he was growing up, he lived and worked on a farm, and that's real labor, you know. Later he was with the FBI for about four years. You get an unusual training in that service, you know. I guess it's all stood him in good stead lately."

During the three days early in 1956 when the campus of the University of Alabama and the town of Tuscaloosa were rocked by mob demonstrations protesting the admittance of a Negro student, Autherine Lucy, to the school, Buford Boone's newspaper carried the ugly story and pictures, and the bare recounting of events and the on-the-spot photographs were eloquent. But Boone added his own concerned call for some firm responsibility and authority, and action which could anticipate something besides abdication. Monday the riots reached their climax. ("Make no mistake of it, the mob here would have killed the girl if it could have gotten its hands on her," Boone says.) Then the Negro girl was suspended from the university and with their demand satisfied, the rioters went home.

On Tuesday Boone said to his fellow townsmen, from the front page of the News: "What a Price for Peace! . . .

"As matters now stand, the University administration and trustees have knuckled under to the pressures and desires of a mob. What is to keep the same mob, if uncontrolled again, from taking over in any other field where it decides to impose its wishes? Apparently nothing.

"What is the answer to a mob? We think that is clear. It lies in firm, decisive action. It lies in the use of whatever force is necessary to restrain and subdue anyone who is violating the law.

"Not a single University student has been arrested on the campus and that is no indictment against the men in uniform, but against higher levels which failed to give them clean-cut authority to go along with responsibility. . . .

"We have a breakdown of law and order, an abject surrender to what is expedient rather than a courageous stand for what is right.

"Yes, there's peace on the University campus this morning. But what a price has been paid for it!"

A little later that month, when the New York Herald Tribune asked Boone for his comments on segregation and the situation in Alabama, he set them down plainly for the Tribune's readers in New York and his own News readers in Tuscaloosa.

". . . The thinking people of the South will pay the price of maintaining respect for law, and for bringing themselves to face the realities of the present. For white Southerners, that price is an agonizing slipping away of some customs and habits as comfortable as old garments. For Negro Southerners, the price is calmness, continued patience and a measure of satisfaction in the ever-so-slow implementation of rights that are theirs as American citizens.

"But white Southerners will not submit to force and intimidation, nor to all-the-way-at-once changes in a way of life. It is silly, in some people's minds, to revere a cow. But the Hindus do. It may not be sensible, intelligent, nor American in the opinions of many for Southerners to think as we do about segregation.

"However, in understanding the problem, it is necessary to recognize a condition that exists, whether right or wrong. For sentiment has coalesced and congealed, over the generations and decades, into a condition. . . .

"Personally, I know that change is here. I am neither ashamed of the past, afraid of the present, nor despondent about the future. I believe law and order will emerge triumphant. And if it doesn't, all is lost."

During that summer, Boone made an appeal to the university and town. First, he asked, "Are we preparing ourselves for problems that are sure to come, or are we just waiting for things to happen and then muddle through with the initiative being left by default in the hands of whatever rabble-rouser should appear?"

Then he proposed a Council of Reason, at which men might work to solve, rather than compound, a few of the human relationship problems bristling all over the South. "A wonderful opportunity now waits for a Council of Reason to work for intelligent, sensible, realistic approaches to these problems."

Then, in January, 1957, the *Tuscaloosa News* publisher was asked to speak at a meeting of the local White Citizens' Council. A friend tells you, "The night he spoke to them, it was all rigged. I couldn't go with him, even as a friend, for it would have looked as if I went as a bodyguard, so all I could do was sit home and see it on television.

"Buford knew what he was getting into, but he thought he ought to go down and tell them what he thought. It was time for somebody to speak out, and he had the opportunity to talk where it might do some good. At least it wouldn't be like talking at some of these meetings where you're baptizing people who are already wet. He'd been asked to speak for thirty minutes; he used twenty-nine. They had said he would be the only speaker of the evening and that the rest of the program would be given over to questions and discussion. But they had roped in this Council member from Arkansas who got up after Buford and talked for over an hour.

"Of course the WCCs say they're all for law and order, no violence. Well, Buford laid it to them that night. He put it on the line: 'What are you going to do when another nigra girl enrolls at the University?' And you could hear, even over the television, shouts from the audience, 'Kill her. Run her off!' "

Boone did not consider himself a hero or a martyr for adopting and discussing a viewpoint different from many of his fellow Alabamians. He simply considered it time for responsible people to adopt a "positive approach to the inevitable."

The following Sunday, Boone published portions of his own talk and that of his fellow speaker's. The parallel, seeing the two talks in print, was deadly. The Council's representative said, in part:

"You know, my friends, this thing tonight is not a small question, it's not the question of whether or not a few snot-nosed nigger younguns will attend the schools with your grandchildren or whether or not a few impudent niggers will ride on the front seat of a bus. Our question that we are confronted with in Alabama tonight is whether or not Christian civilization shall continue to exist on earth or whether or not we shall be enslaved in the Communist conspiracy. . . .

"I, too, am a sort of jack-leg newspaperman. I have been in the habit, I reckon you'd call it. My friends, during the past four years, and particularly after the infamous Supreme Court decision, I have rapidly become ashamed of my profession, trade, habit or what not. . . .

"Now we've got two other messes of trash that have caused us more trouble even than the newspapermen. We've got, I guess, the worst offenders, probably the people that have hurt us the most in the South than any other one people . . . and that is our top-water preacher . . . And then the next one that have hurt you more than anyone else and will hurt us more in the future than all the rest of them put together is the so-called intelligent educator. . . ."

The *Tuscaloosa News* and its staff waited, in the days after Boone's talk to the Council, for the blow at their most vulnerable spot: the paper's circulation. In the following week, they had eight canceled subscriptions.

A soft-spoken man who does not advocate total integration of the public schools in Alabama at this moment, who will give no countenance to defiance of the Supreme Court, who calls for a Council of Reason where communication may be established and progress begun—Buford Boone has earned his Pulitzer Prize and an even more valuable award: the respect of his readers.

These, then, are some of the less widely known newspapers in the South; special pleaders, some of them, for white supremacy or racial tolerance; embattled defenders of the *status quo* or prophets of constructive change. There are many others—the big dailies who deal forthrightly with or look the other way on racial problems, the growing weeklies who must balance the pressures of the community with the pressures of history, the monthlies who are a "wood's-colt" combination of newspaper and magazine.

In the early 1940's, Lillian Smith, who was subsequently to become famous as an author, published from her home in Clayton, Georgia, a magazine first called *North Georgia Review*, and then *South Today*. Concerned with the needs of Southern people of every color, it might be called a forerunner of the present *New South*, published by the Southern Regional Council in Atlanta, and *The Southern Patriot*, issued by the Southern Conference Educational Fund in New Orleans.

Without local precedent, however, is the *Southern School News*, a nonprofit monthly published by the Southern Education Reporting Service and financed by the Ford Foundation. Its goal is "accurate unbiased information" on the subject of school segregation-integration. Its executive director, Don Shoemaker, tells his staff of writers: "We don't want any adjectives."

In each of the eighteen states covered by its detailed accounts on latest developments in desegregation, *Southern School News* has a reporter who collects the facts and figures for his state, distills them into a report which is included in the monthly paper. In its headquarters at Nashville, Tennessee, Southern Education Reporting Service maintains a library whose present files include over fifty-five thousand newspaper articles and more than one thousand magazine articles, speeches, special studies and texts of legal documents relating to segregation. Queries come to the service from writers, government officials, educators, interested citizens, in all parts of the United States and many foreign countries.

By the end of 1956, Shoemaker, who had been an editor in the South for twenty years before accepting the directorship of SERS, was able to comment that Southern newspapers were improving in their objective approach to the subject of segregation. He found that the South's thirty-eight biggest dailies (all but a dozen of which editorially defend segregation) are now playing desegregation stories "straight down the line. . . . The feeling at first was that any news treatment of the problem would be resented by readers, because it was such a highly touchy subject. Now newspapers have found readers don't resent it, and use their own staffs to cover the problem instead of relying on the news services. There is more reporting in depth."

In discussing a fellow North Carolina newspaper writer, Harry Golden once said that he and Nell Battle Lewis, a columnist for the Raleigh *News and Observer*, took directly opposite views on the Supreme Court decision, but what they had in common was "expressed brilliantly by the eminent scholar, Carl F. Wittke, of Western Reserve University: 'Flexibility has kept our democracy strong and made it stable. We need free enterprise in business and industry, and we need free enterprise in ideas about government and its functions. We need a free and independent press, and in an era of mass production more William Allen Whites to get off their chest what they really think . . . the essence of all great religions is mercy, and all the virtues are enwrapped in compassion for one's fellow man and devotion to the beloved community.' Nell Battle Lewis and I stand together on Dean Wittke's principle of 'beloved community' and, in the last analysis, this is what will bring brotherhood to our region and a better life for all its people."

12　The Ham and the Corn

"Leadership is what the South has lacked during this interval since the Supreme Court decision," a newspaper editor tells you. He lights a cigarette and clasps his hands behind his head, tilting back in his big green swivel chair. "Right after the decision there was a void—no one seemed to know just what to say or do. Church men, the school people, the business community—everyone sort of froze. Then the politicians began to move in, and the closer they got, the more they saw that this was for them.

"After all, it had been growing more unpopular for a long time down here to win elections by hollering 'nigger.' Pitchfork Ben Tillman and Vardaman, and even Bilbo, have been dead a good little while. Some of the boys had even come to the point where they were discussing issues right on through their campaigns. But the Supreme Court made all that unneccessary. Their decision on school segregation opened the hunting season again. It put new life back in all the old bogeymen some of us thought were dead and buried. Now we've got the hollering again—they're slicing the ham and serving the corn once more, even if it is a hybrid, Improved, De Luxe corn this time.

"So what we have now is not leadership, but followship. And the art of followship is to make it seem like you've got your feet on the ground and are going somewhere, when actually you've got your ear to the ground and are standing still."

The political aspects of the racial picture in the South have managed to embrace, and frequently absorb, most of the other related issues.

Press-room, pulpit, playground, payroll window: the politicians have made segregation an issue everywhere. Obviously the organizations to preserve and extend segregation were founded with many political overtones, and their influence in the Black Belt states has increased with their membership. One of their chief aims has been to keep the so-called Border States, where councils and committees have proved much less popular and potent, "in line," and at the same time persuade the North

220

to leave settlement of the segregation issue to Southern, rather than national, politics. Senator James Eastland has mourned the fact that those states between the segregated South and the integrated North and Midwest have what he terms "weak-kneed political leaders," for he insists that "if we can win the Border States, I am confident of the outcome. The determination of the South has caused the people of the North to stop and think. Now they say, 'We had better go slowly.' "

Once again, as a reporter whose beat is the Southern region says grudgingly, "The South is winning that same old poker game. The North holds all the cards, but they're being outbluffed. You wait and you'll see. When the chips are down, that's when the Southern politicians stand pat and win the pot: it takes guts and know-how, but they've got both."

In political ability and experience, the South has much to offer the rest of the union. It should be said at once that it is a mistake to assume because there has been loud, long shouting about the Negro, that the South is a monolithic wasteland of medieval thought. There is a tradition of statesmanship in the South which has sometimes been lost sight of amid the more colorful language and antics of the perennial demagogues. (In all sincerity, one suave and able segregation leader you visit can have the motto on his wall: "The politician thinks of the next election. A statesman thinks of the next generation.")

With the paradox you encounter so frequently in the South, there is here, still, the old-fashioned respect for law as a profession, and disregard for it as a means of control; there is the most deep-seated reaction and the most dedicated liberalism. (A newcomer from California says: "I used to think, out there, that there couldn't be any real liberals in the South. Now I'm beginning to believe the best liberals are here. They're the ones who will stick. They've had it. They've gone from something to something—haven't just drifted.")

Continuing the paradox, although the South has been frequently provincial nationally, it has also had a wide international outlook. This, of course, stems in part from the fact that much of the South's economy, because of cotton, was for a long while oriented to Europe. But when Herman Talmadge was elected Senator from Georgia in the 1956 campaign, he was the first Southerner to win a seat in the Senate on a platform of isolationism since Reconstruction days. Those Southern senators and representatives who have often been a thorn-in-the-flesh of both Democratic and Republican administrations on national issues, and certainly on Civil Rights matters, have often been those very men who helped in the establishment of international policy.

There is no discounting Southern "savvy" in that most exclusive of all clubs, the Senate. The Southerners early sized up and seized upon the values of seniority. They have received and administered committee chairmanships zealously. In fact, it might be said that although the South lost the War of Secession at Appomattox it won the War of Succession in Washington.

Perhaps one reason for this knack at winning in the in-fighting is the fact that Southerners have been well trained in factional disputes. Since there has been only one dominant party in the region for as long as its voters can remember, until 1952 and 1956 seemed to shake the structure somewhat—at least on the national selection level—campaigning has often been a matter of personalities rather than issues, with the Democratic primary the decisive battleground.

Then, too, the "Ciceronians," as one man says, "have a heritage of power. They've been in control for a long time now. They're adept in using men and issues; they wear leadership easily. And in this race crisis, they're against violence and ugly talk. People like John Kasper and some of the KKK Kleagles embarrass them. They've held the reins for years and they simply assume that they are going to find a way to remain in power for years to come."

Before the Civil War the Black Belt stamped its image on the national consciousness as The South—unified, solid, indestructible, and achieved this rather remarkable feat mainly through political means. The voices of its powerful men were accepted as speaking for all Southerners, and because many of them were able men—whether or not they were always worthy ones—they were convincing to themselves, their electorate and the North.

War came, and many Southerners were not for secession; parts of the region rebelled against the Confederacy and sent men to the Federal army—but this group of Deep South leaders continued to present the image to the outside world intact. Populism flourished and withered, progressivism had its day, industry and mechanization on the farms gradually changed life throughout the South—but outsiders, and many within the region, as well, continued to believe in a completely homogeneous place and people. And that is true because of one fact that is far less simple than it would appear to be at first glance, even when considered only from a standpoint of politics: the important and pervading presence of the Negro. And so we come in full circle in our discussion.

In 1949, V. O. Key, Jr., concluding his study, *Southern Politics*, certainly a landmark in its field, said, "Until greater emancipation of the white from the Negro is achieved, the southern political and economic system will labor under formidable handicaps. The race issue broadly defined thus must be considered as the number one problem on the southern agenda. Lacking a solution for it, all else fails."

Then came the Supreme Court decision, and the possibility of white and Negro emancipation from mutual bondage—and from the constant, overriding, self-consuming preoccupation with race. Probably it was naïve, in Southerners and Northerners alike, not to have foreseen that before this preoccupation could be overcome, or at least lessened, it might be expected to stage a fierce retaliation. There are too many investments in the present racial patterns for them to be yielded without protest. There are not only the obvious investments of white economics and politics, but subtler ones of prestige and personality, too. So there has been a resurgence of much of the old racism, sometimes wearing its same old robes, more often boasting a new custom-made tailoring—but always vocal and often political in inspiration.

In May, 1956, Jack O'Dowd, then editor of the Florence, South Carolina, Morning News, said in a talk to some fellow citizens of his state: "A few hours after the Supreme Court announced its decision on that May 17, the cry went up from South Carolina and Georgia capitols, and from Southern Senate and Congressional offices in Washington —'We will never consent. We will resist to the end. We will never mix. The Supreme Court cannot force us to desegregate.' . . .

"I am not as interested in starting a movement toward compliance with the court as I am in restraining those who threaten absolute noncompliance with the court or the accepted establishments of society. I argue for the right of reasonable dissent. Because of the hanging back of decent men of character, it is almost impossible to describe the Supreme Court as a legal body with a voice of authority. Our Southland is becoming a place where non-concurrence with the established orthodoxy is cause for rejection and social ostracism. . . ."

(As sad but documentary proof of his words, Editor O'Dowd has been with the Chicago Sun-Times rather than the Florence Morning News for well over a year now.)

In March, 1957, an observer of the Georgia Legislature said, "The session has been dominated by the single obsession that has gripped all Georgia political life since May 17, 1954: race. So constant has the leadership been in its manipulation of the segregation issue that a sizeable number of important issues have been allowed to drift into the background, to the misfortune of the urban citizenry and the gratification of the ruling clique."

To many Southerners, this was perhaps the most frustrating of all aspects of the segregation debate, that as it began in a rush of emotion, it snowballed under its own self-destructive momentum until its avalanche now threatens to overwhelm much that is constructive and necessary to the South. The region must face many problems similar to those of the rest of this country—economic lags, agricultural imbalances, political non-participation, natural-resource conservation, urban improvement, all the deep and thorny problems of a better quality of education for ever-increasing quantities of students, and a host of related matters—but these have been shuttled aside, or given only halfhearted attention, while the "old Ciceronians" turned their mental powers and political prowess to attacks on the Supreme Court, legal evasions, popularization of a problem that will never be easily solved but has always been easily exploited.

"We've the work of the world to do, man's work," a white-haired gentleman of the South's old aristocracy tells you, "and here we are wasting our time debating whether we shall do that work together or separately.

"The South once produced the leaders of this nation—and don't let anyone ever tell you that Madison and such men were for states defying the Supreme Court; Madison gave Andy Jackson—and they were both just as Southern, mind you, as Calhoun—the mental and moral backing for Jackson's forcible resistance to nullification. We can give our nation leadership again—national, not just regional, leadership—but first we've got to rid ourselves of this burden of race. A man or a society with a single obsession can't develop properly. I'm sick of seeing the South betray itself, and hand over its future to those who betray it loudest!"

Somewhere between this man's accusation of betrayal and the news-paperman's term "followship" runs the broad path many politicians in the South have chosen. Some are cynically expedient in their use of segregation as a weapon and a tool. Some are sincerely dedicated to segregation as a method of keeping separate two races they consider totally incompatible. Probably the majority vacillate somewhere between these two viewpoints, wrestle with logic and ideals as seldom as possible, and convince themselves with varying degrees of success of their good fortune that the way of expediency is also the way of virtue in the matter of segregation. And yet—for all the boldness and certainty of their public façade, you cannot talk long with the political leaders of this region, from courthouse steps to legislative halls to administrative mansions, without becoming increasingly aware of a certain troubled fearfulness which permeates the atmosphere.

"We'll never have integration in my state," a Southern congressman flatly asserts, "not in a hundred years." There is some difference between "never" and "a hundred years," and despite his self-confidence the sudden grave thoughtfulness of the congressman's countenance indicates he is aware of the difference.

You sit at dinner in a Southern governor's dining room and bask in the pleasant graciousness which can make the sparkle of lights on state chandelier and crystal and damask seem warm and friendly—until The Subject is mentioned, and there is a moment of silence. Then, like a clear pool suddenly disturbed and muddied by a random pebble, the frown which creases the governor's forehead clouds the atmosphere to the farthest corners of the room. You know that he has said to others, older acquaintances, before you, "I have advocated such segregation legislation as our state has passed for one reason: to avoid bloodshed. We could have had violence, I'm convinced, over this thing, but our action averted it."

Now he tells you: "We've been set back at least ten years by this decision. There's a stiffening of attitude in both the white and Negro community. In my opinion it'll take a decade, or longer, to build the relationships back up again. Very early we called the Negroes in, gave them the broad background, told them what we had in mind on all this situation: they wouldn't meet with us again. The sad part about all this is the number of Negro schools and colleges we have, and yet the more you do, the worse it makes the dilemma."

And you know that you will never know—and worse, this man himself, this leader of capability and charm, will probably never know—precisely what his innermost convictions are on this basic issue of our place and time.

His dining room seems private and well ordered and secure, with its black waiters and white guests and the silver in its proper places. And yet there is a sensation as of people waiting just beyond the folding doors, of eyes staring in from the darkness through the tall windows. Always—out there—beyond the caucus room and the plush office—the people wait. Do they lead the politicians, or do the politicians lead them? This central question and balance of democracy is nowhere more fundamental than in the South in this moment of crisis.

You may seek the answer in one of the Southern legislatures at the special session convened to give that particular state direction in its response to the Supreme Court decision. The morning is already warm, foretelling the heat of the day yet to come, as you wait for the legislators and the members of the public who will discuss pro and con the pending bills designed to preserve segregated schools, without ever stating that purpose. Two women wait near the door, too; one an upcountry rural woman, the other a resident of the capital. Their hair, still damp from the hasty comb of water to hold it in place, is drawn back from their faces, and their cotton dresses are freshly starched.

"Well, the niggers were down here yesterday strutting their stuff before the lawmakers, weren't they?" the hill woman asks you, her face less belligerent than her words. "Don't it make you mad to see niggers uppity like that? But I reckon no matter what they do, we've got to have public schools. I sure hope this legislature here won't do anything to hinder them. I'd rather sit by a nigger all day than have no public schools!" (How often her words come to mind during the rest of the day, during months to follow, when "leaders" assure you and each other that "all the people" are perfectly ready to "close down the schools" before they will send their children to integrated classes. There are places where you believe this may be true, but your certainty wavers as you remember this woman's words when she was confronted with the necessity to choose.)

Inside the great room where the hearings will be held, the legislators appear fresh and casual in seersucker and dacron and Palm Beach suits. They read the morning papers, talk with each other briefly, scan the room with hawk-sharp, knowing eyes. Occasionally an obvious newcomer to the group slaps an old-timer gingerly on the arm, within a limited range of familiarity. One white-haired man in a polka-dot bow tie and navy blue suit appears aloof from the ebb and flow around him as he concentrates on the speaker's stand at the front of the hall.

Then there is the group of not-quite-young men who circulate around the auditorium, clean-shaven, still trim in their summer suits, with only the jowls and the folds under their eyes beginning to sag ever so slightly, and the waistline under their belts beginning to bulge ever so faintly. Their cheeks are pink from steam packs and already tanned from weekends at the beach; they have good clothes and hard eyes and slack mouths. There is something fearful and fearsome about them. These are the young old men who have payments to meet on the house that is a little too large, the car that was a fraction too costly, college and the braces for teen-age teeth just around the corner. They cannot afford unpleasantness at dinner parties, snubs at the men's luncheon clubs on Mondays or Thursdays or in the locker room on Saturday afternoons.

There are the country professionals, already in their shirt sleeves, who thrive on campaigns and controversy, whose ambitions do not extend beyond these halls and the prestige they enjoy in the villages "back home." It is their talent to listen and weigh and trade shrewdly, separate the "fuzzy-minded dreamers" from the "hardheaded realists." They have been around a long time, and they know the breaking point between a man's values and his price.

Under a large sign, "No Smoking, City Ordinance," the lawmakers sit and smoke steadily. Their conversation flows around you:

"Saw old Bob over at the hotel this morning. Didn't have a chance to get with him on that proposition we were talking about last night; he was busier than a nigger writing a check."

"How are the folks up your way on these bills? Over in my county there's right much sentiment for them."

"Everything's under control."

The wink, the nod, the sentence out of one corner of the mouth— these are the currencies of exchange. The public statements begin.

A minister comes to the loud-speaker: "God created the races seggregated. Those who say we should integrate should tell it to the birds. They segregate. Should we interfere with God's plan?"

A young man speaking "as a private citizen": "After socializing in school, these little children will be color blind. They tell us children are not prejudiced. They aren't prejudiced against lightning and other dangerous things, either. That's why we teach them."

"A Jew," someone behind you whispers as the next man walks to the microphone. His companion replies, "The South treats a Jew better than any other part of the country." Most of the legislators know this well-informed, conscientious citizen and several who have been reading the morning papers lay them aside to listen as he talks.

"To enact laws and hope they will not be used perhaps confesses that they contain certain dangers. 'Race' in these bills before us is a dangerous concept. Can it be extended to include a Chinese or Cuban family who might move into town; could it mean a private school for Italians? . . . In our state we have no line of communication between white and Negro people today. Even back in the pioneer days we had negotiations with the Indians, held conferences with their chiefs. We have not conferred with the Negro chiefs. . . . We must realize that it is impossible for a country to grow and prosper where one-third of the people are under-privileged."

The next man is stout and genial. He wears suspenders and a sober black suit. "When they brought the green slaves in from Africa back during the days of the slave trade, they'd saved a lot of them from eating each other. The first moment's security the niggers ever had from neighbors' raids and from the wild animals of the jungle and from hunger, was when they reached these shores."

The state attorney general moves about the floor conferring with some of the legislators, whispering briefly with some of the people who are appearing at the hearing.

A businesslike, able lawyer addresses himself to the issues at stake, and comments on a previous speaker, "I sat here yesterday with amazement and heard a professor from one of our law schools say that the only course we could follow was spineless acquiescence, what we needed was 'good leadership.' Leadership to lead us where? Come down, come down, professor, out of your ivory tower and learn of the grass roots. If you want to preserve the school system, you'd better find out how to do it and preserve segregation. . . . The people of this state have always resisted aggression, whether heralded by the rattle of drums or the soft swish of judicial robes."

A handsome attorney in an immaculate white suit and smart bow tie: "I concur with the foundation stone of the plan we have proposed: that Negroes prefer to associate with those of their own race. Given a fair chance, natural selection of their own race will result in separation in the schools in not less than ninety-nine per cent of the cases. . . . I don't think it's right to compel social contacts. There is nothing quite so dangerous in the human mind as the feeling of helplessness, of coercion. We're recommending legislation we hope will not be used, we expect will not be used. It is an escape valve. . . ."

Late in the afternoon, after the legislators have adjourned the public hearings, you walk back down the street with a young man who has attended both days of the session. "It makes you sick to hear them say one thing and do another," he mourns, with a lack of sophistication and an intensity of feeling that belie his infrequent contacts with the political world. "The same people who spent hours telling how much they hallowed education were the first ones to deride and attack a university professor who had the intelligence and character to stand up and tell them their proposals were unconstitutional and wrong; and their attack wasn't against what he said as much as against the fact that he was a professor. Never has our latent pioneer contempt for learning been more obvious than at these hearings, when people were furious because a teacher, a professor, would dare contradict them. 'We love schools,' they say in one breath, and 'beware the ivory towers,' they say with the next breath.

"Then, of course, the point kept crossing my mind, *if the Negroes* are all so happy, and everyone's so contented, no whites in the state want integration, no Negroes in the state want integration, why pass laws about it? Of course the whole session has a false front, anyway. Passage of the plan was sewed up weeks ago in private conferences all over the state. This just gave anyone who felt real strong about schools or race a chance to come and feel like he'd had his say."

Later, in the elevator of the hotel not far from the capitol, a plump, amused-looking man in a wilted shirt says to another plump, wilted man, "These legislators are getting religion on this thing now. Not only here, everywhere. They're saying their speeches, making some laws, scattering a little vote-bait for the varmints."

Thus Southern legislatures have met and are meeting in sessions characterized by varying degrees of intensity on the segregation issue. South Carolina anticipated the Supreme Court decision almost two years before it was handed down when, in November, 1952, the voters approved a measure, submitted by the General Assembly, to make possible the abolition of public schools in their state.

In 1953, Georgia's legislature adopted the "private school amendment" which allowed for grants from state or local funds to be used for individual educational purposes. Following the 1954 decision, these and even more specific measures providing for closing of public schools, removal of compulsory-attendance laws, private-tuition payments and pupil assignment were passed in state after state.

In referring to the segregation laws passed by the 1956 Georgia General Assembly, Georgia's Attorney General, Eugene Cook, said, "We might as well be candid. Most of these laws will be stricken down by the Courts in due course."

Perhaps one of the most surprising features to many people, in the developing political antagonism to the Supreme Court decision, has been the total-segregation attitude of Virginia. Governor Stanley made an early, rather mild statement suggesting acquiescence to the country's foremost legal body, but a situation soon developed in which every political leader in Virginia seemed to be trying to outdo the other in advocating segregation. Illustrative of how undeviating the opposition to integration came to be in Virginia was this incident: when State Attorney General J. Lindsay Almond, Jr., called for a special session of the legislature in the summer of 1956, saying he was at the end of his rope and needed a legal "weapon" to fight NAACP lawsuits, E. B. Moore, speaker of the Virginia House of Delegates, demanded, "I ask the attorney general to inform the people of Virginia of the exact nature of this 'weapon,' and whether as representing Virginia, he proposes to fight for a continuance of segregated schools for the school term beginning in September, 1956, or does he desire legislation that would permit any form of integration for this coming school year?"

Attorney General Almond replied, "I must say that I am shocked at the unwarranted and unjustified attack Mr. Moore has seen fit to make upon me. For more than five years, I have fought with my back to the wall in an effort to save the public school system of Virginia from destruction. In this fight I have exhausted every available legal defense.

"Throughout this long and heartbreaking struggle, not one hint or suggestion has ever emanated from Mr. Moore. . . . As legal adviser to the state, I consider it my duty to call for every legal weapon available to continue the fight. I charge Mr. Moore with deliberately distorting and misrepresenting my position before the people of Virginia. Whether his motive is political or otherwise, I stand ready to debate the issue with him at any time or place he may select." (Such vehemence, once reserved in the South for uncomplimentary references to mothers, hound dogs and line fences, might indicate the increasing fear of the slightest tolerance on this issue of school integration.) Perhaps the secret of this controversy as to which man was the more devout segregationist lay in a sentence in a news item recounting the exchange of words. "Both Almond and Moore are considered potential candidates for governor of Virginia next year."

And indeed, when Attorney General Almond did announce his candidacy for the governorship some five months later, he mentioned, "For more than five years I have fought to save our public school system from destruction and to defend Virginia's right to govern in her own internal affairs and in the lawful exercise of her inherent and constitutional sovereignty."

A Southern political observer tells you, "Two states have been real disappointments on this integration: Virginia and North Carolina. Personally, I had hoped for some constructive leadership from both of these states—and about all they've given us has been more complicated versions of the same old frenzy. I suppose I had underestimated the absolute control of the Byrd machine in Virginia politics, and overestimated the influence of the university and some of the really outstanding men North Carolina used to have on the national scene."

Disillusionment with Virginia on the part of other Southerners was forcefully stated by the Nashville Tennessean early in 1957, after a Federal judge had ruled that Virginia's placement law was unconstitutional. Under the heading, "So This Is Leadership," the Nashville editor said, "Once

The Ham and the Corn   231

again the futility of trying to evade the Supreme Court's school segregation decisions with legislative gimmicks has been convincingly demonstrated, this time in Virginia.

"There should be no great surprise at Federal Judge Walter Hoffman's ruling that the student placement law enacted in Virginia last year is 'unconstitutional on its face,' for it is part and parcel of a legislative program clearly intended to maintain compulsory segregation in the state's public schools. But it is a timely reminder that those who have urged other Southern states—including our own—to look to the Old Dominion for leadership are pointing down a road that leads nowhere."

Not unexpectedly, the South's loudest official spokesman for segregation has come from Mississippi. And although Senator James O. Eastland is a native of the land of Vardaman and Bilbo, it is a tactical error to assume that he is "just another one of those demagogues" who scatters some "vote-bait" during periodic campaigns back home. Eastland's taste does not run to string ties, kissing sticky babies or defense of lynching. He has been described as "the patron saint of the White Citizens' Councils" and that indicates the nature of his fight against any change in the racial status quo.

His words may often sound hysterical to outsiders, but they are convincing to many of the people in Mississippi. Their combination of grave assurance and audacity is a heady tonic for many people who feel frustrated and uncertain in their own rejection of national ideals and laws. When the Supreme Court handed down its school decision, Eastland made it his business to become leader of the opposition, and no one has yet successfully challenged his position. In speeches before the Citizens' Councils in 1955, Eastland outlined the attack he felt would win public approval for himself, the Councils, and white supremacy. In an unpredictable time, his statements had all the powerful pull of unequivocal gospel.

"There can be no outcome but total and complete victory. Defensive action is the road to destruction and death. We must take the offense. We must carry the message to every section of the United States. Our position is righteous. The great majority of the rank and file of the people of the North believe exactly as we do. The law of nature is on our side.

"The drive for racial amalgamation is both illegal and immoral, and those who would mix little children of both races in our schools are following an illegal, immoral and sinful doctrine."

Urging the Council members to avoid violence, he said, "Violence and lawlessness will hurt this organization. These acts are turned against us by our enemies. They are effectively used to mould public sentiment against us in the North. The South must get public opinion on its side."

Labeling the present moves toward integration as more dangerous than Civil War Reconstruction days, his word was, "It is more dangerous because the present decisions are built upon gradualism; to induce us to agree or to force us to comply step by step.

"In reconstruction there was the attempt to force the hideous monster upon us all at once. Our ancestors rallied and stopped it. Its weakness then was that they attempted to enforce it all at once. It will take special precautions to guard against the gradual acceptance, and the erosion of our rights through the deadly doctrine of gradualism."

To realize how accurately the Senator formulated the "solid" and "respectable" doctrine of defiance for the Deep South, it is only necessary to scan the developments of the two years since some of his speeches were made. "Lawful" disregard for the law has become the rallying cry. One of Senator Eastland's best-known talks was a piece for home consumption in which he revealed some details of his three-year vendetta against President Truman's civil rights program.

"Eastland of Mississippi became the boss of the committee that had all the civil rights bills and ever since then the CIO and these organizations have been yapping that I was arrogant and high-handed with them.

"And so I was. And they said that I broke the law. And so I did. You know, the law says the committee has got to meet once a week. And there I was, chairman of a committee, and there were Northerners up there—Yankees that didn't know anything about the question—who were lined up against us.

"You know what happened? Why, for the three years I was chairman, that committee didn't hold a meeting. . . . We have a rule in the Senate that when you report a bill out of a committee, you have got to have the original bill, got to have the original thing there before you. I was afraid that they'd call a special session of that committee and vote the bills out behind my back.

"You know what happened? I had special pockets put in my pants and for three years I carried those bills around in my pockets everywhere I went, and every one of them was defeated and the CIO and these racial groups yapped and yapped. But their yapping didn't get them anywhere."

His reason for this behavior and this boastfulness over it? "I had to protect the interests of the people of Mississippi." (All the people?)

Against this background, there was natural reaction of consternation on the part of much of the nation when Eastland's seniority brought him, early in 1956, to the chairmanship of the powerful Senate Judiciary Committee. (It is a significant sidelight on Southern and national politics today that the Senate did not feel it could challenge the hallowed rule of seniority in the case of Senator Eastland from Mississippi, who had defied national law and the Supreme Court of the United States on the matter of segregation, but a few months later this same rule of seniority was abandoned in a committee membership involving Senator Kefauver from Tennessee, who had defied Deep South race patterns and asked for respect of the Supreme Court in their ruling on desegregation.)

"With better than five thousand acres of Delta cotton land down here in Mississippi, and a good Senate chairmanship up there in Washington, ole Jim's got it made," a local politician says. "Long as there's a nigger in Dixie, he'll know how to get ballots in the box."

Another political spokesman for segregation, and the man who epitomizes the difference between yesterday's demagogues and today's councilors, is Georgia's newest Senator, Herman Talmadge. The name Talmadge, as handed on by his father "Gene," has been associated with red galluses and spittoons, attacks on Georgia's university system, and virulent racism. Perhaps that is why the public reacts with surprise when, on a national television network, the son is a well-combed, clean-shaven man in his early forties, with a properly folded handkerchief in his pocket and a wrist watch gleaming on his folded arm.

The public outside the South may have been surprised, but it cannot afford to be lulled into wishful thinking. Talmadge has been described as having "a fresh polish but not a fresh horizon." His appearances have adapted to the contemporary world, and so have many of the techniques he employs, but the basic philosophy has remained much the same as that of his father's world.

Herman Talmadge managed his political adaptations so well in 1956 that he eliminated, without the full effort of a campaign, the venerable, widely respected senior Senator from Georgia who had served six consecutive terms in Washington and won chairmanship of the important Senate Foreign Relations Committee. Seventy-eight-year-old Walter F. George had gained the ear of government officials in most areas of the world, but he lost the ear of back-country Georgians—to Herman Talmadge; Senator George had won the respect of many colleagues in both parties in Washington, but he lost the financial backing necessary for a successful campaign in his home state—to Herman Talmadge.

When Herman was in the third grade, George went to Washington as Senator. In the years that followed, George became more and more aware of the world beyond Georgia, while Herman became more and more astute in the ways within Georgia and its two dominant political features: the county unit vote and the Negro.

Early in 1956, the backers of Senator George surveyed and assessed the local situation and the possibilities and probabilities of a campaign, during the long hot Georgia summer, against the younger Talmadge. On May ninth, the Senator withdrew from the race.

A young Southerner, George McMillan, writing about this defeat by default, said, "When Senator George withdrew without a struggle, the earth must have trembled beneath the feet of a host of Southern Senators and Representatives who have been elected, re-elected—and re-elected again—by those complacent coalitions that have so long marked the limited democracy of the deep South."

It seems to be the consensus of opinion that had George decided to run the Senate race, the segregation issue would have been the difficult hurdle for him to clear on his home ground. He would probably have been labeled "moderate" or "weak," and if that seems incredible to Northerners who recall that the Southern Manifesto was introduced into Congress by Senator George, they simply do not understand as yet the strange web of fear and conformity which politics has woven in part of the South. When Talmadge wrote his book, You and Segregation, he made a statement which might have been aimed at Senator George: "No candidate will dare advocate publicly the end of segregation. To do that would mean his sure defeat. However, there is a type candidate who will make deals, sacrifice principles and sell out, while giving lip-service to our cause. Beware that candidate! He is the most dangerous. He is the thief in the night, clothed in garments of sweet lip-service, but whose raiment, we know from costly experience, conceals the deadly dagger of treachery."

Confronted with the prospect of a weary season of campaigning on an issue in which the only new dimension promised to be the volume of shouts growing ever more shrill in their "me-too's," and "me-more-so's," it is small wonder that George withdrew—and became President Eisenhower's personal representative to the North Atlantic Treaty Organization.

Talmadge not only adapted the old issues to new necessities, but he adapted new aspects of the South's economic and industrial life to the old political realities. How successfully he had welded all his accommodations into a single structure was demonstrated by the election in November, 1956, when, against a last-minute opposition entry in the race, he won the unit vote of every one of Georgia's 159 counties. In addition, he had brought into his campaign in an active capacity many of his former opponents, including both of Atlanta's newspapers and some powerful businessmen.

These and other supporters of Talmadge assure you that he has done more for Georgia than "any man before him." As governor he spent 53 per cent of Georgia's income on education, which he estimates to be the highest ratio of any state in the nation. During his administration, he points out, over three and a half million dollars was spent on Negro college expansion, almost one million on schools for the Negro blind and deaf, and a half-million dollars on a Negro psychiatric hospital. He spent money lavishly—but, the majority of Georgians seem to agree, not foolishly.

Ralph McGill, able editor of the *Atlanta Constitution*, has tried to define Talmadge's political character: "Some . . . have seen him as a gallus snapper; a sort of hillbilly clown or character. Nothing could be further from the fact.

"He is a conservative by birth, environment and conscious determination. But since he is intelligent he has not been able to have a closed mind. . . . A guess would be that privately he often is made uncomfortable by this fact. . . . A provincial man with a closed mind can make a 'demagogic' character of himself, but an intelligent man, however conservative, cannot quite agree to destroy himself. Herman Talmadge is no provincial." And elsewhere McGill has said, "Talmadge is not the last Southern demagogue, but only the first of a new and shrewder breed."

Perhaps the person and career of Herman Talmadge demonstrate most clearly the present truce, not always easy, between the old and the new in Georgia and the South. A knowledgeable woman in state politics, who has been around many an election but has spent some of her recent years of inactivity on the local scene trying to gain a larger perspective, confides, during one of the long talk-sessions she feasts on: "There are three directions the politicians can look: back to yesterday—like some of these 'elder statesmen' we've been keeping in Washington—and on the racial issues they're trying to tip tables and resurrect the ghost of Calhoun. Or they can look at today—like the dog-in-the-manger boys who are up in Washington: they've got it made, all they care about now is keeping it. Then there are the few who are looking out to tomorrow. They know that the quick answers which seem so easy right now may be harder to face up to in the next generation.

"They're looking forward to a future, they want to tie in with the best that can come down here. It's tough to know just what that'll be but it's worth looking out for. Only it costs the one thing a politician can least afford: risk."

It is difficult to place some of the Southern political leaders in such neat categories. More and more the feeling increases of a mutual bondage between the supposed leaders and the so-called led. And such a tie is a disservice to democracy precisely to the extent that it is a bondage rather than a mutual trust.

A man who has been a liberal in a vulnerable profession in a Deep South state for some years speaks with feeling about one of the foremost political figures in his state: "He's really so much better than he can let on in this whole damned race issue. He knows nullification and interposition are asinine; he knows that eventually the Supreme Court will be abided by. But he's a practicing politician. He's going to make the noises and follow the moves he has to on this—but not as many as he could.

"Of course, if someone hears about this and begins to write articles about him for the national papers and magazines, he'll be ruined. All a man needs to just about finish him off in an election down here today is the blessing of *Time* or *Life*. That's all his opposition needs to suggest that he's an 'outsider,' an integrationist or a communist—and the words are made to seem interchangeable.

"Hell, the politicians are in a spot. They're following the people on this. If they don't, they can get their heads chopped off and go to New Jersey and be politicians."

The self-propagating need for Southern leadership to constantly prove its devotion to segregation has led to two particularly indigenous developments. Although neither one seems likely to result in any constructive change or innovation whatsoever, this has not diminished their attractiveness to people whose frustrations can always draw ink, if not blood. The first was "interposition." Its birth and warm reception through some of the South reflects the close relationship which often binds together the press and political movements.

As stated in a collection of editorials by James Jackson Kilpatrick, who dusted off the word and movement and introduced them in the current controversy, this is how the revised version of nullification began: "On November 21, 1955, *The Richmond News Leader* launched an editorial campaign that brought an old Constitutional doctrine out of American history and gave it new meaning for this generation.

"It is the doctrine of Interposition.

"In other days, the right of the States to interpose their sovereign powers against encroachment by the Federal Government was expounded by such great men as Jefferson, Madison, Calhoun, and the brilliant but neglected John Taylor of Caroline. In bygone years, the right was asserted not only in the South, but in New England and the Midwest also."

Some three months after the launching of this doctrine, *Southern School News* interviewed Professor Wylie H. Davis of the law school of the University of Texas, who stated, " 'Interposition' is historically nothing more than a political method of achieving nullification. . . . In my candid opinion there is no legal basis whatever for 'interposition' as a nullifying or voiding device. As anything more than a formal and official protest against federal action, the doctrine is a legal absurdity. Of course it was never recognized by the federal courts in any case with respect to rights or immunities created or protected by the U.S. Constitution, treaties, or valid federal statutes. And as a reputable political theory, 'interposition' in the nullification sense was dealt a grievous blow by the Henry Clay-engineered Tariff Compromise of 1833. After that even most of the Southern leaders who championed the right of secession did not contend that a state could both nullify and remain in the Union. Certainly the outcome of the Civil War did not enhance the legal and political luster of 'interposition.' "

At least interposition gave segregationists a fresh and legalistic rallying cry. It provided subject material for orators and editorialists.

The second large political move which was made by the South was the introduction in the House and Senate on March 12, 1956, of a Southern Manifesto.

The importance of this document lay in the fact that it carried the names of nineteen Senators and seventy-seven (later increased to eighty-two) representatives from eleven states, who had concurred—or been pressured into concurring—in these opinions:

". . . We regard the decision of the Supreme Court in the school cases as a clear abuse of judicial power. It climaxes a trend in the federal judiciary undertaking to legislate, in derogation of the authority of Congress, and to encroach upon the reserved rights of the states and the people. . . .

"This unwarranted exercise of power by the court, contrary to the Constitution, is creating chaos and confusion in the states principally affected. It is destroying the amicable relations between the white and Negro races that have been created through 90 years of patient effort by the good people of both races. It has planted hatred and suspicion where there has been heretofore friendship and understanding.

"Without regard to the consent of the governed, outside agitators are threatening immediate and revolutionary changes in our public school systems. If done, this is certain to destroy the system of public education in some of the states. . . .

"We pledge ourselves to use all lawful means to bring about a reversal of this decision which is contrary to the Constitution and to prevent the use of force in its implementation.

"In this trying period, as we all seek to right this wrong, we appeal to our people not to be provoked by the agitators and trouble-makers invading our states and to scrupulously refrain from disorder and lawless acts."

Only two Southern Senators refused to put their names on this call for legal defiance of the law. (Senate Democratic leader Lyndon Johnson and House Speaker Sam Rayburn, both of Texas, were not asked to sign.) They were the two senators from Tennessee, Estes Kefauver and Albert Gore, who both pointed out that the decision of the Supreme Court was "a decision of the highest court in the land."

Twenty-four Southern representatives refused to sign the manifesto. Three of these were from North Carolina—one of whom, Representative Thurmond Chatham, said, "I, personally, will not sign anything that will tear down the power and prestige of the court as the final arbiter of justice. We sometimes forget that, in a country ruled by a dictator, the courts are destroyed first."

During elections later in the year, two of these three North Carolinians who had been critical of the manifesto were defeated for re-election to the House. When one of them, Representative C. Bennett Deane, made his "valedictory speech" in the House, his colleagues in Washington paid him tribute. Twenty-two Southern and Northern representatives hailed his courage and Democratic leader John W. McCormack of Massachusetts, said, "He leaves us not defeated, but the victor. He won a victory by acting in accordance with his conscience." A fellow North Carolinian who had signed the manifesto said, "I've never admired a man so much in all my life, although I took a different position."

Even among the signers there were flurries of protest and disagreement. One of the most confused situations developed in Tennessee when young Representative Ross Bass questioned the "propriety of members of Congress making a public pledge to reverse a decision of the Supreme Court," and then freely endorsed the document which did just that in relation to the school desegregation dispute. Having said he was under political pressure to sign the manifesto, he later explained that that pressure existed in his own fear that failure to sign would be interpreted in the district which he represented as meaning that he favored integration. He said that he regarded the manifesto as a political document intended largely to aid Senator Walter George of Georgia in his effort at re-election in the 1956 campaign.

Although Representative Bass's unclarified position served to illustrate the muddied political waters of the South, and the difficulty of looking forward by moving backward, he pointed up the essential characteristic of the controversial Southern Manifesto: it had no legal status, required no Congressional action, provided no constructive plan for achieving any of its stated purposes at either the local or national level— it was, in short, a political device.

Men in Washington, who might be fearful that their constituents at home could be persuaded that they had not done all in their power to preserve the old racial patterns, could now refer to this concrete document as one of their achievements. Men who needed the bolstering effect of concerted action in defiance of the Supreme Court received that companionship in the manifesto.

"The worst feature of that manifesto," one Southern leader tells you months after its public presentation, "was that it said one thing but did another. While declaring for legal resistance to the Court, it created the very climate for illegal defiance. While condemning violence, it fostered the suspicion and frustration that breed violence. It was supposed to be the product of the deliberations of some skillful gentlemen, but it put them in league with some mighty clumsy thugs they'd like to disown, I imagine.

"Senator Erwin, from North Carolina, said he hoped the statement would have the earnest consideration of reasonable people everywhere and would be a lamp of moderation in these crucial days. Well, maybe it was moderate compared to what might have been written. There was no cry of 'Communist,' there was no 'inflammatory' language. But what it achieved was the silencing of many real 'moderates' down here. People who couldn't be frightened by ranting racists were disturbed by this quieter, legalistic-sounding document—and because it had the weight of political power and authority, it stifled many who might otherwise have taken a stand of 'desegregation is eventually inevitable, we hope it will come slowly but how can we implement its success?' "

Probably the most influential person to approve the manifesto outside the South was a Princeton University professor of jurisprudence, Dr. Alpheus T. Mason, who was quoted by The New York Times as saying that it was a good thing which "at the very least, is calculated to give the

Court and the country pause." In this prediction, Dr. Mason seemed to be accurate, for official calls for "moderation" became increasingly national in scope and popular in theory following the manifesto. The only difficulty lay in the fact that neither black nor white, North nor South, politician nor preacher, held the same working definition of "moderation."

One Southerner, who carries no small influence in his state, sums up his attitude toward the manifesto. "I can't say that I really blame those men whose careers would have been utterly killed by failure to support the Southern Manifesto. But there were many who displayed nothing but a lack of courage. Now our senator is a brilliant man, one of the leaders in the United States Senate. Our governor is without formal education, a hack politician, and he doesn't pretend to be anything else. Both say, of course, that you can't be effective unless you're elected. That's true, and they're in office and I'm not. But I made the decision a long time ago that if I had to go back on what I knew was right, I'd not be elected.

"Damn it all, somebody has to stick to his guns. Like Winston Churchill who kept right on saying what he thought was right but unpopular, and finally he was called back to office when the people came to see he was right. On this situation today, there have to be some who'll be right eight or ten years from now, even though they're unpopular today.

"Our senator signed the Southern Manifesto because he was a damned coward. He'd have had a costly, rough campaign to face if he'd have refused, and of course he said that by staying with the boys and working on the manifesto he helped keep the more moderate view alive; it wasn't as bad as it could have been. Of course the manifesto could have come out and endorsed open lynching!

"But, as I see it"—and for a moment the man pauses and gazes out of the window of his office, his face thoughtful and concerned—"the real harm our senator, and some of the others who signed that document, did, was twofold. First, at the local level, the many people who didn't like the 1954 ruling but decided to try to live by it, now suddenly found these men who were supposedly half-way liberal signing a paper saying that there were legal means by which you could defeat the supreme law of the land. It gave them a false hope of evading integration and prolonged the whole process.

"Second, on a world level, for the names of some of these men, who are known all over the world, and in the countries of the colored peoples especially—for them to appear on such a document couldn't help but lessen our national stature everywhere. I think perhaps the Southern Manifesto marked the low-water point in our controversy since 1954.

Maybe now a few more politicians are screwing their courage 'to the sticking point.' "

"Courage?" the former mayor of a large Southern city says when you broach the subject to him. "That's a commodity we seem to be running short on just now. Sometimes we don't even have the guts to stick with our own political parties; if everything doesn't go just to suit us, we take our marbles and go home—or start a new party. Incidentally, do you know what a Dixiecrat is? A Dixiecrat is a disgruntled Democrat who'll sleep with a Negro but won't eat breakfast with her.

"I know 'em all, from the old-timey lynchers right on down to the present crop of bigots. Why, I saw them beat down this jail here once, a crowd after a Negro who'd already been taken to another city for safe-keeping. I knew nearly every one of the men on the log, and anybody with a pistol and a dime's worth of nerve could have stopped them. But nobody even tried, and they rammed the jail open.

"One rum-head, I told somebody, 'he's not after any Negro, he's trying to get in there to steal something.' He'd worked for me, I knew him. Sure enough, I saw him about an hour later going down the street with a copper still on his shoulder. He'd stolen it from the jail.

"A lot of the fellows carrying on today about the Supreme Court and segregation and all that, are the same way. They don't give a damn about Negroes or whites—it's something else they're after. Votes, I suspect."

Perhaps the Southern governor who has earned the most respect of the most people for his position on the racial question has been Florida's LeRoy Collins. It may be said that Florida, with its non-white population not quite 22 per cent of the total, its specialized agriculture and its large groups of residents who have come from other regions, is not "typical" of the South. True, it is not representative of the Delta South—but in many ways it is very typical of another, different South. And if the same old single planter-type image is not to be stamped on the region in this crisis as it was in the Civil War, we must acknowledge these differences as not being always atypical.

On January 8, 1957, Governor Collins made his inaugural address. After pointing out that Florida is growing so rapidly that from the rank of twentieth among the states in population in 1950, it has now moved to thirteenth, and that new industrial plants are settling in Florida at the rate of one a day, he touched on some of the state's needs—and finally dwelt on the subject of racial integration in the longest and most thorough discussion he devoted to any single topic.

"I do not know the ultimate answer. And I do not believe anyone else does. However, I am convinced that we will not find the answer in some attitudes that are being reflected in various quarters today.

"In the first place, it will do us no good whatever to defy the United States Supreme Court. Actually, this Court is an essential institution for the preservation of our form of government. It is little short of rebellion and anarchy to suggest that any state can isolate and quarantine itself against the effect of a decision of the United States Supreme Court.

"If such a proposal could possibly have any legal efficacy, we would have no Union and the power of the Court to protect the people in the enjoyment of their freedoms would be severely impugned and imperiled. We should frankly admit this and put the true label of demagoguery on any doctrine of nullification. . . .

"It is not easy to say, but it is nevertheless true and I feel that I should stand up and say it: The Supreme Court decisions are the law of the land. And this Nation's strength and Florida's strength are bottomed upon the basic reverse premise that ours is a land of the law. . . .

"As I see it, we must side with truth even though now we may share her wretched crust. History requires that we not stand aside, coward-like, waiting for the multitude to make virtue of our position. The cause is with us now. It requires leadership now, not only from me as Governor but also from you as citizens. . . .

"This is the call of history—a history which grows impatient. Ours is the generation in which great decisions can no longer be passed to the next. We have a State to build—a South to save—a Nation to convince—and a God to serve."

The favorable response of the press throughout Florida to Collins's address indicated their pride in the fact that his was "the first firm official voice raised in the Deep South for moderation and gradual compliance."

Headlines varied according to the sympathies of the papers and reflected the fact that the governor had made appeals to both sides of the question. They ranged from "Mixed Schools Inevitable" to "Segregation to Stay." The Pensacola Journal commented, "Governor Collins, in a message of masterly eloquence, laid down the facts of life in this 1957 democracy in discussing integration." The Miami Herald praised his frankness and vigor; The Jacksonville Journal said his stand "is bound to please no one at the extremes of the problem," but that it should please the majority and Collins "was reaching for the hearts and minds of the people of Florida." The Tampa Morning Tribune gave him the strongest endorsement: "In private life this statement might pass unnoticed, but in politics it takes courage; for it is mortally offensive to a certain bloc of extremists who can make, and have made, trouble for the advocates of temperance and reason in race problems."

"Three years ago, who would have thought that we'd be hailing approval of the Supreme Court of the United States as a great liberal stand?" a young Floridian asks. "But it shows how much your thinking can be modified; now I really think Collins' speech was a step forward."

A rector in Jacksonville, a former New Englander, says, "Collins is the best man in Southern politics on this issue. His religion is definitely behind his present attitude."

An able and well-known political scientist in another part of the state tells you, "Collins is sincere in his concern over this problem. He really bleeds about it. Wishes it had never come up, but takes his Episcopalian beliefs seriously and really has faith in brotherhood. As a boy he was rather poor, worked in a grocery store, all that—graduated from high school, took a degree from Cumberland Law School up in Tennessee. Married the descendant of a former territorial governor; has appointed a pretty high-type of man to office. His leadership, and Florida's progress during the next few years, should be interesting to watch."

A Negro college professor talks with you candidly. "Collins pleased everybody with his inaugural speech when he said justice would prevail. The White Citizens' Councils figure he means their justice, the boycott group in Tallahassee thinks he means their justice, all the Negro and white groups assume he's using their definition—and so everybody feels he's talking to them. If I were a Southern white man in the governor's position, I can see that I would probably do the same thing he's doing. But I'm not a white man. And while I'm pleased that he's taken what stand he has, I could have hoped for a lot more.

"What too many people here, and throughout the South, don't realize is that we can't ever go back. White people say, 'Everything was so peaceful.' Maybe it seemed more peaceful to them than it really was to the rest of us. But Negro people here will never be the same again. Even their leaders couldn't change them back, if they wanted to."

When you meet Governor Collins, you see a slim, unusual-looking man, with eyes so brown they seem to be solid dabs of color in his tanned face. His hair is iron-grey, and when he smiles his face crinkles into dozens of lines around his mouth and eyes. The over-all moderation which one analyst has attributed to Florida might be reflected in its governor's medium height, conservative dress, soft voice and easy courtesy. Yet his eyes are troubled and his mouth becomes more firmly set when he discusses the complex issue of Negro and white relationships.

"This is an enormously difficult problem. Every word in my inaugural address was weighed and labored over. In a talk of that sort, what you say is so easily misinterpreted, taken out of context, used by both sides erroneously. I feel that the great need we have now—the thing we must find—is some leadership for this vast middle group who are inert. They will not arouse themselves to be heard in this matter. They will not say or do anything. Yet it is a matter of basic citizenship that they make their presence felt on this basic issue of our times."

Another Southern governor who has eschewed demagoguery on the racial issue, and followed a steadfast course of "local option" in matters of school desegregation, is Frank Clement of Tennessee. Under pressure from the western counties of his state, where Negro population is heaviest and pro-segregation organizations even went so far as to stage a march on the capitol, the nation's youngest governor has stood steadfast against extremist legislation. As opposed to the monolithic resistance imposed by many of the Southern states on all its counties and communities, the program of Tennessee and Clement has remained one of flexibility and permissiveness.

"His critics say Clement follows a middle course because he has national ambitions," a young politician in Nashville says. "So what? Isn't the national perspective what we have more need of in Southern politics? Actually I think it's Frank's Methodism as much as his ambition that has influenced his approach to the problem. Whatever the cause, it seems to me that he's come closer than any of the eleven Southern governors to the Supreme Court's idea of local solution to integration according to local problems."

Yet a Negro NAACP leader tells you, "Clement let this 1957 legislature pass a series of segregation bills. I can't say I was disappointed in him; I'd never expected very much from him."

A white attorney and community leader of one of Tennessee's largest cities, says, however, "The legislation didn't mean too much, really. The permissiveness still remains, and that's fundamental. It's fundamental democracy."

You remember the legislators all over the South, and the citizens appearing before them one by one; the governors and Senators you have talked with and the little officials whose role looms so large in this particular crisis. You feel hopeful, that if one or two political leaders can break, or bend, some of the bars of fear or conformity or inertia imprisoning them, perhaps there can be a series of solutions to some of the political problems which often seem reduced only to the ham and the corn.

Perhaps the South's political talents need not always be sacrificed to the single specter of race. Perhaps the solid conservatism which is one part of its tradition need not always be rendered churlish by racial struggles, and the imaginative, liberal leaderhip which is another part of its heritage need not always be choked by white supremacy.

When a mountain man down South was asked how he liked a certain speech delivered by one of the political leaders of the region, with native shrewdness he replied, "Now I'll tell you, that talk was just like shearing a hog. There was a hell of a lot of noise and not a thimble full of wool." This is no time for noise, and people who know better have already given us more than enough. Now we need to get down to work and harvest the wool—confront our problems and seek their solutions with the wit and resourcefulness we have too often spent on less constructive causes.

One Southerner has stated the challenge well. United Nations mediator Frank P. Graham, former president of the University of North Carolina and one-time Senator from North Carolina, has said that our need in the future is to create a world in which "democracy is without vulgarity, excellence without ignorance, differences are without hate; where the answer to error is not terror; the way of progress is not subversion, respect for the past is not reaction and the hope of the future not revolution." The South has had its statesmen as well as it demagogues!

13 ⣿ Who Knows the Score?

        If the South has not always had more leisure than any other part of the United States, more time and talent to enjoy its sports or arts, at least that has always seemed to be the case.

"We don't believe in letting work interfere with a good time." One old man, rocking on his veranda under peeling paint on the high ceiling and atop a shaky floorboard or two, smiles at you knowingly. "Course, those who contend that we're all a bunch of lazybones down here are just talking off the top of their heads. We don't mind hard work—for a little while at a time. Our attitude toward work is sort of like that of the country fellow who went to the circus and saw his first giraffe: 'Now look here, let's don't overdo this thing!' "

White Southerners early established a reputation for being hard-riding, hard-fighting, hard-drinking men. If they were gentlemen, this meant hunting and racing blooded horses, dueling to the death, indulging in a toddy or a julep or a flip. If they were frontiersmen and upland farmers, it meant racing on the Greasy Cove Racetrack instead of a well-kept course with "stands for ladies," eye-gouging and skull-cracking in the free-for-alls, and a jug of raw wild brew rather than a decanter of imported nicety.

But all of this helped give birth to the mythical gay and carefree and prodigal Southerner who refused to be burdened by so crass a consideration as money and a livelihood.

Negro Southerners followed somewhat the same path of recreation, only, since most of them could not buy horses, they went on the field hunts for the small game closer home, and they went fishing; they reflected the same violence, only they used a knife instead of silver-mounted pistols, and they got drunk on home-brew.

In this case however, the pastimes did not give birth to a fanciful individualist but to the mythical shiftless, cavorting, fish-fry and cutting-scrape Negro, whose indulgencies were unadorned and therefore socially unacceptable.

246

There were areas where the recreation of white and black overlapped, however, and in whatever amount that mutual good will—about which we presently hear so much—exists today, it surely stems in large part from these shared memories.

"Lordy, I remember swimming with nigra boys from the time I was a little tad. We was all out in the natural free-flowing water then. I reckon it's since we got everything penned off and doctored up that we're more particular."

"I have an unsegregated ball game in my front yard 'most every day," a woman on a plantation in the Deep South says. Her home is surrounded by Negro homes; her only white neighbor has no children the age of her three boys. "The proportions on our team are three to eleven, too—my three against little old black 'Scoot' and 'Tunk' and 'Rius' and the others. They really play hard together. I mean they play and fight and get mad, and go on and play some more. And I'm glad.

"But that doesn't mean we could accept integrating our schools right now. Why here, in this district, we'd have a mass of people on a lower level in education and health and culture—you can't imagine how much lower—for our children to be in class with, and nobody would be better. It's hard! We have to raise their standards for eventual improvement—but meantime, I have to raise my children!"

These people, and many others scattered through the South, flock each Saturday in autumn, when the team is not traveling, to see the state university or the state agricultural or engineering college or one of the other major teams make its bid for football glory. The smell of burning leaves hangs in the blue Indian summer air; there are the cries of old "alums" greeting one another with a Southern mixture of exaggerated joy and affection, and the shrieks of undergraduates cheering for victory which seems, at the moment, somehow important. The sun moves slowly down behind the west wing of the stadium, and the huge oval stands, in the last few minutes of the game, are divided between a bright autumnal light and deep shadow.

"Football's not a game here," a professor at one of the more enthusiastic sports universities scoffs; "it's a state of mind. As a matter of fact, it's a way of life. Now, if we can just get the football lower-case way into competition with the older capital-letter Southern Way, we might really be near the solution of our desegregation problems—at least in the halls of so-called Higher Learning."

Integrated football teams certainly seem to have been successful as far as the students are concerned. A man at the University of Oklahoma says, "We have a Negro freshman on our football team here. When the team went up to Tulsa to play, they were supposed to have a big chicken feast at one of the more fashionable places there. When they went, someone refused to serve the Negro boy. So the whole team got up and left with him. And there was this restaurant left with all that chicken, and all this prepared banquet.

"Well, the management got very upset about it and then went to extremes in the opposite direction: apologized to the whole team as well as to the Negro, wrote letters of apology to the coach and the president of the university and everyone in any way connected with the team, and then did something which was anything but conducive to racial good will: fired the party who had refused to serve the Negro boy. But the interesting thing, of course, was that the team stood together."

In Texas an acquaintance tells you some stories of the 1956–57 football season. "At one town here, during our first year of integration, a Negro player was putting the high school on the map for the first time in several seasons. One day, after he'd made three touchdown runs in a district game and was on a long run for the fourth t.d., leaving all the other players behind, a white man in the crowd grew very excited, jumped up, nudged an old Negro man and shouted, 'Look at him go. Isn't that boy something?' 'Naw,' the older man answered, 'a colored boy always could outrun white boys if you let 'em out in the open.'"

He laughs a hearty Texas laugh and takes a long drink of scalding coffee. "No, at the schools and elsewhere, you can't argue with these sports. And of course, when C. R. Roberts, the big Southern California Negro football player, singlehanded beat the University of Texas in the Rose Bowl, it put the final skids under segregation here.

"At one point in the game, after Roberts got off three t.d.s and then they put in a second-stringer with a Latin American name, one fan said, 'These inferior races sure are beating hell out of us, aren't they?'"

(This reminds you of something a man in Florida told you a while before, "When people I know start talking 'But all Negroes are slow,' I say, 'Like Hank Aaron?'

"Or, 'Negroes are cowards,' I say, 'Like Joe Louis?'

" 'Negroes are stupid.' 'Like Harry Belafonte?'

" 'Negroes are dirty.' 'Like Lena Horne?'

" 'They're shiftless.' 'Like Althea Gibson and Katherine Dunham?'

"And while it may not change their theme, it makes them change the tune a little anyway.")

It has been on policies of sports, particularly football, and segregation, that politicans so far have met their most public opposition to demagoguery. Governor Marvin Griffin found that when football and Georgia's "traditions" were in conflict, the pigskin sometimes proved more potent than politics.

On November 30, 1955, a second vice president of the States' Rights Council of Georgia, Incorporated, sent a telegram from Augusta to Coach Bobby Dodd in Atlanta protesting Georgia Tech's plans to play in the Sugar Bowl. Since bids to this bowl game had been the prize sought for many seasons by every university in the South, this seemed like strange criticism. The objection was that Georgia Tech would be playing against the University of Pittsburgh, whose team was non-segregated. They had a Negro reserve halfback.

On December first, a Georgia Tech official told newsmen: "Our boys voted to play in the Sugar Bowl and we will not break our contract, especially since both Georgia and Tech have played against Negroes before and there has been no criticism."

Robert O. Arnold, chairman of the Georgia Board of Regents, which determines policy of the state colleges and universities, said it would be nothing new for Tech and he wouldn't make an issue of it.

On December second, however, Governor Griffin asked the Board of Regents, including Chairman Arnold, to meet and make provisions to keep "athletic teams of units of the University System of Georgia" from engaging in "contests with other teams where the races are mixed on such teams or where segregation is not required among spectators at such events."

One regent, a Tech alumnus, when informed of Griffin's proposal, declared it "utterly ridiculous."

That day and night, news of the governor's request spread over the campus. About twenty-five hundred students marched from Atlanta's Five Points to the State Capitol, where they broke in and overturned trash cans, scattered sand from the cigarette urns, pulled fire hoses from their racks. Back outside again, they pulled up a little shrubbery, left an ash can on the head of the statue of a Civil War hero, and hanged a dummy labeled "Griffin" from a tree on the Tech campus. Other effigies of the governor were hanged and burned, and there were signs saying, "Grow Up, Griffin," and "We Play Anybody."

A little later, some five hundred other students staged a demonstration at the governor's mansion. This time, some twenty-five state patrol cars and police cars from Atlanta and three adjoining counties were called in, but State Representative M. M. Smith was later given credit for the peaceful dispersal of the students. Himself a Tech graduate and former football player on the team, he made the undergrads a pledge: "We are going to the Sugar Bowl."

After the mob had left, at about three o'clock in the morning, the governor dismissed the whole affair as "just a bunch of college boys having a good time." He said he would not be pressured "on this thing" and would still request a stern athletic segregation policy when the regents met on Monday.

The student president sent a telegram to the student body at the University of Pittsburgh: "The Student body of Georgia Tech sincerely apologizes for the unwarranted action of Georgia's governor. We are looking forward to seeing your entire team and student body at the Sugar Bowl."

Reaction was widespread to Governor Griffin's belief that "The South stands at Armageddon. There is no more difference in compromising the integrity of race on the playing field than in doing so in the classrooms. One break in the dike and the relentless seas will rush in and destroy us."

Georgia's largest paper, *The Atlanta Journal*, reported that letters it received ran about six to one against the governor. Other newspapers throughout the South deplored the situation. In Alabama, *The Montgomery Advertiser* said editorially that Griffin was "making a political football of football. . . . Pitt's negro fullback is about as great a threat to segregation in Georgia as one of the waiters in Governor Griffin's household."

At Georgia Tech, in December, 1955, the students won the immediate victory, for Tech did play in the Sugar Bowl on January second. But the Governor and his backers won the long-range victory, for the regents provided that although all units of the Georgia university system can play racially mixed teams in those states which permit integration, they cannot play desegregated teams in states whose laws require segregation. This, of course, was a direct aim at the Southern bowls, where desegregated teams from outside the South play in the games although the state laws themselves are for segregation. Governor Griffin declared: "More people were looking at the sugar in the bowl than the chocolate in the Pitt." Georgia's move may have helped some Louisiana politicians realize the dichotomy of their position, and not to be outdone in the segregation show, a special session of their legislature passed a law the following August which banned interracial athletics and unsegregated seating at sports events. When some Sugar Bowl officials suggested that a better way would leave the stands segregated and the playing field integrated, the chairman of the Citizens' Council of New Orleans said that to either repeal or alter the law would "nullify and destroy all other segregation measures and [give way to] the wishes of the integrationists and mongrelizers."

The gamble on "all or nothing" won all, for the segregated athletics law went into effect in Louisiana on October 15, 1956. The field secretary for the NAACP, in New Orleans, pointed out that Hitler was criticized for his attitude toward American Negro athletes in the 1936 Olympic Games at Berlin. "Is racial prejudice less offensive in so-called democratic Louisiana than under the German race-ridden dictatorship of Hitler?"

A Tennessee editor commented: "If the people of Louisiana want a law which makes excellence in performance a secondary consideration in sports, that is their privilege, short-sighted though it may be.

"This law, however, stands as a classic example of the extremes to which some people will go in depriving themselves of pleasure as they search for means to achieve their goals."

The sports editor of the *Atlanta Journal and Constitution* said that "the Sugar Bowl, the jewel in the New Year's Day crown of which New Orleans was so proud, is really done for unless the Louisiana legislature takes it all back. When the fire-breathing politicians at Baton Rouge refused to make an exception in their new law against mixed sports and mixed seating, they reduced the game to a strictly local affair. . . . It is the television angle after all that kills the Sugar Bowl as a big show. Television means money. The pulling power of any bowl game, let us say now, is the size of the check given the competing teams.

"Whether the Sugar Bowl will attempt to stage a game with what teams it can interest for a modest fee is a question. New Orleans had it. It was great while it lasted. . . ."

Louisiana State Senator Rainach was jubilant, however. "We are winning the segregation fight. It won't take longer than eight years to consolidate the South against integration. After that the governors of non-southern states will be entering the fight and our victory will be complete." It appeared, however, that Louisiana was losing the baseball fight. The New Orleans Pelicans, once the class of the Southern League, during the summer, 1957, were in the cellar both competitively and financially, due largely to a Negro boycott of their games.

Turmoil over segregation in athletic contests seems to have alternated largely between Georgia and Lousiana. In November, 1956, Georgia was again embroiled in a state-wide controversy over a football game. At first glance, the arrangements for this game at the town of Summerville seemed impeccable: it was sponsored by the local Junior Chamber of Commerce, it was to be between two Negro teams, seating was to be segregated, proceeds were to go to benefit the white-high-school band which received no state support. But, since there was no Negro football field in Chattooga County, the game was scheduled to be played on the gridiron of white Summerville High—whose band was to receive the money from the gate.

A few days prior to the playing of the game, the county sheriff received a wire from a man in Atlanta who identified himself as vice president of one of the Ku Klux Klan groups. He said the proposed contest was forbidden by state law. When school officials asked attorney general Eugene Cook for an opinion, he advised them to call off the game "because of the way the law reads." He pointed out that Georgia law says all state school buildings shall be used by the race for which they were intended and this was interpreted to mean all physical facilities. The game was canceled.

The Jaycees, who estimated they had spent about five hundred dollars promoting the game, and hoped to make about twenty-five hundred dollars for the band, held a two-hour mass meeting of protest on the high-school grounds. They condemned the action of the Klan and the attorney general, and a state senator-elect, Bobby Lee Cook, who was also a Jaycee official, said in a speech that anyone who belongs to the KKK is "inherently and basically a coward" and called the attorney general's ruling not only unjust but illegal. But the game was canceled.

Georgia opinion, as reflected in the majority of its newspapers, once more regretted "this unfortunate event." The Macon News said, "The deplorable situation at Summerville, where school officials have gotten themselves into the position of being intimidated by the Klan and panicked by an unofficial opinion of Att. Gen. Eugene Cook, makes Southern protestations of friendship between the white and Negro races look ridiculous."

The Marietta Daily Journal was angry, too. "Georgia politics, in a ridiculous ruling, reached down into high school athletic ranks with a sickening low when Att. Gen. Eugene Cook ruled out a championship Negro football game in a white high school stadium. . . .

"It's bad enough when politicians interfere with college athletics in the state, but when they 'muscle in' at high school level, the outlook is sad indeed."

But the game was canceled.

Once again, the question arose, who won and who lost in this many-sided struggle? Did the Negro football teams lose? Or the white-high-school band? The Jaycees and the KKKs, what did they lose or win? And the sovereign state of Georgia and its attorney general, how did they fare? What was added to or subtracted from that quality for which we say our games exist: sportsmanship?

The questions could be asked not only of this situation but an accumulating number of similar ones, too.

In Evansville, Indiana, on December twenty-ninth, 1956 the Evansville College athletic director read a statement to a crowd who had come to see Evansville play Mississippi State College in an invitational basketball tournament. "The Mississippi State College basketball team has been ordered home by its school administration," the Indiana director said flatly, "and the reason ascribed is the presence of colored players in this tourney."

Two days later the University of Mississippi joined its companion state institution and walked out of the All-American City Basketball Tournament in Kentucky, because of Negro players on opposing teams.

Harvard University canceled its southern winter basketball tour as a protest against segregation stipulations, although it had no Negro on its varsity squad. The Brooklyn Dodgers baseball team announced that it was canceling its traditional spring exhibition tour of the South. "We're twenty-five Dodgers, some Negroes," its vice president said. "We play and travel together."

In January, 1957, a Georgia state senator introduced a bill to the legislature prohibiting dances, social functions and athletic training involving white persons and Negroes. The senator said he was in favor of doing away with baseball "if they can't get along without Negroes." The legislature defeated the bill, after an opponent pointed out that the wording was so vague in prohibiting "personal and social contact" that it would "make a colored maid liable for pinning a diaper on a baby in Georgia."

The pressure is on in both directions. As political tensions and publicity needs multiply, Southern cities and counties and states cope with such measures of total segregation as those ordinances passed in Montgomery, Alabama, in March, 1957. As reported in Southern School News, the new law made it "unlawful for white and Negro people to play together in any game: baseball, football, basketball, golf, track, dice, cards, dominoes, checkers, pool, billards, or at swimming pools, beaches, lakes or ponds."

But as the emphasis on winning, on professionalism in sports increases, as we get away from the cow pastures to the highly organized track meets, and leave the ponds and creeks behind for the regulation swimming pools, the need for the best athletes available becomes increasingly important to the teams involved. And if that means Negro players, the pressure to overlook pigmentation grows steadily stronger.

A man at a small-town filling station in Louisiana tells you sadly, "They about ruint our Sugar Bowl when they fixed it so those good teams that had niggers on them couldn't play down here."

Leaning an elbow on the window, he confides softly, "Now I'm not for mixing in the schools, and it won't come for a long time here. Ever' once in a while a nigger gets smart here, but he gets back in line pretty soon. But it's coming. It'll come in all the places around and finally Louisiana and Mississippi will have to give in, too. But it'll be ten years anyway. And I wish they'd a-left our Sugar Bowl alone."

A man in Georgia demands bitterly, "What do our state fathers propose to do in regard to our television sets? You can go down the street in any town in Georgia most any night in the week and see a lot of good 'Crackers' watching Negro wrestlers—or boxers, or basketball players, or singers, or actors, oh hell, most anything you can name—and that may get to be suspect pretty soon. I guess the big white fathers will have to 'black out' TV."

In San Antonio a plump stranger at a restaurant joins in ready conversation. "We got 'em in the schools here, but lots of them are smart and don't go. And one thing about it, no niggers are going to play ball this summer. Louisiana fixed that for us. Shreveport is in the Texas League and no niggers can play there."

In a small town not far from Oklahoma's "Little Dixie" corner, a young Baptist minister tells you, "Our high-school basketball team hasn't taken any Negro players yet, and we've been severely beaten by several of the teams in other towns that do have Negroes. There's been a good deal in our local paper about why don't we have Negro players. At a basketball game the other night near here, Baptist University had a Negro on its team. One of the players on a visiting team kept talking about it, standing up on the side lines and cursing and saying, 'Look at that nigger,' calling him 'nigger' every few minutes. Finally one of the University boys couldn't take it any longer. He walked over and just laid that man out with a sock on the jaw. And the referee didn't do a thing about it. They carried the fellow off the court and everyone was so glad nobody said a word, just went ahead and finished the game."

But the summer of 1957 saw a "new look" in the Southern world of segregation and sports. It involved an anachronism that was in the best comic tradition and a potential for trouble that was sobering. On May third, a Chattanooga, Tennessee, newspaper reported: "Hourigan's Homer Beats Woolens." That "homer" was made by a KKK team!

This single hit, in one of the early games of the city's Commercial AA Softball League, was enough "to give the Knights their first victory." Indeed, it gave their sponsors more than that: their first respectability, their first "family-style" publicity—for behind the regulation softball uniforms of the Knights were the old robes of the Ku Klux Klan. Handbills which were distributed in the area said that the motive behind the Klan's sponsorship of a team in this softball league, one of the area's fastest, was a wish to emphasize the Klan's "recreation side" and their interest in "civic good."

The Knoxville News-Sentinel said, "It has been a curious Spring with zany happenings all over. But it remained for Chattanooga to produce about the weirdest of them all.

"Over there the Knights of the Ku Klux Klan fielded a softball team openly to take part in a local commercial league's season. . . . the players came right out under floodlights and went through a game the other night with no nonsense. No kross burned at the plate and not even the umpire was tarred and feathered on klose plays. . . .

"Whether the players actually were Klansmen was not disclosed. But if questioned, presumably they can take the Fifth Amendment."

There were many who suspected that the need for a new reputation, rather than a new recreation, prompted the Klan's action. As they watched the players, with the K's glistening under the night lights, they realized that more than a game was at stake. In a major editorial, the sober and respected Chattanooga Times said, "We can think of nothing which would disgust sincere and intelligent Chattanoogans more than recognition of this divisive secret organization in such a splendid and sportsmanship program as the city softball organization. Whatever may be said for the Klan, sportsmanship is entirely alien to its violent techniques. . . .

"State softball championships sometimes come out of that league. We know Chattanooga does not wish to be represented in the state and Southern softball championship tournaments by the Knights of the Ku Klux Klan. We suspect that the entire Chattanooga softball program will be damaged by this retreat from true sportsmanship."

A week later the Times spoke again: "We have carefully considered our responsibility to keep our readers fully informed—not only on international and national affairs but on those of local and sports interest. We have decided that this responsibility is paramount. . . .

"The night-riding techniques of the Klan are as out of place under the floodlights of a city-owned and city-operated softball field as are those of any other group fostering hatred, division and fear."

Then they asked a most pointed and pertinent question: "Are the great national corporations of Du Pont and Combustion Engineering; Peerless Woolen Mills, part of the huge Burlington Mills; the Chattanooga Gas Company and the Ridgedale merchants prepared to go on with their teams playing ball with the Ku Klux Klan? We do not believe so.

"The Klan's bid for respectability, in this seemingly innocuous move, has not insofar as we know been duplicated over the whole South. . . . The immediate national interest in the fact that Chattanooga has a Klan team in the top softball league has brought newspaper, magazine and television publicity. A well-known TV commentator, showing films of the Tuesday night game between the KKK and Combustion, cuttingly observed to this effect: 'so much for sports in Chattanooga, where they believe that recreation builds character.'

". . . If the Klan is allowed to strengthen and to extend this intrusion into everyday life, there is no telling what ultimate damage may be done. Let those who see clearly stand up and be counted."

Three days later, the Chattanooga Commercial AA Softball League was dissolved after the plants of three national industries withdrew their teams. Du Pont, Combustion Engineering and Peerless Woolen Mills gave no specific reason for their withdrawal, but said that they might try to get a fourth team and form an industrial league.

In this "triple play" it became apparent that in the Klan's effort to establish its white robes in the respectable white-collar world, industry was unwilling to risk its own respectability in the eyes of the world.

Just across the state line in Georgia, a man tells you, "Our governors and our representatives in Washington can make themselves look foolish on this race business, our school men and adminstrators can be made goats of—all over the South—but it's big industry that's really nationally and internationally minded. When the chips are down, they're the boys that aren't going to play fool to somebody's pet prejudice if it's going to cost money or prestige on the larger scene.

"I'm no integrationist, understand, but I hope I'm not blind either. I can see we've got to do better down here. We've got to take the initiative or lose it—and the first thing we've got to do is stop making jackasses of ourselves over some cow-pasture ball game, and we've got to do like those big industries did and stop playing 'footsie' with an outfit like the Klan."

Public recreation is a child of this century, as public education was a child of the last century. When the Supreme Court of the United States, in November, 1955, handed down its ruling which extended the principle of desegregation to public recreational facilities, they underscored the growth and importance of this phase of national life. Since the South has been in the process of becoming urbanized only in very recent years, and since recreation as a large-scale social undertaking develops as a result of large metropolitan areas and needs, this decision could have had meaning in the South only during the last few decades.

One irony, not altogether unique, developed around a United States District Court ruling in Virginia which closely followed the Supreme Court decision. This ruling held that if a state park, or any part of it, were leased by private operators, the state must require that it be operated without discrimination. Such a decision was denounced, of course, as outside meddling and interference in state affairs.

Yet it was "outside interference"—from this same Washington—which had brought the parks into being. Virginia's state park system was established during the depression and, with the aid of the CCC, seven of its nine parks were built at that time. The state of Virginia appropriated fifty thousand dollars for these parks; the Federal government spent more than four million dollars.

Despite the fact that this money had come from the treasury of all the people of the United States, the seven recreation areas were for the use of white people only. As one Southerner put it harshly: "We're like the rest of the world. We don't want the United States Supreme Court down here, just the United States Treasury."

Reaction to the decision on desegregated recreational facilities varied greatly throughout the South. In Atlanta, an able mayor, William B. Hartsfield, displayed leadership in having the city's golf courses opened without restriction. A Negro professor in Atlanta tells you, "The mayor stood firm on this golf course thing. He's a stubborn fellow, a real man. Many another would have panicked and backed down, and nobody would have blamed Hartsfield too much if he had—but he didn't. You see, there's some climate for discussion in Atlanta, even if not in the rest of Georgia. Negroes are involved in the life of Atlanta. I'm reasonably certain that's why there's been no bus strike here."

After Mayor Hartsfield had looked into the situation in many parts

of the South, and decided on Atlanta's policy, he said, "Our action con-
stitutes no precedent and is no bold departure from other Southern
cities, many of which have long since met and solved this situation.
Jacksonville, Nashville, Miami, Pensacola, and New Orleans have allowed
Negroes on their public courses on specified days. Houston, Dallas, Fort
Worth and Louisville have been allowing Negroes to play on public
courses at any time."

In other parts of Georgia, however, the public recreation picture
was different. During the spring of 1956, the State Parks Department
leased a dozen of its parks to private operators, in what was called a
combination effort to further economy and segregation. Attorney General
Eugene Cook explained: "We are pursuing a plan of economy which may
or may not result in economies. But in any event, we would prefer to
plant the park areas in pine seedlings rather than integrate the races in
them."

So it went throughout the South, a pattern of compliance and defiance.
Florida, being the brightest playground of the South, had its own particular dilemmas, especially on the matter of beaches. It was not out of order,
therefore, that a young professor of social science, Lewis M. Killian, of
Florida State University, should summarize, for a group of professional
recreation directors, some of the more acute problems facing them, and
the whole South, in this area of desegregation.

"First is the conflict of values which white society faces. Not only
are such values as adequate public recreation facilities and an efficient
public school system placed in the balance over against the tradition of
segregation. So also are government by law rather than by mob rule;
freedom of speech; the unity of the Christian churches; and the unity
of our democracy. A Negro said to me just the other day, 'This is the
first time I have ever known that white people could be so frightened of
other white people!' In our democracy people have a right to choose their
values, but in facing this problem realistically we must recognize that
choosing some values means sacrificing others. Some price must be paid,
no matter which way we choose.

"A second neglected problem is one of communication—getting
white people to understand what it is Negroes want, why they want it,
and what price they are willing to pay for it; and getting Negroes to understand that white people are not motivated just by hatred and greed, but
by deep-seated beliefs and feelings which they feel are right. I can see no
solution to this problem other than a long, hard process of 'talking it
out' together, even though the roof may threaten to fly off at times!"

The doubts and fears voiced in certain areas of athletics today seem to be decreasing slightly. Time and events will prove, as they have in the past, ameliorating influences.

William Gordon, Negro editor of Atlanta, quotes a young white sports writer: " 'There is more democracy and good race relations in athletics than in any other American institution.' " Then Gordon tells about the young white football player who also liked jazz music and said, "I don't care what color a man's skin is. If he can play music, I'd sit next to him in any band."

And music, of course, is the other realm in which Negro and white have come most closely together in the South, sometimes with closer attention to the score than to each other. The South, with its peculiar experience of two races living in close interdependence and independence, has given the nation the bulk of its truly indigenous music, its paradoxes of joy and sorrow, carefree laughter and burdened faith: jazz and the blues and the spiritual.

Music seems often to have been the bridge which could provide contact between the races, even in times when relationships were undergoing tensions and tightenings. Following the Revolutionary War, in North Carolina, when Negro freedmen were looked on with increasing suspicion, a law was finally passed by the General Assembly in 1812 stating, "It shall not be lawful for the Captain or Commanding Officer of any company of militia to enroll any free Negro or Mulatto in his company." But then it went on to provide "that it shall and may be lawful at all times to enroll a sufficient number of such in any Militia Company as Musicians."

There is a popular and ever-persistent vision of the past in which happy slaves sing merry ditties or plaintive spirituals out in the quarters or—on special occasions—on the wide lawn before the big house. The music not only soothed the master's and mistress's nerves—but their consciences as well. Weren't singing people happy people?

And today, looking back at those days so shrouded in myth, we listen to Dixie and Carry Me Back to Old Virginny and My Old Kentucky Home and tell ourselves that it must have been closer to the movie version than we will admit. But there is always the chilling afterthought: much of the great music has been written out of deep sorrow, rather than lighthearted happiness, and this is the truth which infuses the spirituals and makes them weep for all of us. And the three songs named, those most closely associated with the South in the national mind, were all written by born-and-bred Yankees.

Dan Emmett looked away to Dixie, where he visited once in a while, but he took his stand to "live and die in Dixie" only in his song. James Bland was born in Flushing, Queens, and never lived in Virginny before or after his song about carrying him back—any more than he wore Dem Golden Slippers about which he also wrote. Stephen Foster was a native of Pittsburgh, Pennsylvania, and his old Kentucky Home was Federal Hill, where he visited in 1852. From that visit he mined many of those songs which have established the picture of Old South life in our minds: Swanee River, Old Black Joe and many more.

It is well that those few stout-voiced Southerners who demand to-day that "the South be left alone," "outsiders stay home," have not also suggested that "outsiders'" contributions from the past, and present, be returned. What would happen to the martial spirit, the rebel yell in the South, if we had to send Dixie back up North?

One of the campaigns some branches of the White Citizens' Councils have waged has been against Negro entertainers and Negro music. Publications include pictures of Negro and white singers, actors, musicians as they "fraternize" to "demoralize" America. When Lena Horne headed the NAACP's Christmas Seal campaign, The White Sentinel, published in St. Louis and distributed through the South, devoted a page to the singer and her white friends: "This woman stands high in NAACP circles for two reasons. First she has a long red record and secondly, she is married to a White man. As in the case of Paul Robeson, Lena Horne has been given fame and fortune by White people who buy her records and patronize her shows. She is rewarding her patrons by . . . working with the NAACP to mongrelize America."

In April, 1956, Nat "King" Cole, jazz pianist and ballad singer, returned to his birth-state, Alabama, to perform before a segregated audience. As he sang on the stage of Birmingham's Municipal Auditorium, a white man called, "Let's get that nigger," and a group vaulted the footlights and attacked him. Police, who were in the wings, rescued Cole. When he was unable to continue the program, the audience gave him an ovation and shouted, "We're sorry."

A few nights later, an audience in Raleigh, North Carolina, gave Cole a standing ovation—and voluntarily melted the segregated color lines when they all moved to fill the best front seats together in the thirty-seven-hundred-seat auditorium, which was not quite filled to capacity.

In December, 1956, a group of seventeen boys and girls, with director John Work and their piano accompanist, returned to the South from a two-month concert tour of Europe. They were the Fisk Jubilee Singers, inheritors of a fascinating and inspiring tradition.

The January after the close of the Civil War, a Negro school, Fisk University, was opened in Nashville, Tennessee. As it was for most other institutions at that time, money was "scarce as hen's teeth"; the cupboard was bare. Fortunately the school's treasurer was also a musician. A veteran of Chancellorsville and Gettysburg, George White, a native of New York, had dedicated himself to helping this university. With eleven students, who later grew to twenty-four, he organized a vocal group whose main features were the spirituals of their people, and in October, 1871, they launched on the first of what would become a famous series of tours.

That first year they sometimes endured want and humiliation, but they got many gifts for their school: money and all kinds of supplies and equipment.

"In less than three years' time," one writer, J. B. T. Marsh, says, they brought back to Fisk "nearly one hundred thousand dollars. They had been turned away from hotels, and driven out of railway waiting-rooms because of their color. But they had been received with honor by the President of the United States, they had sung their slave-songs before the Queen of Great Britain, and they had gathered as invited guests about the breakfast-table of her Prime Minister. Their success was as remarkable as their mission was unique."

On the campus at Nashville, built in large part by the performances of these trained and talented singers through the years, the Fisk Jubilee Singers raise their voices in song today. Tenderly, like a mother's lonesome lullaby in a piney-woods cabin; sorrowfully, with a heavy burden of pain and weariness; triumphantly, with the hope of all mankind everywhere—their music fills the silence under the tall magnolias, between the old and new brick buildings. The score from which that music came was written first in the heart and flesh and blood of a people.

Who knows the score in the South today?

Perhaps only those who know the meaning of the legend which one Southern football coach keeps framed on his desk: "An Indian prayer—Great Spirit . . . help me never to judge another until I have walked, for a while, in his moccasins."

14 ⁂ Great Day A-Coming

It is late spring in middle Mississippi, one of those rare moments between winter's chill and dampness and summer's steamy heat, when the air is clean and fragrant and the sun falls gently on your bare arms and on the deserted square of the town where you've paused for lunch.

The courthouse that might appear dingy in other weather seems today mellow with time, and its deserted, trampled lawn, its empty public benches, merely bespeak its daily role as heart of the county stretching around it. Its desertion is only temporary. This is Sunday. Except for a paper boy and a few late churchgoers, the town is still as a tomb.

You kick an empty Coca-Cola bottle aside and sit down on one of the benches. The marble Confederate soldier keeps you silent company. A Negro woman carrying a bundle waits for the green light and as she crosses the street you can hear the heavy shuffle of her feet. Slowly you become aware of the faint sound of singing: a hymn, soft as the spring sun—and sweet. Sweet as honeydew on the tongue, it pours from a brick church on one of the main streets leading off the square. And if you can remember a Southern childhood, a deep nostalgia clutches your throat and tightens your chest. The remembered ritual of Sunday: the fresh, new clothes outside; the certainty within. Hell and heaven forever separate, the black and white, the sheep and goats forever defined.

After a while you go across the square to the town's hotel. It is after church now and there are a few more people on the streets, everyone leisurely in the pleasant air, free of the pressure of school or office until tomorrow. Inside the hotel you are surprised to find the little dining room already crowded. There are a few elderly ladies wearing hats with short veils or clusters of flowers, but most of the diners are family groups—young couples with two or three small squirming boys and girls, older couples with their married children and grandchildren dressed in Sunday navy blues and greys. The tall amber glasses of iced tea, the smell of fried chicken and steamed rice and heaping bowls of vegetables and hot bis-

262

cuits are all familiar—but the locale, the setting, that suggests one of the big changes in the South.

As you are led between the tables and finally seated, you are aware of the decorous inquiry in all the eyes around you. A tentative friend-liness and hostility mix in their gaze until you feel almost an intruder in a family affair. Which, in a sense, you are—for this is the public transfor-mation of something that used to be one of the private rituals. Sunday dinner was the family rite when, hot weather or cool, everyone ate a little too much of the too-rich food and spent the rest of the afternoon in a drowsy stupor digesting the morning paper, the preacher's sermon and the cook's dinner.

But the cook is not in the kitchen any more on Sundays—at least not in many kitchens. In much of the South this simple fact has caused a minor social revolution. Nettie Sue wants to hear her pastor, too. Nettie Sue wants to dress up and seek salvation in the morning instead of at night or in the afternoon. Because of this, several cities have even experi-mented with a nine-o'clock worship service in the white churches so that the housewives may go home in time to fry the okra and cream the corn, slice platters of red tomatoes and boil the butter beans and deep-fry the floured chicken until it crisps to a golden brown. But more and more the small-town cafés, the city hotels, the motel restaurants, are usurping the place of the high-ceilinged old family dining rooms on Sunday, and paper and plastic are replacing damask. And most of those who take dinner at home wash their own dishes or stack them in the electric dishwasher. Nettie Sue is not there any longer on Sunday—and the white families remember this as they sit in their pews; this and a dozen other minor, meaningful changes—and some of them are resigned and some are angry, and a few are glad.

James Weldon Johnson said that "the race question involves the saving of black America's body and white America's soul." Or, as one Kentucky minister tells you, "I'm thinking it's about time we got over the idea of being our brother's keeper and were willing to be our brother's brother for a while."

As the South faces one of its moments of greatest stress, its inner-most strengths and weaknesses suddenly become apparent to all. No-where are the weaknesses more embarrassing, the contradictions more ir-ritating, than in the realm of religion. This is a field in which the region could claim superlatives: more church memberships, higher percentages of attendances—in short, the Bible Belt. And yet . . .

This same Kentuckian says, "For years, generations, we Southerners abstractly said one thing and daily, with as little consciousness of it as was possible, did another. But the Supreme Court decision brought word and act together. 'In the beginning was the word . . . ' Well, we've had the words a long time, now we've got to live up to them. More than that, this decision has brought the Southerner's dichotomy into the open and made him verbalize it. This was the most unforgivable thing of all!"

This dichotomy is not new. While Charlotte, North Carolina, was building its reputation as one of the most churchgoing cities in America, it was also making statistics in having one of the highest crime rates in the country, and this paradox was not uncharacteristic in the region as a whole.

Thirty-seven years ago a man who described the sharecropping system in relation to cotton remarked, "During the hot season about the best thing for croppers to do is to quit work, visit around, and attend the protracted meeting. Then if they haven't killed each other *ad interim*, they are physically fit when the rush of cotton picking begins." The rash of revivals and killings has usually reached a peak in the late summer. It has been claimed that there is no relation between the two facts—and even if this were true, it would perhaps be the most astonishing fact of all, that there could be so little relation between the two.

The South's flair for violence, coupled with its frequent avowals of religion, has been the subject of many studies from social science theses to Broadway musicals. But there seems one thing certain: it has not yet escaped the image of the frontiersman, with Bible in one hand and rifle in the other. What could not be converted remained to be conquered.

In this situation, ministers have had a somewhat ambiguous part to play. White and Negro, it is not surprising that they have sometimes accepted the name of leader but the role of follower. One thing the present crisis seems to have forced on the South is a closer evaluation, conscious or unconscious, of the actual leadership exercised by the clergy. Figurehead or shepherd, theirs has been most acutely the dilemma of how far they might pursue Christianity with effectiveness and where they must withdraw for expediency.

Certainly during the Civil War the Southern ministry mustered beneath the stars and bars. Typical of many churches' statements in the period might be that recorded in the minutes of the General Assembly of the Presbyterian Church in the Confederate States of America, in 1863: "We hesitate not to affirm that it is the peculiar mission of the Southern church to conserve the institution of slavery, and to make it a blessing both to master and slave. We could not, if we would, yield up these four millions of immortal beings to the dictates of fanaticism and to the menaces of military power." To the great national schism were added a series of church schisms, too—the divisions in the major Protestant denominations which are only now beginning to be healed.

The evolution of individual ministers' justifications of slavery has seldom been better described than in a discussion by Peter Cartwright, who preached in the South from 1808 until 1824. "Methodist preachers in those days made it a matter of conscience not to hold their fellow creatures in bondage, if it was practicable to emancipate them, conformably to the laws of the state in which they lived. Methodism increased and spread, and many Methodist preachers, taken from comparative poverty, not able to own a negro, and who preached loudly against it, improved and became popular among slaveholding families, and became personally interested in slave property. They then began to apologize for the evil; then to justify it, on legal principles; then on Bible principles."

A respected Southern historian tells you; "One of the big differences between the Civil War situation and this today is that ninety years ago the ministers were almost unanimously with the Confederacy. Today they are not unanimously on either side, and there are really quite few who are die-hard segregationists. In the Civil War they were officially in the vanguard for secession—now they're against disruption." Or, as one of the leaders of Virginia's pro-segregation Defenders of State Sovereignty and Individual Liberties says: "The worst obstacle we face in the fight to preserve segregated schools in the South is the white preacher. The patriots of Reconstruction had the preachers praying for them instead of working against them."

Almost every large church denomination has gone on record with an official statement condemning segregation. The General Assembly of the Presbyterian Church has taken a firm stand since 1954. In May, 1957, at a meeting in Birmingham, it made the following stern statement: "In this nation, where Christianity and democracy are bywords, it is unthinkable that a Christian should join himself to Klan or Council whose purpose it is to gain its point by intimidation, reprisal and violence, or that he should lift no voice of protest against those who appeal to prejudice and spread fear."

In September, 1956, the world-wide Methodist Conference met on an integrated basis in the South. In the hills of Western North Carolina, where Bishop Asbury had toiled against rugged weather, well-nigh impassable mountains and the hardships of frontier life, and where many a previous camp meeting had made the valleys ring, more than two thousand white and colored delegates from seventy countries gathered to deliberate on the issues of the day. During the very week the council was considering the possibility of making Lake Junaluska world headquarters of Methodism, the state of North Carolina was adopting a stringent new set of laws which would ensure segregation in the schools. No final decision was reached on making a North Carolina site headquarters for a world two-thirds colored and one-third white.

A few days later, the World Methodist Conference issued a strong pledge against "political, economic, educational, social or religious discrimination or segregation" imposed on any race, and called for Methodists everywhere to "initiate, contend for and foster within their own societies a genuine and all-inclusive fellowship." In the summer of 1957, again at Lake Junaluska, Bishop William T. Watkins of Louisville issued a ringing challenge: "We Southerners have a fearful responsibility in the matter of race relations, and we must be careful not to consider it as the same old problem . . . though we have a changeless Christ, we must remember that we preach to a changing world."

Official statements of the Protestant Episcopal Church have been just as unequivocal, the Congregational and Lutheran leaders have stated emphatically against segregation, but most interesting, perhaps, is the fact that the two groups who are precisely opposite in their religious dogma and observance have so far been farthest in the vanguard opening their Southern churches for all the community: the Catholics and the Unitarians. In every Southern city you visit, the one minister all those working for segregation will unanimously condemn, and all those seeking integration will praise, is the Unitarian leader. New Orleans' Archbishop Joseph F. Rummel has become the Roman Catholic voice of deliberate speed in his outspoken condemnation of segregation as "morally wrong and sinful," and his assurance that the parochial schools in New Orleans will integrate. Bishop Vincent S. Waters of North Carolina has faced mob violence as a result of his integration of churches in one town, and has thus gone on record: "As pastor of your souls, I am happy to take the responsibility for any evil which might result from different races worshipping together, but I would be unwilling to take the responsibility of those who refuse to worship God with a person of another race." In San Antonio, Archbishop Robert E. Lucey has been given much credit for the quiet desegregation of local schools. When the Texas legislature, during its spring, 1957, term, had a number of segregation bills under consideration, this spiritual head of Texas Roman Catholics said that "segregationist legislators" should resign, for advocates of segregation are "playing into the hands of Communists . . . showing lack of patriotism, hypocrisy and stupidity."

"You can talk about all the church groups you want to," a Negro leader says, "but in the South you've not scratched the surface till you've included the Baptists."

Today the Southern Baptists are by far the largest regional denomination in America. Between 1940 and 1957, their membership swelled from a little over five million to more than eight and a half million. And each of their widely scattered affiliated thirty thousand churches in twenty-four states, the District of Columbia, Alaska, Mexico and Hawaii, has almost complete local autonomy. This fact has had two current consequences summarized in the words of one Southerner with no church affiliation: "The Catholic clergy have the large advantage, in a local situation, of acting on directives from higher authority. They can pass the buck at the same time they press the issue. The poor Baptist ministers, they have to squirm under their own consciences, knowing they can be taken into quick and direct account for anything they advocate. Certainly this slows them down in taking a stand on anything contrary to the majority of the community. But I also have the feeling that if these Baptists ever really decide to move for integration, the jig will be up. When they decide, individually, to pay the price, the whole cloth will be bought."

Because they are, of all organizations, the quintessence of that individualism which has characterized the South, their disagreements on the matter of segregation may also serve as example of differences which have occurred in all the church groups. Cleavage between Deep and Border South, cleavage along lines of age and education, these are especially evident among Baptists but are probably just as true of the other denominations.

In one town in northern Alabama a man tells you, "Our ministers around here ignore all this race talk. Course the Baptist church is our biggest. The nigra Baptist church is their leading one, too, and their preacher, he's too smart to start talking for this integration. He knows he'd just be talking hisself out of a job. Segregation may've been a handicap on some nigra churches, though I can't see how, but it was sure a big help to most of their preachers. As for the white preachers, they go off to these big get-togethers once a year, subscribe to those general statements some committee writes up, and that makes them feel better; then they come on back home and preach on Revelation like always. Everybody's satisfied."

Although the Southern Baptist Christian Life Commission has urged "Christian statesmen and leaders to use their leadership in positive thought and planning to the end that this crisis in our national history shall not be made the occasion for new and bitter prejudices, but a movement toward a united nation embodying and proclaiming a democracy that will commend freedom to all peoples," there is the feeling among part of the church group that many ministers are providing something less than community leadership in an hour of decision. Here again, the highly individual nature of each congregation can create a gulf between official pronouncement and local practice.

Factors of age and education are important, too. When 1,005 Baptist pastors were recently polled in Tennessee, only 39 per cent favored integration. That figure rose sharply, however, among those who had Bachelor of Divinity degrees, with 79 per cent of this group favoring public school integration. In the group with an eighth-grade education or less, only 9 per cent favored integration. The younger men agreed with the better educated: 61 per cent of the pastors twenty-nine years of age and less were for integration, compared with 16 per cent who were between fifty and fifty-nine years old.

It would be utterly false, of course, to assume that active opposition to integration comes only from the less educated and less wealthy churches, with more elderly members. Without proof, as only a strong impression, it may be that this is the case more often in the border areas outside the Deep South. But within the highly charged atmosphere of the Black Belt, it is obvious that personal convictions of the pastor often coincide with those of his congregation or are not reflected in his church's actions. While pronouncements of the piney-woods church may have less polish than those of the group meeting in a new suburban sanctuary, they often represent a seemingly solid front on racial questions.

A clear example of the division in Southern Baptist ranks occurred in Georgia late in 1956. The Social Service Commission presented a report to the State Baptist Convention recommending acceptance of the Supreme Court decision outlawing segregation in the public schools and calling on Georgia's eight hundred thousand Baptists to help create an attitude whereby school officials could comply with the decision. The report was not adopted, and Dr. Louis D. Newton, an Atlanta minister who led the fight for its defeat, said that it would put "an added burden" on ministers and laymen who are already seeking a solution to the "explosive situation." On the opposite side, another Atlanta minister, Dr. O. Norman Shands, pointed out that there is a "moral obligation on Georgia Baptists to face every moral issue associated with the racial problem."

A decisive group action, which challenged the desegregation struggle at its political and moral levels, was the formal declaration issued by the Richmond, Virginia, Ministers' Association in late February, 1957. Beginning with an affirmation of the moral nature of the world and the richness of Virginia's religious and political heritage, it went on to say, "The point of our concern is that the present Governor and a majority of the Legislature have, in our opinion, seriously impaired the sacred and historic traditions of Virginian democracy and lowered the prestige of the State in the eyes of thoughtful people all across the nation, if not the world, by what we regard as their exceedingly inept handling of the current racial situation.

". . . To cap the whole, the special session of our Legislature has sought to restrict the open, free criticism of its coerced solutions by forbidding unhampered freedom to discuss the matter or to enter litigation over it. Adding insult to injury, it has, furthermore, exempted politicians and political groups from these restrictions."

Response to this ministerial "poaching" on political preserves was explosive. The afternoon paper deplored it as a "muddle-headed mixture of good intentions and poor thinking . . . confusing what is mortal and what is divine." One of the sponsors of House Bill 60 said of the ministers who signed the statement, "The cloak of morality which they drape around their shoulders appears a little thin. Integration has only become a great moral and religious issue to them since the Supreme Court decision. Evidently the Supreme Court has become the new interpreter of God's word." Letters of disagreement to the Richmond papers did not, as a rule, attack the logic or error of the statement as much as they condemned the ministers personally. Calling for "separation of church and state," they generally instructed the ministers to mind their own business.

"I'm for separation of church and state," one young minister tells you, "just like I don't believe in the divine right of kings. But I'm for the separation of Sunday morality from Monday immorality, too, and I don't believe in any divine right of white people, either." He shakes his head sadly as he leads you down the walk toward his church annex. "I'm afraid the habit of segregation is catching. Our people found it was advantageous to segregate one race to an inferior status, now we seem to be discovering that we've found it convenient to segregate one area of our lives from the whole, too. We've fractionalized our lives until the cost has become almost too high to keep the pattern safe: Restricted if it's Hebrew, segregated if it's Negro, isolated if it's leprosy and ignored if it's religious."

A more worldly resident of Richmond says, "The ministers of the

South had better be careful. They're driving an irretrievable wedge between the pulpit and the pew."

What may seem a wedge to one may apparently be a banner to another. "Thank God at least some of the church leadership has finally taken a stand against the political leadership in this state!" a small-town Virginian says, "Some of us had begun to think all the Christians were in the catacombs."

In most Southern states there seems to have been less silence on the part of the clergy opposing integration. In Virginia, pro-segregation church members were urged by the Episcopal chaplain of the Defenders of State Sovereignty and Individual Liberties to remain in groups "where the social gospel is upheld. Submit your token dues and duties, stay in those organizations, find out what they are thinking and doing." This call to bore from within reminds you of something a young minister in North Carolina said several weeks before: "It's not infiltration by Communists the church has to worry about. It's infiltration of commonness. Christians are supposed to be uncommon people, not conformed to this world but transformed by another one. Yet every day we're working to be just like the rest of the community. We've got to decide whether we want to win a popularity contest today or eternal life tomorrow."

A Methodist minister in Georgia probably summarized the general attitude of less rabid segregationists in his profession. When a Negro wanted to join his church, the pastor said that he told him, "Joining our church won't accomplish anything. There are two hundred Negro churches in Atlanta that need you. You in your church, we in ours, will be worshiping the same God. You will be better off and so will we." Then this Christian minister added a most revealing explanation to his congregation (the old Southern compound of unconscious guilt and conscious defiance?): "If that's unchristian, that's still the way I feel."

In Mississippi, Judge T. P. Brady, a Harvard graduate and leader in the Southern movement to organize Citizens' Councils, told a meeting of white people, "This is a clash of principles. We will fail with bullets and bricks. The highest, finest, cleanest non-violent program is necessary if we are to be victorious. Then we will have God and right on our side."

There is the soft-voiced, hard-eyed minister you hear at a WCC meeting in another state. In his gabardine suit and silk necktie, with well-manicured hands, he is quite different from his audience, but in his resentments and surliness he is quite like them. "To me this is far more than a Negro fight. Somebody said, 'Preacher, I wonder why you're taking such an activity in the segregation business,' and I told him, 'Brother, in this we're fighting all the evil influences in the United States. We've come to the place where it's almost a sin to be an American patriot, we have to include the world in the boundaries of our love and devotion. It's a sin to be just an American.'

"I wish I knew how your minister stood on these issues. And why! Do you know?

"Livingstone said that God made the white man and God made the black man, and the devil made the mulatto. I think he was right. Some of these cultured people, high-up church people, who won't let their Persian cats or their pedigreed poodles out without a leash, talk about all this brotherhood among people. Now lions mate with lions, alley cats with alley cats—but they're all members of the cat family.

"The latest facts are that we're having over two hundred mixed marriages a week going on in Chicago and Cook County, Illinois. Now I figure I can be just as Christian and love the people of the world and keep a fence up in my own backyard. What about you?"

"Amen!"

Gradually the gathering takes on a camp-meeting spirit. The program is thrown open to remarks from the floor, but what is said, and the emotion charging it, transforms remarks into testimonials.

"Brother, I just want to tell you, we're thankful for you. We're thankful there's a few God-led ministers left." (One of the interesting features of the division of clergy over this problem is the frequency with which each side assumes it is the minority.)

"The niggers have got skedaddles of money behind them—the NAPC, that Ford Foundation, Falstaff beer, George Burns and Gracie Allen, and Nixon's a-liking them too—but we've got something stronger than money behind us and that's the Lord!"

"My family's been white men in this county since 1820, and I'm not going back on my raising. No preacher nor nobody else can make me do that!"

"Folks, I'm a preacher from over here in the next county. I work in the mills during the week and preach wherever I get a call of a Sunday. But I'm a-telling you, it's time all red-blooded, God-loving, Christ-fearing, spirit-filled men stood up and fought for what they know's right. Won't but one thing unravel this: for the spirit of Jesus Christ to fill everybody—then everybody will be willing to fit into their place and not stir up trouble.

"Brothers, I'm glad to be here tonight. I've enjoyed every hour in WCCs. With the help of the good Lord, and joining ourselves closeter together, we can get this thing going. I invite each and every one of you over to your neighbor town for our Council meeting this Saturday night."

In Kingstree, South Carolina, the men of the Williamsburg Presbyterian Church were more formal and resourceful in their effort to ban any local expression of "dangerous" ideas: ". . . Whereas, at a recent meeting of the Men of the Church group of Harmony Presbytery, a speaker, in a very subtle manner, advocated integration of the white and negro races in our church, which if followed, would violate the law and contravene the customs and beliefs of many members of this organization;

"And whereas, it is believed that there is a group among the leaders of the Presbyterian Church who desire to have integration of the races in the church, and it is feared that others of that group may be procured to speak, and that they will advocate that policy;

"Now therefore, be it resolved by the Men of the Church of Williamsburg Presbyterian Church that the President is requested to screen prospective speakers, to insure that members of the 'integration clique' do not have an opportunity to appear before Men of the Church of Harmony Presbytery."

In response to this action, The Presbyterian Outlook in Richmond, Virginia, observed, "Somebody should tell the men of the Williamsburg Church in Kingstree, S.C., that despite all their efforts, the dyke will not hold. However they may wish that the ideas which they consider dangerous may be kept from their fellows, there is no way to isolate them in our present world. Moreover, by the very fact of the ban which they seek to impose on any discussion calling for integration, the idea gains a status that it would not otherwise have enjoyed. Furthermore, the fact that advocates of segregation and those who inflame the fears of people on this subject are allowed free course, will appeal to previously unresponsive observers as lacking in sportsmanship."

A successful self-made man in one of the South's largest cities tells you during dinner at his club; "I don't know, seems to me like the religious attitude toward this race situation is all out of focus some way. You take what happened at the Episcopal church we belong to out here in the suburbs. We had a request a couple of Christmases ago, by a Negro congregation temporarily without a building, asking if they could use our church for a meeting. The minister put it squarely in the lap of the vestry, although I think he'd have been glad for them to use it. Out of the eleven who were at our vestry meeting I was the only one who spoke out for letting them use our church. They got the double-dip deep-freeze from all the rest. Hell, if they want to worship at Christmas and use our building—not even come with us!—I don't see what else we could do and be Christians but let them come. And you know why the others didn't want them? Because we had a building fund campaign on at the time and some of the vestry were afraid some of the members who lived near the church would see the Negroes going in and wouldn't contribute to the building. Frankly, I haven't had much to do with them since."

Probably the most influential pro-segregation voice in the Southern pulpit today is that of the Reverend Doctor W. A. Criswell, pastor of Dallas's huge and wealthy First Baptist Church. Indicative of the wide differences on this question, the most influential religious leader who has spoken out for integration is also a member of this church: world-renowned evangelist Billy Graham. Early in 1955 Graham took an unequivocal stand against any segregation at his meetings. "Anthing that causes races to feel inferior one to the other or the making of second-rate and second-class citizens is not only un-American, I think it's unchristian."

As for Dr. Criswell, a stirring speaker and able actor, he has been variously described by fellow Baptists in his state as "one of the finest church organizers of our day," as having "a wonderful mind—for the eighteenth century," and as "the Little Pope of Texas." During 1956 and early 1957 he revived the buried bones of Evolution; pronounced the invocation at a convention of Texas Democratic conservatives who endorsed states' rights, criticized the Supreme Court and socialized medicine, and opposed "federal control" of schools and natural resources production; and told twelve hundred delegates at a Southern Baptist Conference in Denver, Colorado, that "colored people need colored ministers and white people need white ministers."

In a speech at a South Carolina Baptist conference on evangelism, Dr. Criswell dealt with desegregation: "This thing they are trying to ram down our throats now is all foolishness; it is idiocy. Who's stirring up all this stuff? Is it God's people or somebody else? I happen to know it is somebody else. If they will leave us alone and stay up there with their dirty shirts, we'll save more souls and do more good than they."

There are Texans who will assure you that if integration comes, Dr. Criswell is ready to turn his church into a parochial school. (An elderly newspaperman has told you in a moment of reverie: "It seems to be the fate of people who have any deep antagonisms to become more and more like the thing they dislike. Take the the Baptists down here in the South: for years they've waged war against the Roman Catholics, criticizing especially their big cathedrals and their separate schools. Now look at the Baptists! Big brick sanctuaries and copper steeples on every Main Street and at every mudhole in the state, and now some are offering to establish private schools in their churches. Pretty soon the only thing the Romans will have that the Baptists don't is the rosary.")

The sentiments expressed by Dr. Criswell on the matter of integration indicate a schism on many issues which exists, perhaps in it most agitated form, in the religion of the South today. On one side is the fundamental evangelical doctrine of faith emphasizing a change of heart—on the other, the evolving gospel of man-seeking-God emphasizing a changed society. "The thing Criswell and men like him, who oppose what we call 'social gospel,' don't seem to understand is this," a young Baptist explains earnestly, "a church has Christians in all stages of development. Supposedly most of its members have already undergone a change of heart. To keep preaching on that level is to stop the growth at kindergarten. But if a changed heart has any reality or meaning, it affects the world around it. Its inner light sheds out to transform some of the dark corners of society, and a social gospel makes use of that light. Really, the two aren't in conflict; the way I look at it, one grows out of the other, and a preacher must admit both."

Few who have spent much time recently in the Deep South would deny that on the racial question its ministers occupy an ever-narrowing beachhead. It would seem that the immovable object is being confronted by the irresistible force, and those who would counsel in wisdom find themselves on perpetual quicksand. They may take a definite stand or they may abdicate. The pressures on those who remain are not always open and brutal, more often they are subtle and in the long run only cruel. A very proper gentleman in one of the Old South cities comes to mind. You remember how, in his modern office, all the venerable forms of gallantry were observed—and yet, something was lacking. Was it the sense of value that lay behind the true old gallantry? Was it simple human warmth without which all courtesy is an empty husk? Anyway, you remember his analysis of the religious-racial situation in his city:

"I would not presume to say what either the clergy or laity thinks on this. How can any man ever tell what another is thinking? I can say only that a few ministers here have taken stands I suppose you could call integrationist—and their flocks have pretty well shown them they wouldn't follow that line. I know that the boards of the various churches here have been studying very closely the record of any new minister in regard to this question, before they call him here.

"Last year the Bishop of the Catholic Church who was born and bred here was transferred. They sent one down from up North, presumably to soften us up on integration. But I suspect, I deeply suspect, that it is we who have softened him up on segregation.

"As for the Jews, there aren't many here and they're too smart to get caught in this. After all, they're only once removed from the attack themselves. One of the best reactionaries we have in the city is a Jew. On the whole, I simply don't believe we're going to let our ministers become too involved in a problem we consider somewhat more political and social than moral."

A former president of the Georgia Council of Churches stated the situation well when he said, "Freedom of speech is not denied by law; it is now denied by fear."

Yet many have broken out of this paralysis of fear—and have spoken and acted. Unlike one woman who cried, "The most Christian things I do I find I'm doing most secretively," they have rejected secrecy. Their decision has not always produced an immediate conflagration of either protest or agreement. A Reformed Lutheran minister tells you a story which illustrates the insulating power of simple apathy. "Four Methodist ministers in Alabama got together and decided to preach a sermon on the race situation. They synchronized their calendars and each gave his sermon the same Sunday. Immediately afterward there was a real fruit-basket-turnover. Every minister was exchanged but one. When that church was asked why it hadn't demanded that its pastor leave, a member replied, 'We know he'd just be sent to another church—and we're afraid the people there might pay some attention to what he says!' "

In situations where moderate church leadership seems to have no demonstrable effect, the words of one editorialist might apply: "The moral judgment now crystallizing about race segregation is akin to that which condemned slavery. It will not be abolished even in the Church at one stroke, but the important thing is that no congregation and no denomination should ever have a clear conscience while conforming to the pattern."

A cloudy conscience is covering much of the South today because of creation of a new group of people—those the Southern Regional Council has called Displaced Parsons. These most recent DP's are interdenominational, of both races, and come from towns scattered throughout the South: the one thing they have in common is their crime—stating an unpopular viewpoint on race.

In Batesburg, South Carolina, the pastor of the Baptist Church, in which Federal Judge George Timmerman is chairman of the Board of Deacons, engaged in a private discussion of integration. He was reported to have commented that he thought segregation wrong. His resignation as pastor followed soon after. A South Carolina woman tells you, "Stafford was so popular, especially with the young people, he's only thirty-four years old himself and was a pilot in the Marine Corps in World War II. He must have had 95 per cent of his church behind him. No one thought he could be dismissed. But he was! Pronto!"

A Baptist minister in Arkansas preached, in late February, 1955, that segregation was sinful. By March twentieth he was working in Memphis. A Methodist minister appointed to the Annual Mississippi Conference made a speech condemning Jim Crow, and the Conference was unable to find a church that would accept him.

One Baptist official in Dallas tells of a young minister at Palestine, Texas, who shook hands with a Negro on a downtown street corner and then had a Vacation Bible School for some Negro children. "Shortly afterwards, when he was fired from his pulpit, one of the church members held up a hand and said, 'This hand has never touched a nigger.'"

In Jesuit Bend, Louisiana, a Negro priest was prevented from saying mass before a white congregation. Archbishop Francis Rummel immediately closed the mission.

All the white ministers who have spoken for calmness or logic or desegregation have not become DP's, of course. In Henderson, Kentucky, when unrest from anti-integration mob demonstrations at nearby Sturgis and Clay provided the fuse for Citizens' Council leadership of a school boycott, the ministerial association organized in opposition. Thirteen local pastors, representing seven churches, attended the first Citizens' Council mass meeting and spoke for calmness and compliance with the supreme law of the land. If they did not bring sanity to the crowd, they at least provided a counterattack and dispelled the illusion of community solidarity behind violent means and illegal ends. During the week which followed, these ministers bolstered words with actions. They worked with parents in an effort to keep the children in school, corrected as much as they could of the erroneous propaganda flooding this town of twenty thousand people, and provided antidotes for the poisonous bigotry spouted by speakers both local and imported. The boycott of Weaverton school failed. In a diary of these events kept by two of the Henderson ministers—C. Sumpter Logan and Theodore A. Braun—and later published in Christian Century, their summary is particularly pertinent:

"We are told that our ministerial association's was the first organized opposition in the south to a white citizens' council. That may or may not be true. Certainly to assume leadership against a movement that has such powerful emotions behind it is like launching a canoe into the worst sort of rip tide. Even so, one can still witness—and our day calls desperately for Christian witness in a great many areas."

When Billy Graham further clarified his stand in support of integration, he spoke with the most far-ranging authority in the Protestant evangelical South. Claiming that the church has been "too silent" about racial tensions, he said, "Its voice has been hushed when it ought to speak out for neighborly love. . . . The churches' job is to create a climate of good will."

In Houston, Texas, a man tells you about the pastor of one of the local Lutheran churches. "Reverand Paul Seastrand's church is in one of those residential districts where Negroes have been expanding more and more into formerly all-white areas. As his locality changed, I suppose the possibility of Negro members in his church became more logical. Seastrand tried to prepare his congregation for that possibility, which eventually became a reality. I think about seventeen-eighteen white members of the church pulled out in protest when a Negro family joined—but I believe twenty and thirty new white members have been added, so it all seems to have balanced out pretty well. It seems to me, however, that the really important feature of this church is the simple fact that it didn't sell its building and run when it was surrounded by the Negro community. In so many of these situations you find the so-called generals leading from the rear—then they're in good position to maneuver a retreat. Not Seastrand. He and his church are going to stick. 'God and one is always a majority.' That's what he said, and he's proved it!"

One of the most frequent cries of anguish in the South today is voiced by a minister without a pulpit, in Alabama: "What can a Southern man who loves his region and his church, his segregationist congregation and his anti-segregation convictions, do here today and still not be cut down by the powers-that-be? We've seen the teachers and preachers speak—and leave. We've seen the college trustees and church boards build the campuses and get rid of the faculty, build the churches and get rid of the ministers. When a group of civic leaders came to me and pleaded with me not to hold an interracial group meeting in one of the city buildings, I was so heartsick I could only say, 'Gentlemen of good will and bad conscience, I abdicate.' "

The pastor of a Christian Church in Little Rock, Arkansas, points out with common sense and uncommon insight some of the ways Southern ministers can reconcile effectiveness with expediency. Young Dr. Colbert S. Cartwright meets you early on a rainy Monday morning at the door to his church and leads you upstairs to his study. One side of the study is lined with well-used books—one glance registers a wide variety of titles—

and the other wall of the room is glass, opening out to the green lawn and the street beyond and the city beyond that. The room reflects the man: unpretentious physically, challenging in a combination of clear insight with broad outlook.

"I believe that some of the events of the past year have shown us there are ways Southern ministers can act and yet not be martyred into Northern exile. I tried to point out in an article in *Christian Century* that we need greater sensitivity to what each situation calls for. We need to remember that imagination and sympathy are Christian virtues as worthy as fortitude and forthrightness. . . .

"Many different types of action are needed. What is of prime importance is that southern white ministers *do* act, carrying out their actions not only with enlightened consciences but with intelligence and imagination."

There are dozens of voices you hear speaking out of anxiety and certainty, frustration and fulfillment, pew and pulpit as Southern churches respond to a time of transition. Some of them say:

"God made white people and black people and it's unchristian to try to correct a mistake of God's."

"I can remember in Baton Rouge, when I was a kid, standing and trembling as the Klan went by, knowing how they hated Catholics. I told some of the folks at my Catholic church here in Memphis the other day, 'You'd better be fighting the prejudice on this Negro thing because next time it may be you they turn against.' "

"The Supreme Court didn't change the principles of the church. It brought out the negligence of the church."

"I was standing with the handful of Home Guard we'd organized to hold off the mob till state troopers could get to Clinton the night of the riots. The mob was angry but pretty disorganized. I remember one man tore off his coat and tie and threw them down on the ground and jumped on them, yelling, 'Christians, kill them! Kill them!' "

"A cross was burned on our church lawn because a group of whites and Negroes met together. Later they honored my yard, too. But you know, a flaming six-foot cross, lighted in recognition of your stand for the things you believe in, is inspiring, not demoralizing, strengthening, not terrifying, humbling, not humiliating. For isn't the cross the symbol of the highest that we know?"

What of the Negro church in the South today?

A Negro carpenter who signed a petition for integration in his Black

Belt county tells how he and other members of the NAACP (before it was outlawed) were punished by boycott and various other pressures of the white community. "We hate to see winter coming with some of our people in the condition they are as far as housing. Myself included, because I am staying in a place where I did not think I would ever live in my life. God help me, He could look down anywhere and see what chickens there are walking under the house. That is the place I stay in.

"But we had the prayers from other people, and our own prayers. We saw we were into it, and we meant to fight it out, not through violence but through prayers and love. Where they hate us, we try to treat them with love and respect. And in that way we know and we feel now that we are breaking it down and I do not think it will be as hard this winter with us as it was last winter."

In his words is suggested the new church which both affects and reflects the new Negro. And the new individual and group grew as inevitably as tomorrow out of the strongest roots of yesterday's church and layman.

Surely no one would dispute the fact that inside the South itself, since 1954, Negro ministers have provided their people's stoutest leadership. This fact is not without precedent. Nat Turner, who, in 1831, led the rebellion now known by his name, was a Negro preacher. (And the furor over segregated churches which he aroused has implications for today: the fear of slave plots which this uprising instilled in the white masters made many wonder whether all church services should not be desegregated so that the white members could keep an eye, and ear, on their fellow worshipers. Today a Negro Sunday-school teacher says, "If they'd come and learn for themselves what we're saying and doing in church, the white folks wouldn't have to gobble up so many lies and rumors about what we want and how we feel.")

During War and Reconstruction, many of the Negro political leaders were also from the churches, but after power was returned into the hands of the Southern whites, most of the Negro ministers found it confortable to accommodate to the power structure entrenched around them.

As the decades passed, this accommodation sometimes seemed to grow stronger, and the preachers often appeared more interested in cajoling money from white people than seeking justice from them. This segregated church, nevertheless, remained the Negro's strongest bastion of belief, self-expression and pride. He might be a janitor on weekdays, but on Sunday he became a deacon or steward.

Economically hobbled, this was one profession the ambitious and superior boy or man could enter without expensive training, if he so desired. (Until quite recently, it was estimated, in proportion to other professions followed, there were six times as many Negro as white ministers.) Like many of the underprivileged whites who were sometimes his counterpart, the Negro minister could claim that college learning was of little consequence compared to a "call." Preparation of the message was secondary to its presentation, and when reason and grammar faltered, emotion and vocal volume were made to suffice.

Myrdal stated thirteen years ago something white Southerners had known instinctively for a century—that the Negro church is an expression of the Negro community. For years that church and community have seemed equally quiescent and acquiescent; perhaps one of the most disturbing developments confronting many white Southerners today is the determined thrust toward equality which has been displayed on the part of this previously immobilized group.

The new awareness, couched in old terms, is apparent even in a brief conversation with a Negro handyman you talk with in Athens, Georgia: "Naw ma'am, naw suh, they don't 'low none of my people to go to the university. But they ought to. And I think the Bible will fulfill itself. Someday they'll do us right, we're just moving in God's good time—but on our own feet! That day'll come. Lots of the older ones are still looking back but the young folks, they're looking up and out."

Probably one of the clearest examples of the new bond between the other world and the outer world in the present Negro religion is that of Wheat Street Baptist Church in Atlanta. In 1954, this famous church opened an interdenominational Christian Education Center which serves many of its community's pressing needs. One of the most important is its nursery, providing care five days a week for over one hundred children whose mothers work. There is a library, a meeting room for Alcoholics Anonymous and civic groups; and courses for adults are offered in first aid, Spanish and other subjects. Special provisions are made for the blind and the deaf; the Center's buses take voters to registration booths. "They gave that place a true name all right," one Atlanta cook says, "when they called it the Center."

Many, both black and white, who sought in the past for economic, political and educational improvements for the Negroes, have deplored the afterlife theme so popular with the majority of Negro preachers. By seeming to ignore present poverty and injustice and counseling instead for humbleness and peacefulness and the triumph of spirit over flesh, they were accused of abdicating their civic and personal responsibilities. Perhaps they often were—but it is indeed ironic that these qualities which the ministers instilled in their congregations are now the very forces which seem to be shaking segregation at its deepest Southern roots. Which brings us to Montgomery, Alabama.

Just as the Negro church seemed to be slipping more and more into an ineffectual role in the community life of its people, a man and a movement dramatically halted that decline and revived the prestige of the pulpit with astounding results. A sociologist tells you, during a breakfast cup of coffee, "We Southerners are always lamenting that no one understands us, and we're at least partially correct. But I'll tell you someone who *does* understand us, if the Northerners don't. That's Martin Luther King, Jr., the Negro minister over in Alabama. He knows just when to apply the pressure and when to let up, and more important, he knows where to bring it to bear: on the soft underbelly of our consciences. He knows the religious traditions that sway Southerners—black and white alike—and he knows that conscience bolstering economics is an unbeatable combination."

The story of Montgomery is deceptively simple in summary. In the early evening of December 1, 1955, Mrs. Rosa Parks, a Negro seamstress, was on her way home from a long day downtown. The front of the bus on which she was riding was already filled with the whites for whom it was reserved by Jim Crow, when another group of passengers came aboard. As usual, the bus driver asked the four Negroes seated nearest the front to stand and let white riders have their seats. As usual, three of the Negroes stood and moved back. Not at all as usual, Mrs. Parks remained in her seat. "My feet hurt," she explained later. A policeman was called, she was placed under arrest, and subsequently released on bond. That was late Thursday.

By Saturday mimeographed leaflets were in circulation, asking Negroes not to ride the buses the following Monday, as a protest against Mrs. Parks's arrest. The Montgomery *Advertiser* received a call from a white woman who thought they should let their readers know "what the niggers are up to." The Sunday paper carried a story about the boycott being planned, and circulated the news among the city's fifty thousand Negroes far more effectively than any method their leaders could have devised. On Monday morning, to the amazement of Negroes and whites alike, the buses were practically empty of Negro passengers. The strike was 90 per cent effective. During the day, the Negro ministers and business and professional leaders of the town met to discuss the one-day boycott and a future course of action. The Montgomery Improvement Association was formed. Twenty-seven-year-old Martin Luther King, Jr., was chosen president. At a hastily called mass meeting that Monday night, more than five thousand Negroes backed a proposal to continue the boycott.

"Right there at first," one leader says, "we'd have settled for so little: a guarantee of courtesy by the bus drivers; seating on a first-come first-served but still segregated basis, and some Negro drivers on Negro buses. The whites wouldn't even assure us common courtesy. So when they wouldn't give us a little, we asked for a lot—and finally we got it!" After that first mass meeting Montgomery was launched on a long, memorable year. As one woman said, "We've always taken pride in being the Cradle of the Confederacy, now I guess we're also the Bassinet of the Boycott."

Such was the formal beginning of Montgomery's nonviolent protest and violent counterattack, of a new name frequenting the national headlines—Dr. King, who adapted to Southern Negro necessities a technique born last century in the eloquent advocacy of New England's Henry Thoreau, nurtured in this century into international power by the flesh and spirit of India's Gandhi, and now returned to America in one of her most vulnerable moments. King says simply, "The basic philosophy undergirding our protest was nonviolence. We refused to pay a dime to be mistreated. Carlyle said, 'No lie can live forever.' We believe that in Montgomery and that is why we could walk and never get weary. We were willing to exchange tired souls for tired feet."

The bus boycott, and its pyramiding effects on white and Negro alike, continued for a year. Then the Supreme Court handed down a decision outlawing Jim Crow on Montgomery buses. It was a tense moment as December 21, 1956, dawned.

In the still hours just before daylight, fog hung heavy over the dome of Alabama's gleaming white state-capitol building. The shrouded streets which stretched away from it through the city of Montgomery were silent. It was easy, in those small hours, to unloose the imagination and wonder if some of the ghosts of 1861 might not be lurking nearby.

As daylight came, warm and springlike, Court Square—at the opposite end of the wide main street leading up to the capitol—began to waken. Around the dry fountain, with its tiers of figurines, plump pigeons strutted on the wet pavement. Traffic began to pick up. The giant wreaths of Christmas lights strung across the street became more visible. And the city buses began to roll in and out of the square, loading and unloading passengers. In the doorways of the dress shops, the men's ready-to-wear and hardware stores, the newsstands and the offices and drugstores, people stood watching the buses. This was the morning when a year-old boycott and a generations-old tradition were to end.

Negroes and whites sat or stood at the central segregated bus stop—

watching; people drove by slowly, peering from their cars to see what was happening on the buses; and men leaning against the parking meters and standing on the street corners in their shirt sleeves watched. This was the morning that segregation on the city buses of Montgomery gasped its last and integration breathed its first, and there was tension implied in both the birth and the death.

The morning went quietly. A couple of cars filled with watchful white men in leather jackets parked on two sides of Court Square for the first hour, then slowly moved away. Groups of well-dressed Negro leaders stood at the central bus stop and rode several of the runs. The Reverend Mr. King entered a bus and took a seat near the front. The day's pattern developed—most of the buses were only partially filled, but the Negroes rode, for the most part, in the middle seats, a few at the very front, a few at the rear; and the whites rode huddled together far to the front. A few whites rode on the back seat on one or two runs; at least one or two sat by Negroes. By late afternoon the word had gone out over town that "Everything's O.K.; nothing happening."

It was the very calmness of that day that was the great news. People who said nothing had happened meant nothing violent, to make headlines. Actually a great deal had happened which might make news for years to come. Before a new year can begin, an old year must end. Before a new era of human dignity can be born, old indignities must die. On December twenty-first, an era as well as a year came to an end in this city. It was important that Alabamians and Americans alike should realize that what was disappearing was as meaningful as what was developing.

For one thing, the familiar cardboard signs spelling out segregation were gone from the buses. Gone too was the custom that had compelled Negroes to pay their fares at the front door and then often get off the bus and climb back on at the rear door. And the abusive language of some of the drivers calling their passengers "black apes" and "damned niggers" was stilled. Most apparent of all, perhaps, the stream of walking women had almost disappeared.

"The real power of the boycott was the Negro women," a housewife in one of the white residential areas said. "Every morning they came by our door here. It was like watching a brook to look out and see them going by steadily for an hour or so every morning and an hour or so every afternoon. And this morning they weren't there. The brook had dried up."

Other things, less tangible but not a whit less real, were gone, too. Their essence might be summed up in the words of one Negro: "Now there isn't any more hang-dog looking at a white man. We face him. We got a proud look. The Supreme Court brought us Negroes one thing we needed:

hope. For a long time it seemed like the only way we'd ever have justice was to die and go to heaven. But suddenly, back in 1954, it began to look like there might be a way-station on the road to heaven. The court had given us a place to find justice, now."

On a street in one of the newer residential suburbs, you could walk along in the pleasant morning between the rows of green lawns and lush pyracantha bushes heavy with clusters of flaming berries, and see a carload of young schoolboys slow down just past you and shout something before they roared away. A Negro woman walked just behind you. Small and lively as a sparrow in her brown coat and brown head-scarf and brown skin, she smiled. "They was just meddlin' me. They have to act theyself up. I don't pay them no mind, when they get throught actin' theyself up, everything be all right." She had no resentment—against the cruel boys in the present or the bus drivers in the past. "They wasn't all bad. Jus' a few real low mean. My bus driver I hadn' seen in a year welcome me back this mornin'. Like my family I work for: they told me to stay off the buses, they didn' blame us for what we's doin'."

A Negro man summed up the remarkable self-control his people had shown in this victory of their boycott. "We don't use the word 'victory.' We don't want to even have the attitude of the word. Like Reverend King told us at one of our meetings, the attitude of 'victory' wouldn't be worthy of us, and it would be a barrier to the growth we hope for in others."

The conduct and accomplishments of the Negroes during the past year have obviously shaken some of the firmest convictions held by the whites. In the beginning of the boycott it was often said that Negroes "can't organize anything but a crap game," and if they did, they "can't hold out." But they did organize, fifty thousand strong, and they didn't develop into an army and they didn't degenerate into a mob. They remained individuals united by a vision. In a region where patience on the long haul is considered a somewhat less colorful personal asset than pride in the instant's dramatic gesture, one of the most astonishing features of this boycott, to white residents, was the daily plodding persistence with which Negroes moved toward their goal.

Then, of course, the white people began to admit the Negroes were organized, but "outsiders" had done it: "Communists," "NAAPCs," "some of Brownell's gang," "troublemakers" in general. And, of course, the Negroes would submit to the old pressures anyway: a few arrests, some bullying, a few bed sheets.

"For a while there, the police would stop your car, maybe two or three times a day," one Negro leader said. " 'Get out, nigger.' You'd show your driving license and they'd ask you all the questions already filled out on it.

Or they'd book you for going twenty-five miles an hour in a twenty-mile speed zone."

But the spirit didn't break and the Negroes were never provoked into retaliation.

"Then white boys would throw water on us, or a Coca-Cola bottle from a car. Or once in a while they'd spit on us. Even in the last few weeks over twenty cars have had acid thrown on them."

Mass arrest of the famous ninety was the whites' real panzer effort at group intimidation that failed and backfired. "For the first time," a professor at a local Negro college tells you, "it became honorable to go to jail. Everybody whose name wasn't on that list felt sort of slighted, like he hadn't done his share. Some of the ones under arrest would call out to them, 'Joe, what you doing, not up here?' " (Strange echo of Ralph Waldo Emerson's visit to Thoreau over a century before, when the latter lay in jail for refusing to pay taxes to a government which permitted slavery. "Henry, why are you here?" "Waldo, why are you not here?")

The final test came when the Ku Klux Klan announced, on the night the Supreme Court handed down its final decision, that it would stage a demonstration in the Negro part of town. Before such a threat the Negro would once have cowered behind closed doors and darkened windows. But this time the Negro community greeted them almost as it would any other parade. As the estimated forty carloads of Ku Kluxers drove by, lights stayed on, doors were ajar, men, women and children watched openly, in silence. It took enormous courage to face this robed and ancient enemy with such nonchalance. In the end it was the Klan that weakened first. Their parade turned into a side street and disappeared. The Kluxers themselves set the final seal of solidarity and emancipation on the Negro citizens.

Perhaps the most insidious enemy the Negro of Montgomery faced was his attitude toward himself. Indoctrinated for generations by assurances of his inferiority, in many cases he was uncertain as to his own power to sustain this movement. One will tell you now, "I wasn't sure how well we'd stick together or how long we'd last. But the people were way out ahead of the leaders at first. Then we all went together and there wasn't any doubt we'd go on as long as necessary."

Under these pressures and doubts, the Negroes have discovered hidden resources within themselves. And one of the sorest problems facing Negroes everywhere was met and solved: the bridging of that great gap between the really learned and the desperately illiterate. A white woman in Montgomery who had taken part in such interracial group meetings as the town had had, said, "You met time and again with the Negro leaders but somehow you felt that you weren't ever touching the real core—

couldn't reach that vast group of Negroes to even know what they were thinking. Even their leaders were isolated from them." But those the Reverend Mr. King calls "the Ph. D.'s and the no-D.'s" were brought together by the boycott.

This was true because from first to last the movement worked through the churches. "The only way you can reach the great mass of Southern Negroes today is through their churches," one clubwoman said, "and the churches were the great power behind the success of this boycott. It had religious meaning from the beginning."

If there have been improvements in the Negro community of a Sunday, perhaps even more important is the change in the Saturday-night world. That cuttings, stabbings and drunkenness have decreased is attested by most of the Negroes and admitted by most of the whites. As the pressures of despair and frustration have been partially supplanted by the pressures of self-respect and hopefulness, some of the destructiveness has been supplanted by better citizenship.

Many of the white community remained, on that December day, far from reconciled to the Negroes' legal victory, however. Two young men at the central bus stop—wild, blue-eyed boys with sun-hardened skins—spoke with each other. "Well Buck, what we gonna do with these damned niggers?" And one of the leaders of the White Citizens' Council said, "The bus situation here is far, far from settled. It can erupt any time. We're doing our best to keep down any violence, but this is a highly charged situation. Some of these boys mean business."

A bulky taxi driver analyzed developments: "It's all looked all right so far. And it may go on quiet enough, if don't nobody get radical. But this thing's touchy. Could be set off any minute. Then who knows what'll happen?"

Another said only, "The South will always remain the South."

When a shotgun blast was fired at the Reverend Mr. King's home on December twenty-third, the pastor did not notify the police. But he mentioned the incident quietly to his congregation during church services in the same manner and spirit he had coped with threats and bombings during the year just passed. "Even if my attackers 'get' me," he said, "they will still have to 'get' fifty thousand other Negroes in Montgomery." He reminded his motionless visitors that "some of us may have to die," but urged his congregation never to falter in the belief that whatever else changed, God's love for all men would continue. "The glory to God that puts man in his place will make brothers of us all."

A tentative proposal was made to start a white bus boycott and organize a white car pool as retaliation against the integrated buses. The illogic of this, in view of the fact that the Negro car pool had been ruled illegal under a state law, seems not to have occurred to the proposers. With characteristic Southern humor someone suggested that the Negroes should run an ad in the local paper: "For Sale—Slightly used old station wagons for new car pools!"

The boycott and Jim Crow on the city buses were both dead. No matter what happened tomorrow in Montgomery, the fact remained that the Negro here would never be the same again. What one of the leaders, a tall, dark, articulate man, says is obviously true: "On December 5, 1955, the Negro in Montgomery grew from a boy to a man. He'll never be the same again. A white man had always said before, 'Boy, go do this,' 'Boy, do that,' and the Negro jumped and did it. Now he says, 'I don't believe I will,' or he does it, but up straight, looking at the white man. Not a boy any more. He grew up."

The image of the frontiersman has always been vivid in the American mind and memory. One of our frequent laments today is for the disappearing frontier which has been so much a part of American history, and the lively religion which was so much a part of its social life. To a visitor in Montgomery there is the suggestion of a new frontiersman. His weapons are those of Thoreau and Gandhi rather than Crockett and Boone, but the wilderness he faces is no less terrifying. Working on the frontiers of a faith and freedom whose meanings and dynamics have been too little explored before this, these new frontiersmen, black and white, may lead us— and some of the colored and white millions of the world—into a new fulfillment of democracy.

Many reports on the Montgomery story have failed to include the all-important fact that what happened there during 1956 was more than a social upheaval, or a legal process, or an economic tug of war. It was a spiritual mobilization.

"We've got a rich and deep resource we've yet to fully comprehend and lay hold of here in the South," an agricultural conservationist tells you. "That's the capacity for faith, the belief in divinity, which our people have —regardless of their color. In the past I know this has sometimes been the source of sophisticated humor; and the faith has often been perverted and destroyed, but now we mustn't waste such valuable ore any longer. As surely as we stopped erosion in their fields, we must stop the erosion of our people's spirits. Religion isn't set apart from reality, and the Negroes in Montgomery proved that—it is reality!"

15   Pistols and Pocketbooks

If Sunday is still a day with a special message and meaning down South in the so-called Bible Belt, Saturday is the other special day of the week in the most violent region in the United States. Saturday night you make whoopee with your friends; Sunday morning you make peace with your Lord. The neighbors and God are both important in Southern life.

Saturday's activities and Sunday's ideals are sometimes in conflict, but this only seems to re-enforce the necessity for each. Only the space of a breath separates *Beale Street Blues* from *Go Down, Moses*, and each can be sung with the same fervor. This weekend pattern of recreation and repentance is not unusual in much of the world, of course—but it is most dramatic where it is least sophisticated, and it is most interesting where the people are least concerned with the paradox.

A few years ago a North Carolina newspaper editor, William T. Polk, wrote a wise and witty book called *Southern Accent*, in which he wrestled with the subject of Southern violence. He said, "The statistics show that Southerners assault, maim and murder one another at a rate which is far in excess of that of any other region, and with a profusion, indifference and abandon which are unique." In drawing some conclusions about this unenviable record, he mentions: ". . . the main cause of the South's pre-eminence is violence committed by Negroes against Negroes . . . an important contributing cause to Southern violence is the easy availability of deadly weapons, especially shotguns and knives. The code of honor has practically nothing to do with violence in the New South, the great bulk of the violence being committed by people who are not interested in honor.

"The South's Anglo-Saxon heritage contributes to its violence. Anglo-Saxons are naturally wild people who haven't been tamed over here as they have been in England. The frontier spirit lingers in the South and makes its contribution to the violence rate.

"The Southern climate contributes to the high rate of crimes of

288

violence, if only by bringing people together more than a colder climate would."

The preponderance of Negro crime, pointed out by Polk, is supported in both fact and fiction. The sad feature of the situation is that one supports and augments the other until a vicious circle is created which holds an iron grip on Negro and white psychology alike. Its manifestations are often minor and subtle, but the effects are cumulative and destructive.

You wander around the narrow, winding streets of St. Augustine, oldest city in the United States, or ride in one of the little horse-drawn carriages between the walls and little yards bright with hibiscus and poinsettias, past the first school, and the most ancient house with its walls of coquina and floors of tabby and the patina of time over all—and the only place in this past-and-present city where you see a Negro depicted is at the Old Jail on the hangman's scaffold. The Negro carriage driver, hunched in his seat under a threadbare, faded top hat, muttering in a whiskey-loosened monologue, waits for you outside the walls and does not seem to notice the dangling effigy.

As you visit at restored Williamsburg in Virginia, where there are tangible reminders of so much that was excellent in our Southern and national heritage, you go through the restored public buildings—and the jail.

"Back then they didn't have no trouble with nigras," a heavy-set, dark-eyed Virginia man tells you as you look in the shadowy rooms and at the stocks and pillory outside. "They had nigras under control in those days, knew the trick it was done by. If a bad one turned up, he was whipped or killed right on the spot by the gentleman that owned him. That way the courts were never bothered with him.

"Of course they did have runaway slaves who were captured and sometimes kept here in this jail till the owner came and got him. But this was mainly a debtor's prison and of course the nigras couldn't borrow or own money. Women the same way, they couldn't borrow money, didn't have a lot of rights. Back then there wasn't so much fuss about the poor whites and the women and the nigras and all that."

If the white man is one of the determinants, conscious or unconscious, in patterns of black violence today, so the black man was an unconscious determinant of much of the early white violence of the South, whose eventual outcome was the bloody upheaval of four years of war.

The climate of militancy was not finished with the finish of the war; it simply turned to informal, rather than formal, ways and means. A South Carolinian, writing some years after Reconstruction, recalled vividly that the silver-mounted twenty-eight-caliber six-shooter he owned was considered quite a formidable weapon in Virginia, but the first time a man in South Carolina saw it he said, "Sonny, if ever you shoot any gentleman in this part of the country with that thing and he finds it out, he'll take it way from you and beat you with it for insultin' him." The writer later remembered that white men carried an average of two pistols each, and at one rally a judge remarked that he had identified one citizen as "a pure Democrat and really high-toned gentleman because he arrived at the meeting wearing four navy-size six-shooters."

In many parts of the South groups of mounted men banded together to aid in the overthrow of Reconstruction government. When they were ordered to disband as rifle clubs, they held meetings, sometimes on horseback, announced themselves dissolved as a military group, and promptly reorganized under such ridiculous names as The First Baptist Church Sewing Circle, The Mounted Baseball Club (with a team of 150), Mother's Little Helpers and The Mounted Brass Band. One, in South Carolina, called itself The Hampton and Tilden Musical Club with four twelve-pounder flutes.

With the arrival of the Ku Klux Klan and the development of lynching, a note alien to most other Southern violence was introduced on the scene: organization. This would perhaps indicate the frequent political and economic affiliations of both these barbarous devices of control, for otherwise the outstanding characteristic of Southern killing has been its extremely personal nature. As one man has said, "We kill only our family or friends. Strangers have little to fear. I heard the story the other day of a man going to kill his grandmother, who said, 'Better me than somebody doesn't love her.'

"As for the Negroes, time after time I've seen them in court, cousins, brothers, friends, bandaged from head to toe, throats cut half open, and when the judge asks what the trouble was, they reply, 'There wasn't no trouble, Judge. Nothing serious!' "

Harry Golden, in his *Carolina Israelite*, had some observations on "Murder, North and South." He said, "In no other field of endeavour is there as great a difference in the pattern of human behavior, north and south, as murder. And this involves every phase of the crime—motive, use of weapon, and post-murder activity. . . .

"Most Northern murders are involved with 'economics,' such as theft, gangster wars, competition among racketeers, all of which is unknown in the South; neither do we ever have murder for insurance, which accounts for many Northern killings. In the South, nine out of every ten murders are over a woman, or what the French call a 'crime of passion.' "

One category overlooked by Mr. Golden is the politically inspired killing, and these have been numerous in the South, ranging from the hotheaded affray on the courthouse lawn during election day to the planned shooting of an opponent for office. You remember a smartly dressed lady at an afternoon party who tells you of childhood remembrances of politics in a Deep South state.

"When I was small, our state was in the grip of one of the very worst demagogues the South ever produced. My father spoke against him during a crucial campaign and was shot at by a man who was quite well known to him. Eventually that man became president of our state college.

"Later, after father died and we were so poor we didn't have two dimes to rub against each other, this man offered my brother a scholarship to the college. 'We've got to see that Lewis, Junior, goes to college,' he said.

" 'My dear man,' mother told him, 'if you'd been a little better shot there wouldn't even be a Lewis, Junior. Here's your hat.' "

The violence of feeling in racial affairs, which seemed to have subsided somewhat during recent years in the South, has flared again as the legal pressures for Negro equality become more firm. The intense emotion engendered in both races, and their air of mutual surprise at the other's dedication, is probably best explained in someone's saying that "integration is more important to Negroes than the white people realize, and segregation is more important to the whites than the Negroes realize."

Harold C. Fleming and John Constable, writing from surveys conducted by the Southern Regional Council in 1956, concluded: "Although most of the pro-segregation groups publicly deplore violence, it has been increasing steadily since the May 17, 1954, decision. Nearly fifty cases of violence or threats of violence were reported in 1955 in the twelve Southern states most directly concerned with desegregation of schools. These cases included the murder of at least three Negroes in Mississippi, the wounding of at least one other, the burning of a Negro church in South Carolina, and several bombings. In these cases, no person has yet been convicted."

In relation to this situation, there was the chilly night in early spring when you attended the organizational meeting of a White Citizens' Council and some of the members spoke their short testimonial lines:

"It's the purpose of the nigger organizations to ram the niggers in the schools down our throat. And if we don't git up and fight and tell them no, we're going to have it. I don't want no violence—that's the last thing we want—but if it comes to that in our homes, we'll have it. Git in the fight, folks, and stay with it!"

A man with slightly greying hair and an open-collared white shirt under his multi-colored jacket: "I'm green at this-here business, but I'll jump in and do what I can. We'll all stick together and fight this."

And one man slightly more sophisticated than the rest:"We hear a lot about all this violence in the South. Now there can't be too much or somebody would get hurt. Why do all these blastings and bombings we hear about occur only in the midnight hours? That's what I would like to know. Why do they occur at midnight and then are not reported until the next morning? Who sets those blasts?

"The Communists have been wanting this violence for a long time. They don't want the state guard, like they had up in Clinton, Tennessee. That's not enough for them. They want the Federal troops! I tell you we can't win this fight by meeting here every few nights and talking. We've got to carry it on aggressively. Got to fight fire with fire."

On the other side there is the Negro man who says bitterly, "White men are now being tried and fined for killing a Negro. Down here, that's progress."

So the talk grows, the emotions accumulate, the incidents increase. Some make national headlines; some barely make local news items. In a small South Carolina town, a Catholic priest is stopped by four white boys on his way to hold religious services for some two hundred Negroes, and told, "We're the authority around here. We don't want white people doing church work among niggers." A little later, during the showing of a film on the life of Christ, the meeting is broken up by pistol shots fired from a passing truck.

In North Alabama, a seventy-nine-year-old Negro preacher is killed when four white men in a convertible drive along the highway stoning Negroes. A ten-pound rock smashes his leg and he is apparently killed as he falls and hits his head on the highway.

In East Texas a Negro community is terrorized by white youths speeding along their roads, firing into mailboxes, cars, cafés, homes. When a six-teen-year-old Negro boy is killed by one of these random shots, the sheriff says, "It's a nasty situation, I tell you for sure."

Who knows of John Earl Reese and the other "nameless" people who have suffered in silence and died without words because of the fearful false doctrines of race? These are the ones that the powerful men of the South, the ones who bemoan violence publicly and condone it secretly, must answer for someday, somewhere.

The list is long: at a small community in South Georgia, a seventy-one-year-old retired farmer shoots and kills a young Negro mother of six children. He said she had "sassed" him. In New Orleans, an eight-foot cross is burned on the grounds of the residence of Archbishop Joseph Rummel. In a small town in northern Florida, a Negro man is spirited out of jail and beaten for allegedly saying,"Hi, honey," to a white schoolteacher. Six days later he is found in Alabama. The local police chief, who said he had been away chasing a speeding car at the time the Negro was taken from his cell, is quoted: "I sure am glad they found him. I figured somebody took him out of here."

A couple of months later, in a neighboring town, a white man tells you, "There's a lot of agitation around down here now. You got to watch out for it. Most of the Southerners want to keep things like they are. Of course we get some nigger-lovers in here from the North, but we also get a lot who hate their guts just like we do. You got to watch these agitators. Take what happened just a few miles from here a little while back. Somebody went into the jail over there and took this nigger out and beat him up good. It was all a frame-up, put on by the NAPC or somebody. When I saw in the news that they found his hat by the roadside a half-mile away, I said, 'Oh-oh!' The last thing a Southern white would let a nigger take out of his cell would be a hat.

"Of course they spattered some blood around the cell, but that didn't fool me none. I know Southern whites, I've lived here fifty years. They don't do a job like that. And another thing, when they got the nigger six miles out in the woods, they wouldn't whup him with any little ole half-wore-out belt. They use stronger medicine than that. No sir, the agitators didn't fool me none on that trick. And it's the nigger-lovers, much as the niggers, that we got to keep an eye on for keeps."

Indeed, it sometimes seems that the harshest violence, short of death, is reserved for some of the white people who have taken a "moderate" or pro-integration position since 1954. Dr. John Hall Jones, minister, educator, counseling psychologist in Birmingham, tells you an incident of the struggle between white and white there. While Jones was leader of the interracial Council on Human Relations in that city, one of his meetings was raided by a group of men whose leader was "Ace" Carter, notorious for his open advocacy and practice of violence. "When Ace and his followers came to our Council meeting that night, we were all pretty nervous, but I was determined to stand between him and that fine, quiet little group of citizens, Negro and white, we had meeting there to discuss some of our mutual problems." Dr. Jones is a tall, white-haired, well-built man with glasses and a scholarly face and a stubborn chin, who talks fluently and observes sharply.

"Ace got as far as the door and I went up to him and laid my hand on his shoulder, tight right on the ligament, and looked him in the eye and said, 'Look here, Ace, you're a mentally sick man, and as a psychologist I wish I could help you. As a Christian you're a spiritually wrong man and as a minister I wish I could help you. But as a citizen, you're a criminal and I want to warn you that the riot squad is alerted and if you cause any trouble you're going to wind up in the hospital or the morgue.' His brother said, 'Come on, Ace, you can't outtalk this guy, let's go.'

"A funny thing, an encouraging thing, I suppose, happened that same night. One of the twenty-four who had come with Ace, a great big burly boy, remembered me from someplace. I have talked to most of the schools and churches in this vicinity sometime during the last few years; perhaps he'd met me during one of those talks. He came up and said,'I didn't know you were part of this bunch, Dr. Jones. I won't let anyone harm you.' And he laid his hand on my arm to identify himself with me. And when I spoke to Ace, and walked out among the crowd, he stayed right behind me.

"Of course the thing we have to remember about these groups is that most of the people who belong to them are neurotics, mentally disturbed, and they won't be able to stick together. Their violence will eventually prove self-destructive."

When Guy Hutchins, former director of several Southern symphony orchestras and then director of a high-school band in Camden, South Carolina, was returning from a television appearance in Charlotte one night late in December, 1956, he had tire trouble and stopped along the highway to change the tire. As he completed the job, he saw a car slowing down near where he was parked. He later said that he threw up his hand and called, "Thank you, but I don't need any help." But the car still slowed, and as he turned to pick up a tool from the ground, he looked up just in time to see men running from the car. They grabbed him, threw a sack over his head and hustled him into the back seat of their car. After a ride along the highway and down some country roads, he was tied to a tree and beaten with a board and tree limbs. The men accused him of speaking in favor of integration in the schools before a Lion's Club auxiliary. Mr. Hutchins' denials were unavailing, but after he promised to leave town with his wife and two young sons he was untied from the tree, with the burlap bag still over his head, and told to run for his life. With a pistol at his throat and threats to "fill him with buckshot," they let him go.

News of this attack on a respected citizen aroused protests and controversy. One of the first arguments concerned the Klan's part in the event. The Grand Dragon of the United States Knights, Ku Klux Klan, was quoted as saying that his organization was represented in the area (during one week the previous month three Negro churches and a Negro home had been burned), but Klansmen, and Hutchins himself, denied involvement in the flogging. Mayor Henry Savage, of Camden, stated the situation well, however, when he said, "Whether it was the Klan or not, when they spread out a sheet they invite thugs to come under it and the responsibility is theirs."

It was a strange anachronism, this experience of the frontier taking place after its victim had just appeared on television, our newest marvel of communication. "It doesn't seem like the twentieth century; it doesn't seem like America," one woman said, after reading the news stories. "Now I suppose some people will start pointing out the killings up North, and gangland beatings there. Well, I hope it makes Mr. Hutchins' bruises feel better to know it was a fellow Southerner who laid them on."

When a white man in eastern North Carolina signed a petition favoring integrated schools, his home was shaken by a dynamite bomb. As in so many cases during the current crisis, this, too, was violence within the white race, rather than between black and white. And *The News and Observer*, in Raleigh, North Carolina, said, "None should be so outraged by this act as those opponents of desegregation who find themselves put in the company of a ready terrorist. But all who honor freedom and recognize it as the basis of our safety should be shocked and ashamed. . . .

"The suppression of opinion is not new in Guilford, though there is no more enlightened county in North Carolina. It was there in the spring of 1860 that Daniel Worth was tried for circulating *The Impending Crisis*, by Hinton Rowan Helper, a North Carolinian whose book against slavery sold only fewer copies than *Uncle Tom's Cabin*. Worth, a sixty-seven-year-old man, was found guilty and 'given the lightest penalty consistent with the law, imprisonment for twelve months.' So the freedom of white men was destroyed before the bloody war to set Negroes free began. . . ."

The editor of *The Fayetteville Observer*, who strongly opposes unsegregated schools, put the matter even more vigorously: "If we had to choose between racially integrated schools and the loss of free speech in North Carolina we'd choose the mixed schools, because as long as the public retains the right of free speech it has the opportunity to examine and correct intelligently any governmental mistakes that may occur. . . .

"It is not much worse to take a man out into the woods and beat him with a leather strap than it is to hound him out of his job so he can't earn a living and support his family. . . . And economic reprisal will rate with flogging as a tactic which will sell the South short in the eyes of the nation which will be the ultimate judge. . . .

"If a tyranny of terror should be permitted in this State no traditions worth guarding would be left to save."

There are some white men in the South who would resist a tyranny of terror with the sword as well as the pen. A thin, wiry, sun-baked Texas reporter tells you about a television program he has been on discussing integration. "I've known nigras all my life. I've gone swimming with them, chopped cotton with them, been possum hunting with them. I don't intend to turn against them on this school business. And I said as much on our television round table.

"Now the interesting thing is this: four of my great great grandfathers were here in 1836. Some of them came with those Tennesseans who arrived in Texas not only not afraid to fight but just spoiling for a fight. Anyway, now we have people coming down from Michigan and Maine and Illinois, anywhere, and they buy a Confederate flag and stick it on their car, and get some boots and spurs they can't walk downstairs in without falling down—and they're the Texans and the Southerners. Some of them were on this TV program with me, and they out-Southerned me all to pieces.

"Well, after the show, I got about twenty crackpot phone calls, threatening, all that business. So I went out and bought a fence rider's rifle. If you don't know what a fence rider's rifle is, it's a thirty-thirty with a twenty-inch barrel. I got it out there in my car now. They cost seventy-five dollars. I bought this one from a wholesaler for fifty-nine dollars. I got twenty-five dollars for being on the program, so it cost me thirty-four dollars to tell this city I used to go possum hunting with nigras. But I'll tell you one thing: I mean business. I want to see somebody try to burn a cross on my lawn while I'm there. If these fellows want a fight, they better count themselves.

"I also got about a dozen phone calls, not talking about the congratulatory ones, but from men who meant business too, saying they'd heard I might have some difficulty and they were ready to help me. This talk of violence down here, somebody call their hand a couple of times, the game would soon be over."

In the matter of retaliations today, an old Negro saying would apply: "White folks do as they pleases and colored folks do as they can." And of course the Negro crime rate is used as one of the chief arguments by many white people against school integration.

The problem of much of the crime in the South, however, is not one of Negro-white integration as much as it is of integration of all the South's people into democratic society. When Justice's traditional blindfold is askew, permitting her to see the color of the person being weighed in her scales, the result is resentment and frustration on the part of the sufferer, and a false system of values for the "victor." And since the resentments cannot be turned against those in power, they are taken home, or to the dance hall, or to church. They are released by a bottle or a razor or the sudden flash of a pistol. And as surely as the whole community has, in some measure, been responsible for this violence, so, in another measure, the whole community suffers its consequences. It involves the greatest waste in the whole extravagant regional or national scene: the waste of human life.

Dr. Blake Smith, of the University Baptist Church in Austin, Texas, says, "I speak as a Southerner. My forbears were slaveholders. I am not proud of that. But the subtlety of this sin in which we are involved is that it creates its own validity. It creates social conditions which make it seem right."

Many people, Negro and white, feel that one of the subtler, but more important, reasons for Negro crime is the Southern white person's attitude to it. All too often if a black person is maimed or killed the reaction is indifference: "Just another nigger knifing." And with a paternalism that is both unjust and debilitating, the criminal is given an inadequate punishment because his crime was against another Negro.

Representative John Bell Williams, of Mississippi, speaking before the House of Representatives in Washington, said that the segregated South sends fewer Negroes to prison in proportion to its over-all Negro population than do the integrated states. After using figures to show that "the per capita crime rate among Negroes in the integrated states is 199 per cent—or double—the rate in the segregated states," he declared that this proves one of two premises: either Negroes are more law abiding in a segregated society, or Southern courts are far more lenient with Negro defendants. "This, in my opinion, puts the lie to the left-wing and NAACP propaganda that a 'reign of terror' against Negroes prevails in the South."

"What these people don't, or won't understand," a Negro man says, "is that we want equality of punishment as well as equality of freedom. We don't want Negro criminals punished beyond all reason when the victim is a white person, or let off with little or no penalty when the victim is colored. It's just another way of saying that white lives are more sacred than black ones."

If Negro violence is an ugly and tragic reality, even more tragic perhaps is the fact that it sometimes reflects white violence on an official level. In the 1947 report of the President's Committee on Civil Rights, J. Edgar Hoover, head of the Federal Bureau of Investigation, was recorded as testifying about the jail in a certan Southern city: "It was seldom that a Negro man or woman was incarcerated who was not given a severe beating, which started off with a pistol whipping and ended with a rubber hose."

The report went on to state that the files of the Department of Justice "abound with evidence of illegal official action in Southern states. In one case, the victim was arrested on a charge of stealing a tire, taken to the courthouse, beaten by three officers with a blackjack until his head was a bloody pulp, and then dragged unconscious through the streets to the jail where he was thrown, dying, onto the floor. In another case a Florida constable arrested a Negro, against whom he bore a personal grudge, beat him brutally with a bullwhip and then forced his victim, in spite of his protestations of being unable to swim, to jump into a river where he drowned."

In another case cited by the committee, eight Negro prisoners in a state highway camp in Georgia were killed by white guards as they allegedly attempted to escape. A grand jury exonerated the warden and the four guards, but one witness testified that the prisoners had not been trying to escape. "I saw them where they fell. Two were crawling under the bunkhouse, two others as they ran under their cells. The only thing they were trying to escape was death."

It is cases such as these which stir the anger of decent men everywhere, these cases of sanctioned official brutality which make protestations of state's rights and regional sanctimony pale beside the pleas for basic human rights.

More Southerners are realizing ever more clearly, however, that violence may win a skirmish, but it will never win a fundamental struggle. Sophisticated advocates of complete segregation sense the incongruity of a kerosene-soaked cross burning on the lawn of a split-level house, in the shadow of the television antennae. Shrewd white-supremacy leaders are trying to convince their followers that in this current conflict pocketbook warfare will by infinitely more effective than pistols. Several Senators have echoed the words of Senator Ellender of Louisiana, who said, "What the South must avoid at all costs is violence, lawlessness, hatred and bloodshed. The outside agitators who seek the subjugation of both the white and Negro races in the South are hovering like greedy vultures for the time when racial antagonisms lead to chaos, the breakdown of governmental authority, and general lawlessness."

Some ministers and community leaders have expressed the same sentiments as the Reverend M. A. Woodson, a Baptist minister in South Carolina, who told a Citizens' Council group, "We must strive to leave for our children a constitutional form of government and a segregated society that works in harmony. . . . We must fight the Communists and related groups with facts and funds and not ammunition and guns."

Certain economic pressures are not new in the South. In the city of Orangeburg, South Carolina, which experienced, during 1955 and 1956, one of the most mutually destructive boycotts by each race against members of the other race that has yet been known in the South, similar action had taken place eighty years before, in 1876. Alfred B. Williams, writing in his history of *Hampton and His Red Shirts* years later, describes the system of certification which white Democrats used in discovering Negroes who were Republican in sympathy. He says that "Orangeburg's blunt adoption of the boycott policy brought a howl from Republicans at the North, but was approved and imitated in the state." In their last-ditch fight to regain control of the state government, it was essential to Southern Democrats that Negroes should either vote Democratic or not at all.

During the campaign of 1892, when Populism was making its early strong claims in the South, various parts of the region felt the squeeze of political pressures in the form of job losses and boycotts, foreclosed mortgages and terminated tenant contracts. Re-enforced by the constantly invoked specter of miscegenation, they were powerful weapons in destroying the possible unification of poor white and poor Negro for mutual political and economic betterment.

Today the same pressures retain much the same power, only now the white advocates of boycott have discovered that it is a two-edged sword and both sides cut deep. In a South which is economically poor enough at best, it is sad to witness an internecine warfare which can only result in loss for everyone.

Negro leaders say that reprisals began in the white community against colored citizens who had signed school-integration petitions, worked with local chapters of the NAACP, or even held membership in that organization. It is certainly true that in several communities there were wholesale losses of jobs by Negro teachers after they had signed petitions to the local school boards. In Selma, Alabama, for instance, sixteen teachers lost their jobs after they had put their names on an integration petition. At

Elloree, South Carolina, some thirty-seven parents, who signed and filed a petition asking for steps to be taken toward integration, felt the heavy hand of credit loss and unemployment. The owner of seventy-three acres of Mississippi Delta land testified that although he could produce as much as a bale and a half of cotton an acre, he could not get loans for operating capital because of his anti-segregation activities.

The other edge of the weapon is, of course, the Negro boycott of white businesses. A white professor of dentistry in Alabama has called integration "a harsh problem for many of us," and urged "hitting the segregationist where he's very, very tender—in the pocketbook." Obviously this is most successful in towns with large Negro populations, and at the crossroads stores which serve rural areas inhabited almost solely by Negroes. There are many small merchants in the Black Belt today who are disturbed by rising racial tensions and Negro migrations, for they know how quietly and completely the stream of dimes and dollars for coffee and kerosene and snuff and soda and fatback and molasses can dry up and close down their small operation.

Other, smaller boycotts have sprung up all over the South and had varying degrees of success. The owner of a soft-drink bottling company at Jackson, Tennessee, after a lawsuit involving school segregation, said that twelve or thirteen Negro merchants canceled their accounts with his firm. In Tallahassee, Florida, there was a Negro boycott of the local bus company.

In Tuskegee, Alabama, in the summer of 1957, the Negroes put the economic squeeze on local white merchants after State Senator Sam Englehardt decided to squeeze most of the Negro residents out of the city voting limits by new zoning laws. Troubled white merchants feared they could not stand up long under this pressure; would-be Negro voters vowed they would no longer stand for disfranchisement.

The instances of whites boycotting whites have been some of the bitterest in this new tactic of warfare. Reports of NAACP contributions, use of Negro performers on television programs, or any other symptoms of sympathy with change in the Negro's present status, have sometimes proved sufficient cause for sanctions against local distributors of national products. A White Citizens' Council leader tells you, "We're fighting the four F's every way we can. Falstaff, Ford, Philip Morris and Philco. I've seen a picture of the Falstaff beer folks giving a check to the N double-ACP. And Ford's got a Fund for the Republic, it's called, that sets up councils in every state where whites and niggers can mix and mingle together. They're supposed to be objective, but in my book they're just objectionable."

Some businessmen in the South are peculiarly vulnerable to a cross-fire in economic pressures. "Cokes" and "Pepsis" and "Seven-Ups" are a part of life as important to Southerners as tea to Englishmen and tequila to Mexicans. Their tart sweetness, their heady coolness, is part of the long morning, the longer afternoon—and the evening after the sun has disappeared and the day has "let down" into brief relaxation and peace. For Negro and white alike, these are the drinks born in the South, satisfying Southern thirst in a particularly satisfying way. But even they can be sacrificed—by the Negro community when there is a report rumored that the local bottler donated twenty-five thousand dollars to the White Citizens' Council; by the white community when the news circulates that a distributor is servicing a Negro firm whose owner has petitioned for school integration. "Lord, it's a fight," one man walking the narrow chalk line says. "We're more likely to lose than win, no matter how we play."

William Gordon, astute managing editor of the large Negro newspaper, *Atlanta Daily World*, wrote, after a visit to Orangeburg, South Carolina, during its boycott difficulties: "As I drove out of this little Southern town one Sunday evening, I trembled at the very idea of how damaging economic pressure could be; how the South, through ignorance and prejudice, has for many years stifled much of its own progress through use of such a method. . . . Economic pressure used against minorities has no basis for survival. And history has a way of repeating itself. Hate groups contain the seeds of their own destruction. Economic pressure, in a dynamic social order, has a habit of cutting both ways."

Sometimes in the South you hear white voices which are impatient of the boycott. It may be a technique particularly difficult for white Southerners, who have often considered patience more of a temporary hardship than a virtue. In writing of some of the railroad conventions before the Civil War, the *Southern Literary Messenger* cited some resolutions "not to buy Northern goods when they can get Southern, *unless the Northern are the cheapest*; not to freight Northern vessels when they can freight Southern, *unless the Northern freight for less*." The *Messenger* remarked that these were reminiscent "of the oath which Neptune and his crew required of us when we first crossed the equator, viz. 'never to eat brown bread instead of white, unless we preferred the brown;' and never to kiss the maid if we could kiss the mistress, unless we liked the maid best.' "

But where, in the contest of pocketbooks, is the glamour, the excitement, the possibility of the pulsing blood which can rise to momentary fierceness and swiftly cool again, giving room for both rage and repentance? This is part of the tension gripping the South: that the new warfare for the old beliefs must divest itself of those very features which made resistance possible. Pistols were tangible things and quick and their punishment was physical; boycotts begin as intangible ideas and are translated into cumulative action, and their aim is atrophy. Pistols require personal encounters; pocketbooks call for concerted, patient, community action—or inaction. It would seem that while pistols appear adapted to many Southern white temperaments coping with the complexities of our bi-racial life, the pocketbook and the boycott seem peculiarly suited to the Negro temperament. Montgomery revealed this fact. A Negro man says, "Economic warfare won't ever solve our troubles down here. But it can do one thing: if everything else fails, it can make the white people stop for a minute and listen to us. And that's a basic thing that's got to happen all over the South. White people have got to stop telling each other and the world what Negroes want; they've got to start listening to us tell what we want. If they'd only do that, they might be surprised how simple our wants are."

The tradition of violence is older than the tradition of segregation in the South. It has had its moments of brutality, and its manifestations of bravery, as the region has sent the cream of its youth off time after time to die in the nation's wars. But it is a tradition of waste, which admits failure of reason in a world of force; and today neither the South nor the country of which it is a vital part can afford any further irreverence for life or the high gift of human reason.

16 ▓ Blood: Red, White and Blue

"Parts of the South are sick today with one of the most pernicious viruses known to man," says a sardonic yet serious gentleman in Lexington, Kentucky. The tweed coat he is wearing accents the flecks of grey in his dark hair, but its casualness is not reflected in the alertness of his thoughts or conversation. "It's a disease of blood, but the infection is in the mind. The fear and anger which have taken possession of some of our white people are rooted in the mystique of blood. That mystique may not be factually accurate but emotionally it's the largest factor in Southern race attitudes today. It's hard to account for, and harder to cope with, but it will have to be recognized before the rest of the country can understand what's going on down here.

"We're hearing all the old talk of white blood and black blood and blue blood, but what we really have is just the same old red blood all of us have always had. It's blood spilled often enough, God knows, in this ancient cause of 'blood superiority'—or should we say this ancient curse?"

In her charming old second-story sitting room, where tall, gilt-framed mirrors reflect the quiet mahogany richness of the room and flawless camellias glow in the dim afternoon light which slants across the coffee table, a lady in New Orleans speaks softly. "Sometimes, when I think of all the cruelty and bloodshed—when I think of the suffering we've brought to each other, in both races, all races—the illness we cause, or permit, or know nothing about——" she spreads white hands in a gesture of inexpressible sorrow and helplessness.

"I remember when I was a child, a little Negro girl I played with—we were the same age, only she was a trifle smaller than I was, and she'd wear my old dresses; and sometimes, when we'd be playing, I remember thinking that it was like playing with a shadow of myself to see her there in my familiar clothes—well, anyway, when we were both about ten, she died of typhoid fever.

"I remember my father saying the city had killed her because the authorities hadn't bothered to test the water down in the Negro part of

303

the little town where we lived. There was a regular epidemic that summer. Why we weren't all destroyed, I'll never know. But I can't forget that child. We gave her mother the white dress I'd worn to be baptized in, and that was what she was buried in."

The red blood flows and the flesh suffers, and the appeals to "pure bloodstreams" stir the world over—and in the South—once more. The blood of life that is real, and the potent blood of myth: these you touch upon, and probe to understand, throughout the region.

A distinguished lawyer in the capital of one Southern state tells you, "The doctor in charge of pediatrics at one of our largest hospitals here desegregated that department several years ago. He couldn't give some of the Negro children who were his patients the care they needed elsewhere, and he simply brought them to this hospital. It has been desegregated ever since. A certain board member who was going through the hospital on an inspection tour one day saw the Negro babies with the white ones and said, 'Why are they here?' 'Because they're sick,' the pediatrician answered. The policy has never been questioned since then."

In a small town in Middle Tennessee, when you ask a resident if there is a Negro doctor for the sizable Negro population there, he replies, "No, but they got an undertaker."

Statistics show that in 1951 a Negro baby born in the United States had seven less years to live than a white baby born the same hour. Yet eventually each would require the same number of months to become the same colored dust.

A very light brown mulatto woman in Austin, Texas, remarks bitterly on the potency of 'Negro' blood. "No matter how many pints of 'white' blood you have in your veins, one drop of 'Negro' blood neutralizes it all, and you're Negro."

In one of the larger Southern cities, a white businessman relates a conversation he has had with one of the Senators from his state. "We'd had the Senator out here for dinner, and after dinner I was telling him about a talk I'd heard Ralph Bunche make a short while before. When I said I thought Bunche was a brilliant man, the Senator said, 'I bet he's got four fifths white blood.' Well, that ended the conversation right there. How can you talk with a person who thinks like that?"

The Group for the Advancement of Psychiatry, meeting in Chicago in mid-1957, included this observation in a report on the psychological aspects of desegregation: "Poor living conditions can breed the spread of disease from menial to boss as easily as from schoolmate to schoolmate, because contagiousness does not discriminate."

Or, as someone said over a decade ago, "Bacteria are broad-minded."

In September, 1956, the South African Medical Council approved a plan by which containers used in the country's blood bank would have more thorough labeling. White labels are to designate the blood received from white donors, and black labels will mark the blood donated by non-whites. The director of the blood transfusion service opposed the move and stated that it had "no justification on scientific grounds."

And in its annual session of spring, 1957, the General Assembly of South Carolina took under consideration a bill requiring all blood banks in the state to inaugurate a system of labeling which would designate whether each donor was a white person or a colored person.

"No man is an island"—and if religious conviction cannot make us believe this, the epidemics of dread disease which for so long plagued mankind can persuade us. White men brought the Indians many early gifts—among them smallpox. It raged through the Southern tribes with more deadly efficiency than many a hostile human foe. To study the colonial history of the South is to realize ever more completely how interwoven in bondage to pain and disease and death were white and red and black men. The horrors of the middle passage might bring death tolls as high as four fifths of the Africans being transported to America for the slave market, but the suffering of many Europeans en route to the New World was only slightly less extreme.

Epidemics of smallpox, cholera and yellow fever ravaged the cities, from the coast inland, during all the years of their growth. As late as 1879, after experiencing three plagues of yellow fever—in 1873, 1878 and 1879—which took the lives of between seven and ten thousand residents, people were saying that the city of Memphis was dead.

In addition, in many of the lowlands, there was the daily experience of a new and extreme climate. A local chronicler, writing about the summer of 1738 in Charles Town, said that for several days in June the temperature had been ninety-eight in the shade. Slaves had dropped dead in the rice fields where they were working under temperatures the writer estimated at 124 or 125 degrees. In a graphic description of events, he says that "in the short space of five hours the body of a pretty corpulent woman who died as she was ironing linen, burst the coffin, so violent was the putrefaction." Dead bodies were wrapped in sheets wrung out in tar and bound with cords. When smallpox threatened to decimate the city during this torrid June, a fast day was appointed by proclamation.

On the antebellum plantations, it was, obviously, to the owner's advantage to have healthy rather than sick slaves. To protect a sizable investment, insure a high rate of return on its labors, and—because the planters were fellow humans with human emotional involvements—to bring some measure of justification to the system itself, white owners were probably fairly solicitous of their black slaves' health.

During the early summer of 1854, when Frederick Law Olmsted was traveling through the large plantation country of Mississippi, he spent a night at the home of an overseer on one of these estates. Of this encounter, Olmsted wrote, "He gave me much overseer's lore about cotton culture, nigger and cattle maladies, the right way to keep sweet potatoes, etc. . . . The room was garnished with pistols and other arms and ammunition, rolls of negro-cloth, shoes and hats, handcuffs, a large medicine chest, and several books on medical and surgical subjects and farriery; while articles of both men's and women's wearing apparel hung against the walls, which were also decorated with some large patent-medicine posters."

Shortly thereafter Olmsted commented, "It is difficult to handle simply as property, a creature possessing human passions and human feelings, however debased and torpid the condition of that creature may be; while, on the other hand, the absolute necessity of dealing with property as a thing, greatly embarrassed a man in any attempt to treat it as a person. And it is the natural result of this complicated state of things, that the system of slave-management is irregular, ambiguous, and contradictory; that it is never either consistently humane or consistently economical." (This ambiguity of attitude still haunts us today, and may be one of the deepest reasons behind some of those paradoxes that are most puzzling to non-Southerners.)

Following the Civil War and Reconstruction and those decades of poverty which pushed the Southern states into the lowest positions on so many statistical totem poles, the health of large segments of both Negro and white population suffered. In a region where winters were for the most part mild and summers were hot, the living seemed easy—but this climate also made it easier for certain parasites and insects to live on human prey. In a region where nature could be abundant and kind with its luscious crops and wide varieties of plants, it could suddenly turn cruel and destructive with raging floods, burning droughts, furious hurricanes. Within many of the people—the poorest, the weakest, the ones most closely squeezed by the elements—these extremes bred a patient, plodding fatalism.

In his study of a Black Belt county in Alabama, *Shadow of the*

Plantation, in 1934, Dr. Charles S. Johnson described some of the Negroes' attitudes and discussions of disease. "Except on the basis of a general health examination it would be impossible to estimate the extent of sickness from various diseases. Complaints are generalized into merely 'feelin' kinda poorly' or 'I ain't no good,' and generalized complaints call for the generalized measures of patent medicines, or home herb remedies. 'Black Draught,' '666,' salts, and castor oil make up a large part of the treatment of disease. Other standard remedies are 'White Wonder Salve,' calomel, and quinine.

"Unless there is some folk pattern of treatment, death may result from sickness which in all probability could be avoided or intelligently treated. As one illiterate mother stated: 'I had one child to die when it was just three days old, but I ain't never knowed what the trouble was. It just cried an' cried for three days and nights and then died.'

"Children die in great numbers and mothers accept their death with a dull and uninquiring fatalism. Some of the expressions back of the infant mortality rates are thus most casual and uninformed: 'I don' had lots of chillun to die. I don't know what ailed them.' "

Those who are unaware of the tremendous changes that have taken place in the South during the last few years could find no more encouraging phase of its life to study than this one of health. But if you can remember when "hookworm" was a dirty word to Southerners, even while it was an undeniable reality, if you can remember a man or woman, black or white, with thin arms and lusterless eyes, who talked of pellagra ("pl'agry") with sad intimacy—then you know that the term "New South" is not without meaning. The accuracy of North Carolina poet John Charles McNeill's picture of a "Tar Heel" diminishes each year:

> Oh, I gits my stren'th from white side meat,
> I sops all de sorghum a nigger kin eat,
> I chaws wheat bread on Saddy night.
> En Sunday's when my jug gits light.

The story of hookworm and the South has many features that are characteristic of other, similar problems in the region. To begin with an irony of unconscious revenge: the American species of this parasite was an import from Africa, brought over by the Negro slaves, and it eventually wreaked havoc on enormous numbers of white Southerners. There is also the interesting fact that for generations some of the region's critics maintained that certain "lower levels" of white people in the South were biologically inferior to other whites, and they intimated that this was an unalterable fact of nature and history. When Dr. Charles W. Stiles, a native of North Carolina, made the discovery of the hookworm in America around the turn of the century, he pointed out that some of the inefficiency of these apparently inadequate white people was doubtless due to this parasite. A New York newspaper announced that the "germ of laziness" had been discovered. Many Southerners felt that their region had been slandered by a native son who would admit that all its people were not ideally healthy and happy. Once again, with human perverseness, it was easier to attack the person who had exposed an evil than to remedy the evil itself.

When Dr. Stiles was able to interest Walter Hines Page and John D. Rockefeller in the fact that two million people in the South were afflicted with this disease, a commission for its extermination was organized in 1909 with an initial gift of a million dollars from Rockefeller. As Dr. Rupert Vance later pointed out, the achievement in abolition of hookworm "was a social no less than a scientific triumph. A lack of interest and organization for public health was met and overcome. Although the South may not realize the debt, it is largely to the early Rockefeller campaigns that the section owes its present county public health organization."

In subsequent intelligence and achievement tests conducted in schools and army camps, it was discovered that persons infected with hookworm rated anywhere from 22 to 33 per cent lower than those free of the parasite. A curable infection, rather than an innate inferiority, proved to be the cause of some of the wide inequalities between "white trash" and "quality."

Today a similar situation often seems to exist in relation to Negro-white health standards, when Negroes are made to appear the perpetrators rather than the victims of illness. There are wide gaps between the two races in this respect. For example, in the 1954 brief prepared by the attorney general of Florida for presentation before the United States Supreme Court, it was stated that, while not quite 2 per cent of the white births in Florida during 1953 were illegitimate, twenty-four per cent of Negro births were illegitimate. "According to the State Board of Health there was a total of 11,459 cases of gonorrhea reported in Florida during 1953 of which 10,206 were among the Negro population."

Certainly there must be forthright recognition and solution of these problems which exist throughout the South. The distressing feature of the situation is that white leadership sometimes seems more eager to recognize than to solve these lags in Negro health. We must admit the acts of illegitimacy, as pointed out above, and then another fact, as stated by another Floridian, Dr. Winston Ehrmann, who has made studies of the social and psychological aspects of illegitimacy: "Better education and economic conditions among Negroes in the South and the consequent changes in their social and family relations would seem to stimulate an increase in statutory marriages and hence a decrease in illegitimacy."

Or, as Dr. Rupert Vance stated in *All These People:* "The problem of Negro health, serious as it is in its economic and social aspects, is nothing of a medical mystery. Excess Negro mortality is made of the elements that cause excess deaths everywhere. It is related to occupational factors found in rough, heavy work, to poor housing, heating, and sanitation, to inadequate nutrition and poor medical care, and to that ignorance which condemns a people to both, when they might secure better."

Too often the attitude toward Negro care is that of a taxi driver in Richmond who tells you, "All this talk of them going to our schools, using our hospitals, would be like me trying to live in a rich man's house. Just feel out of place, wouldn't be comfortable. Why, they don't support the schools. And they've got a hospital right here in the city, we have to keep it going for them. They get to fighting, cutting each other up Friday, Saturday nights, the bandages alone would probably cost a half-million dollars!"

Although many advances have been made in wiping out some of the most dread afflictions, especially since the introduction of the "wonder drugs," much still remains to be done. In the winter of 1955, in an effort to secure more funds for the care of tubercular patients, Alabama's health leaders pointed out the great need for additional facilities. In Montgomery County, site of the state capital, it was stated that there were 742 known cases of tuberculosis, but only 144 beds to care for these patients. The medical director of the Montgomery t.b. hospital said, "There is a much higher rate of incidence of t.b. among Negroes. They tend to get more severe cases and take longer to get well. We had forty-eight names on our waiting list from out of the county at the start of 1955. Average waiting time for white persons was five days before they were admitted. Negroes, on the other hand, averaged a hundred and forty-one days of waiting before they could find a bed. We closed out the year with forty-three persons on our waiting list. Of those, forty-one were Negroes. While waiting, seven persons died. Six were Negroes."

There were seven babies suffering from t.b. at this doctor's sanatorium, and all were Negro children. "No one is born with t.b. It re-

sults simply from breathing in the tuberculosis germ. Living in squalo
and terribly overcrowded, some Negroes are thus more susceptible t
the disease."

Rigidity of segregation in hospitals has varied throughout the South
In 1948, a national committee reporting on segregation in the nation'
capital said, "The segregation of Negroes is worse than it was sixty year
ago. In 1889, the United States Senate asked for a report on the racia
policies of Washington's hospitals, and all of the eleven which the
served the city replied that no person was denied admission on accoun
of 'race, color, or previous condition of servitude.' Now a fourth of th
twelve private hospitals exclude Negroes altogether, and the remainde
allot them a limited number of beds in segregated wards. How rigid th
color bar can be was discovered on a cold winter morning of 1945 by
young colored woman in childbirth. Unable to reach the city hospit
in time, she rushed to a church-supported hospital. But admission wa
refused, and the baby was delivered on the sidewalk in front of the doo
The staff supplied a sheet to cover the mother and child until the cit
ambulance arrived to take them away."

Since that time, of course, conditions have changed back towar
the older "tradition" of non-segregation in Washington and some oth
parts of the South. In 1954, Bishop Vincent Waters, of Raleigh, Nort
Carolina, issued a call "to open all facilities of our Catholic hospita
to Catholic Negroes, in any places where this has not been done alread
and to non-Catholic Negroes as far as extra room may permit. Perm
qualified Negro physicians and surgeons to take care of these patien
whenever possible, especially by offering opportunities for work t
Negroes to help solve their problems." Mercy Hospital, in Charlotte, on
of the state's largest and most modern, became the first in that city t
admit Negro patients.

Statistics on this subject do not always reflect the exact situation i
parts of the South. A resident in one of the northern, more industrialize
counties of a Deep South state, tells you, "I was examining a recer
report on health conditions through the South and naturally turned t
the figures on our city. It didn't have a single hospital listed whe
Negro doctors could practice, or Negro patients could be accommodate
but that's been going on quietly at our hospital for several years. Th
children's ward, for instance, is completely desegregated. But of cours
I'm sure that if the hospital had known of the preparation of such a r
port, they'd have begged the writers, on their knees, not to tell wh
they were doing."

An amusing and revealing example of the subtleties and ramifications in handling these situations in the South lies in the story of Huey Long and Charity Hospital in Louisiana. A political scientist shares it with you: "Long was an atypical Southern demagogue, you know, in that he was not a racist. I have this particular incident thirdhand, but I think it both accurate and meaningful. A Negro woman working in the Long household told Huey one day how none of her people had a chance at the Charity Hospital. They couldn't be nurses or aids there. Well, Huey told her he'd see what he could do. In a few days he went down on an inspection tour. Went all through the hospital and when he was through he called all the personnel and adminstration together and pounded his fist on the table and shouted, 'I'm shocked by what I've just seen here. Nice sweet white girls washing the faces and looking after Negroes. Why aren't there black people here to do this, instead of having our white girls doing these chores?' And I believe it's a matter of record that Charity Hospital has had Negro nurse's aids, at least, ever since."

In mid-1957, Mississippi was caught up in a controversy over the building of a veteran's hospital. When the 1954 legislature authorized the gift of some state land in Jackson for the site of the hospital, it stipulated that transfer should be made by the State Building Commission "on terms and conditions it sees fit." When eleven million dollars was set aside for construction, officials wanted to be certain that the land was still available. Mississippi's segregation "watchdog" group, the State Sovereignty Commission, investigated integration in federal facilities and discovered that the hospital would be integrated. Governor Coleman, as chairman of the building commission as well as the sovereignty commission, said, in response to protests over the donation of land for an integrated facility, "It would put us in a bad light over the country to deny the land and indicate we're willing to deny the veterans these facilities just to prove we're segregationists. There's a great deal of difference between putting grown people together in a hospital and putting children together in a school."

When the sovereignty commission recommended that the land be given for the hospital, the *Jackson Daily News* labeled the event as "Mississippi's Munich Day," and suggested calling the group "the surrender commission," because it had swallowed "the lure of federal funds like a hungry bass at dawn." Veterans' groups favored the governor's stand on proceeding with the hospital's construction, but the Association of Citizens' Councils of Mississippi asked Congress to "enact such legislation as they deem fit to cause veterans hospitals to be operated in conformity with the customs, traditions, and law of the states wherein they are located."

The hardships which Negro doctors have confronted in trying to serve their communities, not only in the South but often in other parts of the country, seem particularly unreasonable. In many hospitals, they may not attend their own patients who are assigned to segregated sections but are required to have a white doctor. Membership in professional societies is often denied them. There is, however, steady progress being made along these lines. In 1955 a study committee of the North Carolina Medical Society called it "unwise and unfair to deny a Negro physician by reason of his color the place in society which he has achieved through his industry, character and tenacity of purpose. To so deny him is, in our opinion, not only a violation of Christian ethics, but also a violation of the tenets of true democracy in which we profess." By a vote of 101 to 34, the Society agreed to admit qualified Negro doctors as scientific fellows. In some other states, Virginia, Texas, Tennessee, Oklahoma, similar progress was made. And in The Negro Potential, published in 1956, Dr. Eli Ginzberg and his associates pointed out: "One important area of employment may present greatly increased opportunities for Negro women in both the North and the South over the next decade—the field of health services. Today many hospitals in the North could not operate without the help of Negro nurses and auxiliaries. There is also scattered evidence in the South that exceptions to segregation are being made in the health fields for properly qualified Negro women. An expanding economy with rising personal incomes will bring increasing demands for social and health services."

It is indeed strange that in the South, where the Negro woman's patience and gentleness have perhaps been most appreciated, even to the extent that many generations of white children have been given over to her care and nurture—here she has been most rigorously barred from the formal dignity of becoming a nurse for hospitalized adults, or those same children she will care for at home.

So we fail to tap human resources which lie all around us; we fail to exert our utmost intelligence or reverence in seeking to alleviate the pain of life and slow the inevitable approach of death, in our mutual mortal bondage to flesh and blood. We are hindered in our smallest acts, or our largest decisions of humanity, by pride, or fear or hate—or simply habit.

A charming, lively lady in South Carolina, with a deep concern for all the people of her state and a flair for conversation, tells you about an encounter she had with a doctor in her city. We shall call him Dr. House-man because that is not his real name. "Dr. Houseman is one of our most prominent specialists. I went to him for a checkup recently and discovered that he has a Negro office woman who is also his secretary, does practically everything in the office. I was so interested when I saw her that I could hardly listen to Dr. Houseman's report on my own state of health.

"Anyway, when he'd finished discussing my diagnosis, I said to him, 'Doctor, I'm certainly pleased to see that you judge people on their abilities and act accordingly.' He asked me what I meant, and when I referred to his stenographer we got to talking about all the current racial awareness, and this question of reputation. Dr. Houseman told me about being on a train from New York not long before, and in the dining car the headwaiter detected his Southern accent and said, 'I'm sorry, you'll have to wait. The only seat we have available just now is with a Negro army officer and I suppose you prefer to wait.'

" 'Not at all,' Dr. Houseman replied. So he sat down, and the Negro officer, who had overheard all this, said, 'Well, isn't it unusual for you from the South to be willing to eat with me?'

" 'Not at all,' the doctor said again, and went ahead and told him of many Negroes he'd rather eat with than many whites.

"Then I asked Dr. Houseman, 'Would you do that in the South?'

" 'No, indeed. A gentleman is never conspicuous.'

"He went on to tell me about his Negro butler-chauffeur, one of his best friends as well as his employee, and one of the most intelligent men he knew. A probing fine mind. Dr. Houseman's getting rather deaf now and he'd really rather sit in front in the car on his way to the office so he could hear better what the chauffeur has to say, but he doesn't, because 'No gentleman is ever conspicuous.' "

The desire to be inconspicuous, the need to be liked by the neighbors, are factors which cannot be neglected in evaluating much of the reaction and inaction on the part of white Southerners today. Sometimes a single act occurs, thoughtless in the "mores of the community" because its origin is in the deeper morals of humanity. And it sets in motion a series of events which are astounding in the glimpse they afford of the forces—destructive and constructive—which lie below the surface of the community. Such was the case of Dr. Deborah Coggins and Madison, Florida.

Along the narrow neck of northern Florida, which connects the large central and southern portion of the state with the northwest panhandle, is a cluster of three rural counties: Madison, Jefferson and Taylor. Jefferson and Madison, bordering on Georgia, are, as their names would indicate, two of the oldest counties in Florida. Formed in 1827, they were part of the old plantation cotton economy in antebellum days, and their population still has a large Negro proportion.

In the summer of 1956, one health officer was serving all three of these counties. That officer was a thirty-two-year-old woman with blonde hair and blue eyes, excellent training and professional reputation, and diverse interests. The wife of a practicing physician in the town of Madison, capital of the county bearing that name, Dr. Deborah Coggins is the mother of three small children; in her spare time she swims, golfs, makes hooked rugs. But caring for the health of an area whose standards are still low—where some one fourth to one third of the births are still by midwife, hookworm and tuberculosis exist in surprising numbers of cases, and the biggest problem is that of much of the South, malnutrition—leaves little spare time. In fact, during August of that year Dr. Coggins was so swamped with work that when Mrs. Ethel Kirkland, a Negro midwife consultant to the Board of Health, came over from Jacksonville to have a conference, Dr. Coggins could not manage to see her for two days. Finally, a meeting at lunchtime on the third day seemed the only solution to the pressures of time and work. Dr. Coggins went to a local restaurant and asked the manager if she and the Negro midwife might use the private dining room. She was advised to ask the cook, and when the cook agreed to the request, everything seemed settled. The doctor and the midwife had lunch and discussed the health problems of the people they served.

The first clouds of the storm that was to follow were not noticed by Dr. Coggins because they gathered in secrecy. No one berated her for breaking the social code—in fact, no one even mentioned the event to her. And then she learned that a petition was being circulated among certain groups of townspeople calling for her dismissal as county health officer.

By September seventh, *The Madison Enterprise-Recorder* felt it necessary to give a front-page summary of "The Coggins Affair:"

"The breaking of our age-old unwritten Southern tradition that white folks and colored folks do not eat from the same table at the same time, is what caused the uproar. Talk started, tongues wagged throughout the day and night, a petition was circulated, somebody put pressure on the county commissioners, and at noon, Wednesday, September 5, 1956, three commissioners, concluding their meeting in an automobile parked by the courthouse, when this writer thought they had adjourned, voted to ask the State Board of Health to recall Mrs. Coggins. She was notified via telephone of the Board's action by Clerk Dale Leslie. The Board did not call her for any questioning or hearing. . . .

"The American way would be to hold an open hearing. . . ."

With an appeal that would carry less obvious weight anywhere outside the South, the editor then went on to list the local families of distinction to whom Deborah Coggins was related by marriage. He called for another hearing at which the doctor would be permitted to appear before the commissioners.

On September twenty-seventh, the commissioners of the three counties met in a joint session and agreed to fire Dr. Coggins. Two days later, at its county seat of Monticello, Jefferson County gave the doctor her first hearing. The Commission Chairman told her: "Lunching with darkies is not very much of a custom in the South. . . . We're sorry this occurred. We'll never get another health officer as good as you, but with the people so strong against you, there's nothing else we can do."

Dr. Coggins told the commission: "Health knows no color boundaries, not even in the South; and I do not feel I have done anything illegal. I didn't just eat with any of them. I ate with a nurse, someone in my own profession."

The commission chairman interrupted her: "What if I ate with my corn-breakers? I guess you'd think that was legal." (Corn-breakers are Negro plow hands.)

The doctor then explained that in Tampa, where she was reared, the county medical society meets each month and "white and Negro doctors eat dinner together. In a medical group this is not the shocking thing it appears to you."

The reply was brief. "We work with them and have them in our homes, but we don't eat with them."

Another Jefferson commissioner said elsewhere that his group felt that making an example of Dr. Coggins would help in retaining Southern traditions and customs. "It was a hard decision to make and hard to explain why we acted as we did."

A few days later, at a meeting of the Madison County commissioners, Dr. Coggins requested that they discuss her dismissal in her presence. Their answer was silence. Then she asked, "Could it be that you think what you did was unjust, illegal, undemocratic or unchristian? Is that why you don't speak? Why are you such cowards?"

Two Madison Countians then arose to speak for Dr. Coggins. The first was Robert H. Browning, county health information officer. Still

on the public payroll, he informed the commissioners that he was un-
afraid of them "individually or collectively. Dr. Coggins has been severely
persecuted. Dr. Coggins has been tormented. The health programs in
three counties have collapsed. I say, 'Is it worth it?' What do you have to
prove? To acquiesce at a time like this would be to sacrifice principle.

"I cannot and will not sacrifice my own integrity and self-respect on
the altar of economic security. What Dr. Coggins did had no more to
do with spreading integration than drinking a cup of Russian tea has to
do with spreading communism.

"If there is one Christian among you, one American, let me hear a
motion to rescind this action. Let me hear it now." Silence.

Then Editor T. C. Merchant, Jr., arose. He spoke of the lies, mis-
representations and slander to which the community had been subjected,
and said, "A physician greater than Deborah Coggins was once criticized
for eating with tax collectors and sinners. I am not attempting to make
any irreverent comparisons, but I sincerely believe that if you fire this
girl today for the reason you have in mind, you will be doing an evil
and unjust act, the memory of which will follow you to your graves."
He then called each of the commissioners by first name and asked them to
"show the world what Southern white men are like."

There was still only silence, until Deborah Coggins finally stood and
cried, "You're all fools, fools! I'm going to stay in Madison, and you
are going to have to look at me for a long time." The hearing was over.

Governor LeRoy Collins stated that he was "sick about" Dr. Coggins's
dismissal. "The action cannot be squared with right and justice and conscience, and if I didn't speak up and say so, I feel I would, by my silence,
condone an evil act." Then he added, "This would never have occurred
two years ago—it is a by-product of the passion aroused by efforts to
coerce integration of the races against the will of the people."

To which the *Tampa Morning Tribune* replied, "Florida is not
responsible for the Supreme Court's decisions. But Florida *is* responsible
for what its own public officials and people do. . . . It is the duty of a
community's leaders to speak for justice, no matter how violently the
bigots howl in the streets. By doing so they become molders, rather than
prisoners, of public opinion. . . .

"We can denounce the Supreme Court decision as much as we
please. We can lament the worsening of race relations it unquestionably
has caused. But let us remember that any act of brutality or injustice
committed in this state does not darken the door of the court—it scars
the conscience and the reputation of Florida."

The scars cut individually, too, wider and deeper than into the life of one doctor. Robert Browning, who had spoken against Dr. Coggins's firing, was released from his job as information officer of the tri-county area, after Jefferson County commissioners wrote the State Board of Health that a "health educator is no longer necessary." Editor Merchant wrote in his Madison paper: "Browning deserves to be treated as the high school civics books say Americans should be treated. His ancestors have lived in Madison County for one hundred years. He is well-educated, well-qualified for his job of bringing better health practices to the people. He should not be run out of this county and away from his home merely because he exercised his American right of free speech." But Mr. Browning was dismissed.

Another supporter of Dr. Coggins, Mrs. Flo Way, a fifth-grade teacher in Monticello, was called before the Jefferson County school board and asked to resign. When she declined and the State School Superintendent pointed out that she had a continuing contract which provided that she could be discharged only for "good and sufficient cause," the matter was dropped.

A few weeks later, editor Merchant, talking with a reporter, said, "I've never thought much about such things. If I thought at all, it was the way Madison thinks, I guess. Until this came along. . . . Of course, I know small towns. They forget quickly. Perhaps this will all blow over, but it has done something to me." And he asked, "Who are these people I live with?"

The town did appear to forget as quickly as possible. With the arrival of the New Year, this small notice appeared in the *Madison Enterprize-Recorder:* "Deborah R. Coggins, M.D., announces the opening of her office for the general practice of medicine. Jan 7, 1957. 702 W. Base St., Madison, Florida."

In the big white house which has been in her husband's family for almost a century, small, friendly, informal Deborah Coggins ponders on some of the things she learned about the people and place where she lives. There is the knowledge that the poor whites and Negroes in these counties are much the same in their need for better health, better education, better opportunity, that often all the whites have to set them apart is their skin. In the homes with servants, Negroes use the same silver and china to eat with, often the same table, but the segregation is a matter of timing: me now, you later. There is the self-appraisal which tells her she is not a crusader. She stumbled into a situation which grew beyond her, and yet made her suddenly aware of issues to which she'd given little previous thought. After all, in a democracy each person should be able to eat with anyone he wished to! And there is remembrance of the ignorance and superstition of some of the midwives with whom she worked—like the one who told her after an especially long and difficult delivery that the mother had eaten clay, and that had made the baby stick. And as she tells a reporter, there is hope and belief that the controversy "may have stirred some respect for the individual, whether he be white or colored. Let's call it human dignity. In the medical profession we draw no color distinction when we treat human ailments."

In Mississippi, P. D. East said in his *Petal Paper*, after Dr. Coggins's dismissal: "You see a constant stream of Klan Kopy in which they point out that Negroes will have to do something about their health problems before they can make any progress, etc. Well, hell's bells, how can they! Witness the incident in Florida. In Hattiesburg there are three hospitals, and a Negro medical doctor cannot practice in either one of them. Yet, we contend the Negro has a serious health problem, which, indeed, he does. But how can he be taught? What inducement is offered a Negro doctor getting out of school to come to Hattiesburg? None whatsoever. Result: Twelve thousand Negroes in the county and two doctors of their race. And then we sit around and wonder what's wrong with so many things in our beloved Southland. Quite basically we slit our own throat and then are shocked and surprised when someone points it out to us."

While townspeople and county commissioners and people over the state were spending time and energy and money considering the case of Dr. Deborah Coggins who had eaten lunch with a Negro fellow worker, the needy of both "black blood" and "white blood" had to suffer the pain and weariness of disease and undernourishment as best they could. For the only certainty in the pain and pride of blood is death, which man's indomitable spirit alone can survive.

17   A Place in the Sun

Two full decades before the famous Forty-Niners began their westward push that was to become an epic in American history, the South had the Twenty-Niners—and its own gold rush to the hills of Georgia.

After 1828 and the discovery of nuggets containing the ore in the Indian nation, people from all corners of the South and East flocked to the North Georgia gold fields. Pressure for the expulsion of the Cherokees from their homeland was inevitably accelerated. Georgia successfully defied the United States government in its encroachments on the freedom of red men and would soon defy it again on the question of freedom for black men. But the dilemma was essentially neither black nor white nor red, but yellow—the color of gold—and green—the color of fertile fields and pleasant hills the white men needed and had the strength to seize.

From its beginnings to the present, the South's chief source of distress seems also to have been its chief economic resource—and that was its people, all of the people. For years it was said that the South's best crop was its babies. But prosperity was doomed as long as part of the population sought—in a basic irreverence for life—to profit from, rather than with, all of the rest of the human neighborhood.

Before the Civil War had quite ended, a Northern general living in South Carolina coined the phrase "the New South." "It's something of a shock to realize that this 'New South' we're always talking about is almost a century old now," the Southern proprietor of a small factory tells you.

Indeed it is difficult to realize how firmly old foundations may support a new façade. Recent events and attitudes which have come as a surprise to much of the rest of the country simply reflect anachronisms which have been accumulating in the South for many years.

Following the Civil War, the South once again displayed cracks in that solid front which has been supposed its most constant characteristic. Rather than resisting new and peaceful invasions by the Yankees, many towns and counties were now hoping for their return as investors of capital, knowledgeable technicians, skilled industrialists. In December, 1868, an advertisement noted by Gilbert Govan and James Livingood in their regional history, *Chattanooga Country*, appeared in a local newspaper. Its headline said, "Wanted Immediately Any Number of Carpet-Baggers to Come to Chattanooga and Settle." An explanation and invitation followed.

"The people of Chattanooga, no longer wishing to stay in the background, and feeling the necessity of immediately developing the vast mineral resources surrounding them, by which they can place themselves on the high road to wealth, prosperity and power, extend a General Invitation to all Carpet-Baggers to leave the bleak winds of the North and come to Chattanooga. . . .

"Those who wish to come can be assured they will not Be Required To Renounce Their Political and Religious Tenets, as the jurisdiction of the Ku Klux and other vermin does not extend over these parts. . . .

"P.S. Those having capital, brains and muscle preferred."

But for some years after the War, the lure of new lands and fresh beginnings in the West far outweighed the prospect of partially used-up land and an inheritance of old problems in the South. Some of the Southerners themselves joined in the westward trek.

Then came the great revival—or as W. J. Cash called it in *The Mind of the South*, a "crusade," a "folk movement"—to redeem the South from ignorance and poverty and its many other problems by taking "a page from the book of Yankeedom" and meeting "the old enemy on his own ground." The conviction grew in the minds of the leaders: "Let us introduce the factory in force. Let us, in particular, build cotton mills, here in the midst of the cotton fields. Let us build a thousand mills—and more than a thousand mills, and erect the South into a great industrial and commercial empire."

Communities raised funds for the construction of factories, "poor whites" came down from the hills and in from the farms. It was a social as well as business enterprise. Too frequently, in these early instances, they discovered that they had only exchanged an old loose poverty for a more up-to-date machine-bound servitude.

Before the turn of the century, merchants in Charleston were able to lift a toast: "South Carolina—a new era of prosperity is about to dawn upon her; increasing commerce, manufactures, agriculture and population are echoes of its coming." This zeal was appropriate to a community which needed Causes as well as cash.

Does this confidence and hope not find an echo today in the almost belligerent enthusiasm of a young businessman in a town in West Tennessee when he says to you, in his paneled office decorated with enlarged photographs of the various scenic attractions in his state, "We're at the threshold of a new day here in the South: business is better every year, industry's moving in—let 'em squawk up North about our pirating their factories; it's about time they felt the pinch that's squeezed us down here all these years. I tell you, the South's getting the feel of folding money again—and we like it. We're about to make a down payment on our rightful place in the sun, and damn it all, we don't intend to have the mortgage on that place foreclosed on us."

Do the old appeals not find numerous, more sophisticated, echoes today in the advertisements which appear directly in the "carpetbagger" press? (And the weight of an old bargain—bring us new means but not new ways of life—is still here, too: while *The New York Times* carries a story in its news section of some Southern leader who has joined his voice to the chorus of those urging Yankees, in effect, to stay home and mind their own business, a half- or full-page advertisement appears in the financial section urging Yankee business to come on down South. States' rights may be the call to colors on the front pages, but it's the states' fights for industry which is the rallying cry on the inner pages.)

In a *Newsweek* advertisement, Mississippi's Governor J. P. Coleman invited readers to "Know Mississippi: Manpower, Materials, Markets. . . . Every effort is made to operate our State government on such a high plane of service, stability and economy that industrialists can know that Mississippi is a sound, safe and outstanding place in which to locate and operate."

In *U.S. News and World Report* the four electric power companies making up The Southern Company used a two-page spread to publicize the growth of the Southern cattle industry, textile and coal production, the football team of Georgia Tech—training engineers for industry, the Cloister as one of many coastline resorts, and the expanding uses of wood and oil. "The march has just begun!" they said. "The last half of the twentieth century belongs to the South!"

To the fast-growing Pacific Northwest and other more prosperous areas, such statements may seem only an ad man's hyperbole, but perhaps they are something more, too. Realizing how handicapped their region was for many years by lack of capital—in 1894, for instance, there were 123 counties in Georgia that had not a single incorporated bank, state or national—and by such fetters as discriminatory freight rates, it is not difficult to realize why the recent upsurge in industrial development brings such satisfaction to Southerners.

Most of the region would appreciate the words of James Street, who probed wittily into the pleasure and pain and paradox of his native land. Shortly before his untimely death in 1954, he said that it is hard to find agreement nowadays as to whether the South is a land of "moonlight or moonshine, Tobacco Road or tobacco factories, Texas Cadillacs or ox carts, Uncle Remus or George Washington Carver, Supreme Court Justice Hugo Black or Senator Claghorn, hydrogen plants or hot air, RFD or TVA, hospitality or hostility, violence or tranquility, Miami or mud, Li'l Abner, Prince Valiant or Pogo."

A constant stream of public oratory, editorial comment and sectional eloquence covers the South's "New Look." Senator Fulbright of Arkansas says, "The South is no longer the nation's No. 1 economic problem; it is now the nation's new economic frontier. The level of economic development in the South is still considerably below that of the rest of the nation. However, we no longer view our difficulties as a national problem, but as a challenge to ourselves; a challenge to develop our potentials to reach the national level of economic development so that the people of the South may share fully in the American standard of living."

And, with the optimism indispensable to a man who had just been presented the Horatio Alger Award in Washington, D.C., by the Secretary of Commerce, a multimillionaire businessman from Mississippi pointed out, "The South's long lag in industrialization is, oddly enough, proving to be a blessing. The new plants and those under construction have profited by advances in design, equipment and production engineering so that they have a tremendous advantage over the obsolescent plants of the older industrial areas of the North.

"South Carolina produces more textiles than Massachusetts; Louisiana produces more chemicals than New York state; Georgia manufactures more paper than Wisconsin; and Baton Rouge, Louisiana, is the most highly concentrated industrial complex in the world."

Of all the Southern states, none has boomed in population like Florida. From its rank as twentieth in the nation in 1950, it has moved in seven short years up to thirteenth in population. Its best cash crop, the tourist trade, accounts for some of this, of course, but the rapid increase of industry has brought many of the permanent settlers. Since there is no water power, iron or coal in Florida, climate has been called "Just about its only raw material." But if a congenial climate can attract highly skilled engineers, chemists, technicians, that is a factor which will prove not only persuasive but decisive with many of the "light" industries the state hopes to secure. So Floridians, far from telling "outsiders" to go home, will be spending upwards of six million dollars during the next two years to persuade them to come home—to their own spot in the sun.

Apparently there was only South-wide satisfaction over a recent announcement of Time, Inc. Although the reporting of current events by the magazine of that name frequently brings shouts of "persecution" and "anti-South" from some areas of the region, there were no protests over the news that *Time* had joined Crown Zellerbach Corporation to form a company for the manufacture, beginning sometime late in 1958, of machine-coated printing paper at a thirty-one-million-dollar mill in Louisiana.

And there was certainly no outcry against the "federal interference" which brought to the seven-state area of the Southeast, alone, in 1956, purchases of goods and services of the government totaling just a little less than five hundred million dollars.

But halt a moment! With all the lost sharecroppers and the new-found payrolls, with all the new banks for both soil and money, with the old optimism couched in new Madison Avenue language—despite all this, and lest we receive a picture of the over-all situation as distorted as the old illusion of limitless moonlight and juleps: in 1954, the nine states with the lowest per capita income of the forty-eight were in the South.

"What too many of us refuse to realize," one man says, "is that the South has to come from way behind just to stay in the race. In relation to the rest of the country in cities and industries, we've just kicked off some old hobbles. Now we can substitute a run for a limp—if we want to."

And here we come again to the familiar dilemma, the fundamental problem which the South must confront before it can find any permanent solution for its many vexations. At the heart of the matter—the Negro, the white, and their old dual pantomime governed now by new necessity.

When Roy Parker, Jr., a young newspaperman in the Roanoke-Chowan River section of North Carolina, became interested in a labor survey that had been taken in the region, the facts were revealing. "The most plentiful commodity of the Roanoke-Chowan isn't tobacco or peanuts—it's people," Mr. Parker said. "That was proved last week when a survey of available Negro labor was taken in Ahoskie. A total of 950 people—727 women and 223 men—signed up. That is about four per cent of the population of Hertford County.

"The labor survey was the idea of Negro leaders. The idea of industry using Negro labor is almost new. In Rich Square an all-Negro plant has been operating for more than a year. It employs only Negro women in the manufacture of pajamas, and is housed in a Negro-owned building."

As Jim Crow was born more recently than many people realize, so the idea of the inferiority of the Negro as a skilled artisan was largely born after the Civil War. Before the War, many of the most able craftsmen in the South were Negroes. Their labor built many of the fine old mansions so cherished today, and laced many a New Orleans balcony with delicate grillwork. But when their competition with white labor became more and more direct, and as opportunities for training in the crafts were lessened, they were increasingly frozen into their role as "hewers of wood and drawers of water."

"The nigger's shiftless," a confident young lawyer in a navy blue pin-stripe suit and a grey felt hat assures you. "Like old Uncle Bud, when Harve Williams offered him a good steady job. 'Nawsuh, Mistah Williams. I'se got a dollar and a half from Miz Mackay last week and seventy-five cents from Mistah Lewis this week. I'se don't want to git too self-supportin'.' They're all like that—no-count unless they're downright hungry or cold. Never look ahead as far as day after tomorrow."

In the same city, another man—somewhat slighter in build and more soft-spoken—who has worked with many groups of laborers in the South, from farm migrants to some of the heavy industries, says, "The jobs of Negro men in Southern industry today all too often lead nowhere. In plants where you do find Negro workers, there is almost no chance for promotion. There are some exceptions, of course, but the incentive for advancement to the supervisory or management status is usually denied Negroes.

"As for the Negro women, their need is to break through the narrow confines of service work to factory jobs and clerical and sales positions."

In its annual race-relations survey, Tuskegee Institute noted for 1956 that "major oil refining companies in the Gulf Coast section are providing for the mobility of Negro employees out of the area of un-skilled jobs upward into other job classifications." Many cities were also showing increased Negro personnel in the post offices. The atomic energy installations at Oak Ridge, Paducah, and on the Savannah were providing a wide range of employment opportunities for qualified Negroes. A reporter in Memphis tells you: "International Harvester is about as well integrated as it could be, I think. It's interesting because that has been its policy from the very beginning. Before the plant opened, the president came down and laid it on the line how employment would be, and after the first day's work, people found he meant it. Some of the white workers didn't, and don't, like it—Negroes in equal jobs, equal pay, promotion on merit. But the wages are good and there's not much anybody can do about it. As for the Negroes in Memphis, it's been a real milestone for them, of course.

"Firestone has been here some longer, and it grew into a policy of non-discrimination. This developed without publicity, and the change has come smoothly."

The Negro's efforts to exchange the pick and shovel for other, more remunerative, implements, has been long and hard. Yet, since 1940, it has been estimated that the proportion of skilled Negro workers in the United States has increased 49 per cent. This pyramiding economic revolution has had many far-reaching effects, but probably the most important has been the rise of what is called the "Negro market."

"We're discovering," a business administration professor in a Southern university tells you, "that if the South is to prosper industrially it needs good workers and some of those workers will have to be our Negroes. We also need that increased purchasing power. Keeping the Negro poor, the South has stayed poor."

In Nashville someone likens the present industrial situation to that which existed at the Vanderbilt University Theological School when they had Negro applications for admission. "Vandy's colors are black and gold, you know, and they receive a great deal of aid from many of the large foundations. It may turn out in our industry that we'll have to do what some people said the school did: take the black to save the gold."

In 1955, the United States Secretary of Labor pointed out in a speech in Nashville: "The South will soon have to realize that its remarkable industrial growth is being threatened by the loss of many of its best-educated and best-trained Negroes, who represent one quarter of the Southern labor force. Unless this area starts now to train its Negro workers, it is going to find that its possibilities for industrial expansion will be sharply curtailed."

And in 1956, Fisk University president Charles S. Johnson said in an article in *The New York Times Magazine:* "We cannot escape the fact that the Negro minority market alone, even when held down by unequal opportunity and limited education to one half its potential, is equal to the total wealth of Canada or to our total foreign exports."

The chairman of the board of directors of one big Southern-born-and-bred industry says, "I spoke up at Vassar College a few months ago. Those girls there just wanted to talk about unions and Negroes. Finally I told them, 'Let's talk about something else. We're not in a turmoil down South, we're working.'

"We've got a million Negroes in my state. All of us in business have something to sell. If we can increase their income ten dollars each per year, any man in his right mind would be a fool not to try to implement such a situation. Those who criticize us so much for what we're trying to do down here should realize we know this.

"The trouble is that the Negro down South today is getting himself in a bind. Nobody loves him. The Negro is getting belligerent, upstage. I know lots of people who don't have a single servant now—too much trouble; too much mouth, too little smile.

"Negroes are going to town. I don't mind carrying the Negro, but not while he's squealing. I'm ready to let him stand on his own. We're interested in the Negroes because we're selfish, like the rest of the country: when he doesn't have enough money to buy our goods, we suffer. We're not in a turmoil down here. Like I said, all we want to do is get to work."

In an article on "The Negro's New Economic Life" in *Fortune* magazine, September, 1956, writer Emmet John Hughes discusses the capital of Georgia as a city unique in the life of the American Negro. "Auburn Avenue in Atlanta lays claim to being the richest Negro street in the world. It is not a pretentious sight, most of its low buildings housing the familiar, drab Negro taverns, barbershops, groceries. But scattered among them there stand: the Atlanta Life Insurance Co., whose $40 million in assets qualifies it as the largest Negro stock company in the U.S.; the Citizens Trust Co., with assets of $7 million, the Negro bank belonging to the Federal Reserve System; the Atlanta *World*, the nation's only Negro daily; the Mutual Federal Savings & Loan Association of Atlanta, with assets of $11 million, the largest such institution south of Washington. . . .

"Atlanta's Negroes and whites have long shown intelligent capacity to work together, notably on housing problems. But common sense and good will have mattered less than a cruder force: Negro purchasing power and credit standing. Negroes, who today can get loans from any Atlanta bank, owe thanks to the Auburn Avenue financial institutions, which, by their own fine records, shattered the myth that the Negro is financially irresponsible."

So the picture of economic opportunity for the Negro varies in the South, as in the rest of the nation, from city to city, from county to county. As one energetic young Negro businessman tells you, "In skilled and unskilled jobs the pattern for us is still the old one, 'Last hired, first fired.' In the matter of enterprise, and starting our own businesses, building our own homes, it's 'Last loaned, first called.' "

As mechanization increases throughout the South and the prospects of automation loom larger throughout the nation, the tenuous grasp of the unskilled and semiskilled Negro on his job becomes even more apparent. And the possibility of increasing his security or improving his prospects through membership in a union is not always open to the Negro.

Traditionally the South has been slow to unionize, and at least part of the reaction to national policy of the unions on integration may be summed up in the comments of two Southern leaders: "First we are white men—then union men." And, "We're good union men, but we're good Southerners."

Rumors of rifts between the national organization and Southern locals have been numerous. Proposals to "secede" from the AFL-CIO have been forthcoming; the launching of a Southern Federation of Labor brought about expulsion of its chairman from his international AFL-CIO local and a withering of the movement. The case of Chattanooga is illustrative of the internal dissension on the question of integration. When that city's Board of Education announced that it would integrate the schools at "the earliest practicable date," the Chattanooga Central Labor Union promptly endorsed the decision. An immediate protest broke out in some of the member locals. Controversy became so hot that the Central Labor Union renounced its earlier commendation of the Board of Education and took a neutral position on school desegregation.

The spring of 1956 seemed particularly turbulent in union handling of this issue. A Detroit union official threw a meeting of a United Auto Workers' local into an uproar when he said, in Memphis, "You're no longer holding meetings for union business—you're meeting to fight integration." There were reports that many Southern organizers were asking the national union officials to soften denunciations of the White Citizens' Councils and take less public stands in favor of integration. "For the sake of our union, don't make our job any harder in the South!"

Those Southern workers who hold membership cards both in a union and a White Citizens' Council appear to have reconciled the differences in the official policies of the two groups. How long that reconciliation can last remains to be seen. (Are the two, perhaps, made even temporarily compatible because of the Southern white worker's deep-seated need for a security he has never known?)

For those who have always been suspicious of unions, their national endorsement of non-segregation has merely deepened the dislike. A plant foreman in one middle South state says, "I tell you, it'll be a thousand years before there's any mixing of any sort in these parts. The Lord never intended it and the people won't stand for it. Why, if we ever put a nigger on the line up here in my section, there'd be a riot. Why can't the Yankee unions understand this? There's no difference a-tall in unionism and communism. They both believe in forcing a feller to do what he don't want to do. I'll tell you right now, there'd never be any unionizing or integrating at this plant, if I had my way."

Former Govenor of Arkansas, Sidney McMath, speaking at a merger convention of the AFL-CIO, said that many of the people fighting for racial segregation had as a corollary objective the destruction of the labor unions in the South. He described the efforts of some of these people as follows: "They concentrate on getting union members signed up in Citizens' Councils. They inflame the union members over the question of segregation in the schools. When the member is in the proper frame of mind, they then remind him that there are Negroes employed in the plant where he works, that there are Negroes in the union to which he belongs. Before the union member knows what is happening to him, he is passing resolutions withdrawing from his internationals on the ground that they permit Negro membership, then he starts circulating petitions to organize an all-white union. When this union member cools off, he finds that he has destroyed the union that has protected his rights and has given his family and him a decent standard of living."

Every phase of the Negro's life—his ability to get a job and how far he can rise on that job, his health, his home, his education, the well-being of his family—is fenced about with the pressures of segregation. That is obvious. Another fact is becoming ever more obvious in the South today, and that is the interdependence of the white and Negro economy.

One of the most interesting features of the Montgomery, Alabama, bus boycott was the fact that physical intimidation failed to break the solid resistance of the Negro community—and so did economic threats. As one person put it: "Our schools may not be integrated, but our dollars sure are." Early in the boycott when the mayor asked the women of Montgomery not to go after their maids, and, if the maid wouldn't walk to work, to fire her, one housewife said, "The Mayor can do his own cooking if he wants to. I'm going after my cook." The Negro women were also well aware of the natural human distaste for mops and ironing boards as long as anyone else can be found to use them. It sometimes seems easier for people to tolerate injustice than to withstand inconvenience.

"They talked about firing all the Negroes in the boycott from their jobs," a Negro man smiles as he remembers. "But then I guess they got to thinking about all those white folks' houses we rent. No payroll, no rent. What would those poor white widows living on their husbands' estates do? And what about those refrigerators and cars and furniture we owed payments on? The storekeepers didn't want all that stuff back. They wanted the money. No, after a little thinking there was very few of us fired from work."

A man in Georgia tells you an incident to illustrate how quickly the green of dollars can render people color blind to black and white. "We had a company down here that used a process peculiarly adapted to nigra labor. They employed nigras only in the plant and used whites in the shipping department. Of course, the nigras got the highest rate of pay and after a little while the whites petitioned to work in the plant proper. They were told they'd have to work with nigras, they said that was O.K. They wanted that dollar thirty-five an hour. People can change mighty fast—if they want to."

One of the most explosive subtopics of conversation and concern in the general subject of segregation has been whether or not the South's resistance to desegregation would in any way curtail the industrial development of the region.

When nationally syndicated financial columnist Sylvia Porter reported, in March, 1956, that the southward march of industry was being slowed by racial tensions, and that several corporations were reconsidering decisions to move South because of the unsettled situation, she probed her pen in a tender spot and received immediate cries of rebuttal.

In an address before the Southern States Industrial Relations Conference, however, the president of the United States Chamber of Commerce, and chairman of the board of the Mississippi School Supply Company, said, "I am merely stating a fact when I say that this issue has created a host of new tensions in major segments of the Southern states. Northern businessmen are thoroughly aware of this. We all know that some Northern concerns have moved South or have thought about moving South to escape tension and in the hopes of conducting their businesses in an orderly, fair and equitable way. I am inclined to the opinion that not very many men will exchange a familiar kind of tension—no matter how irksome—for an unknown kind of tension."

A lawyer in Arkansas tells you, "I imagine the whole South, Mississippi especially, has suffered some slow-down on industry because of school uncertainty. Not because industries are crusaders but because their chief attraction to our region is labor, and if that labor—Negro or white— is in friction with itself, or is leaving the state in large numbers, that's bad. Winthrop Rockefeller, who helped found the Industrial Research Council here in our state, has tried to point out that industry doesn't want to move into situations of turmoil."

In the capital city of one state, a young professional man tells you of a local chamber of commerce conference with the representatives of one company. "They were considering locating here, and if one Negro had been present at that meeting, I believe that would have clinched the decision. This particular enterprise had some government contracts, and a good part of the discussion at the conference was taken up with the hiring of Negroes. Would it be all right? Could they promote them without fear of reprisal? As it turned out, that particular plant did not come here."

One of the most knowledgeable men in the region says: "Industry will have a great influence on this racial situation, of course. So far that influence has been mostly negative—but good in that the power structure boys have said, 'We can't have any of this violence. We're not going to get industry and money down here with race riots.' Oh, they've supported the segregation movements, I'm sure—in many cases, behind the scenes—but at the same time they've gotten the message to the wool-hat fellows that this blood in the street business is out.

"The South's getting accustomed to industry. What many of us haven't realized yet is that even the big plantations are in the modern pattern. They aren't the paternal organizations so much any more. They're getting mechanized, becoming big corporate offices, run with filing cabinets and adding machines like New York Life and the Prudential, and the Negroes aren't sharecroppers as often as they are day laborers. They're learning to use the machines on the farms, too, and pretty soon they'll be learning to use those machines inside."

A political scientist in Florida tells you, "One of the men from the Sperry plant near here said to me, 'What the hell are you Southerners trying to do down here? Don't you know if you pass anything saying you can do away with the public schools that we can't get men to come here from all over the country?'"

With Florida and many of the other Southern states particularly interested in securing industries requiring highly trained technicians, this problem of securing men, who are in short enough supply that they can afford to be choosy about the place where they will live and rear their families, is very real. Governor LeRoy Collins is one of the few Southern governors who has faced this fact publicly. After a tour of Eastern business areas, he said, "Many industrialists have indicated to me, in one way or the other, that their very first consideration in locating new plants is the general atmosphere of the community."

In this realm, as elsewhere, then, the South can choose to wear blinders, adopt a defensive attitude and ignore the waste inherent in segregation and intolerance; or it can adjust a twenty-twenty vision to an aggressive and constructive self-criticism and become, through its own catharsis of self-knowledge, the nation's inspiration.

It can say, as one of its citizens says, "All this talk against the South, this harping on 'racial tension' and 'violence,' is just the same old propaganda. Those people up North are mad because we're getting some of their plants. Unions never have liked the South. They're all teaming up together now to scare industry away from us, to keep those dollars up above the Mason-Dixon line. Nothing in our way of life down here to hurt business, though, and pretty soon everybody'll see that and all the propaganda of these bleeding-heart money-lenders will dry up on the vine."

Or it can consider the words of Opie L. Shelton who, as executive vice president of the Baton Rouge Chamber of Commerce, said to other executives of the Southern Association of this organization, "It is my sincere belief that the greatest single contribution we who serve Southern Chambers of Commerce can make is to work at the individual community level to help ameliorate a situation which so far has been pretty well left up to the extremists of both sides. . . .

"Boycotts, economic reprisals, the possibility of abandoning our public schools, incidents of violence, irresponsible statements—these are new factors which will now be given consideration by industry and business when they consider a Southern location, each to varying degrees."

You travel the South. And in mountain valleys where, not long ago, the world of towns was so remote that a man had to hitch up his wagon and team and take off a day for a trip to "the store," you come across new brick buildings. In suburbs where the rich smell of asphalt is still fresh along the newly paved "lanes" and "drives" and "circles," you find new brick clusters. In wide, untended fields and busy, climbing cities, you discover new brick hives. They are: four-square churches, sprawling factories, consolidated schools, ranch-style homes.

These are the symbols of a new place in the sun. White people own most of them. But Negroes also feel the pull of that "good life" made tangible in brick and chromium. They want to feel the effect of those churches, share in the work and income from those factories, learn in those schoolhouses, and live in homes of their own that bear the stamp of permanence and respectability that attaches to brick!

The South has come so far, can go so much farther. The grandson of a black man born in chattel slavery now carries on his own business behind plate glass and a solid front of white support. The son of a white man who died of pellagra and poverty now heads a multimillion-dollar enterprise. And you know why North Carolina-born Thomas Wolfe could write of America: "It is a fabulous country, the only fabulous country; it is the one place where miracles not only happen, but where they happen all the time."

You visit the great dams of the Tennessee Valley Authority, sweeping bastions of concrete and steel, where the destructive power of a mighty river was harnessed and transformed into a constructive force, and know that in 1956 more than twenty-six hundred visitors from eighty foreign countries came to study the operations of TVA and its multipurpose program. Its enrichment of one part of America was an enrichment for the whole country—for just as the South cannot keep any segment of its people poor without diminishing all of its economy, so these United States cannot afford the waste of human or natural resources at any place or time.

You see and hear and sense the revolution going on in the South right now—farms and factories side by side, Negroes building a new middle-class world for themselves, the forward movements and the backward pulls.

Philip G. Hammer, industrialist of Atlanta, Georgia: "Each new plant coming to the South weakens the hold of the old-style, wool-hat leadership. More important, each new industrial plant presents an opportunity for our young economic leadership to think differently about educational, political, and social problems—to think more clearly about human rights and responsibilities." Industry may become the Trojan horse to penetrate the walls of segregation.

Ralph McGill, of The Atlanta Constitution, has said: "It was, and still is, a puzzling fact that most of those who headed, or were members of, delegations seeking new enterprises never saw themselves as carriers of the virus which was to destroy the status quo in their towns and communities—and also, therefore, the old 'way of life in the South.' They brought new payrolls to their towns. Businesses boomed and new ones came. The delegations basked in the sun of progress. But still they fretted. 'Things are not the same,' they said, shaking their puzzled heads. The organizers and unions came. The Negroes were encouraged to register and vote. The PTA and the community meetings began to hear new and protesting voices about the crowded schools, the town's municipal services. The political contests began to be less and less 'sure' of result. All the while, though deploring the change and declaring to visitors that things were not as they had been, the delegations never saw themselves as makers of the revolution. They sought with a kind of desperation to maintain the status quo—all the while laboring to bring new industries and payrolls which could only accelerate the changes."

In Western North Carolina, a thin mountain woman with arms all bone and muscle, and a level gaze from deep-set brown eyes, tells you simply, "My boy and girl have got life a heap better than I had it at their age. That's proper. I recollect hearing my grandmother say how easy I had it compared to when she was growing up. We all got to make our own way, but we've got the obligation to clear out as much of the underbrush along the way as we can.

"I don't know much about a lot of things going on in the world, but there's a little I've learned: nothing that's living can stand still, it's got to live and grow or die and rot. And there's nothing we can leave behind us, on this side of the grave, but the shape we've helped give to whatever was growing around us."

The shape of its future, its place in the sun: this, truly, will be "Manufactured in the South by Southerners." And if the pitfalls of mistaking inventiveness for inspiration and mechanical ingenuity for human insight can be foreseen and avoided, perhaps the South can bring a new emancipation to all its own and the nation's people: emancipation by and from the machine.

18   Charleston to Houston

It is said that the Mississippi Delta begins in the lobby of the Peabody Hotel in Memphis and ends at Vicksburg. It might also be said that the South begins on the Battery in Charleston and ends in the lobby of the Shamrock Hotel in Houston. For those who have everything "below Mason-Dixon" entrenched in their minds and imaginations as one monolothic mass, the thousand miles between these two hub cities is a journey more in time than in space, an adventure more of discovery than of confirmation.

Atlanta and Dallas may be, by stricter measurements, the regional capitals, and they are lively, hard-working, interesting trade and financial centers, but they lack a certain dedicated individuality which makes Charleston and Houston stand as gateways for entrance or exit to a landscape and a frame of mind. Both are essential to present understanding of the variety of that landscape.

From magnolias to mesquite, from the handsome octagonal clock tower of St. Michael's to the sharp punctuation of a skyscraper against the wide Texas sky; from a reserved, candlelit dinner in an elegant, unobtrusive room, where heavy draperies soften the occasional noises of Meeting (or Broad or Tradd) Street below, to the expansive informality of a pungent barbecue on an acre terrace complete with trees and tile, freezer and fireplace, burning logs and deep-cushioned lounges; from the impenetrable faces of Gullah women along the roads leading into Charleston to the crisp-collared secretaries in an immaculate new Negro office serving the Southwest; from the *grande dame* city of South Carolina with what is known as the oldest Chamber of Commerce organization in the United States, to the high-riding adolescent metropolis of Texas with what must surely be one of the most effective Chambers of Commerce functioning today: from one extreme to the other, this is Charleston to Houston, and both are the South.

The width of their differences, as well as the points of their likeness reflect the rest of the South. Two fundamentals they have in common:

334

egregation and pride. Houston operates the largest segregated school system in the nation, and Charleston's is probably the most adamant. As for their pride, it sometimes seems to non-Charlestonians sheer snobbery, and to non-Houstonians bald boastfulness. But their pride is more similar in its quantity than its sources: Charleston's derives from the fact that it changes as slowly as possible, and Houston's springs from the knowledge it is changing faster than seems probable.

From its Battery, when Charleston looks to the sea it gazes out upon Fort Sumter, and frequently it seems more enamoured of the world that lied there than the one which presently exists all around it. Although the sea is fifty miles away, Houston has made itself the newest and one of the leading ports in the United States with its cargoes of white and black gold. Houston is the largest cotton-shipping port in the United States and the largest oil-shipping port in the world.

"Charlestonians went into a deep-freeze in the eighteenth century," an upcountry South Carolina lawyer laughs. "They decided to stay just the way they were, but the world bypassed them and kept right on changing; they think everything's been a little out of step ever since. It's a city full of chiefs and not enough Indians."

In 1790, Charleston, with a population of 16,359, was the fourth city in the United States. Only Philadelphia, New York and Boston were larger. In 1950, Houston, with 806,701 people, was the fourteenth city in the nation, and first in the South, in population. Even rice, once the major crop on the plantations surrounding Charleston, has moved to Texas, which now produces more of that staple cereal than any other state in the country. Along the narrow winding lanes and alleys of Charleston, with its little secret gardens hidden behind tall iron gates and its houses turning their shoulders to the streets, you feel as if you are walking in the past. Along the wide straight boulevards of Houston, with their reach farther and farther into mushrooming suburbs and countryside and on every steel and brick and concrete structure the stamp of an air-conditioned giant, you feel as if you are riding into the future. Yet such feelings and descriptions are, of course, deceptive in their polarity and simplicity. Cities, like people, choose the myths they wish to perpetuate, and realities at variance with their choice are often buried beneath the myth.

Surely one of the South's most valuable assets today is its consciousness of the past. The past of any people is the root system by which its present flowering must be nourished. But the very value of the past is that it has gone before. Sometimes it seems that the idea of change, rather than any single specific change, is what the South represented by Charleston rejects. In 1898, when a law establishing Jim Crow seating arrangements on trains was under consideration, the Charleston *News and Courier* opposed it. "We have got along fairly well," its editor said, "without such a measure and we can probably get on as well hereafter without it, certainly so extreme a measure should not be adopted and enforced without added and urgent cause."

Within ten years the paper had become a staunch defender of this new status quo, and by now—not quite sixty years later—it is a leader in the fight against abolition of the Jim Crow it was once reluctant to accept. Thomas R. Waring, present editor of *The News and Courier*, has waged a struggle second only to James Byrnes's to present the Southern Gentleman Segregationist's viewpoint to Northern Gentlemen's Groups. (A photograph of Waring and Byrnes together, affable and authoritative in proper after-dinner speaker's tuxedo attire, hangs on the wall of the editor's office.) Waring has been quoted as saying, "If we maintain decency and some semblance of order, we may be able to convince some of the people of the North that we are not a complete bunch of barbarians in the South. It has been a theory of mine, ever since I started trying to pierce the paper curtain, that people of the North simply have not been allowed to be educated on this thing and do not know how far we may be goaded on this segregation issue."

In an article in *Harper's* magazine Mr. Waring probably reached his widest audience. It is not only integration but democracy itself which disturbs Mr. Waring. Advising that he and his newspaper have always taken "a dim view of small 'd' democracy," he makes a favorite point, that the United States is not a democracy but a republic. He is reluctant to bring religion to bear in this sordid disagreement. "We believe that religion has more sides than the social doctrines which so many church leaders today seem to have put up at the top of their lists. If worship must await solution of the race problem, many a church will be dark in the years ahead. . . . *The News and Courier* is not among those on either side of the race issue who believe in quoting scripture on the color line. Despite the many Bible texts one hears on the subject, we are convinced that God has not yet revealed the ultimate intentions on race."

Thomas Waring speaks for a number of people in the South today, certainly not as large a number as he might wish for, but not a small enough number to dismiss under a casual label, either. With 275 years of family background in Charleston, he speaks from both the past and present of that city with a courteous coolness which makes clear its assumption that

:o be introduced in Charleston, or the human race, is not necessarily to be
accepted. Like predestination in theology, those not born into the realm
of acceptance must earn a somewhat lesser grace. "The Negroes already
have their rights; they are demanding that whites be forced to associate
with Negroes. Association is a privilege, not a right. . . . Respect and
acceptance must be earned, not demanded. Until this elementary fact is
understood throughout the country, the South will be fighting a lone
battle to preserve decency, integrity and life itself."

And yet . . .

It was in this city of Charleston, it was in this very family of Waring,
that a United States District Judge found the South Carolina plan for a
white Democratic primary not in accord with the Constitution of the
United States and said, "I cannot see where the skies will fall if South
Carolina is put in the same class" with other states which permitted
Negroes to vote in the primary. "It is time for South Carolina to rejoin
the Union. It is time to fall in step with the other states and to adopt the
American way of conducting elections."

In Charleston, because of old residential and labor patterns, Negroes
and whites live in much closer proximity than in the newer city of Hous-
on, but the chasm between communication of the races is also deeper and
wider in Charleston. You remember what one man tells you: "Just a
bunch of people living in the same block, that's not a community. But
people working together to make a better block for everyone who lives
here, that's a community."

A Negro leader in Houston seems to have a keen awareness of this.
Slim and erect, white-haired, proud of his modern, efficient business,
quietly dispassionate in conversation, he talks with you in the cool inner
sanctum of his office. "Texas Negroes have initiated four of the five main
lawsuits to abolish discrimination. The white primary, equal educational opportunities, equalization of teachers' salaries and one of the key
suits on school integration, Herman Sweatt's case, all started in this
state.

"Now that we have won lawsuits, however, we don't expect the
schools to all be desegregated at once. We know the residential patterns
will influence that. But there can be beginnings. There's no way that a
Negro child coming up in the segregated schools we've known can be
equal educationally to white students. White people have expected us to
be a superior race.

"One of the most significant things in America is the fact that Negro
purchasing power is now sixteen billion dollars a year. Well, down here the

oil companies have started developing filling stations leased and operated by Negroes. Then the automobile companies have started hiring Negro salesmen. The Negro salesman of one make of car won an award here recently for selling the most cars of any salesman in the region. You see for years the South has been biting off its nose to spoil its face by keeping one-fourth of its population poor.

"Personally, as I grow older, and a little wiser perhaps, I don't carry race around with me any more. I'm a Negro by biological accident; in my case by choice, too. Two of my grandparents were white. But that's all aside—as someone has said, ancestors are like rutabagas anyway, all under ground. What isn't aside is the fact that Negro or white, the man who lets race pressure him loses—spiritually, physically, mentally. It's a great load lifted when a man can lay down the burden of race."

He has made an important point: just as there is no room, in the common struggle for a better South and nation, for the Professional Southerner, so there is no room for the Professional Negro. The national Negro magazine, *Ebony*, wrote an editorial in March, 1957, on this subject, in which it said, "The black man's obsession with his problem can hinder his personal development just as a white man's hatred for black men can reduce his usefulness as a citizen . . . the Bunches, the Kitts and the Davises have passed out of the narrow world of Negroes into the broad universe of man. . . . Being a part-time Negro does not mean the denial of racial heritage. It does not mean the rejection of racial traits or the loss of valued traditions. It does mean, however, that he who demands first class citizenship must be prepared to put citizenship first, race second."

Then there is the regional reporter who tells you, late one night over waffles in a Toddle House, "Everything in Florida and Texas is going up. Everything in Mississippi and South Carolina is going along. That's the story in a nutshell—and it's tough to crack."

Charleston to Houston—the beauty and sadness, the anger and the gentle joy, the waste and the potential of a South where innocence and evil still coexist in a world bounded by belief in a righteous God and a resourceful Satan. "A depressingly high rate of self-destruction prevails among those who ponder about the South and put down their reflections in books," V. O. Key, Jr., has said. He speaks of the "fatal frustration" which follows an attempt to understand and convey what we would term the variety and paradox of the region.

Why, then, the constant attempts? Why *this* attempt? At the end of our journey, we come full circle to the beginning, and looking back we may answer in two ways: in the tired phrase, "Because travel—even next oor—is so broadening; you meet such interesting people." Or, in the words of a French clerk in 1606: "The wonder that far exceedeth all others is that in one and the selfsame kind of creature, I mean in Man, are found more variety than in other things created."

The problems with which the South is wrestling today are the issues of mankind everywhere in every time, the problems with the big names, like "justice" and "liberty" and "reverence for life." And as the externals—roads, army, mass communications—are steadily decreasing the South's sectionalism, the internals—emotions, old allegiances and fears—suddenly increase that sectionalism. In a time of transition, we remember the words an old Smoky Mountaineer used to describe a friend: "That's a heap of man. He lays down a long shadow."

A man must stand up before he can make a full shadow—and he must be backed by light. The need cries out today for people who are willing to seek a light and cast a long shadow. There are men and women particularly remembered from this journey, not always because of agreement or disagreement but because they made an effort to communicate as one human to another, because they seemed to echo the sentiments of many besides themselves—or because they spoke from the lonely depths of their own experiences and convictions. Along each phase of our journey, someone laying down a long shadow, dark or bright, across his corner of the South:

The Dawn Comes up Like Thunder:

An Alabama planter, fat but not flabby where the heavy buckle on his belt bites into the flesh around his waist, says, as he stands looking at a row of Negro houses on his fertile farm, "None of 'em can do a damn thing for themselves. I've grown up with 'em, worked with 'em, hired 'em all my life. I know. They won't pay their taxes, won't pay the doctors, half the time won't go to schools they've already got. Come to me for everything. They may not be licking bootstraps any more, but they've not learned yet to pull themselves up by them, either. I saw Pete there down at the courthouse last week. 'You paid your taxes, Pete?' 'Nawsuh.' 'You going to pay them?' 'Yassuh.' Of course he won't. I asked him what he was doing at the courthouse then. 'Come to vote.' 'How'd you get on the books, Pete?' 'I'se been to school the last fo' months.' 'Learning what?' 'Learning the Constitution.' They know that Constitution every which-way, backwards, forwards, sideways, they know it! And they'd never have been stirred up about it if it hadn't been for this N double-A C P. They're putting words in their mouths and action in their hearts. I don't know what the end of it'll be, but it don't look good."

And in Florida a Negro speaking at a voting league rally: "There's one thing the Negro has that the white man wants but can't get unless you give it to him. That's your vote. He can take your home, your family, your possessions, even your life, and often nothing can be done about it. But the law prohibits him from going into the voting booth with you. He can offer you a million dollars for your vote, but he can't get it unless you give it to him."

The parking-lot attendant, at an excellent restaurant in one of the largest seaboard Southern cities, pauses on a balmy night: "All this trouble other places, talk about the Supreme Court and schools and all that, we don't have no trouble here. When we elected our sheriff a few years back, he went down into niggertown his first day in office, said, 'Show me your meanest nigger.' They pointed him out. The sheriff drew his little pistol, bang, bang, bang. A dead nigger. They had to call the hearse. 'That's just to show you,' sheriff said. 'You know what's right and what's wrong, but when you get into trouble around here you're always wrong and I'm right—so you better stay out.' And he meant it. He was good to them, too. One of them come to him, tell him they had a sick child, needed money, he'd say, 'I'll get you work.' And he'd find them a job, or loan them money out of his pocket. He looked out after them but he wouldn't stand for any trouble.

"Let one of them get out of line, sheriff comes out of his office, looks at the feller. 'You know what I do to bad niggers?' And he pats that pistol on his hip, little ole bitty thing not *that* long. 'Now I'm not telling you again that we don't want any more swill or sass. Don't ever let me see you around here again or your burial insurance will be paid up.'

"The day one tries to go to a white school here, that'll be the day there's a skinned nigger. Skin them the way they do each other, with a shiv. Make a shiv, take four of those one-side-sharp razor blades and put one between each finger, dull side out. Walk up to a feller, say 'hi' and rake that across his face or an artery, he's in a bad way. A policeman comes, the blades are thrown away, no weapon around. Like I say, though, we don't look for any trouble around here, don't have no background for it."

And a country minister in Kentucky, with a Scottish burr he has never lost and a ready laugh he has never stifled: "What the South needs today is a poet. You can't have great movements till the poets get mad. Bobby Burns said, 'A man's a man for a' that,' and set Scotland on its ear

It's awful to be on Southern campuses and feel the liberalism, then come out and the fence falls. The terrible part of this whole controversy is not what segregation does to the Negro—that's bad enough, God knows—but what it does to me, how it limits my freedom as much as his.

"The churches are suffering from respectability. The Methodists don't sing Methodist Pie any more; Baptists don't shout; in the Presbyterian church all the Calvinists are dead; even the Holy Rollers are turning to brick. And of course the church is the key to solve all this pride and prejudice of race—both the white and Negro church. I'm like the Salvation Army man who said he had religion and felt so good he could knock hell out of the drummer. Don't fence the church in! Give it room to breathe! The wife of one of America's great religious leaders told me recently that the worst sin of the church today was mediocrity. Mediocre preachers, mediocre believers. But we've got a chance to rise above that today in the South!

"Another thing that troubles me: no one laughs much any more. As long as people can laugh, they can go through anything. I've heard escapees from the Nazi concentration camps tell how a single flash of humor could keep them going. We can come through anything as long as we know how to laugh and to sing."

You Have Heard Their Voices:

A tall thin Negro publisher does not talk much about his paper, but about the law, in which he made an outstanding record at the Midwestern university from which he received his degree, but which he found difficult to practice in a border South city. "When you're a Negro lawyer, you've got to know more law than the judge and all the other lawyers together. You've got to be on time. You can't ever lose your temper. You can't ever brag on winning or making a point. If the judge is friendly and asks you, outside the courtroom, how you're doing, you say, 'I'm struggling along, judge, struggling along.' No matter whether you like it or not, you're a Negro first and a lawyer second."

A white lawyer from Washington tells some of the folks at home, in a county seat farther south, about "conditions" in the capital: "Well, nobody knows how the integration in Washington is coming along. The nigras are 63 per cent of the population. You can figure it out for yourself. The minority doesn't stand a chance caught between the nigras and the Jews. There's been a new club formed up in Washington: the NAPWPG. That's the National Association for Protection of White Protestants and Gentiles."

Dr. Charles S. Johnson, scholarly and courteous and wise, on a ho
July morning in the summer of '56: "In this period of crisis, there is a larg
number of immobilized people—but there's nothing unique to this situa
tion. The vast middle group in the United States, as well as the South, i
just now enjoying a momentary peace between wars, economic upheaval
they don't want to be disturbed for anything. It's like getting up in th
morning—so hard to make the break. Hope if they don't notice, thes
problems will all go away. Of course they won't go away and eventuall
these people will take the right stand. And we must remember somethin
Frederick Douglass used to say: 'The dust flies but the earth remains.' "

Black Earth and White Cotton:

"What folks up North don't understand is that down here in Mi
sissippi the nigras and whites live this thing out together day by da
Why, Aunt Martha up the road there, she has a voice in how things a
managed. All the tenants I had on one farm a few years back were eithe
her children or her grandchildren. She taught me a lot. For instance: ther
was one season when we had an awful heavy rainfall. The only times
would clear were on Saturdays and Sundays. Finally I put the tractors i
the fields Saturdays and Sundays. After a couple of weeks, Aunt Marth
stopped me in the road one day. She was up in her eighties then. 'I wan
to talk to you, Mister David.' 'Go ahead, Aunt Martha. I want to he:
anything you got to say.' 'Mister David, you been running those tracto
on Sunday. You know that's against the Lord's will. If you don't stop, I'ı
going to take my folks and leave your farm.' I knew she would do it, to
and all the others would follow her. I couldn't have that. 'All right, Au:
Martha, I won't plant any more on Sunday.' Well, my little girl told m
mother, who believed like Aunt Martha about working on Sunday. An
Mama said, 'I want to meet that woman.' Next time she came out fro
town she went to see Aunt Martha, carried her a present. And you knov
it cleared up every Monday after I made that promise to Aunt Martha.
never put any more tractors or men in the fields on Sunday. I figure
maybe she taught me a lesson.

"You see nigras out in one of those big fields toting those big sack
picking cotton, you needn't feel sorry for them. The ones that live he
like cotton picking better than any work they do. Nobody can get ar
house-help during picking time; the schools close down for a while. Ever
body in the fields. It pays pretty high, and then it's social, too. All in tl
field working, visiting together. Sometimes they pretend they are cars-
Cadillac, Lincoln, Buick—and race to see who can finish a row first. . .

I don't know about the solution to all this trouble today—but I know we all got to go on living together for a long time."

Green Hills, Green Hopes:

A lean, handsome gentleman with white hair and stern shoulders and eyes stands beside the long cattle barn on his sprawling ancestral farm. "The hope of the South lies in cattle and trees. Our fathers knew how to thin corn but not how to thin trees. They'd go down with cotton and rise up with trees: after they'd have four or five bad years with cotton, flood, drought, boll weevil or price drop, and be flat broke, they'd pull out of it by cutting a hundred or so acres of trees and planting more cotton. Cotton mad. It gets in the blood. What we need now is planting grass and trees, selective cutting, an annual crop, something year by year, not boom and bust and boom again."

At a moment when it often seems that the differences in people are most exploited to keep them separate, the basic needs of men are also binding them together more surely than ever—individual to individual, region to region, country to country. In December, 1956, two items appeared in Southern publications. The first, in *Southern School News*, was from Oklahoma. "The Atoka County Citizens' Advisory Committee gave up a plan it had proposed earlier for a special poll on election day, November 6, to sound out public sentiment on the integration issue. Atoka County is one of two Oklahoma counties with Negro populations which have not desegregated their schools. Paul Mungle, Atoka dairyman and committee secretary, said the group received considerable support for the proposal. But he explained that, with the arrival of long-awaited rains, members were too busy with fall crops to work out details of the special vote." And *The Birmingham News* reported: "Alabama Has Ties With Thailand. Water is beginning to flow on farms and towns in Thailand in Southeast Asia today and Americans—mainly Alabamians—are getting credit for it. The U.S. Geological Survey, especially the Alabama division . . . supplied much of the technical know-how that is helping Thailanders develop their water resources." It appears that in his struggle for harmony with the natural world around him, man may learn that water is thicker than blood.

Alphabet Stew:

"The only trouble about writers writing about the South," says a good-natured community leader in North Carolina, "is that they have to make their material interesting, 'colorful.' Defiance and conflict are more vivid than quiet constructive patience. Probably that's why we hear more about the White Citizens' Councils than the Southern Regional Council. The first has a larger membership, the latter has an older history, and which has the most stamina remains to be seen. Personally, I know it's inevitable that the purposes of the SRC will eventually prevail because they are in harmony with our national ideals."

The Southern Regional Council is the most effective interracial all-Southern organization working for an end of segregation in the South today. Its present director, young, intelligent, tough-minded Harold C. Fleming, says that its greatest strength lies in the fact that "it is made up of Southerners, people who have been there." Himself a native of rural Georgia, he knows whereof he speaks when he mentions men and women all over the region who have undergone the upheaval of inner change and learned to "accept all people as human beings."

How did this "organization of Southerners of both races working together in the interest of all the people of the South" begin? "As a successor of the Southwide Commission on Interracial Cooperation, the Southern Regional Council goes back, in friendship and reputation, to 1919. A group of leading Southerners representing both races, many occupations, all faiths and denominations, met in 1943 to discuss the problems and promise of the region. They decided that a strong new regional organization was needed, in which Southerners themselves could join together in a cooperative effort to solve their common problems. The result was the Southern Regional Council."

The Council itself is composed of a board of some eighty Southerners who are respected residents of thirteen states and many communities. Their program has been concerned with employment of Negro policemen, impartial law enforcement, newspaper handling of racial news, community self-surveys and conferences on such common causes as health, housing, education and orderly adjustment to the Supreme Court decision on education. Voluntarily affiliated with the Council are interracial organizations in twelve Southern states, with local interests and autonomy. Quietly, with varying degrees of effectiveness but a seemingly constant sincerity, they work toward an affirmative answer to the question posed by one state group: "Does the South have a future, or only a past?"

George Mitchell, for many years director of the SRC, has been called one of the men who knows most about the several Souths, past and present. He prefers allegory to pedantry, deed to word. "Don't toss six pink people, six brown people, in a room, lock them up and say, 'Talk, now you're interracial.' But put six pink school teachers and six brown school teachers in a room to work for higher pay for teachers, you're interracial." Or, "The white church women of the South have always carried the conscience of this region. They shove a few men in front to look good, then they get busy and do the work. And they get their energy and purpose and morality from the church." Or, "The nation had a game once called Plantations and Cogwheels. The South played Plantations while the North played Cogwheels. The players got in a fight. Cogwheels won. Now ten of the Southern states are predominately industrial, but they're still running by plantation standards. They've switched games, but not rules."

Fleming, Mitchell's successor, re-enforces his democratic ideals with hardheaded ideas, and undergirds the emotional good will of dedicated amateurs with level-eyed professional practicality. This is to be expected from a man whose interest in racial relations received impetus during war in the Pacific when he was a captain in charge of a Negro quarter-master company. "Going out of the South made me aware of the racial problem and my Army experience made me think about it deeply for the first time. I lived, ate and slept with it every day." His attitude, and that of the Council, toward the current Southern crisis is simple: "The question is no longer whether the South must solve its racial problem, but when, how and at what cost, or damage, to the economy and the human beings involved." To lessen the cost and damage, and enrich the economy and people involved, is the purpose of this group of Southern-ers, pink and brown.

Look Down That Lonesome Road:

It has been suggested that much of the solution to Southern racial problems may come from Northerners who are moving South to live. This has the virtue of simplicity but the drawback of unreality in many actual situations. "We've got a name for the Yankees that come down and bend over backward trying to please the plantation Southerners," a professor in Tennessee says. "We call them 'white handkerchief heads.'"

A Negro educator who has made extensive studies in the area of industry and race: "A man told me recently that a Yankee who came South had to be quiet for the first ten years; the next five years he could have an opinion occasionally if he apologized. Personally, I think our hope for leadership among these outsiders lies with the young chemical engi-neers and their like, men who have had to be bribed considerably before they'd move out of their native region, men who have no fears for their jobs and can speak out on education or any other subject. You know, the Yankees may win the Civil War yet."

A Southern leader of interracial conferences: "A friend from New York came down recently, sat at our dinner table with an octogenarian judge from the adjoining county who was eating, talking with Negroes. As soon as dinner was over the judge made a talk to our little group, all against intermarriage and its dangers. The visitor was shocked. The Negroes weren't. They were utterly relaxed, knew all about this sort of situation. But the Northerner wanted everybody perfect, straight across the board.

"You know what we need today is more situations in which it's easy for people to go ahead and do the right thing. People do pretty much what is expected of them. That's a lot why the South is acting the way it is today. On the street in Greenville, Mississippi, act one way; come here to one of our group meetings, eat with Negroes, act an altogether different way."

And a teacher in middle Florida, where the influx is very apparent: "When Northerners come South, I've noticed one of four things usually happens. First, they feel very strongly on the race issue, come down and say so-and-so should be done. They get rebuffed several times, finally fit into the framework and begin to function like the rest of us: as they can. Second, are those who have no particular feelings on this or any other subject, and never will have unless it directly concerns them right now. Third, those who outdo the Southerners. Fourth, the ones who come down all fired up with the subject, learn a little about the Negro's statistics, his health and sex life, and recoil in shock. Puritanism asserts itself and they swing to the horrified opposite extreme."

The Southerners who have gone out and then returned are sometimes stoutest in their advocacy of desegregation. A lawyer and his wife, who have known the penance of isolation since returning to Alabama after a government career, can say, "We came back because it's our briar-patch and we love it, even if the briars do scratch a little deep sometimes. A year ago I didn't see how I could bear to live here another month, I wanted to leave so bad. Then the boycott in Montgomery came and it was a wonderful thing to see a cowed people stand up and gain confidence. Almost unbelievable, and all possible because they worked through their churches. My friends write me from other parts of the country about the grey life, Reisman, conformity. I tell them to come down South and they'll get all the excitement they need. I think really we're living in a wonderful period. We have a chance to do something, mean something."

Sugar and Spice and Plenty of Backbone:

One of the great adventures of the South has been the discovery of freedom by its women. In 1897, one of its aristocratic daughters published her first novel. "I had made my break for good and all; I was free," Ellen Glasgow later said. How free she was may be indicated by a single sentence of this First Lady of Virginia: "The Southerner learned to read, to write and to preach before he learned to think—there was, indeed, no need for thinking when everybody thought alike, or, rather, when to think differently meant to be ostracized."

It has been surprising, the number of women who were eager to think, willing to be ostracized. One of the most eloquent on the subject of people, black and white, has been Lillian Smith, of Georgia. An attractive lady of obvious "quality" and no less obvious courage, in her book dealing with the Supreme Court school decision, *Now Is the Time*, she brings particular insight to two of her dearest subjects: the rights of children, and the blunting of white sensibilities under segregation. "Chief Justice Warren, who spoke for a unanimous court, did not clutter his pages with legal precedents. He based the decision on a truth more important than precedents: a child's right to learn. He stated, for the first time in the history of a country's highest court, that a child's feelings are important to a nation; that shame and rejection can block a mind from learning, hence segregation is a barrier to human growth which no state in our democracy can maintain legally in its public school system." And, later on: "If only we who are white could *feel* what Negroes have gone through: the day-by-day, hour-by-hour humiliation which this system of segregation has inflicted on them; the lack of security of body and mind; the poverty and discrimination they have endured. Perhaps this dulling of the white person's imagination and sympathy has been one of the worst consequences of segregation. It has put a third skin on too many minds and hearts."

Another woman of sugar and spice and backbone in good measure lives in Charlottesville, Virginia. "A stout-hearted woman, an ever-present prick to the consciences of a good many Virginians," an Episcopal minister has said. A correspondent wrote her that she was "an ignorant, overeducated blabbermouth," and many others have called her "a traitor to the South," "a frustrated woman in search of excitement," "a hireling of the NAACP." A segregation leader in Charlottesville will tell you, "I know of her, that's all. Know she's got a husband that teaches what I call play-acting at the university and that she's a troublemaker. I think she was born in Africa maybe, her folks might have been missionaries or something."

It seems unlikely that anyone in Virginia really thinks Sarah Patton Boyle was born in Africa, or anywhere else outside the Old Dominion, for hers is one of the most deeply, respectably rooted family trees in the state. A cousin was General George (Blood and Guts) Patton, during World War II. During the Civil War, one grandfather served as a personal scout for General Robert E. Lee, and the other grandfather rode in the rank of colonel under Stonewall Jackson. She is a top-echelon "insider" in the South, and perhaps for that reason all the more to be feared by the Professional Insiders with lesser credentials.

When the first Negro student applied for admission to the University of Virginia, about seven years ago, Mrs. Boyle became interested for the first time in the subject of segregation. Talking with fellow citizens, black and white, she began to realize that a whole area of Southern experience had been blocked off from her life. Since that time she has worked to fill in some of the gaps, for herself and others. In an article in *The Saturday Evening Post*, somewhat misleadingly entitled "Southerners Will *Like* Integration," she tried to show that the background of hospitality and warmth, which is part of the South, provides a reservoir of good will which will make integration less difficult than we think, if we will only attempt it in good faith and high hope. This article thrust her into the front lines of an attack for which she later confessed she was ill prepared.

Petite, vivacious, with greying hair and a youthful smile, little or no make-up, glasses on a black ribbon around her neck and a pleasant Virginia accent in her speech, Mrs. Boyle has been one of the main sparks behind the interracial Council on Human Relations and its efforts to provide communication between the two races as the Federal court orders desegregation in Charlottesville schools. Some would consider it a tribute to her effectiveness that a six-foot cross was burned on her lawn. (At home alone with one of her two schoolboy sons, she sent him out to take a photograph of the flaming cross, then doused it with water and made a statement to the press: "I trust that a continuance of these outrages will arouse the public to a realization that the state's course of defiance of the Supreme Court is one which fosters lawlessness.")

"Bleeding heart? Do-gooder?" Sarah Patton Boyle laughs musically. "I'd rather have a bleeding heart than a hardened heart, and I'd rather be a do-gooder than a do-nothinger. It's weariness, the wet-blanketing of friends, enervating disgust that are the main enemies of liberal Virginians now. It's hard to keep one's fire roaring in this unending drizzle, this delay."

In a letter to the *Richmond Times-Dispatch*, she said, "The time has come when one is ashamed to go unscathed. It is now insufferable to be comfortable, unattacked and secure. I can remember with what gay pride my grandparents bore their poverty following the Civil War. Are there no white Southerners left who will take punishment with pride? Isn't there, for any of us, solace enough in knowing that we stand for what we believe?"

"You see"—Sarah Boyle fixes you with bright, clear eyes—"being 'impractical' is often the highest practicality of all. Jesus' admonition, 'Love your enemies,' is the most realistic suggestion ever offered, for love consumes fear and makes true defeat impossible!"

The Blue, the Grey and the Khaki:

A young professor of history, reared in the Deep South, living now in the Middle South: "I did a complete about-face in my thinking on racial matters, and one of the things that marked that change occurred during the war. It was when transportation was so overcrowded everywhere, I was waiting for a bus one day. A group of Negro soldiers was waiting, too, a little distance away from me. Some of them had combat ribbons on their uniforms. When the bus finally came, the driver wouldn't let those boys on in their turn, let all the white people file in ahead of them. Then there weren't any more places left so he drove off and left the Negro soldiers standing there. Well, there I was, a perfect composite of all the old nineteenth-century beliefs, but it was such a gross unfairness I had just witnessed that I couldn't help but think, especially with the Negroes wearing the uniform of our country. That's the first conscious, concrete episode I can remember in my general shift of thinking on this matter of racial equality."

A young musician in Kentucky: "You know in the opera *Norma* the hero is ready to die for the woman he won't live with. Sometimes it seems to me that we Southerners are like that: we'd rather die for our problems than live with them. Probably it's because war is always so much simpler than peace."

The Embattled Ivory Towers:

From Charleston to Houston, the names of unknown villages suddenly become national symbols of violence; in a new struggle for independence they will be remembered as beachheads won or lost because of the presence or absence of courage on the part of local citizens. Hoxie, Mansfield, Sturgis, Clay, Clinton: towns where main streets became battlegrounds overnight, and the pupils learned their lessons of citizenship in the schoolyards rather than the classrooms.

The ivory towers are embattled in the South, but the heart of the matter lies in the thousands of public schools. Already harassed by overcrowding and understaffing and a deep public indifference which seeks to hide under solemn platitudes its poverty of imagination and concern, now these burdened institutions must assume this new load of national conscience and sectional conflict focusing on the issue of school desegregation. In these towns, for a few days, a few months, civics moved out of the dusty textbooks into the dust of human turmoil.

A resident of one of these trouble spots says, "You live in a town all your life, nice and peaceable, everything rocking along, you think you know everybody, know what your town's like, what your country's like—till a handful of nigra kids start to go to a white high school. Suddenly you don't know anybody; everything's crazy, shot to hell. You're not only a town of fine patriotic citizens, you're a town of hoodlums, too. It chills you right down to the marrow. You can't forget it easy."

Clinton: small town in the hills of East Tennessee, may stand as symbol for all the towns which have made black headlines with white violence. In the fall and winter of 1956, Clinton became the focal point for citizens everywhere who had interest either in integration or segregation—or, as local Baptist minister, Paul Turner, said in one sermon, "the disintegration of our body politic and our community." Clinton's conflict epitomizes many of the deepest characteristics of the region and most of the complexity infusing the racial issue in the South today. It dramatized, in a time of often-waning confidence in the importance of individual acts and beliefs, the fact that a single person can still change the tide in the course of human events. Although the mob, and its brief reign in the city, was the big story, news-wise, of what happened in Clinton, the really important events were wrought by individuals.

Among these was John Kasper. Anyone who asks, for better or worse, "What can one person do?" should study the meteoric career of this Yankee who came South to be a professional segregationist, this college-bred bookseller who became leader for uneducated mountain people who had little left for pride but the bleach of their skins, this fanatic who preached defiance of the highest authority of our land. There is general agreement in Clinton today that if Kasper had not come down from

Washington, D.C., on August 25, 1956, and started his personal campaign
to oppose the Federally ordered entrance of twelve Negroes into the high
school of about eight hundred whites, integration would have taken
place without event. Without someone to articulate and mobilize the
differences and frustrations and dislikes that are latent in every town,
most ready to rise to the surface during moments of crisis and change,
peace might have been preserved. But John Kasper was eager both to
articulate and mobilize—and he found a core of ready helpers both within
and without Clinton.

The individual perhaps most precisely opposed to Kasper was the
high-school principal, D. J. Brittain, Jr. Not only during the first furious
weeks of attempts to expel the Negroes or close the school, but through
the following months of harassment and intimidation, this "ordinary"
man displayed the extraordinary fortitude we Americans like to consider
our special hidden virtue. Thin, bespectacled, almost frail in appearance,
this man withstood with iron determination the daily onslaughts of those
who would wreck his school.

Actually the pattern of Kasper's defeat and Brittain's steadfastness
was indicated in the earliest sequence of events, when a mob of between
two and three thousand demonstrated during the Labor Day weekend
against school integration and were confronted by forty-seven citizens
who had banded themselves into a Home Guard. Before the Highway
Patrol arrived that Saturday night, followed by the National Guard the
next day, these individuals had taken a stand rarely necessary in
America any more: the defense of their community against mob rule. And
the strangeness was increased by the fact that the enemies were neighbors.

"What many Americans don't realize," says Horace V. Wells, Jr.,
editor of the Clinton Courier-News and one of the staunch leaders opposing Kasper and those who have succeeded him, "is that this wasn't a clash
between the Negroes and whites, that is in its largest sense. It was
mainly a struggle between a majority of white citizens who wanted to
obey an order of the Federal court to desegregate Clinton High School
and a minority of white people who tried to defy that order." Editor
Wells probably summed up the attitude of that majority when he wrote
in his paper: "In obeying the law, we believe that all laws must be obeyed—
not just those we like. If individuals are allowed to select the laws they
want to obey and are left free to ignore those to which they object, we
would have no government, no freedom, no individual liberties or
rights—we would merely have chaos and anarchy."

Other individuals who shaped the course of events in Clinton were two young attorneys, Buford Lewallen, son of the popular and prosperous mayor, and one-time Speaker of the House in the Tennessee Legislature, and Leo Grant, Jr., from nearby Oak Ridge, a veteran of Korea "with a Silver Star and several wounds and lots of guts," as a friend says. Together these two, who in another situation might be considered men in grey flannel suits, led in rounding up the doctors, preachers, shopkeepers and assorted citizens who formed Clinton's posse against the desperadoes.

And crucial to the final outcome of integration at Clinton was a walk taken by one of its leading ministers just before Christmas. Late in November a stalemate had been reached in the situation at the high school. The Negro pupils were still in school, a Federal injunction had curtailed Kasper's activities, but a small gang, estimated by teachers at between forty and fifty out of more than seven hundred white students, had concentrated on making life unbearable for the dozen Negroes. The school faculty pointed out in a joint statement: "The activities of this small group in our school have been of a vicious nature, obviously prompted by a mature person." But by the last Wednesday of November they had achieved part of their goal—the Negro children were staying away from school.

"We'd had all we could bear," one Negro mother said. "We wanted some assurance our children wouldn't be harmed before we let them walk into that school again."

Principal Brittain gave the Negro youngsters the same support he had provided since school opened, but the school board said it could not make the guarantee the Negro parents wanted. Local police seemed ineffective and Federal authorities made no public move to meet the crisis. The Negro children were out of school and the White Citizens' Council members were triumphant.

Then, on Monday, December third, the Reverend Paul W. Turner sent word to the Negro children that if they wanted to return to school he would come and walk with them. The next morning the thirty-three-year-old minister walked past the big solid First Baptist Church where he had preached for eight years, down the main street decorated with lights and garlands and good-will greetings for the Christmas season, around the corner at the old brick courthouse where Kasper had only recently been acquitted in his second trial for inciting to riot, and down the street to the high school serving both the town and surrounding Anderson County. A block beyond the school building a steep hill rises. The Reverend Turner now had two fellow townsmen walking with him: Sidney Davis and

Leo Burnett, and the three of them climbed about halfway up the hill. There they were met by six Negro boys and girls. The little group went down the hill, past a huddle of perhaps fifty jeering white people, and the children went safely into the school. Davis and Burnett went back about their day's business, and Turner started for his church. Some of the gang outside the school followed him. A block away a half dozen of them closed in. In the broad daylight of an unseasonably warm winter morning, on a downtown sidewalk in front of a small, well-occupied office building, the minister of the town's largest church was beaten up. Before the police arrived his blood had spattered the car near which he stood, and stained the sidewalk.

News of the attack blazed through Clinton like a leaf-fire. There were two immediate results. School was closed (a teacher had also been shoved around by two non-students who had entered the building during the morning and asked where they could find one of the Negroes). But there was also a city election taking place that day, with a White Citizens' Council candidate for mayor and the Council testing for the first time its real strength in the town. And although the school closed, the city polls stayed open—and instead of activity dwindling during the afternoon as is usual in small-town elections, there was actually a waiting line at times. The man and the event and the moment had met with rare fortuitousness that morning. Many citizens had many explanations for what happens when a man takes the right step at the right time:

"Remember, we're not called the Bible Belt without reason. Turner wasn't just anyone getting mauled. He was a symbol, too. What happened to him, happened to us all—and it waked us up."

"Somebody had to do it. And it wasn't going to be my husband and it wasn't going to be any of the others that have businesses here in town. Most of us had shaken our heads over the Citizens' Council and what it stood for, but we'd gone right ahead pussy-footing and passing the buck. Paul Turner stuck his neck out for all of us."

"You might call Paul the catalytic agent we needed to bring this whole thing into the open. The whole White Citizens' Council ticket for mayor and aldermen was defeated four to one. People who'd been afraid to speak up before spoke out with their ballots."

These men in their small-town offices and stores, these women in their neat yards and living rooms, these casual conversationalists along the streets, made vivid the fact that sometimes the most important step a citizen of a democracy can take is that short walk to the voting booth. And Paul Turner, in his modest brick house filled with the buoyant sound of two small children, does not talk glibly or heroically about what happened that day. Six feet, blue-eyed, friendly and relaxed: "Back in the fall when the first violence came, I didn't see what I could do to be effective except through my pulpit. The community didn't realize what was happening. We were all caught off guard. Action at the state level was the only answer. But this time we knew better what was going on. Someone had to make a move or those people would win the day—and I guess I was elected. As things developed during the week and the Negro children were intimidated out of school, I began to think what I could do. First, of course, I could preach to my congregation about it on Sunday, Then on Monday I could act. And that's what I did."

Another resident tells about the two men who walked with the Reverend Turner. "Sid Davis is an attorney here in Clinton. He was on his way over to Knoxville that morning when he heard his minister was going to bring the Negro children back to school. Sid is absolutely fearless. Maybe foolhardy. But he just went over and told Turner he'd go along. As for Leo Burnett, he's an accountant down here at the hosiery mill, not a member of Turner's church. But he got an idea of what this was all about before most of the rest of us. He was one of those John Kasper talked with when he first came down from Washington back in August. Leo was out washing his car, mowing his lawn, or something, and this stranger came up and asked him if he believed in integration. Leo said no. Then Kasper went on to tell him about the tyranny of the Supreme Court, that it was like it was back in the days of England against the colonies. Leo told Kasper he might be against integration but hell, he didn't want to start a revolution and for Kasper to get out of his yard."

Many facets of the Clinton situation are reflected in that encounter. Chief among them is the dilemma of the great immobilized group, not only in Clinton but throughout the South, which does not want integration but does want to abide by the law. Faced on one hand with the immovable object of Federal law, and on the other with the apparently irresistible force of elements which are always ready to resort to violence, they have been caught in a vacuum, without leadership and perhaps without precedent. Probably 90 per cent of the people of Clinton prefer segregation in the schools. Yet the overwhelming majority of their children accepted the Negro students into their midst with good will; they elected one Negro girl vice president of her homeroom, and when the school was closed, the Student Council passed a resolution asking that classes be resumed as soon as possible and on an integrated basis. The parents themselves rejected the segregationist organization at the polls.

For those who can accept the reality that democracy is not perfection attained but a process working on the premise of perfectibility, it may not be premature to say that the story of Clinton contains cause for quiet optimism.

"I used to think of myself as a segregationist," one man confides. "Now I'm not so sure. It's come to more than a matter of labels, anyway. Whatever else I may or may not think I am, I know I'm for law and order."

Individuals who acted in a crisis: the Negro community knows who they are. "Principal Brittain and all the teachers—they've been fine to the children," one Negro woman says.

Or one of the Negro girls who walked to school December fourth: "Reverend Turner was wonderful. When we came down the hill and saw some people waiting there outside the school he just kept saying to us, 'Don't be afraid. Don't be afraid. I won't let them hurt you.'" The girl's mother listens with tears brimming in her wide brown eyes. "He knows courage all right. But I think he must have had something else, too. Mr. Turner must know love."

Then there were the Negro students who made, each day, that walk down Foley Hill and into the long corridors of the high school. There were the parents who let them go, and waited for them to return. There were the Negro citizens who heard bombs explode in their yards and felt a blast of dynamite shake their homes. "You wouldn't think folks could be so mean." One of the Negro men shakes his head. "But they're the few. They'll pass. The good folks will win out, take the long run."

This time of decision may force us to abandon the romantic fiction that all our heroes walk in twenty-league boots with never a misstep. Those who led the way to law and order in Clinton wear ordinary human shoes—and sometimes falter. But on May 17, 1957, they must have felt a deep satisfaction in the knowledge that they had not submitted democracy to mobocracy and had not sacrificed principle to expediency. On May seventeenth, exactly three years after the Supreme Court had handed down its decision, Bobby Cain, seventeen, walked with eighty-eight other seniors into the gymnasium of Clinton High School. There he became the first Negro ever to graduate from an integrated public school in Tennessee. The class valedictorian said: "During this year we [seniors] have learned to look for the truth in an unprejudiced manner . . . we have lived in fellowship . . . we will miss this fellowship now that we go our many ways after graduation."

Many problems lie ahead of Clinton and its high school, of course. But it has met and answered the crucial question: whether or not to use its energies working to implement the law, or to spend its resources working to evade and subvert the law. Having decided on the constructive course, it can now move on to the solution of other problems, just that much ahead of those who, in similar situations of small Negro enrollment and inadequate facilities, will not listen to logic, but berate and delay and sacrifice their schools to their prejudices.

Pressure on the Press:

Mabel Norris Reese is a tall, handsome woman with dark eyes, dark hair slashed with glimpses of grey, and capable hands. When you meet her in the office of the weekly newspaper she edits in Florida, *The Mount Dora Topic*, she is wearing a brown flannel skirt and a tailored shirt with cuff links; her ready smile reveals beautiful white teeth, as even as her crisp, unemotional words. She is one of the white lady editors of the South (Hazel Brannon Smith of Mississippi is another) who has dared to challenge on his own ground a powerful sheriff and his administration of justice.

In November, 1954, Mabel Norris Reese learned that the five children of a fruit picker from South Carolina, Allen Platt, had been ordered out of the white school at Mt. Dora because Sheriff Willis McCall didn't like "the looks of a girl's nose."

"Our sheriff's more than a segregationist," one resident of Mt. Dora says, "he's a top-water racist. He's been in office since 1944 and he has quite a history with Negro cases. The most celebrated, I suppose, was our Lake County rape case: after the Supreme Court reversed the conviction of some Negro boys for raping a white woman, the sheriff shot two of the prisoners, killed them. He said they were trying to escape. And even after the Platt case first came to public attention, there was another fruit picker run out of town on the accusation that the two boys in school were part Negro."

Mrs. Reese and Sheriff McCall had had their differences before and when she discovered the Platts, bewildered over the children's ouster from school and insistent that they were part Croatan Indian, with no Negro blood, she began a long and costly struggle for what appeared to her to be simple justice. Platt wrote an appeal to Governor Collins: "Mr. McCall is sheriff of Lake County and I am told that it is dangerous in this county to antagonize him and that many law-abiding citizens are afraid of him. My experience with him shows this to be true. I am helpless under those conditions. I have no other recourse but to appeal to you to make a thorough investigation."

During the year that followed, investigations were made, with little result. The Platts filed suit to compel the Lake County board to enroll their children in white schools. Then a small reign of terror began, during which Allen Platt and his family moved several times and endured attempts to burn their home, shotgun blasts and attacks on their children. They secured an attorney who charged that Sheriff McCall had indicated he would not protect the Platts from this violence, and in reply the sheriff told one newspaper, "I'll be just as good to them as any other niggers I know of. I can't baby-sit with them. I can't go out and live with them."

Sheriff McCall couldn't live with Mrs. Reese and her family, either, and bombs were exploded on her lawn, loads of dead fish and garbage were dumped in front of her house in a quiet residential area, windows at the newspaper office were broken and her watchdog was poisoned. "We've never fully recovered from the blows we received, mostly the curtailment of our commercial printing," Mrs. Reese says. "But we're managing. And the courts have ruled that the Platts can go to white schools; they're in a church-operated school here now, and I believe the people of Mt. Dora are more aware of constitutional liberties, and practical justice, than they were before this case came up." Her credo she summed up several months ago: "To me a newspaper, whether in a small town or large town, tells the news. It sounds the warning of danger to the rights, the peace, the prosperity of the community's citizens."

The Ham and the Corn:

Meeting in special session in July, 1956, the Florida legislature had under consideration five bills designed to help maintain segregation in the schools without ever stating their purpose. The bills passed the Senate unanimously and went to the House of Representatives. As they came to a vote, the green lights on the long display board at the front of the House chamber flashed with monotonous acquiescence. Then, suddenly, a single red light signaled "No." It stood opposite the name of John B. Orr, Jr., from Dade (Miami) County, and Orr stood alone among his fellow legislators, opposing circumvention of the Supreme Court.

When the excitement created by this rare and disturbing move had died down a little, the thirty-six-year-old Florida-born-and-reared politician arose on a point of personal privilege and said he would like to state his position. Silence fell in the House and, as one reporter said, "For the next quarter hour John Orr got something that few men ever get from a state legislature—the complete and undivided attention of every member of the House." With compelling sincerity, this pioneer voice in Southern legislative halls read a statement which must have impressed even the most hostile of its listeners with the depth of its feeling and the courage of its conviction. In essence, John Orr, standing on the blue carpeting of the House, under the Great Seal of the State of Florida, before the public balconies and the battery of desks manned by his colleagues, said,

"I favor the gradual integration of our public-school system. I believe that had we devoted as much energy, time, and talent to discovering means to live under the law instead of in defiance of it, we could have discovered a way. I believe segregation is morally wrong. . . . If we hope to maintain our leadership among the free peoples of the world, if we hope to give hope to those subjugated peoples behind the Iron and Bamboo Curtains, we must demonstrate by our acts as well as our words that our democratic form of government places no artificial barriers on the opportunity to live and work with our fellow man. . . .

"For us to set an example of hypocrisy and deceit—of disrespect for our laws—will surely do more harm to our children than will result from their being seated in a classroom next to one whose skin is of a different hue."

This was the burden of Orr's earnest message that hot July morning. He closed with words in which he staked his political future against the principles by which he lived. "When we finally have to face up to this problem, and we surely will be required to, I hope that God gives us the wisdom and strength to conquer prejudice and bigotry and to renew our faith in our Constitution. Meantime, I will take solace in the prayer our chaplain delivered last Tuesday: 'Help us, thus, to see that it is better to fail in a just cause that will ultimately succeed, than to succeed in an unrighteous case that will ultimately fail.' "

There was a deep stillness in the room as John Orr walked back to his seat. Then a fellow member of the House, also from Miami, arose and said, "I hope if I am ever faced with the same problem on any subject, I have the same courage."

Reaction was strong. Editorials commended and condemned, an effort was made to unseat him, another to expel him from the Democratic Party. When it became known that Orr had made a small contribution to the NAACP and received a membership card in return, a second wave of critical questioning swept across the state. In November he had to stand the test of re-election to his seat, and there were those who said Jack Orr had killed his own chances ever to win public office again. Letters began to arrive by the hundreds, but the odds were about eighteen to one in favor of the young legislator.

Cordial and informal, slightly heavy-set as befits a former football player, blue-eyed and sandy-haired John Orr tells you a little about the aftermath of his vote against segregation. "Before I could get back to Miami from Tallahassee, someone had called our home and begun threatening my family, and I didn't know what to expect when I left the train. A friend and I stopped by a restaurant to eat a bite on the way home and we ran into the president of one of the largest companies in Florida. He had reason not to like me; I'd made talks opposing his company in relation to bills before the legislature at various times. Anyway he was one of the old Southerners from a long background, and as he stood up and came toward me I wondered what was going to happen. He congratulated me on my vote! Then he said he had all the Southern prejudices that anyone spending a lifetime here has, and he wouldn't have voted as I did, but he knew he was wrong. And he said next time he voted he would not vote with his prejudices but for me—because he believed I had done what I did from a conscience. Well, you can imagine how much that meant to me at that particular moment!"

Throughout the summer and the fall campaign, came letters of vilification ("White nigger—you better leave Florida!") and praise ("What is significant is that you have shown that there are some men left at least who can afford the luxury of integrity. In so doing you have galvanized the faith of a lot of people of little faith"). Segregation was made the only real issue in the November race. "Everywhere I spoke I reiterated my position that segregation is morally wrong," Orr says. He received 104,000 votes; his opponent 77,000.

In a state-wide election, Orr admits his chances would be slim for the next few years, but he has faith in the long-term future. "In a few years, when schools are integrated and none of the terrible things predicted by the rabble-rousers have come to pass, people will see that I am right. They will see that the South and the nation is improved. Then who knows?" He smiles, not with a politician's quick facileness but with a statesman's confident hope.

Who Knows the Score:

Perhaps it would be difficult to find a more dramatic example of the "new Negro" in the "new South" than that of the man sometimes called "Mister Beale Street." It has been said that "Will Handy put the blues to music, but George Lee froze them into words." Today Handy is dead and blues are part of the musical history of America and George Washington Lee is one of the most astute Negro leaders in the South. He has been for several years a director in the richest Negro enterprise in the world, Atlanta Life Insurance Company, a board member of Memphis's only Negro bank, a national officer in the Negro Elks, and a leader who put Memphis ahead of every Negro community in the nation in subscribing to war-bond drives during World War II. He is a potent political force.

Slim, slightly less than six feet, agile, quick to laugh and promptly sober again, now in his early sixties, Lee's biography is symbolic in itself. Born in a sharecropper's shack in Mississippi, he progressed from cotton picking to clerking in a white man's store, and at seventeen migrated to the river-queen city of Memphis. He worked as a bellhop, went to college, and then, during World War I, won a lieutenant's rank and served overseas. When he came home, he went to work in the insurance business. He became a successful businessman, then turned to writing. He published a biography of Beale Street and a novel and a collection of short stories. More than any single person he has, perhaps, helped keep alive the Beale Street of yesterday. "Pewee's Place," he has written of the night spot where so many of the blues songs had their beginning in the mind and fingers of Will Handy, "offered Handy just the kind of emotional environment he needed. Negroes from the cotton fields and sweltering river bottoms came there to lay down their burdens of work and woe and step into a neat, lazy shuffle, to raise their voices in wailing melody while weariness, nostalgia and abandon combined to shape their impromptu songs." Probably more than any other single person, he has helped change Beale Street from the old, violent irresponsibility into a new center of commercial and political awareness. Personifying both that gay past and the more adult present, Lieutenant Lee, as he is known in most of Memphis, faces you across his desk in the office with a door standing open to Beale Street. At once expansive and reticent, he is a rare combination of the shrewd and the lyrical, the poet and the politician, the orator and the insurance salesman. He knows the practical means of securing votes, but he also knows the deeper meaning behind the process of voting.

"I wouldn't trade Memphis for any other city in the South for

Negroes," he says. "Of course I wouldn't trade Memphis for any city anywhere—I could have, many times, with offers from up North, but I want to stay down here.

"The Negro's growing, the whites are growing, too. I believe in the power of the ballot in a free land, but I emphasize to my people not only civil rights but civil responsibilities." Good-by, Beale St. Blues!

Great Day A-Coming:

Darkness had fallen over the little town in Mississippi. The young minister turned on the light in his study. His voice was calm and soft and its accent confirmed the fact that he had spent most of his life in this town and surrounding countryside. His church, the largest in town, had not yet yielded to the fashion for remodeling with thick carpeting and indirect lights, and the main auditorium seemed bare, almost stark, with its dark wooden seats and oiled floors. In this sanctuary, a few Sundays before, the blond, deliberate pastor had stood and told his congregation some important racial truths. His sermon was not about integration—that would have been a purely academic discussion ("I know we won't have integration in this part of Mississippi now.")—but it was about common attitudes and everyday practices which must be reconsidered and altered before there can be any hope for lasting change.

"One Sunday morning, during my regular service, I asked my congregation to all bow their heads. Then I said, 'Now, for a moment, just imagine that you're a Negro. You're a Negro in Mississippi today. You can't . . .' And I went down quite a list of things we take for granted that we couldn't do if we were Negroes. I asked them, in the light of this, to search their consciences.

"A few days later a member of my congregation phoned me. 'Do you love the niggers?' she asked. 'I do.' 'Would you let one come in your house?' 'I already have.' 'Would you bring him in your living room?' 'Of course.' That was when I decided my congregation should know how I stood on this, and I prepared my sermon. I called it 'A View of the Race Issue,' and there was a big crowd to hear it. Here, on this very street, I've heard Bilbo preach hate against the Negroes such as you couldn't imagine, using oaths to describe them, so you can understand why I was a little nervous that morning I gave my sermon."

It was not so much what the minister said that was meaningful, but where he said it, and to whom. A child must crawl before it walks, and a community must accept all its people as equal human creatures before it will accept them as first-class citizens. "The Negro is a diamond in the rough. He is a human being made in the image of God. The inexperienced eye would not realize the value of a diamond if he saw it in the rough, and would not offer you a dollar for one as large as a marble. And, yet, when that same diamond is properly cut and polished, it will bring a fortune. The same is true with minds and hearts, darkened by prejudice, they do not see the value of another race of human beings that live among us. . . . Don't forget it, there is a just God on the throne and everybody who ever took a rotten penny from an illiterate Negro had better get ready to pay, for he will. There are people who have built their palaces on the bones of Negro tenants. . . . My brother said that when he was overseas, on the front line in the Signal Corps, he ran right into a German machine-gun nest. He thought to himself, 'This is where I die.' Suddenly, there was a burst of machine-gun fire from behind. He turned quickly and saw that an American Negro had saved his life by blasting the Germans. Then, from another direction, another volley rang out and cut the Negro down. He toppled backward into a ditch. My brother leaped into the ditch and took the Negro's head in his lap. The rich, red American blood gushed out. He was dead, but my brother is still alive, and he said, 'Every time I see the face of a black man, there is only love in my heart for him.' "

After the sermon, there was a momentary pause and then that Mississippi audience came forward and congratulated its pastor. "I suppose there were a few who didn't shake my hand, but they never mentioned it to me. You see, this is so close to my heart, and everyone knows it. I was an orphan, grew up in the homes of others, and I saw Negroes work all year, get something called food and something called clothes, seldom any money. The white man grew rich, the black man stayed poor. Things like that boil up inside me and I wonder at the patience of the Lord and I have to do what I can."

Pistols and Pocketbooks:

A visitor to Sumter County, in Georgia, will have no difficulty finding Andersonville. Andersonville is a silent spot, marked by grass and trees and monuments. Beneath the grass lie the bodies of more than thirteen thousand Yankees who died in prison here during bloody war between the states. Deep holes still pockmark the earth where the prison stockade stood, where diseased, wounded, starving men dug with their hands in search of water. It is a sad place, a desolate reminder of the ultimate results of hate and violence.

Only a few miles distant, in the same county, is another landmark founded on principles precisely opposed to those which produced Andersonville, the principles of love and nonviolence. Yet it has created one of the keenest crises in the South in this matter of pistols and pocketbooks. "Welcome to Koinonia," the sign says. It bears the picture of a cross and two hands clasped in friendship; now it also bears several bullet holes.

"What is Koinonia?" its residents explain. "Sounds like Greek to you? Well, you're right. Pronounced Koin-oh-NEE-ah, it occurs frequently throughout the New Testament and means 'a fellowship or a community.' The early church was sometimes called a 'koinonia.' That's what Koinonia Farms seeks to be today. We have all come together here, seeking to walk in God's ways and to worship Him according to the dictates of our conscience. It was for this reason also that our forefathers came to America. For this reason General Oglethorpe and his little band of ex-prisoners settled in Georgia."

Koinonia was founded in 1942 by Dr. Clarence L. Jordan, who saw it grow to a community of sixty members, Negro and white, with eleven hundred acres of farmland, crops of cotton, peanuts and pecans, four thousand hens and other livestock. Many people in the surrounding county and the nearby town of Americus did not understand the philosophy which prompted people to pool all their worldly resources and receive from a common fund only what they needed. Even though Negroes did not hold full membership in the organization, many white neighbors could not understand their being part of the fellowship. There were occasional tensions between the farm and the townspeople. But Clarence Jordan is a native Georgian, from the nearby town of Talboton, Ph.D. graduate of the Southern Baptist Theological Seminary in Louisville and an ordained Baptist minister with a degree in agriculture from the University of Georgia. With assistant, Conrad Browne, an alumnus of the Divinity School of the University of Chicago, and Virginia-born Norman Long, president of the group, he introduced improved methods of poultry care into the area and Sumter County today has the highest egg production of any county in Georgia. When a neighbor's house burned down, members of Koinonia helped him rebuild it. Negro sharecroppers in trouble, often financial difficulties, came to Koinonia for advice and aid. The farm had a high credit rating in Americus, and over the years the residents of Americus learned to tolerate, almost appreciate, the "different ones" in their midst— or, at least, so it seemed.

Then Dr. Jordan, along with another graduate of the Univeristy of Georgia, indicated that he would be willing to sign the applications of two Negro students who sought admission to Georgia State College. He conferred with the president of the college and the executive secretary of the

Board of Regents. "We were very kindly received, but the secretary told us it was a big problem, and asked that we give him a few days to think it over. This was agreed upon, and he thanked us very profusely for the Christian spirit in which we had come." By the time Jordan had returned to Americus, however, he found that someone in the state administration "had already called up the sheriff down here to find out about 'This Jordan fellow' and what he was up to." The local paper carried headlines to the effect that a Koinonia resident had signed applications of Negroes to enter Georgia Business College. Threatening telephone calls began, the first insurance cancellation came through, and a pattern of boycotts and bombings, shootings and burnings, began which has continued intermittently ever since.

In June, 1956, a heavy-caliber pistol was fired into the Roadside Market where Koinonia marketed many of its products. On July twenty-third, an explosion did some three thousand dollars' damage to the market and on January 14, 1957, it and all its equipment was destroyed by explosion and fire. An empty dwelling house on the farm was burned and an attempt was made on the barn of a sympathetic neighbor. During January and February and March, shotgun blasts from passing cars were fired into the homes, narrowly missing some of the children, including Clarence Jordan's daughter, Eleanor, a student at the University of Georgia. Crosses were burned before the homes of neighbors who had been friendly to Koinonia. Unarmed watchmen, standing in front of the farm, were fired upon.

Simultaneously, the local boycott became almost complete. All insurance policies were canceled, local gins would not gin the farm's cotton, supplies and services of all descriptions were cut off, and despite what Jordan terms "a perfect record of payments over fourteen years," the Citizens Bank of Americus cut off his credit. An interracial summer camp for children was placed under court injunction and thereby closed. In February, a seventy-car KKK delegation visited Koinonia and offered to buy the farm, whose value has been estimated as being at least $150,000. Members of the single-K tried to explain to the robed members of the triple-K that under ordinary circumstances they would listen to any reasonable offer, but that under present circumstances to sell would be to surrender. Pressure by pistol and pocketbook continued.

The Sumter County and Americus Ministerial Association, the Georgia Council of Churches and the United Church Women of Georgia have condemned the violence against Koinonia. "Several people in Americus have told us they'd like to help," one of the residents of the farm says, "but they don't dare let their sympathy be made public." Well-wishers from various parts of the country have sent in contributions, and the farm's mail-order business has increased, but with capital losses mounting and income for support of the families decreasing as crops are changed to cope with the strait jacket of the boycotts, the accusations of accumulating wealth from national publicity seem particularly ridiculous.

Physically, the farm itself is a simple cluster of buildings, frame and cement block, set in the midst of level to gently rolling fields. Its guiding spirit, Clarence Jordan, is a well-built man of forty-four, with powerful muscles and weighing not quite two hundred pounds. "Jordan's a realist, along with his idealism," one man in Atlanta tells you. "They've evacuated all the children from Koinonia now, and most of the Negroes, but I believe Jordan will stay on. He's not going to let Americus and Sumter County bury its conscience so easily."

Koinonia has stirred the conscience of much of the South. A man in Mississippi tells you, "I don't give a damn about Koinonia itself as such, but I know it stands for all of us and a right we have: the right to be silly in our neighbor's eyes. I think it's silly to be a pacifist, like Jordan, but I feel like going over there and helping in his right to be different from me."

And a newspaperman, native of Virginia, says, "Koinonia is probably not a very practical experiment—but it has a right to exist and prosper if America means anything at all."

The most astonishing aspect of Koinonia and Americus is the upside-down fearfulness. For despite the bombs and the bullets and the boycotts turned against them, the residents of the beleaguered farm seem somehow calmer, more certain, freer of suspicion, than the residents around them who have all the physical weapons and most of the outward powers apparently on their side. Fear is a treacherous weapon, and those who would turn its sharp edge against others frequently discover, to their dismay, that instead of committing murder they have committed hari-kari.

Blood: Red, White and Blue:

In a second-story office overlooking the Main Street of the little East Tennessee town of Newport, there is a reception room filled with patients waiting to see the doctor. There are two white men—one in overalls, the other in neat khaki work clothes—and three white women, one holding a child. There are three Negroes—a young woman and a middle-aged one, and a man. They all wait together patiently, talking once in a while of their crops and ailments, for different as they are in many other ways, these people have two things in common: their hurt flesh and the doctor they have sought out to help them.

Dr. Dennis Branch is small and thin, with greying hair and goatee, courtly manners and ready humor. Also, he is a Negro. "Ninety per cent of my patients are white," he says matter-of-factly. "When folks are desperate, they'll try anybody." He chuckles, then goes on more seriously. "No, I guess what counts is the fact that I've been here forty-three, nearly forty-four, years now, and they trust me. Ever since I first came to this town, I've treated white people, here and up in the mountains, too, back when I had to use a horse and buggy to get there."

When Dennis Branch, young M.D. with a brand-new shingle, came to this county seat in the shadow of the Great Smokies, in 1914, he had six hundred dollars and hopes to move on in a few months, and Cocke County had few roads but hopes for some development to attract outside visitors. The doctor forgot his plans to leave, and in the late nineteen twenties, when funds were being collected to secure a national park in the Great Smoky Mountains which bordered part of Cocke County, Dr. Branch made a donation large enough to be a real sacrifice for him. By the time the park had ben created, the doctor was an entrenched citizen of Newport.

The white doctors of the town worked with him, often on cases where kerosene lamps and corn-shuck mattresses provided the physical equipment. One of the most brilliant of these physicians, a student of literature and breeder of fine livestock, Dr. John Stanbery, said, "Dr. Branch has a black skin and the whitest heart of any man I know." At his death, Dr. Stanbery left his Negro colleague a collection of cherished surgical instruments.

Dr. Branch bridged a difficult gap to become accepted by both the town's civic leaders and the reticent hill people as well. Perhaps he had learned tact and human nature when he was growing up in Raleigh, North Carolina, working as a bootblack and later as a Pullman porter to pay his way through Shaw University. Never sacrificing his dignity to flatter white feelings, never sacrificing his common sense to exploit his role of leadership, he made it difficult for the people in his corner of Tennessee to mouth easy clichés against Negroes. Through the years many a conversation might begin, "Nigras are all so shiftless——" to be quickly ended when someone said, "But look at Doc Branch."

He became a standard for the Negro community and a challenge to the white citizenry. And the Negro leaders at nearby Morristown College made him a trustee of their institution, and the white members of the Newport Chamber of Commerce made him a vice president of their organization.

But the real achievement, the quiet drama of Dennis Branch's life, is in that steady stream of humanity which crosses his threshold every day in the week. (When his only son, Dennis, Jr., died at the age of seventeen, the doctor started spending part of every Sunday at his office, too, and as patients learned this, many would come by to make a call that day.) As you watch and listen during a long, crowded day in this office, see lean, weather-bitten Anglo-Saxons, quiet-spoken rural Negroes, gregarious townspeople, both black and white, come and go, you realize that color bars which are in effect on the streets outside have melted here.

"You been waiting on my family forty years, Doc," one elderly white man says. "Now I want you to give me something for this high blood that's bothering me."

And a white woman in a pretty summer dress: "I'm working up in Ohio now, Dr. Branch, but every time I come home on a vacation I like for you to give me a check-up."

One white woman, who needs to sign some paper, cannot write, and Dr. Branch's secretary, a pleasant, efficient girl, fills in the necessary writing and shows the woman where to mark her "x." There is no apparent sense of superiority on either side of the color line, and this simple transaction illustrates some important facts about the upland South today.

A maintenance engineer from the street department rolls up a shirt sleeve and presents his arm to the doctor. "I've tried them all, and Dr. Branch is the only one can seem to do any good for me. So I've been coming to him for over thirty years now."

When the day is finished, and the work-worn rooms of the office are empty of their flow of traffic, the doctor wearily takes the stethoscope from around his neck and hangs his white coat on the wall. His seventy-one years, and the long hours of the day just finished, seem to weigh heavily upon him for a moment. Then he smiles, and speaks of his patients. "They're fine, plain folks. If doctors ever begin to think the color of a man's skin is more important than the color of his blood, we might as well look to the Lord and be dismissed. But I know that'll never happen now. I know the white doctors in this town. I know the way the world's moving. We're getting rid of a lot of the old diseases, in our minds as well as our bodies. I can take the Lord and do anything—and so can anybody else in this world that wants to."

A Place in the Sun:

Seeking their own particular place in the sun, the Vikings and Phoe-
nicians traveled the uncharted waters of the ancient world; nomads
trekked across deserts and founded cities and left new deserts in their wake;
Romans built an empire and Englishmen established colonies around
the world, and settlers immigrated to a new land called America. With
those first arrivees came the seeds of the nation's highest achievements
and deepest dilemmas. For example, the single year of 1619 brought the
infant colony at Jamestown three such pregnant innovations: the arrival
of English girls who would become wives of the settlers, introduction of
the first Negroes into Virginia, and a meeting of the House of Burgesses
which was the first representative legislative assembly in the New World.

Seeking their place in the sun, the people of the world, the colored
billions who have looked in the ugly face of famine too often, and walked
with poverty and devastation and ignorance too long, now stir. Their
stirring is a slight shiver, a distant rumble, an infant challenge. Here, in the
richest, freest land on earth, it echoes faintly—but it will not be dismissed. And the colored peoples in this land seek to walk the last and
hardest mile toward full realization of their democracy.

A young Negro reporter from Minnesota, born and reared in the
South, returns from travels across America and to some of the teeming
countries of the Far East, and talks with a group of young Negroes on
their college campus in the South. You watch the attentive faces of these
boys and girls and see the growing determination in their faces as Carl
Rowan links their own desire for equality of justice and opportunity to
the growing hunger in all parts of the world for dignity.

"Man everywhere is at war with what he's always been at war with:
ignorance. Also arrogance and laziness and sheer stupidity. But the thing
that's stirring the hearts of people in Mandalay is essentially the same
thing that's stirring the hearts of people in Montgomery, Alabama."

That gallant South, which has placed such a glory in pride, should be
the most able to appreciate this craving on the part of the humiliated
for a measure of pride. That instinctive South, which has proved there
are battles men will fight regardless of the odds or cost, should understand most clearly this dedicated instinct on the part of the deprived
toward a better life. That South, which has suffered war on its own fields
and years of misunderstanding and generations of want, should be most
committed to the fulfillment of these needs everywhere. And that fertile
South, which has nourished and seen wasted such a variety of living
things, should most passionately recognize that reverence for life which

is a universal supplication. As there are several Souths, their legacy to the present includes several traditions. If, in this crucial time of choice, the majority of the region will turn to its oldest, it finest, its most fundamental tradition—which, indeed, it helped write into the very bulwark of the nation: the tradition of human worth and every individual's rights—then the South may become the real frontier for a renewed vision of democracy.

From the backward pull may come the forward thrust that will help determine a world policy in the age of the atom. In discussing a recent book by a British visitor to America, Mr. Gerald Johnson said, in *The New York Herald Tribune Book Review*, "There is no escape clause in his estimate of the South. He did not overlook its beauty, but its melancholy depressed and its bitterness repelled him. He arrived there at the moment when racial desegregation was becoming the dominant interest, and the violence of the reaction appalled him, as it has appalled many others. He made no allowance for the fact that he was on the scene of an ethnological experiment without parallel in human history—the consciously planned upgrading of a racial minority in the presence of a majority to which it is alien not merely in geographical origin, but even in color. This is a tricky and difficult enterprise, but if it is carried through successfully it will be a greater triumph of self-government than the establishment of the Republic."

That forward thrust, that "triumph of self-government," will not, cannot, come, however, without a great deal of work and a rare use of intelligence. The cunning of the little foxes must be undercut by shrewd implementation of ideals. The loudness of negativism and prejudice must be canceled out by the clarity of constructive action. In a moment when logic seems to be playing hide-and-seek, emotions seem also to have run amuck and grown more calloused. It has been well said that what the situation demands is a combination of soft hearts and hard heads. Affirmation is necessary, particularly among those who live in the South and must daily confront the small problems and help implement the large promises of the place and people around them. But that affirmation must be grounded in reality, in thorough knowledge of the strength of its antagonists, in basic appraisal of what is present and what is possible.

We in the South do not need any more Pilates to wash their hands of our stubbornness and travail and turn to less thorny problems, as occurred in 1876 at the end of Reconstruction; instead, black and white, we need pilots, many of them, from within and without the South, who will extend a grip of friendship and reason in a time of doubt and dismay. Journeying up and down and through these thirteen states, you see the steel cobweb of electric power lines crisscrossing the face of the South, releasing it from bondage as surely as the Fourteenth Amendment did in the past. You observe the outstretched antennae of the television aerials on plantation houses and ranch-style subdivisions and tar-papered shacks, binding the South to the rest of the union more surely than the post-bellum oath of allegiance ever did. The South and the nation are one today, as they always have been. When, at the turn of the century, this nation took up "the white man's burden," it laid down some of its right to indignation at the South for "the Negro problem." Both believed in the white man's supremacy. Where abolition had been the source of the Southern Bourbon's aversion, immigration became the fountainhead of the Boston Brahmin's aversion. That, today, is why both the nation and the South have the right, indeed the responsibility, to point to flaws in each other, and yet each must work to eliminate its own wrongs, beginning where it is, moving along—and along—and along.

While we recognize the granite resistance and the glacial pace of change which exists in some parts of the South, it is not necessary to yield to the toal pessimism of visitors who come, who see, who are conquered. We must realize that in December, 1956, the National Opinion Research Center could release these factual findings, in *Scientific American:*

"Among the three aspects of integration, the North is least tolerant toward residential proximity, while the South is more tolerant toward this than toward desegregation in schools or transportation. . . . A Charolotte, N.C., housewife said, 'I don't mind living beside them but I don't want the children going to school with them. I just don't.' On the other hand, a Brooklyn housewife said: 'I approve of them. They should have the same rights. But I wouldn't want to live with them.' . . .

"The rigid views of the segregationists are matched for consistency, strength and intensity by those who favor integration, and the gap would appear irreconcilable.

"However, the statistics take on new meaning when viewed in historical perspective. They are very different today from what they were in 1942, when the same questions were asked in the first NORC survey on the subject. In the North, support for school integration has risen among whites from 40 per cent in 1942 to 61 per cent now. In the South only one white person in 50 spoke up for school integration then; today the figure is one in seven. The proportion of Southern whites who would allow Negroes equal facilities on buses has jumped from 4 to 27 per cent. The South of today has moved far from its earlier position."

When Jonathan Daniels made his revealing journey of discovery through the South almost two decades ago, he said, "In the complicated South, all that is wanted is the simple remedy." Today the complications seem to have increased—but many people are still looking for that capsule cure-all.

It will not be found. And the sooner the search for a facile answer, a patent-medicine prescription, is abandoned, the sooner we may release the energies of our soberest intelligence and most joyous faith into the slow but irrevocable mainstream of human development.

In the heart of the New South stands a new city, Oak Ridge. The schools at Oak Ridge desegregated the year after the Supreme Court handed down its decision. Integration was accomplished quietly and successfully.

"Oak Ridge is different," some people say. "The schools are run by Federal authority. The government can say what's to be done and that settles it."

"Oak Ridge is different. Lots of people from all parts of the country living there. There's no solid South structure."

Oak Ridge *is* different. Perhaps the anachronism of discussing mankind in terms of black and white is particularly apparent in this town of the split atom, in this age of the massive bomb.

"The question used to be *how* people lived," a displaced Alabamian in one of the long, anonymous Oak Ridge buildings says, "now the question is, *if* we live." He hesitates. "Actually I suppose the two are one: how we live determines if we live."

The dilemma of the world, in microcosm in the South, is as simple and involved as that.